T0349015

Inside Copilot

Inside Copilot is designed to teach users to master Copilot, Microsoft's generative AI assistant. Learn prompt engineering and use cases for Copilot in many Microsoft products at beginner, intermediate, and expert levels. Perfect for any professionals who find their schedules packed with repetitive computer tasks, Copilot can automatically generate PowerPoint presentations, draft emails on Outlook, write code on GitHub, and more. Both companies and individuals can learn to utilize Copilot to significantly speed up processes and gain an advantage.

More information about this series at https://link.springer.com/bookseries/17432.

Microsoft Copilot for Power Apps

Transforming App Development with AI Assistance

Rezwanur Rahman

Apress®

Microsoft Copilot for Power Apps: Transforming App Development with AI Assistance

Rezwanur Rahman
Innsbruck, Austria

ISBN-13 (pbk): 979-8-8688-0511-0   ISBN-13 (electronic): 979-8-8688-0512-7
https://doi.org/10.1007/979-8-8688-0512-7

Managing Director, Apress Media LLC: Welmoed Spahr
Acquisitions Editor: Ryan Byrnes
Development Editor: Laura Berendson
Editorial Assistant: Gryffin Winkler
Copy Editor: Kezia Endsley

Cover designed by eStudioCalamar

Distributed to the book trade worldwide by Springer Science+Business Media New York, 1 New York Plaza, Suite 4600, New York, NY 10004-1562, USA. Phone 1-800-SPRINGER, fax (201) 348-4505, e-mail orders-ny@springer-sbm.com, or visit www.springeronline.com. Apress Media, LLC is a California LLC and the sole member (owner) is Springer Science + Business Media Finance Inc (SSBM Finance Inc). SSBM Finance Inc is a **Delaware** corporation.

For information on translations, please e-mail booktranslations@springernature.com; for reprint, paperback, or audio rights, please e-mail bookpermissions@springernature.com.

Apress titles may be purchased in bulk for academic, corporate, or promotional use. eBook versions and licenses are also available for most titles. For more information, reference our Print and eBook Bulk Sales web page at http://www.apress.com/bulk-sales.

Any source code or other supplementary material referenced by the author in this book is available to readers on GitHub. For more detailed information, please visit https://www.apress.com/gp/services/source-code.

If disposing of this product, please recycle the paper

Dedicated to my lovely and beautiful wife, Mobaswira Farzana Munia. Thank you for your support and love!

Table of Contents

About the Author

 **Rezwanur Rahman,** the visionary CEO and managing director of Backend Emerging Business Limited (Backend EBL), stands at the forefront of the tech world as an expert cloud solution architect. His accolades include being a Microsoft MVP in Microsoft Copilot & Microsoft 365 development and a Microsoft Certified Trainer (MCT), reflecting his deep-seated passion for innovation and software development. Rezwanur's academic journey began at the American International University-Bangladesh (AIUB), where he specialized in software engineering, laying a strong foundation for his illustrious career.

Rezwanur's professional trajectory is marked by pivotal roles, including senior technical lead (escalation engineer) for Microsoft 365 Global Support at Microsoft and technical evangelist-intern at Microsoft Bangladesh. These positions equipped him with a profound understanding of modern technology trends and their practical applications.

In 2018, Rezwanur made history as the first Bangladeshi to receive the Windows Insider MVP award. This was followed by the prestigious Microsoft Most Valuable Professional (Microsoft MVP) award in Microsoft 365 Development in 2021, showcasing his unwavering dedication to pushing technological boundaries, particularly within Microsoft platforms.

Rezwanur's expertise extends globally through his participation in renowned international speaking events like Microsoft Ignite, Microsoft AI Tour, Global Power Platform Bootcamp, M365 Developer Conferences, TeamsNations, GraphDevDay, and Global AI Bootcamps. These engagements have allowed him to share his insights and knowledge with a worldwide audience.

His involvement in cybersecurity, through collaborations with the Bangladesh Grey Hat Hackers and Cybersecurity Alliance-Bangladesh, adds another layer to his professional portfolio, emphasizing his commitment to promoting secure and ethical technological practices.

Driven by a desire to share his extensive knowledge and experience, Rezwanur authored *Mastering Copilot for Power Apps: Transforming App Development with AI Assistance*. This book aims to demystify the integration of AI in app development, particularly through tools like Copilot in Power Apps, offering readers a comprehensive guide, from basic concepts to advanced applications.

Residing in Tirol, Austria, Rezwanur continues to be inspired by the potential of technology to innovate and transform, remaining at the cutting edge of the tech industry.

About the Technical Reviewer

Kanwal Khipple is a dynamic leader, seasoned Power Platform expert, and CEO of 2toLead, a premier Microsoft consulting firm. With two decades of experience driving digital transformation and enabling organizations to maximize their investment in Microsoft 365, Kanwal is renowned for his deep expertise in user experience design, employee engagement, and modern workplace strategies.

As a passionate advocate for technology adoption and innovation, Kanwal has guided countless organizations through complex migrations, modernizations, and change management initiatives. His approach is grounded in empathy, creativity, and a strong focus on aligning technology with business goals to deliver exceptional value.

Kanwal is also a sought-after speaker, known for his engaging storytelling and practical insights on technical implementation, leadership, and user experience. His thought leadership extends beyond the stage to his influential writing, where he frequently shares best practices, case studies, and actionable advice for organizations navigating their digital journeys.

When he's not driving transformation in the digital workplace, Kanwal is dedicated to fostering an inclusive environment within his organization and the broader tech community. He is a mentor, a leader, and an advocate for continuous learning and generosity as key business values.

Acknowledgments

My deepest gratitude goes to my parents and parents-in-law for their steadfast support and love. Their encouragement has been a constant source of strength. I am also immensely grateful to my younger sister, Zarin Tasnim, and my beautiful wife, Mobaswira Farzana Munia, whose understanding and patience have been invaluable.

I wish to express my sincere appreciation to my technical reviewer, Kanwal Khipple, for his meticulous insights and feedback, which have significantly enhanced the quality of this work. A special acknowledgement to Apress, the publisher, for choosing me to write this book and for their consistent support throughout the process.

A heartfelt thanks to all the teams at Microsoft Bangladesh, Microsoft Deutschland, and the Microsoft Global Headquarters. Your trust in my abilities has been a tremendous motivation. Special thanks to EMEA Lead, Community Program Management at Microsoft, Alice Piras, for her exceptional support and guidance. Additionally, I am grateful to the Microsoft Product Groups (PG) for their collaborative spirit, and to the senior product manager Microsoft 365 Copilot and Microsoft Graph at Microsoft, Fabian Williams, for his outstanding leadership.

I am deeply thankful to my fellow Microsoft MVP colleagues. Your continuous support and willingness to share knowledge have greatly enriched my learning experience.

Lastly, I am profoundly appreciative of my friend and legal advisor, lawyer Mag. Stefan Gamsjäger. His wise counsel, steadfast support, and assistance in making crucial decisions have been essential throughout this journey.

Thank you all for your invaluable contributions and unwavering support.

Introduction

Welcome to *Microsoft Copilot for Power Apps*, a comprehensive resource designed to guide you through the innovative capabilities and practical applications of Microsoft's latest AI-driven assistant for Power Apps. This book is crafted for developers, IT professionals, and business users who aim to harness the power of AI to streamline their app development processes and enhance productivity.

What This Book Is About

Microsoft Copilot for Power Apps explores the transformative potential of integrating AI into app development through Microsoft Copilot. The book covers the functionalities, benefits, and prospects of using Copilot within the Power Apps ecosystem. It provides step-by-step instructions, case studies, and best practices to help you maximize the use of this powerful tool.

Who This Book Is For

Whether you are a seasoned developer looking to incorporate AI into your workflow, a business user aiming to create efficient applications without extensive coding knowledge, or an IT professional responsible for deploying and managing enterprise applications, this book offers valuable insights and practical guidance tailored to your needs.

Structure of the Book

The book is structured to take you on a journey from understanding the basics of Microsoft Copilot to mastering its advanced features and applications. Here's a brief overview of what each chapter covers:

Chapter 1: Unveiling Copilot: A New Era in Power Apps

This chapter provides an overview of Copilot, its core features, and the benefits it offers to Power Apps users. You'll learn about the evolution of AI in app development and how Copilot stands out as a game-changer.

Chapter 2: Embarking on the Copilot Journey

This chapter describes the process for setting up and optimizing Microsoft Copilot for Power Apps, focusing on simple deployment due to its online service model. It covers the different licensing options, setting up a conducive testing and development environment, and troubleshooting issues related to proxy servers.

Chapter 3: Mastering the Core: Copilot's Engine Room

Focused on the AI Builder at the heart of Microsoft Copilot, this chapter explains how AI Builder helps developers build and launch AI models quickly using an accessible low-code approach. It details how Microsoft Azure services enhance the architecture of Copilot, making AI accessible to all developers.

Chapter 4: Crafting Power Apps with Copilot: The Essentials

This chapter guides you through the process of building functional and aesthetically pleasing Power Apps using Microsoft Copilot. It covers the distinctions between Canvas and model-driven apps, and explains how to automate modifications and adjust UI components using straightforward, natural language commands.

Chapter 5: Advanced Customizations and Automation with Copilot

This chapter introduces advanced customization techniques, including optimizing layouts, employing grid systems, and integrating diverse data sources. It also explores the powerful capabilities of Copilot functionalities such as Copilot Chat, Copilot Studio, and Copilot Answer.

Chapter 6: Advanced UI/UX Techniques in Power Apps Development

This chapter explains how to integrate advanced AI capabilities into Power Apps using AI Builder. It covers adding AI models like text recognition, sentiment analysis, and document processing to your applications, enhancing their functionality and user experience.

Chapter 7: Dynamic Content, Comments, and Copilot Customization in Power Apps

This chapter demonstrates how to create dynamic and engaging user interfaces (UI) with Copilot, focusing on practical implementation by designing modern menus and crafting sophisticated UIs for canvas apps in tablet format.

Chapter 8: Integrating Diverse Data Sources and Media in Power Apps

This chapter focuses on enhancing Power Apps by integrating multiple data sources such as Microsoft Dataverse, SharePoint, and Azure SQL. It covers creating and customizing Dataverse tables, connecting to external data repositories, and managing multimedia elements, including images, videos, and pen input controls. These integrations empower developers to build data-driven, dynamic applications that offer a richer, interactive experience for users.

Chapter 9: Introducing AI Builder in Power Apps

This chapter explores AI Builder, guiding you on how to enhance Power Apps with artificial intelligence to automate processes, predict outcomes, and extract insights from data—all without requiring advanced AI expertise. It covers both prebuilt and custom AI models, including text recognition, sentiment analysis, and object detection, offering versatile tools for business applications. With this integration, you'll be able to create smarter, proactive apps that streamline workflows, improve decision-making, and add valuable intelligence to everyday tasks.

Chapter 10: Advanced Techniques with AI Builder and Conditional Formatting

This chapter guides you through advanced techniques for enhancing Power Apps with AI Builder and conditional formatting. It introduces custom AI prompts, enabling you to add tailored, intelligent features to your applications, and demonstrates how conditional formatting can be applied to make data-driven visual adjustments, creating a more responsive and visually intuitive user experience. You'll also learn to leverage Copilot for creating and refining conditional formatting rules, streamlining complex tasks without requiring deep technical expertise.

Chapter 11: Revolutionizing Power Apps UI with Microsoft Copilot: A Complete Project

This chapter showcases how to use Microsoft Copilot to transform Power Apps UI, guiding you through a complete project. It covers the creation of a modern, dynamic user interface with collapsible menus, a theme-switching toggle, and a responsive layout. By following these steps, you'll learn to craft Power Apps that are visually appealing, interactive, and adaptable to different user preferences, providing a professional, modern look to your applications.

Chapter 12: Visions of the Future: Copilot's Evolving Landscape

This chapter explores the latest trends poised to transform app development, including AI integration, low-code/no-code platforms, cross-platform development, AR and VR technologies, and blockchain. This chapter also discusses future innovations in Copilot technology.

Chapter 13: Copilot Success Stories: Lessons from the Field

This chapter showcases how various industries have successfully implemented Copilot, highlighting the challenges they faced and the solutions they devised. It emphasizes strategic planning, effective data governance, and change management.

Chapter 14: Comprehensive Resources

The final chapter provides essential resources to support your journey with Microsoft Copilot for Power Apps. It includes key terms and definitions and online resources for further learning, and it highlights thriving online communities for sharing ideas and accessing support.

What You'll Learn

By the end of this book, you will have a thorough understanding of how to leverage Microsoft Copilot to enhance your Power Apps projects. You will be equipped with the knowledge to implement AI-driven solutions, optimize your workflows, and create applications that are both powerful and user-friendly.

I hope this book inspires you to explore new possibilities with Microsoft Copilot and empowers you to build innovative applications that drive success in your organization. Let's embark on this exciting journey together and unlock the full potential of AI in app development.

CHAPTER 1

Unveiling Copilot: A New Era in Power Apps

Have you ever wondered what it would be like if building apps was as simple as talking through an idea? What if you didn't have to write lines and lines of code, but instead, you could simply speak to an AI program, whose only purpose was to turn your thoughts into binaries? This is not some futuristic idea anymore—this is the reality in which we are now living.

Fundamentally, Microsoft Copilot, which is part of Power Apps, changes everything for low-code application development. You are no longer tethered by the boundaries of coding languages. Think of Copilot as your digital friend who speaks fluent code and knows that you do not. Instead of simply listening to your requests, it anticipates what you need before you even think of it, offering suggestions that can make you more efficient.

Now is the time to envision greater possibilities, strive for bigger goals, and reach new heights.

© Rezwanur Rahman 2024
R. Rahman, *Microsoft Copilot for Power Apps*, Inside Copilot,
https://doi.org/10.1007/979-8-8688-0512-7_1

Decoding the Copilot Phenomenon

In this modern-day story of technological revolution, Microsoft 365 Copilot is a front-runner—meaning a giant leap from hitherto practiced ways of engaging with and drawing on artificial intelligence (AI) to boost software development. These transformations—the Copilot Revolution, more generally—embody the most radical synthesis of AI with human expertise, breaking many of the traditional practices of software development. The essence of Microsoft 365 Copilot is an AI assistant that has human capabilities in the software building field. It's beyond what automated coding traditionally defines: it provides predictive analytics, design guidance, and smart help in problem-solving. This integration will practically bring out a new role in the sense that Copilot will become more of a collaborator in the development process than just a tool. Figure 1-1 shows the various Copilot logos.

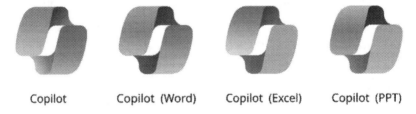

Copilot   Copilot (Word)   Copilot (Excel)   Copilot (PPT)

Figure 1-1. *Copilot in different Microsoft product environments*

And, of course, what Copilot brings to the platform is one of the most fascinating aspects of this integration. It's democratizing software development. With intuitive suggestions and an easy-to-use interface, Copilot makes it significantly simpler to write software. This opens the door to a much broader range of contributors—people who previously didn't code are now becoming developers and making substantial contributions. Consequently, we can expect greater diversity and innovation in software development approaches.

Copilot's main strength is its ability to be flexible and customizable to your needs. Based on your interactions with Copilot, it tailors the experience by tuning suggestions to you. In the development environment, different users have different preferences and different project requirements, and as Copilot learns more about you, your experience of using Copilot will evolve. Copilot will become tailored to your personal preferences and the latest trends in the language.

The implications are profound, prompting us to envision a future where AI integrates into the creative and development processes, collaborating with human expertise and innovation. This partnership could transform the software development landscape, making software more adaptable to market shifts and driving exploration of new technological horizons.

The Genesis of Copilot: Origin and Evolution

Amid the rapidly evolving landscape of digital technology and AI, the arrival of Microsoft 365 Copilot marks a significant milestone, closely tied to advancements in AI, especially in natural language processing championed by OpenAI. The story of Microsoft 365 Copilot unfolds alongside OpenAI's models, with a key chapter focusing on Generative Pre-trained Transformers (GPT), particularly GPT-4 and Bing GPT-4.

GPT-4 is the journey that was started with GPT-1 in 2018, a monumental AI model that produced human-like text. It laid the foundation for later releases, such as GPT-2 and GPT-3, further pushing the frontier of what AI could do with text generation and natural language understanding. The gargantuan GPT-3 model had 175 billion parameters, trained on enormous and diverse datasets to make it fluent in producing text across a range of topics.

In 2023, GPT-4 built on this, taking a step change toward greater sophistication. With further parameters, now believed to exceed a trillion in number, and new techniques of training, the output can interpret and generate text with so much subtlety and complexity like no other before it. In other words, GPT-4 could understand context better and produce accurate content between these domains from both the receiver's and producer's view of the text, most accurately, and for more than one language. It also made the processing more efficient and, accordingly, more relevant for integration with a suite of applications, which is where Microsoft 365 Copilot came into play.

At the same time, Bing GPT-4 came into being, taking another important stride. Bing GPT-4 is a special version of GPT-4 developed for the search engine application, which incorporates the latest language skills into GPT-4 but more specifically tuned to the requirements of web search and information finding. In its latest version, it has improved natural language capabilities in understanding and summarizing information from web pages. It gives users more relevant, context-aware responses to their search queries and can serve up the search experience in a much more conversational—some would say interactive—way.

A great contribution for the development of the work was with the integration of GPT-4, in particular Bing GPT-4, within the suite of Microsoft's productivity tools. This capitalized on the advanced AI technology of OpenAI with more intuitive, efficient, and powerful tools for office productivity and collaboration, using OpenAI and its API in the tools.

Creating Microsoft 365 Copilot meant seamlessly bringing together GPT-4 and Bing GPT-4 into one of the most used suites across the world. The challenges were met across several disciplines, right from the integration of AI into the Microsoft suite to staying user-focused, and at the same time, ensuring stringent data privacy and security. This provided very useful feedback in addressing these challenges and refining the tool from the early adopters taking part in the beta test.

The launch of Microsoft 365 Copilot presents a new era in the history of office productivity software. But the range isn't just productivity around changed work and collaboration modes; it's also the emergence of new forms of work, all super-powered by GPT-4 and Bing GPT-4. Over time, with subsequent maturing, Copilot for Microsoft 365 highlights an emerging time when workspaces will slowly be infiltrated by AI tools that help humans break new frontiers of creativity and innovation. The story of Microsoft 365 Copilot is mingled with AI, using the human capacity of creativity to improve the work frontiers still changing in the digital era.

How Microsoft 365 Copilot Works

Microsoft 365 features one of the most promoted innovations so far, the AI-powered productivity toolset. Microsoft 365 takes full advantage of the integration Microsoft has done with Microsoft 365 apps and provides a completely new experience. Copilot interacts with users as they use familiar products like Outlook or Word, which provides a far more powerful, AI-powered experience.

Let's look at how Copilot works and powers a new type of AI-assisted experience for everyday tasks. Figure 1-2 presents the technical flowchart for Microsoft 365 Copilot.

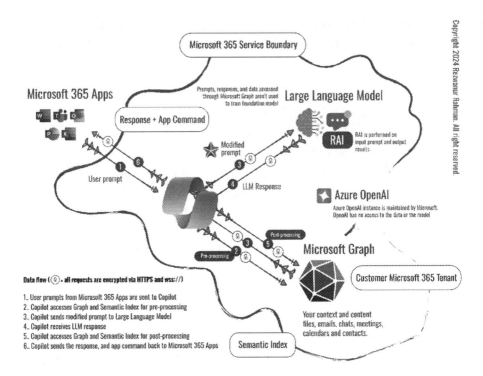

Figure 1-2. *Technical flowchart of Copilot background*

For example, when a user is composing an email in Outlook or writing a document in Word, their input triggers a very complex AI-powered backend process. The prompt is then encrypted and sent to the Copilot service when issued.

Upon receipt, Copilot engages the Microsoft Graph API, a robust interface that interlinks Microsoft's cloud services. The user prompt receives a first semantic analysis, extending with context metadata derived from the user's data ecosystem around Microsoft, including emails, files, meetings, social connections, and other resources. This ensures that the response from AI is not only syntactically perfect but that it considers the context of the historical data pattern and the history of the user's usage.

The richer prompt, now semantically grounded, is securely forwarded to the Large Language Model (LLM), GPT-4, or specifically Bing GPT-4. Forwarding occurs with more encryption at the time of sending the path and the data to retain the user's privacy. The LLM is managing this using a powerful set of algorithms, together with a model of potentially over a trillion parameters, to allow the generation of natural language with nuanced understanding. With expanded capabilities of GPT-4, it can identify the intention described by a prompt and express an answer that is coherent and corresponds to the context provided by that prompt. The response is then sent back to Copilot by the LLM for post-processing.

Here, in outputs of the AI, the Microsoft Graph and Semantic Index are reused to perfectly align the respective final response according to the needs of the user for security and privacy standards. The response matches the command structure of the application and fits into the workflow of the user within the Microsoft 365 app.

Eventually, the processed and refined response that may need application commands is sent back to the originating Microsoft 365 app. These responses are all provided within the view of the user, enabling them to be empowered with AI-based assistance that will increase productivity and smooth decision-making, all at the comfort of their software learning environment. They are encapsulated end-to-end within a secure and privacy-centric framework using state-of-the-art encryption and strong interaction protocols, which safeguard users' data while enabling advanced AI-enhanced user experiences.

Knowledge Note   In the Microsoft 365 Copilot system, the AI doesn't merely process text; it understands context by leveraging semantic indexing. This means when the AI encounters terms like "quarterly review," it doesn't just see words—it sees past documents, emails, and meetings related to your company's quarterly performance, drawing on a rich tapestry of user-specific data to inform its response. This level of contextual awareness is a leap forward in making AI an intuitive extension of natural workflows.

Different Ways to Customize Microsoft Copilot for Microsoft 365

Copilot provides a range of extensibility options, enabling users to enhance, customize, and personalize using plugins and Graph connectors. The following sections take a deeper look and differentiate the different ways users can extend the capabilities of Copilot.

Plugins are exciting. They let you add new features, such as an integration with Microsoft Teams' message extensions or Power Platform's connector. Your enterprise data can be easily accessed within the Copilot for Microsoft 365 environment by using connectors.

You can customize Copilot for Microsoft 365 with the smarts of external services, apps, and data. Choose the tools and SDKs that are right for the way you work, then hit the ground running, creating your connector or plugins.

Figure 1-3 shows the flowchart of Copilot's extensibility options.

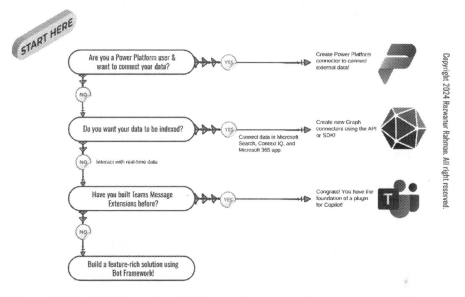

Figure 1-3. *Copilot extensibility options at a glance*

- No-code or low-code developers familiar with Power Platform can optimally access external data in Power Platform through Microsoft Power Platform connectors. This is particularly advantageous for those also using Copilot, as these connectors offer a streamlined solution.

- Within Microsoft 365, Graph connectors offer you a seamless way to integrate unstructured corporate data such as Microsoft search data, Context IQ, and Microsoft 365 app data. This integration using Graph connectors extends all the features available in Microsoft Graph to work with your data.

- For structured data from outside sources, you can integrate with Message Extensions and apply logic with the Bot Framework. If you already have Message Extension apps for Teams, half the work is done. You

9

simply ensure that your app manifest is updated
and meets all the necessary requirements before it is
published as a plugin.

When deciding on the best approach for your project, even skilled
programmers who lean toward high-level programming should consider
certain factors. This consideration remains crucial regardless of a
preference for no-code or low-code alternatives.

Data Types

Think about the characteristics of your data, including its organization,
expected amount and frequency of use, and the access needs it entails.
Table 1-1 shows the comparison of data characteristics across connectors
and plugins.

Table 1-1. *Comparison of Data Characteristics Across Connectors
and Plugins*

	Graph Connectors	**Message Extension Plugins**	**Copilot Studio Plugins**
Structure	Unstructured or flattened data	Structured data	Structured data
Data volume	Up to 5M items per connection	Suitable for high volume data (over 5M)	Suitable for high volume data (over 5M)
Data activity	Up to 20 requests per second	Suitable for high activity (over 20 req/ sec.)	Suitable for high volume data (over 5M)
Summarize/ act	Summarize only (Copilot analyzes and extracts key information)	Summarize + Act (with Adaptive Card, a user can modify the data)	Summarize only

Figure 1-4 shows an example of writable data with a message extension. This plugin handles a product inventory. Copilot queries the data from the inventory and shows the results in Adaptive Card, where it lets the user change the stock.

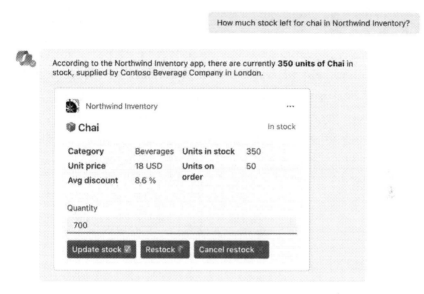

Figure 1-4. *Example of a plugin used for Northwind Inventory. Image Source: Microsoft*

Tip You can find the sample code for the Northwind Inventory plugin at https://learn.microsoft.com/en-us/ microsoft-365-copilot/extensibility/samples#teams- message-extension-samples.

Copilot's Distinctive Features and Competitive Edge

A major leap in office productivity, Microsoft 365 Copilot features advanced artificial intelligence that changes how people interact with technology in the work environment. At the heart of Copilot's groundbreaking innovation is its deep AI integration, converting standard office tools into intelligent assistants. This integration surpasses a simple layering of AI on top of existing tools, instead representing a rethinking of how office applications should work, that is, automating the ordinary experiences and delivering insight that was otherwise only available with specialized expertise. Figure 1-5 shows a comprehensive diagram of Microsoft Copilot's integration into the Microsoft product ecosystem.

Figure 1-5. *Microsoft Copilot in the Microsoft product ecosystem.*
Image Source: https://switchedon.bowdark.com/copilots-
everywhere-understanding-microsofts-copilot-strategy-
f5d576cef81b

**Word with Copilot—Advanced Natural Language
Processing (NLP):** Microsoft 365 Copilot in Word
combines Word and Copilot, ensuring state-of-
the-art capabilities with pioneering NLP technique
advancements, along with innovative architecture
layered atop deep learning. This AI helps users
make documents more impactful and coherent

than ever before. From rephrasing and following preferred style, to generating a contextually relevant content at each interaction that only improves, this AI does everything, improving each time and giving suggestions far superior to the current writing style of the user. The product will ensure that Word remains the top choice for professional writing, whether for educators, business professionals, or any other users.

Excel with Copilot—Predictive Analytics and Data Modeling: The Copilot algorithms empowered with intelligence in Excel give it the ability to deliver predictive insights and analyze patterns in data—in other words, permitting users to do forecasting, trend analysis, and scenario modeling, all without having to go through intensive statistics or analytics training. The software also works in autopilot to visualize your data, suggesting the best ways it would be represented graphically. With the capability to interpret complex datasets, Excel is transformed from just a mere spreadsheet application into a powerful analytical tool essential for making informed business and research decisions.

PowerPoint with Copilot—Intelligent Design and Content Assistance: Copilot for PowerPoint acts as your intelligent designer and content editor, always at your service. Leveraging the latest AI algorithms, it enhances the appearance of your PowerPoint slides progressively. By analyzing the content of each slide, Copilot offers suggestions on layout, theme, and visual enhancements that best complement your material. Instead of relying on excessive animations or poor color choices, Copilot steers you toward more effective design decisions. Text formatting and legibility are automated, ensuring clarity and professionalism. Additionally, relevant images and graphics are recommended to enrich your presentation. Copilot even assists in structuring your content within each slide, improving overall organization. Beyond merely providing tools for slide creation, Copilot offers comprehensive support for crafting a polished and cohesive presentation. Power presenters, particularly educators, marketers, and business professionals, find its predictive design assistance invaluable.

Outlook with Copilot—AI-Enhanced Communication and Scheduling: Copilot assists with drafting messages during work hours by suggesting quick and concise responses based on incoming emails, a process powered by advanced natural language processing (NLP). It also learns from user interactions to improve future suggestions. Additionally, Copilot integrates with the Outlook calendar and contacts to further enhance its functionality. For instance, if a user has a meeting, Copilot uses NLP to identify who should be included in the communication and suggest relevant participants. It can also analyze the organizational chart to recommend appropriate contacts. Furthermore, Copilot can check the availability of all participants and propose optimal meeting times, coordinating schedules seamlessly between users.

Teams with Copilot—Enhanced Collaboration and Meeting Efficiency: Copilot on Teams introduces a new offering enabled by new AI capabilities that enhances the virtual collaboration experience. It provides real-time transcription and translation services by utilizing advanced speech recognition and NLP technology, which encourages open, yet sensitivity-controlled communications with different global teams. AI-powered meeting analytics summarize, identify key points, and track action items so valuable insights from meetings aren't lost. This technology makes Teams a smart hub in collaboration and productivity.

OneNote with Copilot—Smart Information Management: OneNote makes more sense with AI integration because of its NLP that entails AI-powered organization and retrieval through classification algorithms, which are used to categorize your notes, tag main information, and make suggestions for associated notes during up-and-coming meetings or projects. This level of AI integration transforms OneNote from a simple note-taking tool into a robust system that intelligently manages notes, resources, and tasks, making it an invaluable asset for researchers, students, and knowledge workers.

SharePoint with Copilot—AI-Powered Document Management and Collaboration: With Copilot in SharePoint, teams get a range of capabilities based on AI to take their managing of documents and collaboration to a new level. Powerful machine-learning algorithms enable optimized searches that deliver results faster and more accurately. It features categorization through AI and management of doc libraries for easy access and collaboration. It avails the projects and collaborations to be very dynamic and efficient at the facility by keeping the document in SharePoint.

Security and Compliance—Ensuring Data Integrity and Privacy: The most crucial aspect is security and compliance. The platform, which is based on AI models and algorithms, ensures data security and privacy of the users. It guarantees that all information used with this tool is kept securely in a decentralized manner. Copilot has these securities to align with what the world protections have demanded when handling customer-sensitive data, like GDPR for privacy maintenance and proper data management.

Integration with Azure, Dynamics 365, Power BI, and Power Automate:

- **Azure:** Provides a scalable cloud infrastructure to run the AI and ML computations that power Copilot, ensuring high performance and reliability.

- **Dynamics 365:** Integrates Copilot into CRM and ERP systems, enhancing customer relationship management and streamlining operations with AI-driven insights.

- **Power BI:** Empowers data analysis with Copilot, offering advanced visualization and reporting capabilities.

- **Power Automate:** Leverages Copilot to automate workflows and processes, improving efficiency across various tasks.

Enhance Microsoft Copilot for Microsoft 365

With Copilot for Microsoft 365, developers can tailor AI to the core audience that they support in the Microsoft 365 environment.

It is packed with valuable capabilities designed to help work processes through a set of text, insight, predictive analysis, memory, language translation, and creative content services. It does this by indexing and tapping into the content of an organization through Microsoft Graph—documents, chat histories, and emails that users have access to. Figure 1-6 shows how natural language works with Microsoft Copilot in Microsoft 365.

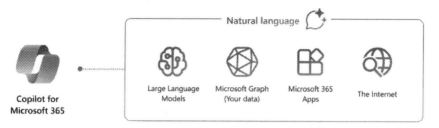

Figure 1-6. *How natural language works with Copilot for Microsoft 365. Image Source: Microsoft Learn*

Microsoft 365 doesn't just provide apps and data formats—many business processes require more, and Microsoft has built extensibility into Copilot. Copilot is already rich with AI capabilities, and with Copilot extensibility, you can enhance Copilot for Microsoft 365 by adding custom capabilities and expert knowledge specific to your organization and its users, all powered by AI. You can turn your app into a plugin to expand what Copilot can do and increase productivity across the numerous tasks and workflows people carry out every day. By using Microsoft Graph connectors to bring your enterprise data and content into Copilot, you can also make your organization's knowledge available to Copilot. Figure 1-7 shows the extensibility graph of Microsoft Copilot.

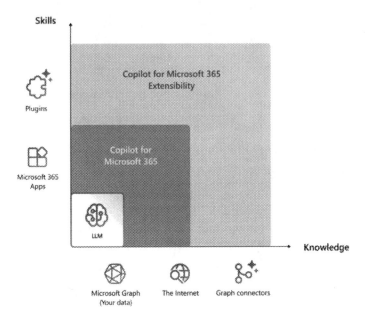

Figure 1-7. *Extensibility graph of Microsoft Copilot. Image Source: Microsoft Learn*

Using Copilot for Microsoft 365, you enhance the performance of your apps and data with AI, by:

- Enhancing the data assets of your organization with the best AI in the market.

- Helping your users complete their tasks smoothly, from beginning to end.

- Benefiting from top-notch security, compliance, and privacy policies.

Customize Copilot for Your Use Case!

Copilot's extensibility enhances the productivity of your collaborative environment by merging vital data, widely used tools, and trusted procedures with a common platform where teams typically gather, learn, and conduct work. Whether developing a new application specifically for Copilot or integrating an already existing one, the possibilities are broad. The following sections give specific examples of what you can develop for your organization.

Managing Engineering Team's Tasks

Let's say your engineering team uses a project management application. You now can build a custom tool to track outstanding tickets. Users could ask about the status of all the tickets assigned to them and Copilot could grab that data and present it in their custom extension. Figure 1-8 shows a visual example of how an engineering team can track issues using Microsoft Copilot.

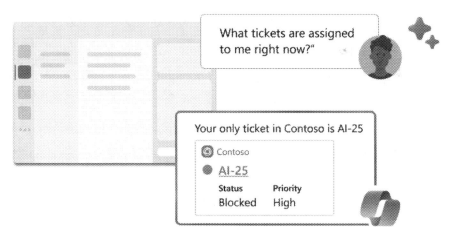

Figure 1-8. *Visual example of issue tracking for engineering team. Image Source: Microsoft Learn*

Enterprise Knowledge Sharing

Imagine a global company with knowledge that is distributed through many different formats—including documents, emails, and chat transcripts—and stored in many different systems. Microsoft Graph connectors create a universal solution by bringing that data together into one single interface that can be searched efficiently. This means you get—presuming your organization's data is available in Graph—your organization's collective intelligence at your fingertips.

Product Inventory for Ecommerce

You can use Copilot to check the stock level of certain products and develop your own in-house inventory management tool by linking it to your product database.

Integrating Data with the Applications

Copilot for Microsoft 365 can be enhanced in two ways:

- By adding skills to Copilot through *plugins.*

- By linking it with organizational data through Graph *connectors.*

Let's discuss plugins and connectors in more detail. Figure 1-9 illustrates the technical flowchart of how Microsoft Graph connector and plugins work with Microsoft Copilot.

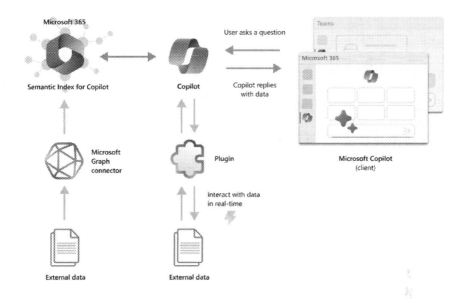

Figure 1-9. *Technical flowchart of how plugins and Microsoft Graph connector work*

Plugins

You can help your users do things with your web service by using Copilot plugins. Users can interact with your web service in natural language by using plugins:

- Get near real-time information. For example, keep up with the latest news about a new product launch.

- Access data through links. For example, generate a report on the service tickets assigned to a particular team member.

- Do tasks cross application. For example, start a new assignment in your organization's task management system.

You can build plugins with a Microsoft Teams message extension or a connector for the Power platform. If you already have a message extension or a Power platform connector, you're most of the way to having a Copilot plugin.

Microsoft Graph Connectors

When you integrate Graph connectors into the Microsoft 365 Copilot framework, they significantly enhance accessibility and engagement with your corporate data. Utilizing these connectors allows you to:

- Maximize the value of your external datasets with Copilot by providing it with the capability to pull data from various sources and aggregate, consequently empowering your capability in analytics.

- Turn Copilot into a true research assistant that can pull, summarize, and explore your favorite datasets to provide a natural question-and-answer functionality.

- Infuse intelligent Copilot capabilities into solutions as part of the search experience for Microsoft Search or as an intelligent form-filler within Context IQ—whatever path your users take to information access, you can make it a better one.

Implementing a Graph connector is a three-step process:

1. Create a connection.

2. Configure your data schema.

3. Channel your data into Microsoft Graph.

This ensures that each data entry adheres to your established schema to optimize discoverability in the Microsoft 365 ecosystem.

Extensibility Preview Support

Plugins are currently in preview mode and only work with Microsoft 365 Chat for Teams. Figure 1-10 shows Microsoft Copilot inside the Microsoft Teams app.

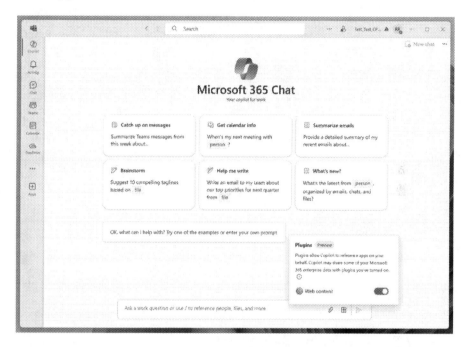

Figure 1-10. *Copilot inside the Microsoft Teams app*

Graph connectors are currently supported by Microsoft 365 Chat experiences in Teams, Microsoft 365 (Office) app, and Microsoft Bing.

Integration Mastery: Copilot Meets Power Apps

Integrating Microsoft 365 Copilot with Power Apps marks a leap forward in application development by marrying the easy, low-code capabilities of Power Apps with the most powerful artificial intelligence features from Copilot. These integrations are, in fact, very helpful in inculcating the development of powerful, user-friendly applications, revolutionizing the development space by providing users with the ability to develop functionally rich applications with intelligence. Figure 1-11 shows the illustration for Copilot in Microsoft Power Apps.

Figure 1-11. *Copilot in Microsoft Power Apps*

AI-Powered Code Generation: One of the most outstanding features of Copilot in Power Apps is its ability to generate code on common app scenarios and tasks, benefitting users who may not be conversant with syntax or formulas in coding. The user writes a request in natural language, such as "create a form to submit feedback" or "show a pie chart of sales by region," and Copilot interprets it into the required code and components.

This function helps reduce the development time needed and affords users more time to concentrate on designing the application and its logic rather than getting lost in the maze of programming.

Code Suggestions and Best Practices: Copilot improves the quality and performance of the application by giving alternative code with the best practices. Users can skim through various options in an order of moments, understand the reasoning for each suggestion, and observe how the functionality will be affected in the app. For example, when a user needs to add emailing capabilities, Copilot will suggest various ways, like adding connectors, and will list pros and cons for every one of them. Copilot provides guided assistance to the user for making the right decisions in ways to make their application more usable, secure, and cost-effective.

Debugging and Troubleshooting Assistance: Another great benefit of Copilot is that it can debug and troubleshoot applications. It helps identify errors, bugs, and all kinds of problems with the code, logic, or design of the application and offers solutions. For example, when prompted for a command like "fix the error in the gallery," Copilot may be able to diagnose the error because of a data source mismatch or incorrect filter conditions, as well as provide probable fixes. This feature is invaluable in ensuring that apps are not only functional but also reliable and free from errors.

Personalized and Context-Aware Recommendations: Copilot goes way beyond integrated generic help with Power Apps. It helps the apps learn from a user's coding style and preferences, thereby giving suggestions that are contextual and personalized. This aspect of learning with Copilot means that, as users interact with it, its suggestions become more personalized and impactful, thereby enhancing productivity and the app development experience.

Streamlining Complex Development Tasks: The AI-driven capabilities of Copilot help unravel the struggle to interweave complex processes, thus making it easier for users to add advanced features without them needing to have deep technical knowledge. This democratizes app development in the sense that any user can develop sophisticated applications that suit specific business requirements.

Enhancing Business Process Automation and Analytics: Moreover, integration is central to the automation of business processes and analytics. With AI-driven insights, Copilot can automate repetitive tasks inside applications and support businesses by providing analytical capabilities to businesses from their applications. This takes Power Apps from just being app development software to being a tool for strategic business analysis and automation.

Seamless Integration: Bridging Copilot with Power Apps

With the integration of Copilot and Power Apps, Microsoft 365 Copilot is a huge step forward in application development. Combining the power of Copilot's advanced AI with the simple, low-code Power Apps platform makes it possible for developers to create powerful, user-friendly applications in a whole new way. The result? Microsoft delivers on the Power Apps promise to empower business developers to create functionally rich and intelligent applications that have the potential to change the solutions people can build.

> **Facilitating Low-Code Development with AI:** Power Apps allows users to build custom applications for a very wide set of business needs. Copilot adds AI to the app-building experience. Using the latest machine learning algorithms and natural language processing, Copilot becomes a hands-on partner in performing sophisticated coding tasks. It automates mundane coding tasks, suggests code, and offers insights that will enable users to make data-driven decisions.

> **Intuitive AI-Driven Code Generation:** One of the most exciting features of this integration is Copilot's ability to generate code from natural language inputs. With the capability to describe the problem users need to solve and what they need to build in plain English (or your native language), users can get Copilot to "create a customer feedback form" or "design a dashboard for sales data," and it will convert this into Power Apps code. This is a game-

changer. If you're not an experienced developer or want to accelerate your learning, this tool allows you to focus on what your app should do and how it should look, while the technology handles the complex coding tasks.

Connecting Data Sources: A first and vital step in this seamless integration is to connect data sources. Power Apps allows a variety of data sources, including Excel, SharePoint, SQL Server, Common Data Service, Dynamics 365, and more commonly used by organizations. Users can also write custom connectors to connect to data that may not be officially supported by the platform, such as a custom service at an organization with RESTful endpoints. Copilot helps in choosing the right data sources, tables, and fields and makes suggestions based on the app's usage, as well as its functionality, in addition to helping define the relationships between data sources. This is crucial for showing and manipulating related data in the app.

Optimizing Code and Enhancing App Quality: Copilot goes beyond code generation by suggesting multiple variants of code that enhance compression and practicability, leading to improved efficiency and user-friendliness in applications. It recommends practical solutions, explaining their essence and implications, helping developers choose the most effective options. These recommendations guide developers in creating high-quality applications that are robust and scalable.

**Debugging and Personalized Development
Experience:** Copilot helps in debugging errors in
Power Apps by identifying them multiple times
and offering solutions, whether the issue lies in the
code, logic, or design. The suggestions adapt based
on the user's interactions, ensuring a customized
development experience. This adaptive approach
not only boosts productivity but also creates a more
intuitive way of interacting with development.

**Simplifying Complex Development Tasks and
Enhancing Business Processes:** The integration
simplifies complex app development tasks that were
previously hindered by the low-code limitations
of Power Apps. With Copilot, users can now
implement complex data models or integrate API-
enabled services, significantly expanding the range
of functions that Power Apps can easily achieve.
Additionally, the integration automates intricate
business processes and enables Power Apps to drive
data-driven decisions effectively. As a result, Power
Apps evolves beyond a simple app development
tool, becoming a strategic platform for business
automation and decision-making.

Case Studies: Successful Integration Scenarios

Right now, not many organizations are using Microsoft 365 Copilot for
Power Apps by Microsoft. This is one of the newest and possibly most
innovative products that Microsoft has debuted and as a result there are

only a few early adopters. Because of the newness of Copilot, it is very hard to find actual organizations that are implementing Copilot in Power Apps, so I have instead created some fictional but realistic scenarios to show its possibilities.

Case Study 1

This case study delves into the transformation journey of an emerging ecommerce platform grappling with complexities in managing inventory. The inventory system was very poor at the onset of the company; it led to overstocking and below-optimal communication with suppliers. In response, the company strategically overhauled their approach to inventory management to deploy an innovative solution that involved Power Apps and would integrate seamlessly with Copilot's AI technology.

This integration was a game-changer. It introduced a predictive stock management system, which leveraged advanced algorithms to forecast demand accurately and adjust inventory levels proactively. This AI-driven approach enabled the ecommerce retailer to anticipate market trends and consumer preferences, ensuring that the right products were available at the right time.

It also combined the automated supplier ordering process. This system resulted in automatically initiated supplier orders for actualized inventory information and predictive analytics, which led to a very efficient supply chain process. It streamlined the entire communication process with the suppliers, minimizing human errors and reducing the administrative pressure on staff. Great results were experienced from this strategic implementation. This helped the ecommerce platform reduce overstock by 40 percent, further saving on storage and inventory costs and deterioration. Better inventory turnover implies better resource utilization, considering that products do not stay as long in storage and quickly go down the supply chain. This transformation not only optimized the company's operational efficiency but also enhanced customer satisfaction by ensuring that product availability was aligned with consumer demand.

The most outstanding point of this case study is the possibility of integrating advanced technologies such as Power Apps and Copilot AI in the management of inventories in ecommerce businesses. The company embraced these innovative strategies to overcome the challenges it was facing and, at the same time, made sustainability plans toward competitive advantages amid the changing trends experienced in the online retail market.

Case Study 2

This case study looks at how a regional healthcare network—struggling to better manage hard-copy patient data and seeking useful ways to improve the appointment scheduling process—changed strategies to include the use of technology. The network was doing the right thing but needed a better way to start systems with technology. This transformation was performed in the heart of the old system—construction of a new system from scratch using Power Apps, integrated with Copilot AI. That's the development of a new and sophisticated application to address the main challenges: the possibility to analyze intricate patient data and optimize planning complicated by the countless factors of an appointment.

The integration of AI into the system was an advancement in patient data management. This is because the AI-based software feature analyzed massive patient data accurately and at a very high speed. This further helped in informed decision-making for patient care with an established framework of data analysis. Very importantly, all this also increased the level of security measures for patient data. The systems were more confidential, strictly following healthcare regulations.

Another major improvement in the system was the optimization of appointment scheduling. AI assessed data parameters such as patient flow, busy hours, and resource availability to allocate appointments more effectively. This not only optimized resource utilization but also significantly reduced patient waiting times, both of which otherwise compromised operational efficiency. The results of this initiative were impressive: increased efficiency in handling patients and a significant decrease in waiting times.

Such improvements not only increased patient satisfaction but also streamlined the health provider's workload. These strongly developing security protocols further built a higher level of trust and reliability among the patients about the safety of their sensitive health information.

In general, with the use of an approach, it can be said that this case study illustrates the positive consequences and success of integrating individualized technology solutions, such as Power Apps, in advancing and adding value to healthcare operations. This regional health network not only managed to fix its initial hiccups but also set new benchmarks for operational excellence and patient-centric care.

Case Study 3

This case study profiles the strategic evolution of a company that manufactures a certain range of products and faced critical challenges in relation to the optimization of logistics and production scheduling. This company operates through global supply chains, and there is a critical need for advanced solutions to increase operational efficiency while reducing expenses.

Confronted with this challenge, the company decided to apply Power Apps together with Copilot AI and develop an AI-based product tailored to logistics and production scheduling. Integration of AI into the logistics and scheduling systems was crucial.

Through AI integration, the company analyzed larger sets of information that spanned each stage of the supply chain and production processes. This often led to better forecasts, optimized schedules, and an improved allocation of resources.

An AI-based tool would make such forecasts and suggest proactive measures so that the supply chain remained smooth. One of the critical elements to this change was in logistics. The AI system revealed the best routes, taking into consideration how the transportation cost would be realized. These issues were related to costs, time, and environmental implications. This made it much easier to plan shipments strategically later, hence more money was saved and sustainability was achieved.

The improvement in production scheduling was also remarkable. Based on real-time data prediction, AI enabled the company to fit its schedules through the dynamic nature. This flexibility allowed the manufacturer to be prompt in responding to market demands, reducing downtime and waste, which boosted overall production efficiency. The results observed during the application of this AI-powered tool were evident.

The company realized a 30 percent gain in production efficiency, and this was a massive improvement in operational ability. Further, process optimization resulted in noticeable cuts in costs, positively affecting the bottom line.

This case study, therefore, reinforces that technology integration in the manufacturing sector, such as Power Apps and Copilot AI, has the potential to be transformational. By embracing this innovative approach, this mid-sized manufacturing company not only addressed logistical and scheduling challenges but also gained a competitive edge in the global market by achieving greater efficiency and cost competitiveness.

Summary

In this chapter, I introduced you to the revolutionary impact of Microsoft 365 Copilot on low-code application development, highlighting how it empowers you to create software more easily with advanced AI capabilities. You learned how Copilot can generate code, provide predictive analytics, and enhance your experience by tailoring suggestions to your preferences.

Chapter 2 explores the practical steps needed to set up, configure, and optimize Copilot for Power Apps. I cover the essential prerequisites, licensing options, and system requirements, ensuring that you have everything needed to maximize your development experience.

Embarking on the Copilot Journey

The previous chapter explored the innovative features and benefits of Copilot, a state-of-the-art tool that helps developers create complex and smart applications. This chapter aims to offer a comprehensive guide on how to install, configure, and optimize Copilot for maximum performance.

This chapter provides guidelines, one after the other, for the successful installation of Copilot over Power Platform, including prerequisites and system checks in relation to compatibility. This chapter provides further information on customizations based on individual needs and project-specific requirements, focusing on setting up the appropriate environment variables and integration points.

Streamlined Setup: From Installation to Execution

Microsoft Copilot for Power Apps is a radical departure from the standard models, mostly due to its approach as a purely online service. This distinction is key for users who are used to the old installation methods. In contrast with traditional applications that demand a list of installation steps, Copilot for Power Apps is available online (from the Microsoft 365 Portal) without installation requirements. This certainly means that from

© Rezwanur Rahman 2024
R. Rahman, *Microsoft Copilot for Power Apps*, Inside Copilot,
https://doi.org/10.1007/979-8-8688-0512-7_2

this online service model, the whole dynamics of the user experience, insofar as business application development and management are concerned, will change entirely. Its immediate availability is the major benefit of the model. It allows users to run Copilot for Power Apps at full functionality without the installation delays and complexities of software. This allows a quick start to developing and managing applications, which is important in accelerated business environments.

Copilot for Power Apps has no requirements like the standard desktop software requirements from a technical perspective and is all about licensing. No installation is required; you do not have to worry about the compatibility of the system, disk space, or the hardware. You must have the right kind of licensing power to access and use the service. Details of these licensing needs and detailed information on system and account requirements are presented in detail in this book.

With this service being available online, it confers advantages in the form of real-time updates and feature enhancements without the user having to do anything. The fact that Copilot for Power Apps forms a part of the continuous Microsoft update cycle means that users are always working with the latest version, and therefore with the most current tools and functionalities. This is critical to being on the edge in app development and deployment.

The cloud-based architecture of Copilot for Power Apps further supports collaborative development environments. Since the service is delivered over the Internet, access to it must be multi-user in nature. It easily allows for collaboration among different teams in the same organization. Teams can work together at the same time in projects from different geographical locations, exploiting shared development enabled by the cloud to close projects in record time.

The focus of this book is particularly on exploring the different important subtleties and features of Copilot for Power Apps. It is a powerful tool and is a merger of automation and intelligence, whereby all sorts of applications are customized to be most efficient and effective within the platform of Power Apps. The following sections explore each application in more detail to help you understand the different features, how to use them in different use cases, and best practices so that you're able to get the best out of Copilot for Power Apps.

It should, however, be noted that this is just part of the larger Copilot ecosystem. It is in this context that successive chapters of this book bring to light Copilot for Microsoft 365 and Copilot Studio. These features complement the capabilities of Copilot for Power Apps in articulating the suite's ability to redefine the way users engage with technology when observed across different Microsoft platforms. Traveling through these chapters should be informative and insightful, but above all, bring you to an enriched experience in the field of digital solutions.

Long story short:

- Copilot for Power Apps does not require desktop software for app design or development.

- There are no requirements in terms of system compatibility, storage, memory, graphics, or physical hardware.

- You can use any modern browser to design Copilot and Power Apps.

- A stable Internet connection is essential to avoid technical problems.

Licensing Overview

Before moving to what is required to use Microsoft Copilot for Power Apps, let's talk about licensing Power Apps and Copilot.

One common question, which many of my friends and colleagues have asked me, is "Do I need Microsoft 365 licenses to develop Microsoft Power Apps?"

You do not need a Microsoft 365 license to use or build Power Apps applications. Microsoft 365 is a suite of productive apps such as Outlook, Word, Excel, PowerPoint, and so on. These apps can be hooked to Power Apps, but that is not required. You can also develop Power Apps without Microsoft 365 licensing. The following list discusses the plans where you can start developing Power Apps:

- **Power Apps Developer Plan:** Among the many app development options, Microsoft has provided a complimentary Power Apps Developer Plan that has been very helpful for educational purposes and immense skill development . It has a complete, dedicated environment for app development, testing, and experimentation using Power Apps, Power Automate, and new functionalities on the *Dataverse*. The plan is meant for personal use, and everyone gets their individual usage environment, which is on a non-production capacity.

- **Power Apps Trials:** Power Apps has a variety of trial plans that allow you to utilize the entire parts of the application, which means you can try the full capabilities of Power Apps before you buy. Generally, a trial is for 30 days, and it has the maximum Power Apps features.

- **Pay-As-You-Go Plan:** By using the pay-as-you-go model, you can access Power Apps through an Azure subscription and pay only for the resources consumed. In this model, there is no need for any upfront commitment to software purchases, license purchases, or infrastructure provisioning.

- **Directly purchase Power Apps licenses:** You can also directly acquire Power Apps licenses independently of any Microsoft 365 subscriptions. This path is ideally suited for those with a heavy reliance on Power Apps or those planning to deploy applications in a production environment.

Table 2-1 provides a comprehensive overview of the Power Apps licensing options, highlighting their key features, approximate pricing, and inherent limitations.

Table 2-1. *Comprehensive Overview of Power Apps Licensing Options with Key Features*

Licensing Option	Description and Key Features	Approx. Pricing (USD)	Limitations
Microsoft 365 and Dynamics 365 Entitlements	Microsoft 365 and Dynamics 365 Entitlements	Included in Microsoft 365/ Dynamics 365 subscriptions	Features dependent on specific Microsoft 365/ Dynamics 365 plan
Connectors Usage	Connects apps to various data sources; includes standard and premium connectors	Included in respective Power Apps/ Automate licenses	Premium connectors only available with specific licenses; standard connectors offer limited capabilities
Trial Plans	Short-term, full-featured access to Power Apps and Power Automate for evaluation purposes	Free	30 days for Power Apps, 90 days for Power Automate; limited features compared to full licenses

(*continued*)

Table 2-1. (*continued*)

Licensing Option	Description and Key Features	Approx. Pricing (USD)	Limitations
Developer Plan	Provides a full-featured development environment for individual learning and experimentation	Free	For individual development only; not suitable for production use
Per App Plan	Allows the use of one app or portal per user; suitable for targeted business solutions	Around $5-10/user/app/month	Restricted to one app or portal per user; not for extensive app portfolios
Pay-As-You-Go Plan	Flexible, usage-based payment model linked to an Azure subscription	Variable; based on usage	Costs can vary greatly based on usage; requires Azure subscription management
Dataverse Plans in Microsoft 365	Limited use of Dataverse for data storage and management with select Microsoft 365 licenses	Included in select Microsoft 365 plans	Cannot create custom apps with Power Apps or use premium connectors with Power Automate
Power Automate Hosted RPA Add-On	Provides capacity for automated workflows with a single RPA bot and a VM	Pricing varies	Limited to one bot per license; additional bots require additional licenses

(*continued*)

Table 2-1. (*continued*)

Licensing Option	Description and Key Features	Approx. Pricing (USD)	Limitations
Microsoft Copilot Studio Licensing	AI-driven bot creation and deployment with a monthly message quota for interactions	Pricing varies	Limited to 25,000 AI messages/month; additional messages incur extra costs
Purchase Options	Licenses available through Power Apps website, Microsoft 365 admin center, or via Microsoft partners	Varies based on plan and channel	Choice of plan and purchasing channel affects pricing and features available

Power Apps Without Microsoft 365: Key Limitations

If you develop Power Apps applications without a Microsoft 365 license, you will be very limited in many ways—in particular, how you can connect and manage data. The following lists explain these limitations in more detail.

Limited integration with Microsoft 365 Services:

- You can't integrate your Power Apps with Microsoft 365 services, such as SharePoint, Outlook, Excel Online, or Teams.

- This limits the ability of these platforms to be used for data storage, user management, and collaboration within your Power Apps.

Data storage and management:

- The place where the app stores data is offered through Microsoft 365—either in SharePoint lists or with Excel Online—the most common sources of data consumed by Power Apps users.

- With the absence of them, you will need to look for alternative resources—data sources like SQL Server, some other databases, or any storage solution provided by a third party.

User authentication and management:

- Microsoft 365 provides a unified identity service (Microsoft Entra ID, previously Azure Active Directory) for authentication and user management.

- Without Microsoft 365, managing user access and authentication for your Power Apps can be more complex, possibly requiring separate identity services or custom solutions.

Collaboration and workflow integration:

- Power Apps frequently interface with Power Automate to enable flow automation. Although Power Automate can be acquired independently, its Microsoft 365 services complement automation and changes.

- Before Microsoft 365, any processes that required Microsoft services, like email notifications through Outlook or data processing with Excel, respectively, would require scads of programming to automate the process.

Access to pre-built templates:

- With Power Apps comes a whole range of pre-built templates to work with Microsoft 365 services.

- They are not very useful without an attached Microsoft 365 license, which could require even more custom development.

Limited access to certain features:

- Some Power Apps features and connectors are designed specifically for Microsoft 365 services. Without access to these services, the full range of Power Apps features may not be available.

Data governance and compliance:

- Data governance and compliance tools and policies are offered through Microsoft 365. The value proposition means that data governance (including data loss prevention—DLP—and retention policies) and compliance policies available with the Microsoft 365 might be of importance to applications that deal with sensitive/regulated data.

- If you built a Power App that processes data that falls within certain regulatory requirements, building a Power App outside the Microsoft 365 ecosystem might require you to do extra work to meet the regulatory compliance needs.

You must evaluate your needs and decide whether the benefits are worth these limitations. If you are using just the standalone products or not having the applications integrate much with Microsoft 365's services, this might be a non-issue.

Prerequisites for the AI Features in Power Apps

For these functionalities in Power Apps to operate appropriately, a range of technical provisions is necessary to enable maximum use of the AI Copilot functions. This will ensure that such advanced features are smoothly integrated and operate in the right manner. The guidelines herein are to aid users in the configuration of their setup to ensure that effective harnessing of AI Copilot capabilities in Power Apps is realized.

> **Regional requirements**: Your Power Apps environment should be located within the United States region. This enables the AI Copilot features to be available and used to their full capacity.
>
> **Browser language setting**: This should be set to "English (United States)" so that the AI Copilot features and interfaces are guaranteed to be presented in a language compatible with full support.
>
> **Microsoft Dataverse database**: Ensure that an active Microsoft Dataverse database is part of your environment. One key repository for data storage and management that AI Copilot uses across different applications and functionalities it has within Power Apps is Dataverse. The chapter discusses the Dataverse database in more detail later. (See the next section for answers to common questions.)
>
> **Activating AI Builder**: AI Builder is a feature of Microsoft Power Apps that brings artificial intelligence capabilities to the Power Apps

platform. It lets users enhance their apps, automate workflows, and examine data in a more productive and accurate way. AI Builder must be enabled in your environment to use the AI models or controls that include AI models. This can be done by following these steps:

1. Sign in to the Power Platform Admin Center. This is your central hub for managing various aspects of your Power Apps environment. Figure 2-1 shows the Power Platform Admin Center.

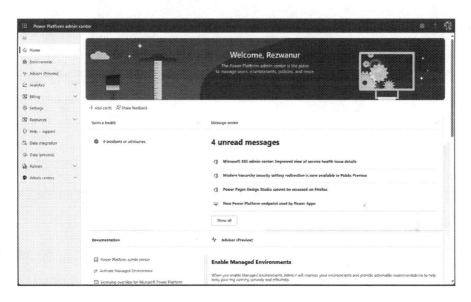

Figure 2-1. *Preview of the Microsoft Power Platform Admin Center*

2. Navigate to Environments and select the specific environment you want to configure for AI Copilot. Figure 2-2 shows the list of the environments.

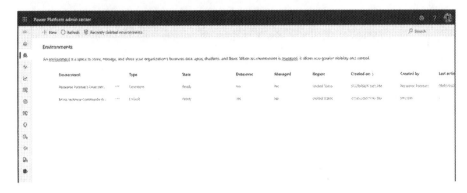

Figure 2-2. *Environments page of the Power Platform Admin Center*

3. Choose Settings ➤ Product ➤ Features. Figure 2-3
    shows the settings for an environment.

Figure 2-3. *Environments Settings page*

4. On the Features settings page, locate the section
    labeled AI Builder. You can enable or disable the
    AI Builder preview models. Enabling AI Builder is
    crucial as it provides the necessary framework and
    tools for AI functionalities within your Power Apps
    environment. Figure 2-4 shows the Features page.

Figure 2-4. *Feature page of environment*

Quick Q/A Session

1. **Can I use AI Builder outside of the United States?**

   For those of you not in the United States, wondering
   if you can use AI Builder, the answer is yes! AI
   Builder is available in India, France, United Arab
   Emirates, Germany, and the United States. However,
   some AI models may perform worse, based on the
   region and languages of your data.

   For more details, you can check out the AI Builder
   regional availability documentation at `https://`
   `learn.microsoft.com/en-us/power-platform-`
   `release-plan/2021wave1/ai-builder/ai-builder-`
   `availability-new-regions`.

2. **Can I use a language other than English in AI Builder?**

Yes, you can use other languages besides English in AI Builder. AI Builder supports 73 languages for text recognition and 12 languages for sentiment analysis. You can also create your own custom models using data in any language. However, some features, such as the business card reader and receipt processing, are currently optimized for English only.

For more details, you can check out the AI Builder language availability documentation at: `https://learn.microsoft.com/en-us/power-platform-release-plan/2021wave2/ai-builder/form-processing-new-language-support`.

3. **Can I use AI Builder without the Microsoft Dataverse Database?**

To make sure that AI Builder is working properly with Power Apps, it requires a database from the Microsoft Dataverse to be tightly integrated, so it can leverage all the features that AI Builder has to offer. In other words, one database is required for AI Builder to function in Power Apps—the Dataverse Database.

Setting Up a Test and Development Space

When you think about it, you probably will find that even when developing software or doing IT professionally, you usually perform testing on a trial tenant first before doing it on your operational tenant, which stores and handles actual data. You can say doing things on the live tenant is a precautionary measure.

It's best to set up a test environment, motivated by several key reasons beyond the initial purpose. These reasons include:

1. **Support for Power Apps beginners:** This approach helps newcomers to Power Apps, providing them with a dedicated space to learn and experiment. This provides a secured and controlled environment whereby the newcomer can explore the features and functionalities of Power Apps, practice with application construction, and gain confidence without the fear of damaging real-world data or systems.

2. **Guidance on acquiring Microsoft 365 licenses for free:** You can acquire a Microsoft 365 license for free, when the work is research and development.

3. **A platform for app development and testing:** This is a complete platform for users to develop and test their applications before deploying within their main tenant. Users can test their applications prior to mainstream integration, which ensures that apps work as intended in the operational context, and do not disrupt operational procedures or data flow. It is useful to developers who can build their apps, test features, and resolve findings all in one go, in a managed environment.

4. **Safe tenant settings modification:** Changing the tenant settings in the primary, operational environment is not without its risks, and it hampers real-time data processing. It is, therefore, crucial to have a test environment that supports safe trials and extensive testing of the adjusted tenant settings.

The changes in this area should be implemented in this test area first to ensure that they are effective and reliable. The subsequent step is critical in maintaining stability and operational integrity for the primary tenant before any putative changes are implemented.

Sign Up for M365 Dev Plan

You can set up a new Microsoft 365 E5 instant sandbox tenant through the Microsoft 365 Developer Program by following these steps:

1. Open your browser and visit `https://developer.microsoft.com/en-us/microsoft-365/dev-program`. Figure 2-5 shows the homepage of Microsoft 365 Developer program.

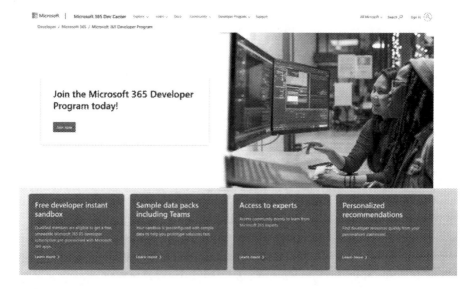

Figure 2-5. *Homepage of Microsoft 365 Developer program*

The Microsoft 365 E5 instant sandbox, as part of the Microsoft 365 Developer Program, includes a comprehensive environment aimed at enabling developers to quickly start building and testing their solutions. Here are the key components included in the instant sandbox:

- **A complete Microsoft 365 E5 Developer environment:** This sandbox comes preloaded with a Microsoft 365 E5 subscription with 25 users, including 16 sample users. This setup is designed to allow developers to start experimenting and building solutions immediately, without the need for extensive configuration.

- **Administrative control:** Developers have the power to act as their own administrators, facilitating the prototyping of apps and solutions with minimal setup.

- **Sample data packs:** Central to the instant sandbox are the preinstalled sample data packs, which include:

  - **Microsoft Graph user, mail, and calendar data:** Featuring 16 sample users with user data and content, this data pack enables developers to model solutions with user mailboxes, calendar events, and integration into a Teams developer environment with simulated chats and team memberships.

- **Teams sample data pack:** This pack is tailored to a developer environment with preconfigured Teams app sideloading, five sample teams, channels, tabs, and chat sessions built around the 16 sample users. It also includes the Teams Developer portal, pre-installed and pinned, aiding in the creation of Teams app manifest and app package, as well as offering a card editor and a React control library.

- **SharePoint framework sample data:** Developers can choose from six site templates to install and evaluate as custom solutions for their organization, with one template preinstalled in the instant sandbox.

On the same page, you can see what's included in the licensing information, as shown in Figure 2-6.

Figure 2-6. *Microsoft 365 E5 instant sandbox page*

2. Click Join Now to reach the Sign In page, as shown in Figure 2-7. If you have an unregistered Microsoft account (Hotmail, Outlook, Live), sign in to continue. Otherwise, select Create One to create a new account.

Figure 2-7. *Sign in page for a Microsoft account*

3. You will see the page shown in Figure 2-8 next. Click Get a New Email Address, as shown in Figure 2-8.

Figure 2-8. *Creating a new Microsoft email address*

4. Choose a name for your email address, select the desired domain, and then proceed by clicking Next. In this instance, I named the email address powerapps.newbook@outlook.com. Figure 2-9 shows this step.

Figure 2-9. *Creating the username of the email address*

5. Type a password, as shown in Figure 2-10, and then
    click Next.

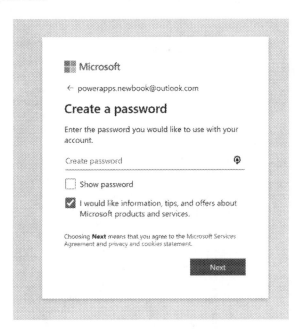

Figure 2-10. *Creating a password for the email address*

6. The next page will prompt you for your Country and Date of Birth, as shown in Figure 2-11. Fill them in and proceed.

Figure 2-11. *Fill in the Country and Date of Birth*

7. Super! The account is done! You will see the page shown in Figure 2-12.

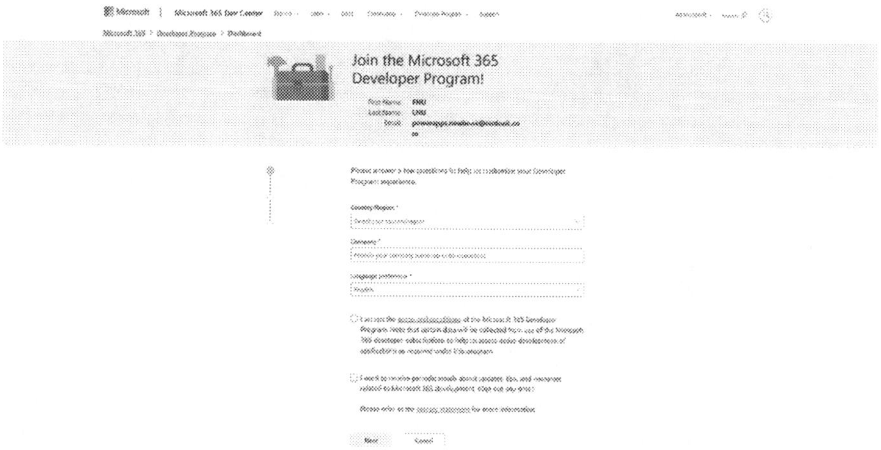

Figure 2-12. *Dashboard setup page for the Microsoft 365 Developer Program*

8. Next, you need to choose the Country, Company, and Language. For this example, choose the Country: United States, Company: *Your_Company_ Name* (If you do not have a real company, just use an imaginary name), and Language Preference: English. Accept the terms and conditions and click Next!

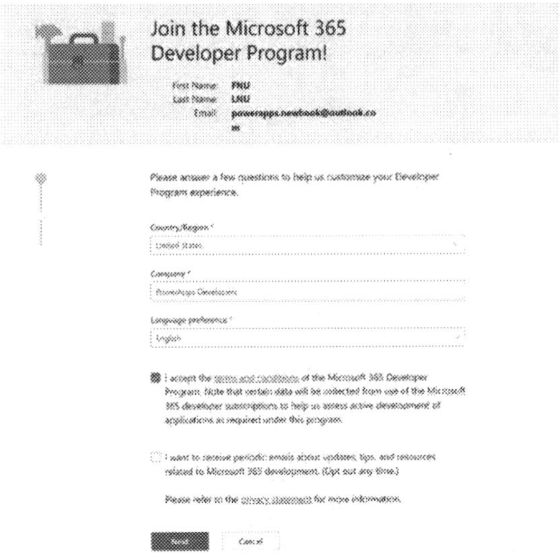

Figure 2-13. *Fill in a Country, Company, and Language for the tenant*

9. The next page will ask you a question. Choose your answer and proceed. I selected Personal Projects, as shown in Figure 2-14.

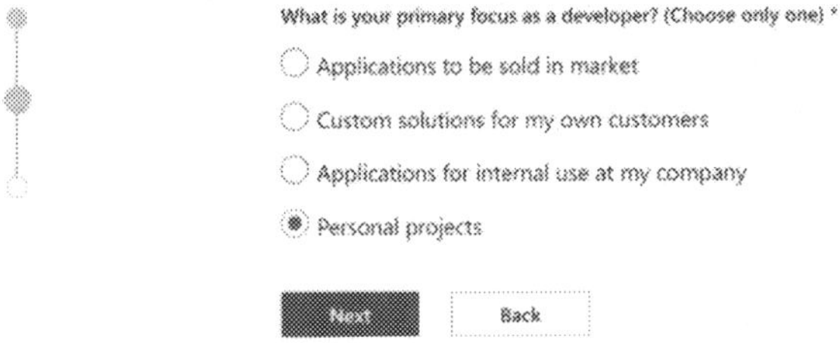

Figure 2-14. *Selecting the answer for the question about primary focus*

10. The next question will ask about your interested areas. Choose your interests, as shown in Figure 2-15. Additionally, you need to confirm your human identity by completing a reCAPTCHA verification. When you're done, click Save.

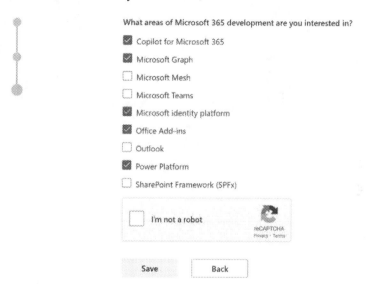

Figure 2-15. *Choose your areas of interest for Microsoft 365 development*

11. Superb! The sign up is complete. You will see the page shown in Figure 2-16. Select Instant Sandbox and click Next.

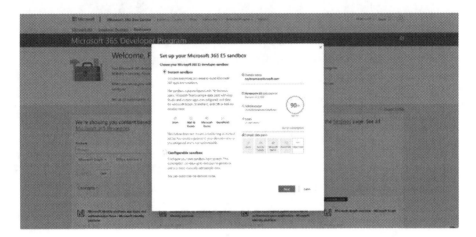

Figure 2-16. *Microsoft 365 Developer Sandbox setup page*

12.   On the next page, you will be asked for the region
      for your data center, the admin username, and a
      password. I selected the North America (United
      States – CA) region and provided a username and
      password to gain access as an administrator. See
      Figure 2-17.

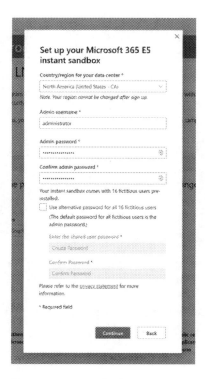

Figure 2-17. *Select the country, admin username, and password*

13.   Next, it will ask for a phone number for verification.
       Enter a valid number and wait for the verification
       code. See Figure 2-18.

Figure 2-18. *Phone number verification modal box*

14.   You are done! You will see the Microsoft 365
Developer dashboard shown in Figure 2-19.

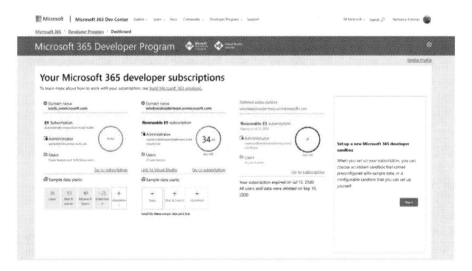

Figure 2-19. *Microsoft 365 Developer subscriptions dashboard*

15. When you click Go to Subscription, the browser will
     redirect you to the Microsoft 365 portal, as shown in
     Figure 2-20.

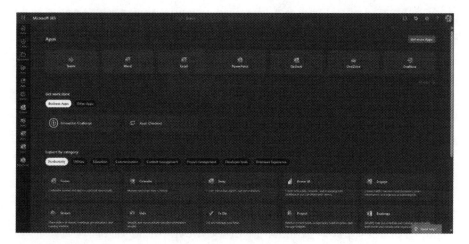

Figure 2-20. *Microsoft 365 Apps Portal*

Signing Up for Microsoft Power Apps Dev Plan

Understanding the difference between the Microsoft 365 Developer E5
license and the Power Apps Developer Plan is very important.

The Microsoft 365 Developer E5 license is an enterprise subscription
built for anyone with diverse, advanced development needs in an
organization, including Power Apps. Best suited for organizational
subscriptions where one needs all solutions in a single environment,
strong security is envisaged, and the features available for application
development are vast and under one organizational setup.

The Power Apps Developer Plan is meant for individual developers,
and it's free. It enables the development and testing of Power Apps in a
focused environment with access to paid features; however, the apps that

are developed under this plan cannot be used in production. This plan allows you to experiment and learn something new with certain limits in data capacity and execution.

The Power Apps Developer Plan is also available to any user who has a Microsoft 365 Developer E5 license. This dual approach allows users to get the combination of enterprise-level services (through the E5 license) and have their secure, isolated environment for development and testing (through the Developer Plan). Note that the apps developed in the Power Apps Developer Plan are test and development applications. They are not supposed to be used in the production environment.

To sign up for Microsoft Power Apps Developer Plan, follow these instructions:

1. Open your browser and visit `https://aka.ms/PowerAppsdevplan`. You will see the homepage, as shown in Figure 2-21.

Figure 2-21. *Homepage of the Microsoft Power Apps Developer Plan website*

Curious to know what's included in the license plan? You can:

- Access the complete environment/sandbox with all features used to create and test apps.

- Connect many data sources, such as custom connectors and on-premises data.

- Use the limited amount of capacity for Dataverse to store and manage your data.

- Develop model-driven and Canvas apps within Power Apps, including Power Automate for workflow automation.

Remember, this license plan is for dev/test use only. You can't use this for your production/official apps.

2. Click Get Started for Free to see the page shown in Figure 2-22.

Figure 2-22. *Sign up page for Microsoft Power Apps for Developer*

3. Type your newly created email address. The page
   will tell you to sign in, as shown in Figure 2-23.

Figure 2-23. *Sign in option after entering the email address*

4. After signing in, click Create Account. You will see
   the option shown in Figure 2-24.

Figure 2-24. *Confirmation details after signing up*

5. That's it. The setup is done! You can see the Power
    Apps page in Figure 2-25.

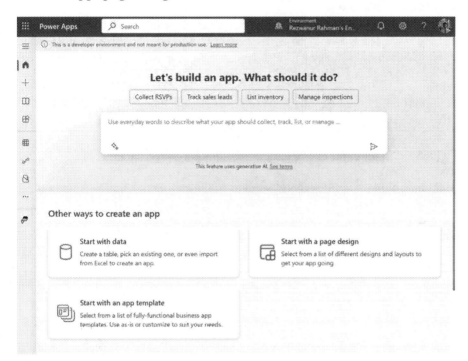

Figure 2-25. *Portal page of Power Apps Developers*

System Requirements, Limits, and Configure Values

When you want to create apps with Power Apps, you need to be aware of the system requirements, boundaries, and configuration settings of Power Apps. This section covers some of these essential requirements.

Table 2-2 lists the platforms that can run apps with the Power Apps mobile app.

Table 2-2. *Supported Platforms That Can Run Apps by Power Apps*

Platform	Version
iOS	The latest version of iOS is always the recommended version to run Power Apps mobile. The previous version is the minimum required.
Android	The latest version of Android is always the recommended version to run Power Apps mobile. The previous three versions are the minimum required to run Power Apps mobile.
Windows	Windows 10 version 17763.0 or later.

Table 2-3 lists the Power Apps-compatible browsers.

Table 2-3. *Supported Browsers That Can Run Apps by Power Apps*

Platform	Version	App Type
Microsoft Edge	Latest three major releases	Model-driven apps, Canvas apps, app and component designers
Google Chrome	Latest three major releases	Model-driven apps, Canvas apps, app and component designers.
Mozilla Firefox	Latest three major releases	Model-driven apps and Canvas apps
Apple Safari	13 and later	Model-driven apps and Canvas apps

Table 2-4 lists the supported operating systems for browsers running Power Apps.

Table 2-4. *Supported Operating Systems for Browsers That Can Run Apps by Power Apps*

Platform	Version	App Type
Windows	Windows 10 or later	Model-driven apps, Canvas apps, app and component designers*
MacOS	10.13 or later	Model-driven apps, Canvas apps, app and component designers*
iOS	iOS 13 or later	Model-driven apps and Canvas apps**
Android	10 and later	Model-driven apps and Canvas apps**

*App and component designers include Power Apps Studio, model-driven app designer, and model-driven custom page designer.

**Using the web browser on a phone to run a model-driven app isn't supported.

Table 2-5 lists the single outgoing request limits.

Table 2-5. *Single Outgoing Request Limits*

Name	Limit
Timeout	180 Seconds
Retry attempt	4

Note   The retry value may vary. For certain error conditions, it's not necessary to retry.

Required Services

Table 2-6 lists the services that Power Apps uses to communicate and what they do. Your network *should not* prevent these services from working.

Table 2-6. *Services Required for Working with Power Apps*

Domain(s)	Protocols	Users
api.bap.microsoft.com *.api.bap.microsoft.com	https	Environment permissions management
management.azure.com	https	Power Apps Management Service
msmanaged-na.azure-apim.net	https	Runtime of Connectors/APIs
login.microsoft.com login.windows.net login.microsoftonline.com secure.aadcdn. microsoftonline-p.com *.odc.officeapps.live.com	https	Microsoft Authentication Library
graph.microsoft.comgraph. windows.net	https	Azure Graph: To get user info (for example, profile photo)
*.azure-apim.net	https	API Hubs: Different subdomains for each locale

(*continued*)

Table 2-6. (*continued*)

Domain(s)	Protocols	Users
*.Power Apps.com	https	create.Power Apps.com, content.Power Apps.com, apps.Power Apps.com, make.Power Apps.com, *gateway.prod.island. Power Apps.com, and *gateway.prod.cm.Power Apps.com
*.azureedge.net	https	create.Power Apps.com, content.Power Apps.com, and make.Power Apps.com
*.ces.microsoftcloud.com	https	Access to net promoter score (NPS) and surveys
*.blob.core.windows.net	https	Blob storage
*.flow.microsoft.com *.powerautomate.com	https	create.Power Apps.com, content.Power Apps.com, and make.Power Apps.com

(*continued*)

Table 2-6. (*continued*)

Domain(s)	Protocols	Users
`http://*.crm#.dynamics.` `com` and `https://*.crm#.` `dynamics.com`	`http` and `https`	Required for environments access. Includes integration and static Content Delivery Network (CDN) content endpoints. Replace # in `http://*.` `crm#.dynamics.com` and `https://*.crm#.` `dynamics.com` with your region's number: • Asia/Pacific: 5 • Canada: 3 • Europe, Africa, and Middle East: 15 and 4 • France: 12 • Germany: 16 • India: 8 • Japan: 7 • North America: No number • Oceania: 6 • Singapore: 20 • South Africa: 14 • South America: 2 • Switzerland: 17 • UAE: 15 • United Kingdom: 11 • Dynamics 365 US Government: 9

(*continued*)

Table 2-6. (*continued*)

Domain(s)	Protocols	Users
eu-mobile.events.data.microsoft.com/Collector/3.0	https	European region telemetry endpoint for model-driven apps
browser.pipe.aria.microsoft.com	https	Rest of the world telemetry endpoint for model-driven apps
localhost	http	Power App Mobile
127.0.0.1	https	Power App Mobile
ecs.office.com	https	Retrieve feature flags for Power Apps
augloop.office.com*.augloop.office.com	WSS	Power Apps Studio Copilot
config.edge.skype.com	https	Retrieve feature flags for Power Apps (backup)
api.powerplatform.com*.powerplatform.com	https	Required for Power Platform API connectivity used internally by Microsoft products, and Power Platform programmability and extensibility
*.sharepointonline.com	https	Retrieve assets for presenting the header that appears at the top of app playing experiences
ris.api.iris.microsoft.comeudb.ris.api.iris.microsoft.com	https	Record user action in response to Power Apps in-app campaigns
arc.msn.comarc-emea.msn.com	https	Record user viewing of Power Apps in-app campaigns

---

Note   If you're using a VPN, you must configure it to *exclude* localhost from tunneling for Power Apps Mobile.

Deprecated Endpoints

Microsoft does not supporting the listed endpoints. I include the old and new endpoints in Table 2-7.

Table 2-7. *Deprecated Endpoints and New Endpoints List*

Deprecated Endpoint	New Endpoint
web.Power Apps.com/apps/{yourAppGuid}	apps.Power Apps.com/play/{yourAppGuid}
web.Power Apps.com/apps/{yourAppGuid}/open	apps.Power Apps.com/play/{yourAppGuid}

Embedding Limits for Canvas Apps

Power Apps doesn't support the nested embedding of Canvas apps in native desktop, mobile, or other non-browser clients.

Table 2-8 lists some of the examples where embedding a Canvas app is and isn't supported.

Table 2-8. *Embedding Limits for Canvas Apps*

Power Apps Embedding Scenario	Supported Clients	Unsupported Clients
A Canvas app embedded in a SharePoint page	Web	Teams desktop Teams mobile
A Canvas app embedded in a SharePoint page that is added as a tab in a Microsoft Teams channel	Web	Teams desktop Teams mobile
A Canvas app used as a custom form in the SharePoint page	Web	Teams desktop Teams mobile
A Canvas app used as a custom form in the SharePoint page that is added to a Teams team	Web	Teams desktop Teams mobile SharePoint mobile
A Power BI report that is added to Teams, or a SharePoint site	Web	Teams desktop Teams mobile SharePoint mobile
A model-driven form that is added to Teams	Web	Teams desktop Teams mobile
A canvas app is embedded in a third-party client	Third-party web client that iframe's an app	Third-party native client via WebView
A Canvas app in a Unified Service Desk	None	Unified Service Desk Desktop app

Note   Remember, pricing and features can change, and it's best to check the official Microsoft Power Apps website for the most current information. The official website is `https://learn.microsoft.com/en-us/power-apps/powerapps-overview`.

Proxies

Using a proxy with Power Apps can cause problems and is unsupported. If something doesn't seem to be working, turn the proxy off and see if that does the trick.

Some proxies (such as Zscaler and Blue Coat) change requests coming to Power Apps by removing some headers (CORS or authentication headers) in their outgoing responses. The app in question relies on the said headers for it to load. Some proxies (e.g., Microsoft Defender for Cloud Apps and McAfee) can tamper with URL links of an application or an embedded one by intercepting it.

For example, Dynamics 365 runs under the domain `org.crm.dynamics.com`, and the Canvas app runs under the domain `apps.PowerApps.com`. In this case, the platform does not support a proxy that changes these domains to a different domain like `mycustomdomain.com`. This can lead to unexpected behavior when the platform tries to get the tokens needed to run the app.

Summary

This chapter guided you through the setup, configuration, and licensing of Microsoft Copilot for Power Apps, highlighting its streamlined online service model and the ease of integrating with Microsoft 365. You learned about the various licensing options, the prerequisites for activating

AI features, and the importance of preparing a solid development environment. This foundation ensures that you can effectively leverage Copilot's capabilities for rapid, AI-driven application development.

As you move to Chapter 3, I take you deeper into the core technology behind Copilot. This chapter explores the powerful AI Builder that drives Copilot, showing how it revolutionizes code development with its low-code interface and seamless integration with Microsoft's Power Platform. I also introduce you to the AI models at the heart of Copilot, their applications in real-world business scenarios, and the advanced technologies that make Copilot a smart, intuitive tool for developers like you.

CHAPTER 3

Mastering the Core: Copilot's Engine Room

What new, magical technology from Microsoft makes Copilot so incredible? How does this magic operate behind the scenes to transform complex programming tasks into simple, intuitive experiences? This chapter looks closely at the sophisticated technology that makes Copilot such a powerful assistant—AI Builder.

Why is AI Builder a crucial component of this breakthrough? This chapter explores these key connections and their functions. I guide you through this adaptability, showing how Copilot, equipped with AI Builder, stands out as a versatile software development tool.

Are you curious about Copilot's intelligence? This chapter also introduces AI algorithms that form the core of Copilot. What happens when these AI algorithms face real-world problems? This chapter also presents AI-based solutions to real-world problems in three case studies. I show that AI-based solutions are theoretical, efficient, and practical, with actual demos planned in upcoming chapters.

© Rezwanur Rahman 2024
R. Rahman, *Microsoft Copilot for Power Apps*, Inside Copilot, https://doi.org/10.1007/979-8-8688-0512-7_3

You are about to gain a deeper understanding of Copilot, appreciate its underlying features, and learn how to be creative with what you have already learned. Are you ready to enter the Copilot Control Room and learn more about how these features affect your development needs? Then, let's proceed.

Harnessing the Power: Key Features Unlocked

This section explains further how the introduction of AI Builder has revolutionized the field of application development. This leads to the next segment, which calls for more elaborate studies about these powerful tools perfectly integrate into the Copilot ecosystem, delivering greater power to developers.

AI Builder: Revolutionizing Code Development

If Copilot is the co-pilot, AI Builder is the pilot. AI Builder is the powerhouse of Copilot; it brings Copilot alive and works on code suggestions based upon natural language, given the query and context. AI Builder is a low-code platform that allows users to create and deploy AI models without writing any code. Hosted on the Microsoft Azure platform, AI Builder provides more than 90 pre-built AI models and empowers users to build AI from scratch, including developing customized AI scenarios such as sentiment analysis, object detection, forms processing, and text recognition. Figure 3-1 shows the components of AI Builder.

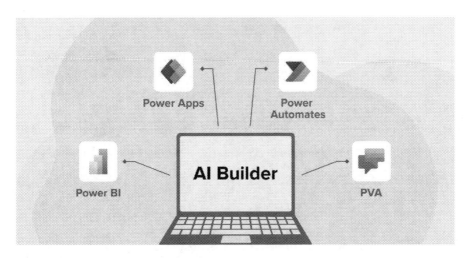

Figure 3-1. *AI Builder is compatible with all Power Platform applications*

AI Builder is fed with data from different sources, including Excel files, SharePoint lists, SQL databases, and Power Apps collections, among others. From there, users can choose an AI scenario, and further personalization is done to meet their exact needs. From there, AI Builder will train and evaluate the model, after which a score is given to grade its performance. After that, the model can be published, ready for use inside Power Apps and Power Automate or in applications developed inside Dynamics 365. Refer to Figure 3-2.

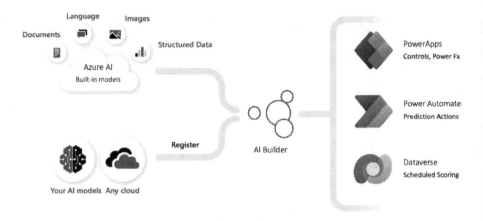

Figure 3-2. *Technical structure of AI Builder*

The most important benefit of AI Builder is that it makes AI accessible to everyone. It does not matter if the person does not know much about coding. No experience in coding is necessary—AI Builder provides a guide to develop an AI model in a few clicks and adds it quickly to the workflows or processes. The models are built in the AI Builder cloud, ensuring they are consistent, secure, compliant, and scalable, as they benefit from the Microsoft Azure best practices.

Core Features of AI Builder in General

This section explores the core capabilities of AI Builder, a solution in the Copilot ecosystem that enables all users, no matter their technical level, to easily develop artificial intelligence.

- **Low-code interface:** AI Builder brings to Power Platform a low code/no code approach, which makes it easy to build AI models and reach more Power Platform customers with the ability to gain value from AI without requiring that they be programmers.

With easy and intuitive visual tools, AI Builder delivers out-of-the-box scenarios that are immediately pre-built and instantly available.

- **Integration with Microsoft Power Platform:** AI Builder natively integrates with the following Microsoft Power Platform products: Power Apps, Power Automate, and Dynamics 365. This allows the direct implementation of AI models within business applications to simplify workflow processes and enable more efficient decision-making.

- **Pre-built AI scenarios:** AI Builder includes a wide range of ready-to-use AI capabilities through pre-built AI scenarios. These scenarios cover everything from sentiment analysis to object detection and form processing to text recognition. They offer ready-to-run AI capabilities that can be trivially set up and operational without requiring deep AI knowledge or coding competence.

- **Custom AI model support:** In addition to all these pre-built scenarios, AI Builder facilitates the development of a custom AI model. From bespoke models that meet specific business needs, you can harness the spectrum of cognitive services and machine learning provided by Microsoft Azure.

- **Data ingestion and processing:** AI Builder handles the source data, and for data ingestion and processing, you can use Excel, SharePoint Lists, SQL databases, CDS on Azure, and Power Apps collections as the sources. This means whatever the data source AI model wants for training and validation it gets easily from the source.

Key Technical Features of AI Builder

First, it's important to understand the primary building blocks of AI Builder that elevate it from merely a low-code platform to a robust and useful AI development tool for the Copilot network. Those include the following:

- **Model training and testing:** AI Builder operates in an automated process for both training and evaluating the model, ensuring that its users are provided with a very efficient system for their AI development. It trains not only the models given but also evaluates their efficiency with the given data, providing suggestions for enhancing accuracy and effectiveness.

- **Performance scoring and feedback:** As a built-in feature of AI Builder, the scoring system ensures that quality and effectiveness are not compromised in any AI model.

- **Seamless workflow integration:** AI Builder creates a design that benefits integration. AI models built with this platform can be easily used in the Power Apps, Power Automate, and Dynamics 365 applications to add AI capabilities.

- **Security, compliance, and scalability:** Microsoft Azure's use of AI Builder ensures that it offers the most secure, fully compliant, and scalable AI models. In the process, it ensures that you are offered the most powerful and highly secured and reliable AI implementations.

- **Democratization of AI:** AI Builder democratizes AI by making model buildings accessible to more people. Because more people are building models, the world of AI has become more widespread. You no longer need to be a technical person to build models, giving it greater reach.

AI Builder for Business Intelligence

AI Builder allows you to develop and use artificial intelligence models that enhance your business operations. You can choose from a wide variety of pre-built models for the most common business situations or tailor a model so that it works according to your current business process, as shown in Figure 3-3. AI Builder in Power Apps helps your business streamline processes and get insights from your data.

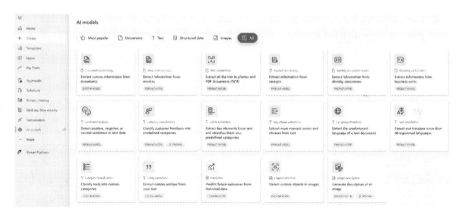

Figure 3-3. *AI models in Power Apps*

Add Intelligence to Your business

You can use AI easily by connecting it to Power Apps and Power Automate. To harness AI for your business, follow these steps:

- **Model selection:** Begin by choosing the appropriate AI model type from a broad array of AI solutions tailored to meet specific business requirements.

- **Data integration:** Select and connect the data relevant to your business from the provided options to inform your AI model.

- **Model customization:** Customize your chosen model to improve its performance, ensuring that it aligns with your business objectives.

- **Model training:** Engage in an automated training process that educates your AI model on resolving specific business challenges, such as recognizing products in images using your tailored data. Once trained, your model can deliver actionable insights, such as predictions or identifying objects within an image.

- **Insight application:** Leverage the insights generated by your AI model within Power Platform to develop innovative solutions that cater to your business needs, all without requiring coding expertise. This could include automating document processing with Power Automate or creating a Power Apps application that predicts supplier compliance issues.

Licensing Overview

AI Builder is a capacity-based license. The capacity is calculated with respect to the service credits or AI Builder credits. You must have at least one Power Apps, Power Automate, or Dynamics 365 license, with the capability to set up the Microsoft Power Platform environment.

AI Builder credits are needed to use AI Builder features in an environment. This is how it works:

- **Credits source:** AI Builder credits are obtained through AI Builder capacity add-on purchases or included with certain user licenses.

- **Credits allocation:** Credits can be assigned to specific environments or remain unallocated at the organization level. Administrators can control the use of unallocated credits via Power Platform admin settings.

- **Environment usage:** Environments use credits from allocated or unallocated sources to access AI Builder features.

- **Monthly reset:** Credit consumption resets monthly, with usage tied to AI Builder model executions in Power Automate flows, Power Apps applications, and model training.

- **Usage monitoring:** Administrators can track credit consumption to stay updated on monthly usage.

- **Overage consequences:** Exceeding credit limits leads to restricted features, initially blocking model editing and creation, and eventually stopping model runs. Additional credits must be purchased or reallocated to resolve overages.

- **Trial access:** AI Builder trials are available for organizations without credits, with capacity linked to individual users without needing allocation.

Chapter 9 includes a hands-on, practical example of using AI Builder tailored for administrators.

Prompts

You might think that a prompt is just a simple instruction, and you would be correct. But it is also more than that. In this section, I introduce you to the concepts of prompt engineering and many other important concepts you need in order to build more effective applications that can generate text from inputs.

What Is a Prompt?

A *prompt* is a set of instructions, or a question posed in natural language, for large language models (LLMs) like ChatGPT. It instructs the LLM what task it must perform. It is like giving a model a "starting point" or a cue word/brief to start generation. The prompt does not only tell the model the topic to talk about, but it also often explains *how* to talk about it (e.g., start a discussion or an essay, solve a problem, write a poem, etc.). This process is often called *instruction tuning*. The prompt is structural and content input so the model can start generating text. The art and the science of writing and optimizing prompts used by a model is called *prompt engineering*. AI Builder provides a prompt builder in which the maker writes, evaluates, saves, and uses prompts to generate text.

Instruction Tuning

Instruction tuning is when you take instructions and give them to the model along with the output for that instruction. The thought here is that by giving the model the instruction text with the output, the model will be much more likely to follow those instructions. The model is simply learning how to understand the instruction prompts so that it can produce the right output.

Prompt Engineering

Prompt engineering is the art and science of crafting and refining these prompts to get the best possible output from a model. You could conduct a set of trials that involve paraphrasing the prompt in such a way as to guide the model toward generating more accurate, creative, or appropriate responses. This makes prompt engineering an indispensable task, since even subtle changes in a prompt can lead to very different outputs. It is a skill that includes understanding how the model works, a mix between what's been done and strategic thinking.

Why It Matters

Prompt engineering and *instruction tuning* are essential because they help developers make the most of LLMs. They allow developers to interact with the model clearly, concisely, and aligned with their goals. Whether they use them for creative writing, complex problem solving, or code generation, effective prompts produce better, more helpful outputs. It is a mutual benefit: the more you improve your prompts to communicate with these models, the more they will assist you in various tasks.

Copilot Prompts

Copilot prompts instruct Copilot to make sense of and fulfill your requests. Usually, Copilot prompts have four parts: goal, context, expectations, and source. Details on each of these are shown in Figure 3-4.

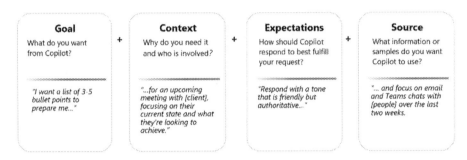

Figure 3-4. *Copilot prompt with an example*

The complexity of a prompt can vary, but at its core, it must have a clear goal. For more precise results, you can include additional elements. Often, to achieve the desired outcome, it is necessary to provide more than just the goal. Here is how a prompt might look in Microsoft 365 chat, incorporating a goal and a source:

```
Write a summary of all emails from Stefan Gamsjäger from the
last 3 months.
```

Here is an example that includes a goal, context, and expectations:

```
Create an outline of an Italian cooking book. The book is for
Asian people who love cooking and want to learn something new.
The tone should be friendly and open.
```

Note   Typically, you will respond to the initial results with a follow-up prompt. Expect a bit of a dialogue as you refine your queries to achieve the desired outcomes.

Copilot is built on Large Language Models (LLMs) that are connected to your Microsoft 365 apps and data. This connection allows Copilot to go beyond the capabilities of other LLM-powered chatbots by accessing data from Microsoft 365 apps and your internal resources, such as articles, reports, emails, presentations, and more. With Copilot, you can create or edit content, ask questions, summarize information, and catch up on things more efficiently:

- **Catch up:** If you need to get up to speed on a meeting's details, you can use Copilot in Teams to ask, what questions were raised during yesterday's meeting? or What were the key ideas discussed?

- **Create:** To assemble a presentation on time management, initiate a prompt with Copilot in PowerPoint: Create a brief presentation about Windows 11. If you need to craft a reply to an email about a project launch, use Copilot in Outlook: Compose an email congratulating the project lead and team on their successful launch.

- **Ask:** Planning a holiday? Query Copilot with, Suggest ideas for a 3-day trip to Innsbruck.

- **Edit:** In Word, direct Copilot to refine a paragraph by selecting it and activating the Rewrite with Copilot option. Enhance a PowerPoint slide by requesting, Incorporate an image of a target with arrows.

- **For Enterprise users:** Copilot offers significant
  business advantages for enterprise-licensed users by
  linking LLMs with internal company data. Business
  clients might employ prompts such as:

```
Outline a training course for onboarding partners to
BackendEBL.
What is the latest update from Munia?
Generate a project kick-off presentation based on our
recent discussions.
```

Be sure to meticulously assess and validate the responses provided by Copilot. Copilot relies on Large Language Models (LLMs), which are sophisticated tools engineered to anticipate and generate text. However, occasional inaccuracies may arise in Copilot's responses due to the vast and multifaceted nature of LLMs. It is *imperative* to scrutinize Copilot's output and corroborate it with reliable sources.

Using the exact prompt multiple times may yield differing responses. As LLMs continue to evolve and assimilate new information, the outcomes generated in response to a previously used prompt may vary.

Always employ Copilot in a manner that is respectful, ethical, and compliant with the law. Avoid utilizing Copilot for any purpose that could potentially inflict harm upon yourself or others.

Microsoft Copilot presents a multitude of opportunities. You can learn more prompts from Copilot Lab at `https://copilot.cloud.microsoft/en-US/prompts`, or follow the QR code in Figure 3-5.

Figure 3-5. *Access to Copilot lab*

In Chapters 10 and 11, you learn how to create a custom prompt, how to create a GPT prompt, how to share the prompt, and how to use the prompt in Power Apps, with a full project demo!

AI Models

AI Builder in Power Platform provides a choice of AI models meant for easy integration into business applications to bring automation and insights without deep technical expertise. These models range from automating routine tasks, such as form processing, to custom predictions that are precisely tailored to your business data. AI Builder enables businesses, whether using AI for the first time or having expert capabilities, to adopt AI to increase efficiency and make even more informed decisions across various functions of the business by fostering innovation.

AI Models in Business Contexts

AI Builder offers different model types for your versatile business needs. You can use custom AI Builder object detection models to find products from images precisely. You can:

- Find products in an image in an effective and customized way through an AI Builder model for object detection.

- Start getting efficiencies in automating expense reports using the pre-built AI Builder receipt scanning model.

- Start creating marketing campaigns with insights from historical data to predict the most effective campaign using a prediction model designed around the context of your business.

These tailored solutions give better output in terms of productivity and improved decision-making in various scenarios.

Table 3-1 defines key features of AI models in AI Builder with respect to model categorization, their handling capabilities for the type of data used, and customization choice.

- **Data type:** This describes the kind of data that every model deals with, be it documents, text, structured data, or images, hence specifying the area of AI application.

- **Build type:** This indicates the readiness of the model, meaning it can be a pre-built model ready for use in business tasks or customizable—needed to be built, trained, and published—according to your specific needs. Custom models are for businesses with unique scenarios in their data, and pre-built models are for businesses needing universal scenarios.

Table 3-1. *Key Features of AI Models in AI Builder with Respect to Model Categorization*

Data Type	Model Type	AI Template Table UniqueName Mapping	Build Type
Documents	Business card reader	`BusinessCard`	Pre-built
Documents	Document processing	`DocumentScanning,` (`DocumentLayoutAnalysis` is used during training)	Custom
Documents	Text recognition	`TextRecognition`	`Pre-built`
Documents	Receipt processing	`ReceiptScanning`	`Pre-built`
Documents	Invoice processing	`InvoiceProcessing`	Pre-built
Documents	ID reader	`IdentityDocument`	Pre-built
Text	Text generation	`GptPowerPrompt,`	Pre-built
Text	Category classification	`TextClassificationV2`	Pre-built (preview) and custom
Text	Entity extraction	`EntityExtraction`	Pre-built and custom
Text	Key phrase extraction	`KeyPhraseExtraction`	Pre-built
Text	Language detection	`LanguageDetection`	Pre-built
Text	Sentiment analysis	`SentimentAnalysis`	Pre-built
Text	Text translation	`TextTranslation`	Pre-built

(continued)

Table 3-1. (*continued*)

Data Type	Model Type	AI Template Table UniqueName Mapping	Build Type
Structured data	Prediction	`BinaryPrediction,` `GenericPrediction`	Custom
Images	Object detection	`ObjectDetection,`	Custom
Images	Image description	`ImageDescription`	Pre-built (preview)
Images	Text recognition	`TextRecognition`	Pre-built

Typical Business Situations

AI Builder includes a repository of many AI models that require no coding or data understanding. Table 3-2 shows some common business situations and the recommended model types to address them.

Table 3-2. *Common Business Situations and Recommended Model Types*

Business Scenario	Model Type
Automate customer application processing	Document processing
Automate expense reports	Receipt processing
Categorize user feedback based on focus	Category classification
Extract insights from product reviews	Entity extraction
Identify language of text	Language detection
Identify and classify customer feedback	Sentiment analysis
Translate support requests into your language	Text translation

(*continued*)

Table 3-2. (*continued*)

Business Scenario	Model Type
Identify fraudulent transactions	Prediction
Get alerted to social media posts referencing your brand	Key phrase extraction
Automate contact list	Business card reader
Automate inventory taking	Object detection
Take a photo of text and save it to a database	Text recognition

Overview of Pre-built AI Models

Pre-built AI models are excellent for adding intelligence to your apps and flows without having to gather data and train and deploy your AI models prior to use. For example, in Power Apps, you can add a component that uses a pre-built AI model to extract contact information from business cards. You can use a pre-built Power Automate model to determine whether customer feedback is positive or negative.

AI Builder has pre-built models that you can use in Power Automate and Power Apps. Here are the pre-built models that AI Builder currently offers:

- Invoice processing

- Text recognition

- Sentiment analysis

- Receipt processing

- Entity extraction

- ID reader

- Key phrase extraction

- Business card reader

- Category classification

- Text generation (preview) (deprecated)

- Language detection

- Text translation

- Image description (preview)

Overview of Custom AI Models

Businesses with various features can benefit from Custom AI models that exploit proprietary data to precisely address requirements of document processing, text analysis, and image recognition.

Designed to meet the peculiar demands of every business, these models empower data-handling and decision-making processes in Power Automate and Power Apps with the power of AI Builder.

- **Document processing:** Extracts tailored information from documents, matching specific business needs.

- **Category classification:** Classifies text into defined categories, customized for each business.

- **Entity extraction:** Identifies and extracts bespoke entities from text tailored to unique business contexts.

- **Prediction:** Uses historical data to predict future outcomes, customized for predictive accuracy in business operations.

- **Object detection:** Detects specified objects within images, customized to recognize unique business items.

- **Azure Machine learning models:** Allows businesses to bring in and utilize their custom models, offering flexibility in AI application.

Benefits of AI Builder

Here are some key benefits of using Microsoft AI Builder:

- **Easy to use:** AI Builder's user experience is outstanding. It features an intuitive interface that provides an easy-to-understand process for anyone to enhance their application with intelligent features. This ease of use minimizes the complexity of the solution to eliminate barriers to entry regarding the user's technical abilities. AI Builder is designed for everyone.

- **Integration with Power Platform:** AI Builder tightly integrates with the Microsoft Power Platform with strong integration points into Power Apps, Power Automate, and Power Virtual Agents. This makes it a perfect solution to infuse intelligence into apps you are building end-to-end—by automating tasks, orchestrating workflows, and helping with chatbots, to name just a few. This tight integration brings the power of artificial intelligence directly into the way you work today to significantly enhance what you can deliver and the quality of the user experience.

- **Pre-built AI models:** AI Builder offers an array of pre-built AI models to cater to the most common business scenarios, such as form processing, object detection, prediction, text classification, and others. It gives you an easy way for models to be customized and retrained with the user's data, therefore allowing the development process to be much faster than it currently is.

- **Customizability:** AI Builder offers users a variety of pre-built models and tools for building custom models to meet a given business's specific needs. Users can train these, for instance, with their data, ensuring the AI solution is relevant and effective in their unique scenario.

- **Data processing and analysis:** With this feature, AI Builder automatically processes and analyzes input data from images, forms, and text, among other sources. It enables businesses to automate data entry and obtain insights on unstructured data to facilitate informed decisions based on AI-driven analyses.

- **Improved efficiency and productivity:** AI Builder enhances the efficiency and effectiveness of human capabilities when it automates repetitive tasks. It processes information rapidly, eliminates manual errors, and deploys human resources to more thoughtful tasks.

- **No code/low code development:** AI Builder allows no-code/low-code Power Platform implementation, whereby users can develop their artificial intelligence solutions and implement them without having to code from scratch. This, therefore, means democratizing AI development in such a way that business analysts and other users who are non-technical can develop solutions.

- **Scalability:** AI Builder solutions are scalable and can be adjusted according to the size of the business. Small, medium, and even large businesses can be assured that AI Builder will help them with their processing needs, whether for a few documents daily or for analyzing thousands of images.

- **Security and compliance:** As part of Microsoft's cloud ecosystem, AI Builder benefits from Microsoft's robust security and compliance features. These ensure that data used within AI Builder is handled securely and in compliance with relevant regulations.

- **Continuous improvement:** Microsoft constantly develops AI Builder, adding new features, models, and improvements. This, in turn, means that users can count on the ever-increasing and improving capabilities of AI; hence, it is up to date with the latest in modern achievements in the development of AI.

Businesses with distinctive attributes can significantly benefit from custom AI models, which leverage proprietary data to specifically address requirements in document processing, text analysis, and image recognition.

AI Unveiled: The Intelligence Behind Copilot

This section uncovers the intelligence behind Copilot—a fusion of machine learning, natural language processing, and predictive analytics. These core technologies synergistically enhance Copilot's functionality, making it not just a tool but a smart companion in the digital landscape.

Core Technologies Behind AI Builder

1. **Advanced NLP and transformer models**

    Built on top of the revolutionary NLP technologies, Microsoft Copilot for Power Apps is powered by transformer models. The underlying models of the GPT series and similar architectures understand input better and give context to the new human-like text that they generate.

    - **Transformer architecture:** Central to these models is the transformer architecture, which applies mechanisms of self-attention to weigh the importance of words within input data. Through this, the model can produce results that are highly relevant and context-aware. For Copilot, this means understanding the user intent well enough to produce the corresponding Power Fx code and app components.

    - **Fine-tuning on domain-specific data:** While the transformer models are made available pre-trained on a huge corpus of text data, a domain fine model aims at bettering its performance in domain-specialized tasks. For the datasets Copilot can have, it would be the Power Apps projects, Power Fx formulas, and user interface settings that Microsoft curates. This domain-specific training ensures the outputs of the model are not only syntactically correct but semantically valid in the context of Power Apps development.

2. **Integration with Power Fx and Power Apps Studio**

A key piece of Copilot involves its integration with Power Fx and Power Apps Studio. Power Fx is a low-code language modeled after Excel formulas, created for providing simplicity with unparalleled power in app development.

- **Code generation and interpretation:** Copilot can understand and generate Power Fx code, including the parsing of the natural language inputs into Power Fx syntax. It requires a deep integration with Power Apps Studio's development environment so Copilot can insert code directly in the app under development.

- **Real-time contextual analysis:** As developers are going about building their application, Copilot is analyzing in real-time the existing state of an application, including UI layout, data bindings, and existing Power Fx formulas. The analysis is accomplished using advanced algorithms that are cognizant of an application's structure and the logic applied, and that provide contextually relevant suggestions for the code writers.

3. **Machine Learning techniques for continuous improvement**

   Copilot learns from user interactions over time and refines its abilities using state-of-the-art machine learning technologies.

   - **Feedback loops:** Copilot suggestions receive user feedback, which turns into extremely valuable data used to train AI models. Whether a suggestion is accepted, modified, or rejected leads to more fine-tuning of the future model outputs. A well-designed feedback loop must yield meaningful and relevant data without usurping the user's experience or encroaching on their privacy.

   - **Reinforcement Learning (RL):** Beyond supervised learning from labeled datasets, Copilot may use RL techniques to further fine-tune its suggestions based on user interactions. In an RL framework, the model learns to make decisions that maximize a reward signal, for example, by generating a piece of Power Fx code (e.g., suggesting the user will accept). This provides the possibility for Copilot to adapt to the structural guidelines of personal developer preferences and organizational patterns over time.

4. **System architecture and data privacy**

   Ensuring Copilot's functionality while maintaining data privacy and security is a complex challenge that involves sophisticated system architecture choices.

- **Secure data processing:** Copilot processes sensitive information, including proprietary business logic and data structures. This, in turn, means that sensitive data should be encrypted both at rest and in transit, with strict access controls, and processed data locally within a user's environment to minimize the exposure of that data.

- **Model training and anonymization:** All data used to train AI models and that Copilot uses must be anonymized and aggregated to avoid any possibility of reverse engineering, which may lead to sensitive information exposure. These include differential privacy techniques, where noise is added to the training data to protect individual data points but still allow the model to learn only general patterns.

Advanced Integration of Azure Services in Copilot for Power Apps Architecture

1. **Azure Machine Learning (Azure ML) for model development and deployment**

   Azure Machine Learning is integral to the development and deployment of Copilot's custom NLP models, because it provides a complete environment for model training, fine-tuning, and scalable deployment.

   - **Custom model training**: Azure ML is central to training the custom NLP models that underpin Copilot. This provides a powerful environment for experimentation, training, and fine-tuning of models on domain-specific data containing a large volume of Power Apps usage data, Power Fx code samples, and user interface interactions. Supporting a range of machine learning frameworks and languages, Copilot allows its team to pick the right tool for the job at each stage.

- **Deployment and scaling of models**: Deployment of this model can be done at a production level using the Azure ML platform after training. It is designed to manage the model lifecycle with versioning and model monitoring. Capable of deploying models as web services on Azure Container Instances (ACI) or Azure Kubernetes Service (AKS), the Copilot AI backend can dynamically scale up and down with demand.

2. **Azure Cognitive Services for enhanced capabilities**

Azure Cognitive Services give Copilot plenty of enrichment, particularly with the advanced capabilities of language understanding and processing, which help in interpreting and executing user commands accurately.

- **Language understanding and processing**: Copilot is likely to exploit Azure Cognitive Services, where the language service is interested in delivering pre-built models with capabilities in the detection of the language, translation, and recognition of entities. This is used to increase the overall understanding of the natural language inputs. These pre-built models provide necessary functionalities such as language detection, translation, and entity recognition to interpret user commands accurately and in context.

3. **Azure Kubernetes Service (AKS) for microservices orchestration**

    Azure Kubernetes Service (AKS) helps in the easy orchestration and management of the microservices-based architecture of Copilot with a guaranteed capability to scale quickly and effectively, including reliable performance across the diversity in functionality.

    - **Service orchestration and management**: The microservices architecture that Copilot is based on uses AKS orchestration to enable updates to be rolled out at scale, ensuring resiliency in managing various aspects of the app development process (e.g., UI generation, Power Fx code generation, and user inputs processing). First, AKS provides automated scaling, self-healing, and load balancing to make it easier for users to manage complex interactions between the services offered by Copilot. First, AKS provides automated scaling, self-healing, and load balancing to make it easier for users to manage complex interactions between the services provided by Copilot.

4. **Azure DevOps for Continuous Integration and Delivery (CI/CD)**

   Azure DevOps tunes the development pipeline for Copilot to become a continuous integration and delivery (CI/CD) medium of swift, reliable updates for the platform.

   - **Streamlined development pipeline**: Azure DevOps supports the development lifecycle of Copilot from code commits to deployment. It enables the team to automate builds, tests, and deployments, ensuring updates for Copilot are delivered quickly and reliably to users, whether they are bug fixes, new features, or improvements to the code or the neural model.

5. **Leveraging Azure Data Services for insights and analytics**

   Azure Data Services enrich Copilot with advanced insights and analytics that drive a sophisticated data management process, iteratively honing AI models on user interaction and feedback.

   - **Data storage and analysis**: The data services Copilot makes critical use of to store data and interact with it include Azure Cosmos DB, which is used to store user-generated data to be replicated globally, and Azure Blob Storage, which is for large-scale unstructured data storage. Further analytics can be conducted with Azure Synapse Analytics or Azure Databricks to gain even more insights for the continuous improvement of the given service.

- **Feedback loop and model retraining**: The architecture includes mechanisms to capture real-time direct user feedback from inside the Power Apps environment. This feedback is stored and processed in Azure using Azure Data Services to continually inform active model retraining within Azure ML, ensuring the AI models of Copilot adapt and improve over time based on actual use.

6. **Security and compliance with Azure**

   To ensure that it upholds the recognized international standards of user data protection and privacy, Azure puts strong measures in place to ensure that Copilot is safe and compliant.

   - **Robust security measures**: Part of the default functionality that Azure provides is network security, IAM, identity, and access management, as well as encryption services, all undergirding Copilot's data and user interaction. Azure also complies with the largest portfolio of international and industry standards, a sample of which includes GDPR and HIPAA.

Frequently Asked Questions
AI Builder

1. **What is AI Builder and how does it revolutionize code development?**

    AI Builder is a low-code platform in Microsoft Copilot that helps developers get suggested code from natural language queries and their respective context. It revolutionizes the way code is developed with native integrations for Microsoft Azure and its cognitive services. Democratization of AI ensures that more people are empowered with the opportunity to access advanced capabilities, and this leads to improved efficiency in development and innovation.

2. **How does AI Builder integrate with Microsoft Power Platform?**

    AI Builder is natively integrated with Microsoft Power Platform, which includes Power Apps, Power Automate, and Dynamics 365. It enables customers to apply AI models in a very easy way to their business applications, thereby bringing intelligence into the workflow and decision-making. This helps support a vast range of pre-built and custom AI scenarios, as users can easily configure and deploy them to enhance their businesses solutions.

3. **What are some of the pre-built AI scenarios provided by AI Builder?**

    The offering ships with pre-built AI scenarios, such as sentiment analysis, object detection, form processing, and text recognition. These scenarios come ready to be used, enabling users with simple substitution of input data for their models, to add AI capabilities to their applications without building then from scratch, therefore shortening the time for deployment and decreasing the barrier of entry for using AI technologies.

4. **Can AI Builder support custom AI model development?**

    AI Builder supports the creation of custom AI models. Users can bring use their business knowledge to develop and train models using Microsoft Azure's cognitive services and the ability to add machine learning capabilities. With AI Builder it is also possible to incorporate AI into more highly specific unique scenarios that cannot be addressed by pre-built models.

5. **What is the significance of prompt engineering in the context of AI Builder?**

    Prompt engineering is just like talking to AI. AI Builder understands this "talk" by shaping the queries so that the inputs are converted to highly precise, creative, and exact responses. This can unlock AI's potential to the fullest and ensure AI really delivers what you want.

113

6. **How does AI Builder ensure the security and compliance of its AI models?**

    To guarantee the security and compliance of the AI models, AI Builder uses a secure deployment on the Microsoft Azure cloud architecture, which provides best practices for cloud security, compliance, and scalability. Some of the best practices of the cloud provider that ensure security and compliance to AI Builder are data encryption (both when in transport and at rest), implementing strict access controls, and meeting the regulations and standards of specific industries. AI Builder ensures security and reliability to the customer through the strict cloud provider platform, which is being used for all the customer's AI needs.

7. **What role does Azure Machine Learning play in Copilot's functionality?**

    Azure Machine Learning is instrumental in developing and deploying the custom NLP models that power Copilot, providing a comprehensive environment for model training, fine-tuning, and deployment. It supports various machine learning frameworks and languages, facilitating the creation of scalable, efficient models tailored to specific functions within Copilot.

8. **How does Copilot use Azure Kubernetes Service (AKS)?**

    Copilot uses AKS to orchestrate and manage its microservices architecture. In this way, AKS makes it possible for the good scaling, self-healing, and automatic load balancing of its services so that they can scale and perform with excellence. It does this by handling complex interactions required around the development of applications.

9. **What continuous improvement mechanisms are incorporated into Copilot?**

Copilot incorporates mechanisms through which its system evolves, including feedback loops with users and learning through reinforcement techniques. The AI models adjust and fine-tune their outputs based on how a user interacts with them. The intention is to make their suggestions more accurate and closer to the expectations of the users with each round of interaction.

10. **How does Copilot maintain data privacy and security?**

Copilot takes your privacy seriously, with leading system architecture choices applying encryption, access control, and local data processing. It also uses anonymization and aggregation techniques in model training to ensure the safe use of sensitive data in compliance with data protection regulations.

Power Fx

1. **What is Power Fx and where is it used?**

Power Fx is a low-code data manipulation and expression language used across the Microsoft Power Platform, including Power Apps, Power

Automate, and Power Virtual Agents. Its syntax and functions are highly reminiscent of Excel formulas, which makes it approachable to business users, analysts, and other non-technical developers. Power Fx is used to define logic, manipulate data, and integrate external data sources within these applications.

2. **How does Power Fx compare to traditional programming languages?**

   Power Fx is specifically designed for the low-code environment of the Microsoft Power Platform, focusing on ease of use and integration with Microsoft services. Unlike traditional programming languages that require extensive coding knowledge, Power Fx uses a declarative syntax like Excel formulas. This makes it easier for non-developers to create complex business applications, workflows, and chatbots by writing expressions that define logic and operations.

3. **Can Power Fx be used for complex applications?**

   Yes, Power Fx can support complex application development within the Power Platform's scope. It provides a wide range of functions and operators that can manage complex data manipulation, logic, and integration tasks. However, the complexity that Power Fx can manage is within the context of the Power Platform's capabilities, and for some highly complex scenarios, external code or Azure functions might be required.

4. **How do I learn Power Fx?**

You can learning Power Fx by using various resources provided by Microsoft and the community. Microsoft offers documentation, tutorials , and learning paths on the official Power Platform documentation site. Additionally, there are community forums, video tutorials, and online courses available. Since Power Fx shares similarities with Excel formulas, users with Excel experience may find it easier to pick up.

Summary

This chapter took you deep into the technological core of Microsoft Copilot, focusing on the pivotal role of AI Builder in transforming complex programming tasks into intuitive experiences. It explored how AI Builder integrates with the Microsoft Power Platform, enabling even non-technical users to create powerful AI models. It also highlighted the integration of advanced NLP and machine learning technologies that make Copilot a versatile development tool.

As you move to Chapter 4, you'll shift from understanding the underlying technology to applying it practically. In that chapter, I guide you through the step-by-step process of building your first Power App using Copilot. You will learn about key app design principles, how to leverage Copilot for app customization, and the fundamentals of creating user-friendly, visually appealing applications. This hands-on approach will help you apply the concepts in this chapter to real-world app development.

CHAPTER 4

Crafting Power Apps with Copilot: The Essentials

The previous chapter explored the core technology behind Microsoft Copilot, revealing how AI Builder simplifies complex programming tasks. You saw how advanced AI models and integration with the Microsoft Power Platform enable developers of all skill levels to create powerful, scalable solutions.

This chapter takes you from understanding the technology to applying it in practice. In this chapter, I walk you through the hands-on process of building your first Power App using Copilot. You'll learn how to apply key design principles, customize your app, and create a user-friendly, visually appealing interface. By the end of this chapter, you'll have the practical skills needed to bring your ideas to life.

Building Your First App: A Step-By-Step Process

Before diving into Power Apps development, it is important to understand the types of Power Apps available. Power Apps can be divided into two main categories: Canvas apps and model-driven apps.

© Rezwanur Rahman 2024
R. Rahman, *Microsoft Copilot for Power Apps*, Inside Copilot,
https://doi.org/10.1007/979-8-8688-0512-7_4

- **Canvas apps** allow for greater customization of the user interface layout and design. They are ideal for creating lightweight applications that can integrate with multiple data sources.

- **Model-driven** apps rely on the Common Data Service to facilitate the creation of forms, processes, and business rules. They are well-suited for complex applications that demand extensive data modeling and logic implementation.

This example shows how to build a simple Canvas app in Power Apps using Microsoft Copilot:

1. To build applications in Power Apps, you need to browse the Microsoft Power Apps website at `https://make.powerapps.com/`. Log in with your credentials, which you created in Chapter 2 (you can also use your own licensed credentials). You will then see the page shown in Figure 4-1.

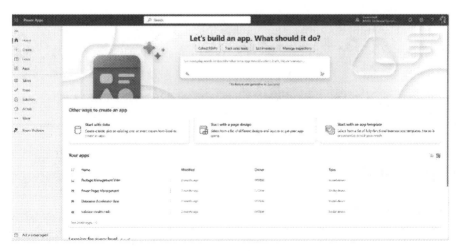

Figure 4-1. *The welcome page of Power Apps after logging in*

2. Let's look at this page in detail. Follow along with
    Figure 4-2.

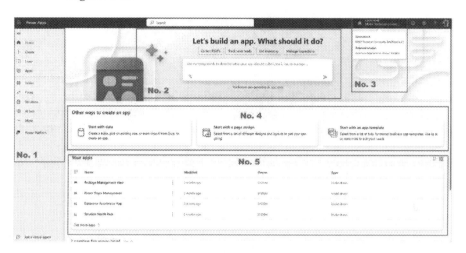

Figure 4-2. *Explanation of the Power Apps portal*

a. On the left side is a column (No. 1 in Figure 4-2).
    You have access to a range of functionalities from
    this. You can create new Power Apps, access your
    previously published apps, generate new tables,
    create new flows, initiate new AI models through the
    AI hub, and establish connections and data flows,
    among other features. See Figure 4-3.

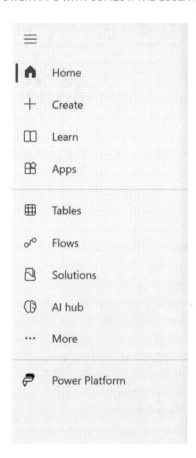

Figure 4-3. *Left sidebar with all the important functionalities*

    b. In the top-center of the page, marked as No. 2 in
       Figure 4-2, there is a large text field. This field
       is designed for inputting commands in natural
       language, which are then directed to Microsoft
       Copilot, as shown in Figure 4-4. Above this field, you
       will find example commands to guide you.

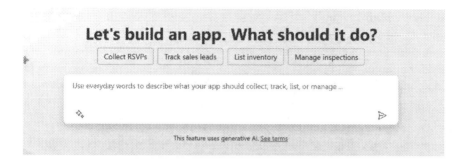

Figure 4-4. *Text field to converse with Copilot via Power Apps*

c. On the right side of the page, the currently active
   Power Apps environment is displayed. By clicking
   Environment (No. 3 in Figure 4-2), you can view
   other environments associated with this tenant (see
   Figure 4-5). Additionally, it is possible to switch
   environments from this section if needed.

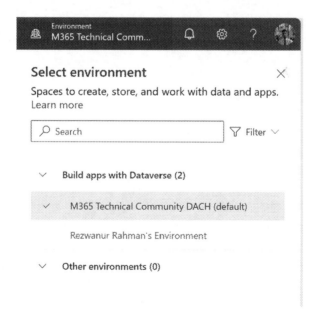

Figure 4-5. *Environment selection option in Power Apps*

d. In the center of the page, a segment titled Other Ways
to Create an App appears, as shown in Figure 4-6.
It offers various suggestions for app development
approaches. The options include creating apps using
Excel Data, Power BI data, or custom tables. You also
have the flexibility to craft apps with distinct layouts
or designs. Moreover, you can develop business
applications utilizing app templates.

Figure 4-6. *Other app creation options*

e. In the lower-center position of the Power Apps
portal, you can find the list of apps that you created
from this account, as shown in Figure 4-7.

Figure 4-7. *The list of apps to be created can be found under*
this account

3. For this example, I create a Personal Organizer app
using this command:

```
Design an app that helps users manage their daily tasks.
Include features for adding, editing, and deleting tasks.
```

4. Press Enter to run the command, as shown in
    Figure 4-8.

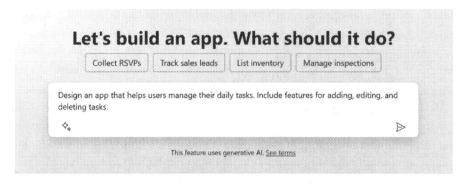

Figure 4-8. *Command to create a Power App using Copilot*

5. The app preview creation process will require a few
    seconds. You will be presented with the page shown
    in Figure 4-9.

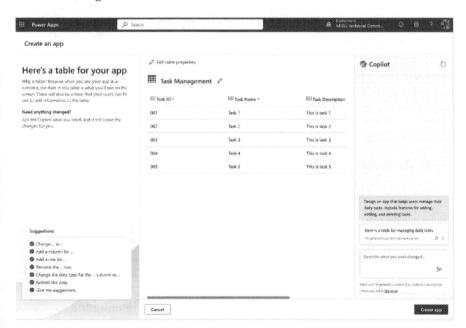

Figure 4-9. *Page that previews the app and its table*

Let's look at this page in detail:

- On the left side, AI suggestions are visible, providing guidance on how to effectively command Copilot.

- Centered on the page is the table generated by Copilot. For manual adjustments, you can click Edit Table Properties to edit the table.

- The Copilot sidebar, situated on the right side, allows for table editing through the input of commands.

6. I now attempt to interact with Copilot by issuing commands to modify the app table.

   I will add a new column to the table named Status, containing the values Open, Pending, and Closed. Here is the command (also shown in Figure 4-10):

```
Add a column named Status with the value Open, Pending
and Closed
```

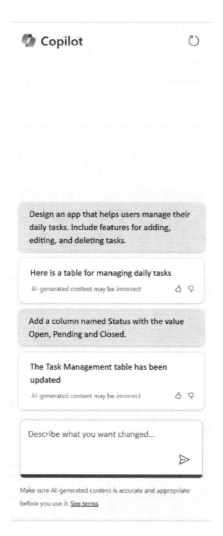

Figure 4-10. *Creating a column named Status with different values*

In a few seconds, a confirmation message appears
noting that the table has been updated. You can
find the column in the table as well, as shown in
Figure 4-11.

🖉 Edit table properties

▦ Task Management 🖉

🔢 Task ID ∨	🔤 Task Name ∨	🔤 Task Description ∨	📅 Task Due D... ∨	☰ Status ∨
001	Task 1	This is task 1	1/1/2022	Open
002	Task 2	This is task 2	1/2/2022	Open
003	Task 3	This is task 3	1/3/2022	Open
004	Task 4	This is task 4	1/4/2022	Open
005	Task 5	This is task 5	1/5/2022	Open

Figure 4-11. *A newly created column named Status is shown in the table*

> 7. This is sample data that was provided by Copilot. I work on that data to build the apps. After that, you click the Create App button to finalize the app. You will see the finalizing page, as shown in Figure 4-12, which will take a few minutes to appear.

Thanks, Rezwanur!
We're creating an app for you.

Getting things ready...

Figure 4-12. *Finalizing page of Power Apps*

128

8. Upon successful creation of the app, the screen in
   Figure 4-13 will be displayed.

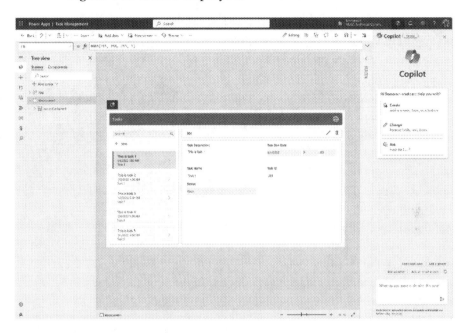

Figure 4-13. *Power Apps project page*

This is the basic app that I created with Copilot. Let's now explore some design principles that you can implement with Copilot.

Design Principles for Beginners

As you progress in your journey through app development with Power Apps and Copilot, it is time to explore the fundamental principles of design. These principles are the building blocks for creating apps that are not only functional but also user-friendly and visually appealing. This section covers some essential topics such as layout, navigation, color schemes, and user interaction. It also discusses how mastering these elements contributes to crafting engaging experiences for your users.

Additionally, I explore how Copilot can assist you in applying these principles, ensuring that even beginners can achieve professional-looking results with confidence. Let's dive into the world of design fundamentals and discover how they shape the apps you create.

Return to the Power Apps project page, as shown in Figure 4-14.

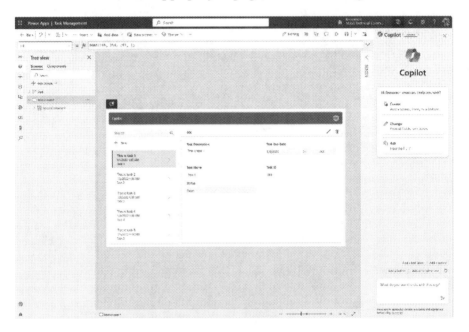

Figure 4-14. *Power Apps project page*

Let's look at this page in detail before moving on:

- On the left side, you can access an array of controls specifically designed for Power Apps. This area also offers options for incorporating external data, media, power automation, variables, and advanced tools. Moreover, the Tree View section displays all the screens and components. By selecting the New Screen option, you can easily add more screens to your app, which I explore in more detail in subsequent steps. Refer to Figure 4-15.

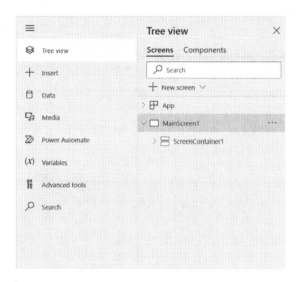

Figure 4-15. *The left sidebar of Power Apps, containing controls, data, media, automation, and many other options*

- In the center of the screen, you will see the live app preview displaying data sourced from the Microsoft Dataverse table you previously explored, as shown in Figure 4-16.

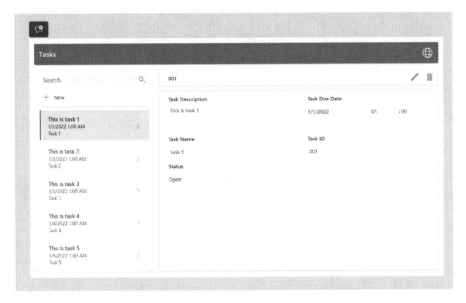

Figure 4-16. *App preview created by Microsoft Copilot*

- On the right side, two default options are available,
  providing access to the properties of any selected
  control or component, as shown in Figure 4-17. For
  instance, if I select the main screen of the application,
  I can view and modify the properties of MainScreen1,
  such as changing the background color or adding
  images. This section also allows you to configure
  advanced features. Adjacent to this, there is the Copilot
  section, where interactions can be conducted through
  conversation to perform various tasks.

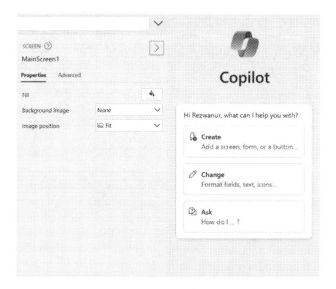

Figure 4-17. *Copilot and control properties option in the right sidebar*

Now is the moment to start modifying the app. This example initially relies on Copilot to change, add, or delete components before proceeding with manual adjustments. Before you give Copilot commands, it is crucial to have a clear understanding of the changes you want to implement. Review the app to identify the necessary modifications, as shown in Figure 4-18.

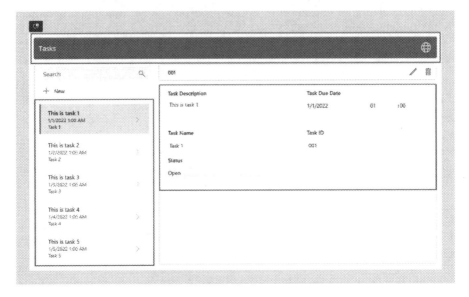

Figure 4-18. *Identifying the app grids*

- At the top of the app, there is a blue layout where the app's name is displayed, along with any additional buttons such as a Back, Next, or Close button. I also show you how to change the color of the layout through Copilot.

- On the left side, there is a container displaying all tasks, which includes the task name, date and time, and a description. The current layout needs to be adjusted so that the task name serves as the headline (right now, the description is in that spot).

- In the middle of the app, where all the task information is visible, I show you how to enhance this section by incorporating more details. This includes adding Microsoft Entra ID users (formerly known as Azure Active Directory users), a Copilot Chat button, and a custom text field for entering additional notes.

Changing the Background Color of Component, Container with Copilot

This section explains how to change the color of the header container through Copilot. First you need to understand what is inside the container. See Figure 4-19.

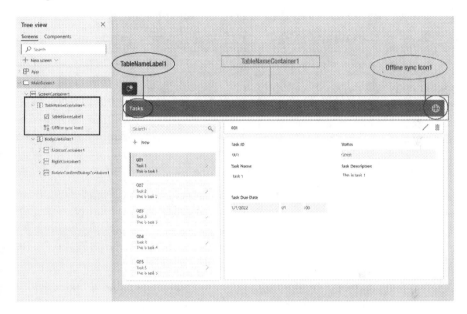

Figure 4-19. *Checking the components inside the container*

The components in the container are highlighted on the left side, marked in black. Each component has its own set of properties, such as background color, position, padding, height, width, and additional advanced settings. Therefore, if you change the background color of TableNameContainer1, it will only affect the background of TableNameContainer1, leaving the properties of other components inside the container unchanged.

> **Note** It is essential to remember that whenever there is a need
> to modify a component, style, or any other element within the app
> through Copilot, you should specify the name of the component. This
> way, Copilot can make the necessary adjustments directly.

Now let's change the color of the whole blue container. I provide
the following command to Copilot to change the color (also shown in
Figure 4-20):

```
Change the background color of TableNameLabel1,
TableNameContainer1 and Offline sync Icon1 blue to brown.
```

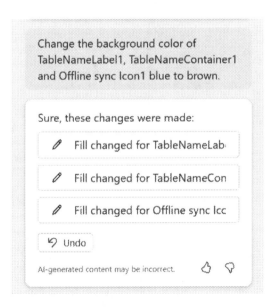

Figure 4-20. *Conversation with Copilot to change the color of Power
Apps components*

This yields the outcome shown in Figure 4-21.

Figure 4-21. *Outcome after the Copilot prompt to change the component's background color*

Experimental Proof:

I will now change the background color of only one component inside the container.

The Copilot command that I am using now is (see Figure 4-22):

```
Change the background color of TableNameLabel1 brown to green.
```

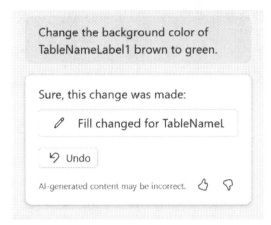

Figure 4-22. *Copilot prompt to change only one component*

The result is shown in Figure 4-23.

Figure 4-23. *Outcome after the Copilot prompt to change only one component*

Here, it is evident that the background color of `TableNameLabel1` has been changed to green, while the other colors have remained brown. As this is an experiment, I revert to brown again.

I will now change the background of the app main screen container. The default name of the main screen container in Power Apps platform is `ScreenContainer1`. I will push the following command to Copilot to change the `ScreenContainer1` background color, as shown in Figure 4-24.

`Change the background color of ScreenContainer1 to Orange.`

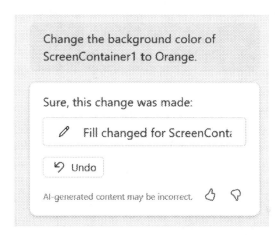

Figure 4-24. *The Copilot prompt to change the background color*

The outcome is shown in Figure 4-25.

Figure 4-25. *Outcome after the Copilot prompt to change only one component*

Note   In Power Apps, every element—containers, text fields, images, media, and buttons—are placed within a screen, which is called *screen container*. The screen that is set to run or debug first within the app is known as the main screen on the Power Apps platform.

Changing the Text or Label Properties with Copilot

This section shows how Copilot can help you change the text or label properties with a natural command.

To change the text, you need to know the name of the label, textbox, or text field. This is similar to changing the color of components.

As an example, I change the value of the text component named NewRecordLabel1. The value is New, and I will change the value called Add My New Item, as shown in Figure 4-26.

Figure 4-26. *NewRecordLabel1 component*

Place the following prompt in Copilot, as shown in Figure 4-27:

Change the NewRecordLabel1 text to "Add my new item".

Figure 4-27. *Changing the text value using Copilot*

It will just take a few seconds to make this change. The result is shown in Figure 4-28.

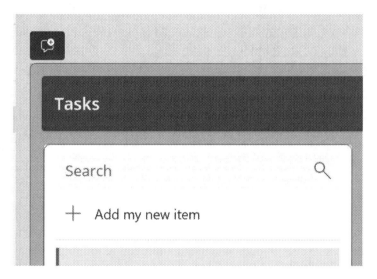

Figure 4-28. *Outcome after the Copilot prompt to change the text value*

Now, let's send multiple queries in a single command. For example, you can change the font, font style, font size, and text alignment using a single command, as shown in Figure 4-29. The command I used follows:

Change the NewRecordLavel1 font to "Dancing Script", font style should be Bold, font size should be 15 and text alignment should be center.

Change the NewRecordLavel1 font to "Dancing Script", font style should be Bold, font size should be 15 and text alignment should be center.

Sure, this change was made:

✏ Font changed for NewRecor

✏ FontWeight changed for Ne

✏ Size changed for NewRecor

✏ Align changed for NewReco

Show less

↩ Undo

Ai-generated content may be incorrect. 👍 👎

Figure 4-29. *Copilot prompt to change all the font properties at one time*

The outcome is fantastic, as shown in Figure 4-30.

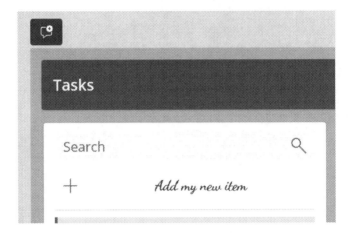

Figure 4-30. *Outcome after the Copilot prompt to change all the font properties*

Adding a Text Field or Label with Copilot

This section shows how to add two different labels in this application. One is in TableNameContainer1 and the other is in Form1, which is inside BodyContainer1, as shown in Figure 4-31. The command is as follows:

Create two text labels, one is inside the TableNameContainer1, and another is inside Form1 below the Task Due Date, the value or text is TableNameContainer1 = "My Personal App" and Form1 = "Copyright 2024 – Rezwanur Rahman".

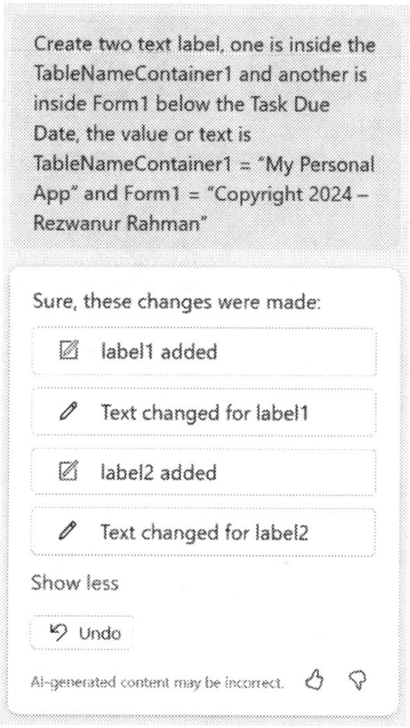

Figure 4-31. *Copilot prompt to add a text label to the Power Apps project*

Copilot has successfully created these labels, as shown in Figure 4-32.

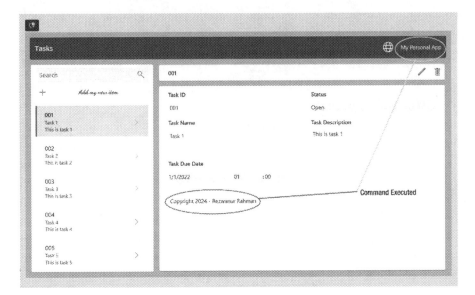

Figure 4-32. *The outcome after the Copilot prompt to add two labels to a different container*

Now let's modify the fonts and font styles displayed in the list container. First, you need to identify the names of the components involved, as shown in Figure 4-33.

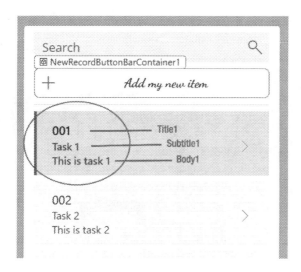

Figure 4-33. *Finding the name of the components*

To find the name of the component, click it. It will automatically be highlighted in the tree view on the left sidebar, and its name will appear as shown in Figure 4-34. At the same time, the right sidebar will display the option's properties, including the type of the component and its name, as shown in Figure 4-35.

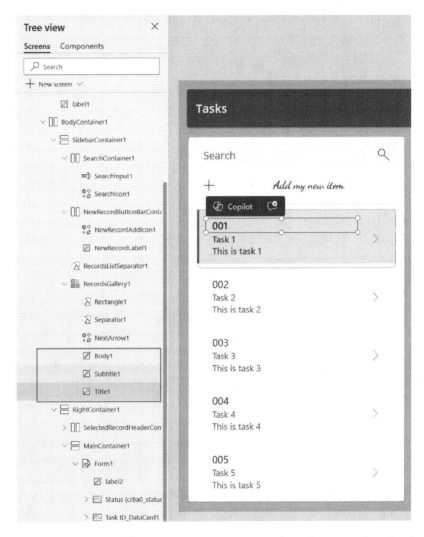

Figure 4-34. *Locate the component name using the tree view in the left sidebar*

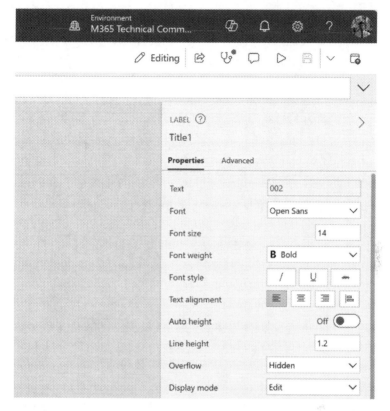

Figure 4-35. *Locate the component name from the properties*

You can push the following command to Copilot to change the font and font style, as shown in Figure 4-36.

```
Change the Title1, Subtitle1 and Body1 font to "Dancing
Script", Title1 font style should be Bold, font size should be
15, Subtitle1 and Body1 should be okay.
```

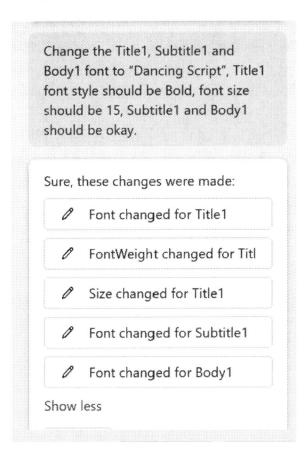

Figure 4-36. *Copilot prompt to change font style and size for titles and subtitles*

You will get the result shown in Figure 4-37.

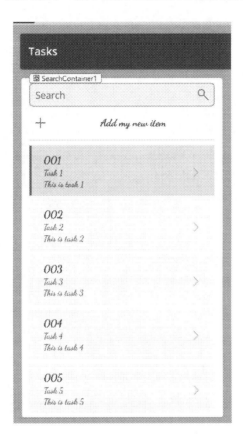

Figure 4-37. *Outcome after the Copilot prompt to change the font family and the size for the title and body*

Note   Changing certain text or labels via Copilot with simple commands is not always possible, as some labels are tied to functions (fx) or formulas. This topic is covered in detail in Chapter 6.

Adding Components with Copilot

Learning to effectively utilize Copilot is a key design principle in Power Apps. With Copilot acting as your assistant, there is no need for manual additions of components, screens, or media—Copilot can handle these tasks on your behalf. Moreover, employing multiple screens, linking them, and facilitating data sharing across these screens are crucial design strategies. It is considered poor practice to display all data on a single page.

Then next section shows you how to use Copilot to add components to your application.

Adding a Screen with a Copilot Prompt

To add a second screen to the app project using Copilot, you send a prompt like this to Copilot, as shown in Figure 4-38:

```
Create a Screen named Screen2.
```

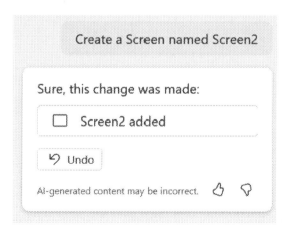

Figure 4-38. *Copilot prompts to create screens in Power Apps*

You can provide any other name for the screen. Screen2 is used for this specific project only. After a few seconds, you'll see a blank screen named Screen2, as shown in Figure 4-39.

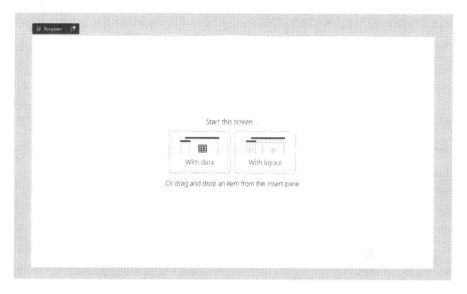

Figure 4-39. *Outcome after the Copilot prompt to create a new screen in the existing Power Apps project*

Connect a Screen to a Screen Using Copilot

It is time to tailor the page, and there are three customization options available to you:

1. Incorporate data into this screen from Microsoft Excel, Power BI, or Microsoft Dataverse.

2. Focus on adding layouts now and adjust the data at a later stage.

3. Utilize the Insert pane on the left side to drag and drop items directly onto the page.

I am using Copilot for this project, so I will not be using any other tools. I direct Copilot to create a ScreenContainer, and within that, I add a button that links to the main screen. The command for these actions follows:

Create a new Screen Container named ScreenContainer2 and inside that, create a back arrow and connect it with MainScreen1.

Figure 4-40 shows the command prompt.

Figure 4-40. *Copilot prompt to create a container with a back icon and connect it to MainScreen1*

As shown in Figure 4-41, Copilot has created the ScreenContainer and a back arrow button and connected it to the MainScreen1.

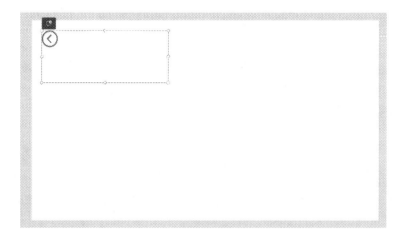

Figure 4-41. *Outcome after the Copilot prompt to create a new screen and a back button connected to MainScreen1*

You can verify this connection in two ways:

1. To launch the app, simply click the Run button or press F5. Afterwards, by clicking the back arrow, you will be redirected to the main screen. See Figure 4-42.

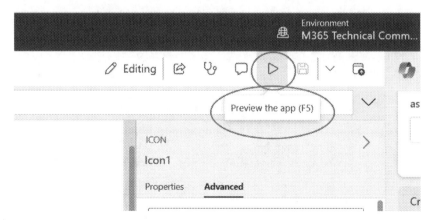

Figure 4-42. *Preview option in Power Apps*

2. Alternatively, by selecting the back arrow, you will notice the function (fx) displayed in the upper-left corner. Here, you can see that Copilot has already set up an `OnSelect` event linked to the `Navigate` (`MainScreen1`) function, as shown in Figure 4-43. This function is explored in detail in Chapter 6.

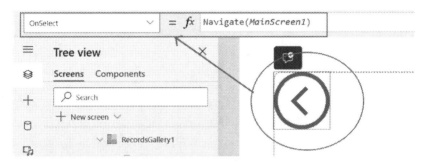

Figure 4-43. *Checking the function from the top bar*

Next, let's adjust the container. Note in Figure 4-41 that the size and padding of the container are not set properly. Let's make it a header. To do this, I use the following Copilot prompt (see Figure 4-44 also):

```
Change the Container6 size (Width = 1366 & Height = 80),
padding (Top =0, Bottom = 0, Left = 25, Right = 0)
```

Change the Container6 size (Width =
1366 & Height = 80), padding (Top
=0, Bottom = 0, Left = 25, Right = 0)

Sure, this change was made:

✏ Width changed for Containe

✏ Height changed for Contain

✏ PaddingTop changed for Co

✏ PaddingBottom changed for

✏ PaddingLeft changed for Co

✏ PaddingRight changed for C

Show less

↺ Undo

AI-generated content may be incorrect. 👍 👎

Figure 4-44. *Copilot prompt to adjust the container size*

The changes are shown in Figure 4-45.

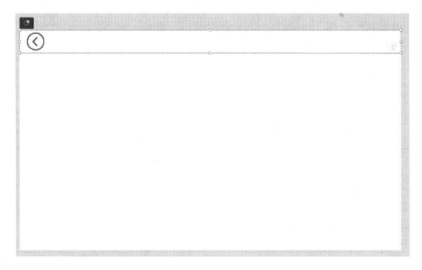

Figure 4-45. *Adjusted container size through Copilot prompt*

EXERCISE 4-01

Using Figure 4-46, try the following:

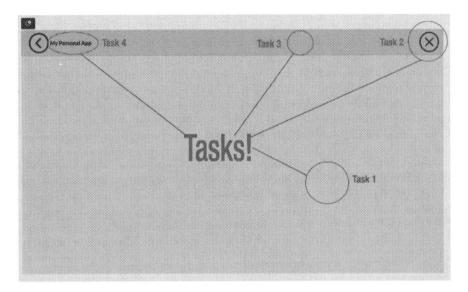

Figure 4-46. *Task for Exercise 1*

Your objective is to modify the second screen in Figure 4-46, utilizing only Copilot to make changes. Here are the tasks:

- **Task 1**: Change the background color of the screen container through Copilot.

  Hint: The color code is RGBA (253, 222, 207, 1)

- **Task 2**: Add a Cancel button on the right side of header panel and color it.

  Hint: This is not a button. Power Apps have the default icon called Cancel. The color code is RGBA (118, 0, 0, 1).

- **Task 3:** Change the background color of the header container.

  Hint: The color code is RGBA (250, 155, 112, 1)

- **Task 4:** Add the label and value it My Personal App; also color it.

  Hint: The color code is RGBA (118, 0, 0, 1)

Save the project using the upper-right Save button or press Ctrl+S. Refer to Figure 4-47.

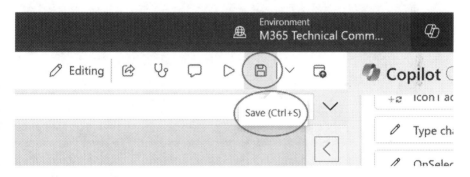

Figure 4-47. *The Save option for Power Apps project*

Summary

In this chapter, I showed you how to apply the technology behind Microsoft Copilot to build your first Canvas app. The chapter focused on essential design principles, explored how to modify app components, and explained how to enhance the app's user interface using natural language commands with Copilot. This gives you a solid foundation for creating user-friendly and visually appealing apps.

Chapter 5 takes you deeper into integrating various data sources, including Microsoft Dataverse, SQL Server, and Excel with Power Apps. You'll learn how to use connectors, understand data types, and harness the power of automation with Power Automate. Chapter 5 will enhance your ability to create dynamic, data-driven applications, building on the skills you developed in this chapter.

CHAPTER 5

Advanced Customizations and Automation with Copilot

In the previous chapter, you gained practical experience in creating and customizing a Canvas app using Microsoft Copilot. You learned how to design user-friendly interfaces, modify app components, and apply essential design principles through natural language commands.

This chapter shifts focus to the integration of various data sources with Power Apps. You'll explore how to connect to Microsoft Dataverse, SQL Server, and Excel, and learn about the importance of data types in building robust applications. Additionally, I introduce you to the automation features of Power Automate, allowing you to streamline processes and enhance the functionality of your apps. By the end of this chapter, you'll be well-equipped to create dynamic, data-driven applications that leverage the full potential of Power Apps.

© Rezwanur Rahman 2024
R. Rahman, *Microsoft Copilot for Power Apps*, Inside Copilot,
https://doi.org/10.1007/979-8-8688-0512-7_5

Analytical Prowess: Data Insights for Beginners

Until now, the example application has been developed without incorporating any specific databases or data sources. It is crucial to explore the data sources that are compatible with Power Apps and understand how to integrate Microsoft Copilot into the workflow.

Power Apps use data sources to work properly, and these sources contain the data that your apps need. Imagine these sources as big, digital libraries that can live online, which means you can get to them from anywhere.

Say you have a list of information in a Microsoft Excel file. You can keep this file on OneDrive for Business or on another online storage place and link it to your Power Apps. To make this connection, you need special tools called *connectors*. This chapter discusses this process.

Understanding the Supported Data Sources for Power Apps

Understanding the data sources supported in Power Apps is particularly important. Power Apps is designed to be plugged into many different types of data sources: Microsoft services such as SharePoint, SQL Server, and Dynamics 365, as well as external databases through connectors. Power Apps also supports custom connectors and APIs, which allows developers to connect to any data source desired. Such flexibility allows users to fully create functional apps, custom-fitted to their needs.

This chapter covers four of the most popular and frequently used Microsoft products for data storage with Canvas Power Apps.

Microsoft Dataverse

Microsoft Dataverse has evolved as a database as a service in developing secure databases. This application can work with apps as well as flows and is compatible with a lot of components from Power Platform. You also get multi-dimensional and high-level configurability to enable Power Apps, Power Automate, and Power BI that is easy to maintain.

Microsoft Dataverse can be aligned with other Microsoft services to create a suitable solution to address the demands that arise from business processes. You can also deliver data at scale, as it offers features that can be leveraged to build applications. The user interface is also interesting, appealing, and convenient to use. You can now leverage Microsoft Dataverse to provide custom data solutions, all with very little or no code.

Why Use Dataverse?

Dataverse tables offer a secure, cloud-based solution for data storage, presenting a business-centric way to define and utilize data within apps. If you are evaluating whether Dataverse tables are the right choice for your needs, consider their advantages:

- **Simplified management:** The cloud stores both metadata and data, eliminating the need to manage storage details.

- **Enhanced security:** Data is securely stored, accessible only to users with permission. Role-based security controls allow you to manage table access by different organization members.

- **Integration with Dynamics 365:** Dataverse tables incorporate data from Dynamics 365 apps, facilitating the development of apps that leverage your Dynamics 365 data and enhancing them through Power Apps.

- **Detailed metadata:** Power Apps directly utilize data types and relationships.

- **Built-in logic and validation:** Support for calculated columns, business rules, workflows, and business process flows ensure high-data quality and drives business processes.

- **Productivity enhancements:** Microsoft Excel add-ins for tables boost productivity and data access.

Microsoft SQL

Microsoft SQL Server is a powerful and widely used database solution that functions as the primary data source for Power Apps. It can handle large scale, secure, and comprehensive data management tasks; it also enables developers to build high-performance, data-driven applications with complex data operations. With SQL Server connected to Power Apps, users can utilize elaborate queries, transactions, as well as data analytics in their custom business applications.

This integration supports real-time access and manipulation of information so that Power Apps can effectively interact with huge amounts of data stored in SQL server databases. Such seamless connection between Microsoft SQL Server and Power Apps allows organizations to leverage their information for better decision-making processes and increasing productivity through improved efficiency. SQL Server then becomes an indispensable component when developing enterprise level software.

Microsoft Excel

Power Apps can use Microsoft Excel spreadsheets as sources of data so that it becomes more convenient and flexible for you to develop apps. Power Apps is seamlessly integrated into Excel, which is used for organizing, analyzing, and storing data. It allows your Excel spreadsheets saved in OneDrive for Business or SharePoint to be turned into live data sources.

You can then simply pull and manipulate this information anytime on your app interface. In other words, Excel's extensive calculation and analysis capabilities can be utilized directly within Power Apps projects, enabling creation of dynamic applications that are responsive to various business needs. This method is especially useful when it comes to rapid prototyping as well as converting existing spreadsheets into interactive mobile friendly apps with the least amount of effort.

Microsoft Lists

By using Microsoft Lists as the data sources to Power Apps, you can manage and work with your structured information in new and creative ways. Empower your team to achieve more with Microsoft Lists, which is a simple, smart, and flexible application to track information and organize work. When used with Microsoft Power Apps, Lists becomes even smarter. Use Microsoft Lists to manage structured data. You can connect your lists to Power Apps to build custom applications to interact with your list data in ways that you cannot with just the standard forms and views. You can also transform your lists into apps that facilitate collaboration and data collection with your team members.

Lists in Power Apps makes it quite easy for your organization to build lists-based applications that are tailored to your specific processes and projects using the Microsoft 365 suite of productivity apps and services. You have the platform to create custom solutions that automate and simplify daily operations and build more effective and insightful ways of working, all within the Microsoft 365 ecosystem you are already employing.

As I am focusing on Microsoft Copilot or AI Builder within Power Apps for robust, enterprise-level applications, Microsoft Dataverse is the recommended choice due to its deep integration and support for a wide range of AI functionalities.

Understanding the Data Types

One hot topic in any software development and data analytics area, namely creation of Power Apps, is understanding data types. Data types describe the values you can store and the operations you can do with them. You work with text, numbers, true/false values, dates, and more complex things every day. Each has its own rules and purpose.

Obviously, it should be no surprise that working across platforms like Microsoft Dataverse, SQL Server, or Excel in Power Apps does require you to understand data types. If you skip over this part or have a weak understanding of what they are and what they do, you will run into trouble when designing your application and working with your data, as well as when working with the formulas and operations your app contains. You need to account for all kinds of data in your systems, from simple contact info to complex transaction records. That necessitates deep knowledge of the data types in your application.

This section discusses the different data types and their characteristics, how to use them, and where they fit into the Power Apps environment. Knowing the data types that are available will allow you to better organize your data and create dynamic, powerful, and efficient applications in Power Apps.

To start, review the differences between the data types in Microsoft Power Apps, Microsoft Dataverse, and Microsoft Power Fx, as explained in Table 5-1.

Table 5-1. *Difference Between Power Apps, Microsoft Dataverse, and Microsoft Power Fx Data Types*

Aspect	Microsoft Power Apps	Microsoft Dataverse	Microsoft Power Fx
Primary use	App development and user interface creation	Data storage and management in a unified format	Formula language for logic and data manipulation in Power Apps
Focus	User interaction, interface elements	Data integrity, interoperability across Microsoft services	Calculations, data manipulation, logic
Data type examples	Text, multiline text, integer, date/time	Text, integer, currency, date and time, complex types like lookups and choice	Like Power Apps but used in formula context; supports logical, text, numeric, date/time
Application context	Building and customizing applications	Centralized data platform for Dynamics 365, Power Apps, and other Microsoft services	Enhancing app functionality with custom logic and formulas

Power Apps Data Types

Power Apps includes a canvas for users to drag and drop various controls, forms, and media to create custom applications. The data types in Power Apps are designed to be straightforward, enabling the handling of basic input and display of data in the apps. The textual data types are listed in Table 5-2.

Table 5-2. *Textual Data Types in Power Apps*

Data Types	Description	Use Cases
Text	Stores plain text, up to a maximum length specified by the data source.	Names, descriptions, or any textual content.
Multiline Text	Like Text but optimized for longer texts.	Comments, product descriptions, etc.
HTML	Stores HTML content.	Rich text formatting, embedded content.

The numeric data types are listed in Table 5-3.

Table 5-3. *Numeric Data Types in Power Apps*

Data Types	Description	Use Cases
Number	Stores whole numbers without decimals.	Age, quantity, identifier numbers
Decimal	Stores numbers with decimals.	Prices, averages, precise measurements
Currency	Like Decimal but used for monetary values.	Financial transactions, pricing

The date and time data types are listed in Table 5-4.

Table 5-4. *Date and Time Data Types in Power Apps*

Data Types	Description	Use Cases
Date	Stores dates without time.	Birthdays, due dates
Time	Stores time without dates.	Schedules, opening hours
DateTime	Stores both date and time.	Event dates, timestamps

The logical data type is listed in Table 5-5.

Table 5-5. *Logical Data Type in Power Apps*

Data Types	Description	Use Cases
Boolean	Stores true or false values.	Conditions, toggles, switches

The complex data types are listed in Table 5-6.

Table 5-6. *Complex Data Types in Power Apps*

Data Types	Description	Use Cases
Image	Stores image data.	Product images, profile pictures
File	Stores a file in its native format.	Documents, spreadsheets, PDFs
Lookup	References data from another table.	Relational data modeling
Email	Stores email addresses.	Contact information
Choice	Allows selection from a predefined list of text values.	Enums, status fields, categories

You can find more information about the Power Apps controls and common data types at `https://learn.microsoft.com/en-us/power-apps/maker/canvas-apps/reference-properties`.

Microsoft Dataverse Data Types

Microsoft Dataverse facilitates the customization of data types through various formats. These formats can be tailored using either the Solution Explorer interface or through API operations. The following sections delve into the specifics of data type formats, covering:

- Supported formats by data type

- Format conversions

- Format validations

You can find detailed information on Microsoft's official website: `https://learn.microsoft.com/en-us/power-apps/developer/data-platform/data-type-format-conversions`

Supported Formats by Data Type

Tables 5-7, 5-8, 5-9, and 5-10 lists the different formats that each data type can have.

Table 5-7. *Text Data Type Formats in Microsoft Dataverse*

Format Name	Description	Available to App Maker?	Notes
Text	Standard text column filled with alphanumeric characters	Yes	Default format value for the text column
Text Area	Text column supporting line breaks and containing alphanumeric characters	Yes	
Email	The text includes a hyperlink to launch the user's email application	Yes	
URL	The text features a hyperlink that opens the specified page. Text lacking a valid protocol prefix will automatically have https:// added to its beginning	Yes	
Ticker Symbol	In most languages, the text serves as a link that opens the MSN Money website, displaying stock price details for the represented ticker symbol	Yes	
Phone	Columns are designed to be clickable, initiating phone calls when selected	Yes	
JSON	Stores text in JSON format	Yes (API only)	Only in non-SQL stores like Audit
Rich Text	Allows rich text formatting, including HTML markup	Yes (API only)	
Version Number	Stores the version number for rows	No	System use only

Table 5-8. *Multiline Text Data Types in Microsoft Dataverse*

Format Name	Description	Available to App Maker?	Notes
Text	Basic text column containing alphanumeric characters	Yes	
Text Area	Text column that supports line breaks and alphanumeric characters	Yes	
Email	For internal use only	No	
JSON	Stores text using JSON formatting	Yes (API only)	Only in non-SQL stores like Log
RichText	Supports rich text formatting, including HTML markup	Yes (API only)	
InternalExtentData	Displays a simple numeric value	No	System use only
None/string. Empty	Basic text column containing alphanumeric characters	Yes	Default format value for whole number column

***Table* 5-9.** *Whole Number Data Types in Microsoft Dataverse*

Format Name	Description
Duration	This field is displayed as a drop-down as there will be several available duration values. The list of these values is from one minute to three days. The duration is kept in the database in minutes. So, you display predefined intervals for users to select. This interval, for example, can be 1 minute, 15 minutes, 30 minutes, or any other duration in minutes. As well as predefined intervals, users can also enter the type of time duration they are trying to capture. For example, in the specified field they can type "1 hour" or "2 days" and it will be able to display it as "60 minutes" and "2880 minutes," respectively.
Timezone	This option gets a drop-down list of all the time zones using Time Zone Codes and stores them as the step name. Every time zone has an integer value. For (GMT-08:00) Pacific Time (US and Canada), the time zone name is stored as 4 in the step name. Model-driven apps will display the time zone by these codes and for Canvas apps, you just get the number it is stored as.
Language	This option shows the list of languages provisioned for your organization. Using an LCID code, the values are stored as a number. Language codes can be four-digit or five-digit locale IDs. If the LCID is in the chart shown in Locale ID (LCID), it is a valid LCID. The model-driven apps have the language as the language name, while the Canvas apps have the number stored.
Locale	This represents a value associated with a particular locale, utilizing ISO standard values.

Table 5-10. *Date and Time Data Types in Microsoft Dataverse*

Format Name	Description	Available to App Maker?
Date Only	This setting records the date only, defaulting the time to 00:00:00, whether set to User Local or Time-Zone Independent	Yes
Date and Time	Date and time format	Yes

Format Conversion

You can only switch to a format from the same data type you selected. If you want to change the format, the existing table definitions (for example, maxsize) are maintained if there is a corresponding one with the new format. If the incoming payload to the table creator API did not specify the format, and there is a format that you want to maintain, you can switch it by setting the desired format in the FormatName column in an API call. I recommend you not directly update the Format column because Dataverse will ignore any new format selections you make.

Note   Right now, the API only does format conversions. A format change does not update any of the data that is currently in a column, so after a format change, users may see encoding differences in their data that they will need to address after the fact.

As mentioned in Table 5-10, there are some restrictions to format conversions:

- JSON formatting is allowed only when a table is used logically in non-SQL storage, such as with logs.

- If data is stored as emailbody and internalextentdata and you try to convert them to any other format, it will ignore the setting and not give an error.

- If data is stored in another format and you try to convert them into `emailbody` or `internalextentdata`, it will throw an error.

- Converting from `Date Only` to `DateTime` is not allowed, but if you set the Date Only field to User Local or Time-Zone Independent, it will convert it into `DateTime`, but the seconds field returned will be 00:00.

If you change the data type to an incompatible format, the following error is displayed:

```
The format <<formatname>> is not valid for the <<datatype>>
type column <<columnname>> of table <<tablename>>. For example,
the format datetime is not valid for the text type column.
```

Microsoft Power Fx Data Types

Power Fx utilizes human-friendly text that is easy to read. It is a low-code language for writing directly into an Excel-like Formula bar or text window, just shorter and more readable than Excel. The language is simple and less verbose, so the most common programming tasks are easy for makers and developers. It can satisfy all levels of development, from no-code for beginners to pro-code for experts, and do so without creating artificial walls or seams for learning and reimplementation. This enables diverse sets of skills and diverse teams to work together.

Note   Microsoft Power Fx has been introduced as the updated name for the formula language used in Canvas apps.

When an app that was developed using Canvas connects to an external data source, it translates each of the data types from that source into the data types that are compatible with Canvas apps. Power Fx's data types are listed in Table 5-11.

Table 5-11. Data Types of Microsoft Power Fx

Data Type	Description	Examples
Boolean	A simple Bool true/false value, which you can use directly in `If`, `Filter`, etc. functions without a need to compare it.	`true`

Color	A color specification, including an alpha channel.	`Color.Red`
		`ColorValue( "#102030" )`
		`RGBA( 255, 128, 0, 0.5 )`

Currency	A bool true/false value, which you can use directly in `if` and `filter` functions if the condition in those functions is met without needing to compare its value.	`123` `4.56`
Date	A date without time, in the user's app time zone.	`Date( 2019, 5, 16 )`
DateTime	A date with time, in the user's app time zone.	`DateTimeValue( "May 16, 2019 1:23:09 PM" )`
Decimal	A number of very high precision. Only a number resulting from base 10 operations with no noticeable rounding errors can be accurately represented. Also, it has a limited range.	`123` `Decimal( "1.2345" )`
GUID	Globally Unique Identifier	`GUID()` `GUID( "123e4567-e89b-12d3-a456-426655440000" )`

Hyperlink	A text string that holds a hyperlink.	`"https://powerapps.` `microsoft.com"`

Image	A Universal Resource Identifier (URI) text string to an image in .jpeg, .png, .svg, .gif, or other common web-image formats.	MyImage added as an app resource
		`"https://northwindtraders.`
		`com/logo.jpg"`
		`"appres://`
		`blobmanager/7b12ffa2..."`

Media	A URI text string to a video or audio recording.	MyVideo added as an app resource
		`"https://northwindtraders.`
		`com/intro.mp4"`
		`"appres://`
		`blobmanager/3ba411c..."`

Number or Float	A number with standard precision, capable of base 2 operations and possessing a wide range.	`123`
		`8.903e121`
		`1.234e200`

Choice	A choice from a predefined set of options, each associated with a numeric value. It pairs a localizable text label, visible within the app, with this numeric value, which is stored and utilized for comparisons.	`ThisItem.OrderStatus`

(continued)

177

Table 5-11. (*continued*)

Data Type	Description	Examples
Record	A record of data values. This compound data type encapsulates instances of other data types specified within this topic.	{ Company: "Northwind Traders", Staff: 35, NonProfit: false }
Record reference	A reference to a record in a table. Such references are often used with polymorphic lookups.	First(Accounts).Owner
Table	This compound data type defines a table of records, where each record consists of fields with uniform names and data types. Omitted fields are considered blank. It encompasses instances of other data types specified within this context.	Table({ FirstName: "Rezwanur", LastName: "Rahman" }, { FirstName: "Mobaswira", LastName: "Farzana" })
Text	A Unicode text string.	"Hello, World"
Time	A time without a date, presented in the time zone of the application's user.	Time(111, 223, 745)

Two option	A choice in a list of two choices, along with a Boolean value. This field type pairs a human readable label for the app, with a Boolean value used internally to evaluate the comparison.	`ThisItem.Taxable`
Untyped object	Represents an object of an unspecified type. The underlying object may be of any existing type and can be converted into compatible types using functions such as `Boolean()`, `Value()`, and `Table()`, among others.	`ParseJSON("{ ""Field"" : 1234 }").Field`

Blank Values

Every data type can assume a blank value, which means it has no value at all. In database terminology, this is commonly referred to as a *null*.

To assign a blank value to a variable or field within Canvas apps, you can use the Blank function in conjunction with the Set or Patch function. For instance, executing Set(x, Blank()) will clear any existing value in the global variable x.

To check if a value is blank, you can use the IsBlank function. Moreover, the Coalesce function allows you to substitute any blank values with alternative non-blank values.

Given that the concept of blank is universally applicable across data types, data types such as Boolean and Two option inherently support a third state, representing the blank condition.

Embedded Text

In a formula, text strings are encapsulated within double quotes. To denote a single double quote within the text string, pair two double quotes consecutively. As shown in Figure 5-1, consider applying the subsequent formula to the OnSelect property of a Button control:

```
Notify( "Rezwanur said ""Hello Readers!""" )
```

When the button is pressed, this formula triggers the display of a banner. The initial and final double quotes are not shown because they serve to enclose the text string. Meanwhile, the double quotes that are doubled up around "Hello, Readers!" are condensed into a single double quote within the displayed message.

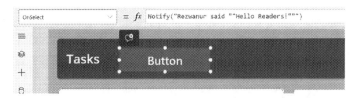

Figure 5-1. *Assigning an OnSelect property to the Power Apps button*

String Interpolation

String interpolation lets you put formulas directly inside a text string. This is sometimes more convenient and easier to understand than using the concatenate function or the & operator. Add a dollar sign $ before the text string and put the formula in curly braces { }. If you want to include a curly brace in your text string, use double curly braces: {{ or }}. String interpolation works everywhere a regular text string will work.

Suppose you have designed a Canvas app that is supposed to maintain swags for an event. You want to add a message that indicates the current stock of t-shirts and stickers.

Suppose that you have the global variable Tshirts set to 3 and the global variable Stickers set to 4. You can use string interpolation to do this:

```
$"We have {TShirts} TShirts, {Stickers} stickers, yielding
{TShirts+Stickers} items total."
```

The formula would look something like this. When you press Enter, it will return "We have 3 TShirts, 4 Stickers, yielding 7 items total" where you can insert TShirts and Stickers inside the text using the curly braces. Similarly, the result of the formula part TShirts+Stickers will replace the first set of curly braces with TShirts+Stickers. The spaces and everything else around the curly braces are left as is.

You can use functions and operators in embedded formulas. The only condition is that the formula's result can be converted to a text string. For example, this formula uses NickName or FirstName in a greeting:

```
$"Welcome {Coalesce( NickName, FirstName )}, it's great to
meet you!" )
```

If NickName equals "Rezwanur", this formula returns the text string Welcome Rezwanur, it's great to meet you! However, if NickName is blank and FirstName equals "Rahman" this formula returns Welcome Rahman, it's great to meet you! instead.

You can add normal text strings to the formula inside the string interpolation. For example, if you do not use NickName or FirstName, you can use "Friend" instead:

```
$"Welcome {Coalesce( NickName, FirstName, "Friend" )}!"
```

You can also nest string interpolations. Consider the following example—the First, Middle, and Last names are concatenated into a greeting. The name elements have the correct number of spaces between them, even if some of them are empty, as shown in Table 5-12. The Coalesce function will convert an empty string inside the inner string interpolation to "Friend".

```
$"Welcome {Coalesce( Trim( $"{First} {Middle} {Last}"}),
"Friend" )}!"
```

Table 5-12. *String Interpolations*

First	Middle	Last	Result
Rezwanur	R.	Rahman	Welcome Rezwanur R. Rahman!
Rezwanur	*blank*	Rahman	Welcome Rezwanur Rahman!
blank	*Blank*	Rahman	Welcome Rahman!
blank	*Blank*	*blank*	Welcome Friend!

Newlines

Text strings that are inserted in other text can have line breaks. For instance, think about setting the Text property of a Label control to this:

```
"Microsoft Copilot Book
Microsoft Power Apps Book
Microsoft Github Book"
```

This formula results in three lines shown in the `label` control, as shown in Figure 5-2.

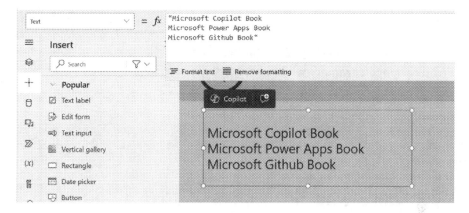

Figure 5-2. *Newlines result for text label control*

Numbers

Power Fx offers support for two types of numbers: `Decimal` and `Float`, also known as Number and Currency.

Note   Currently, Power Apps supports only the Float data type for numerical values, but there are plans to introduce support for the Decimal type soon. I am exploring the Decimal type ahead of this update.

`Decimal` is an exceptionally viable choice for most business calculations. It represents numbers in base 10 exactly; 0.1 does not have a rounding error while performing arithmetic. Its range is more than enough for any business purpose—up to 1028 and it supports up to 28 digits of precision. Therefore, the `Decimal` type is the default numeric type for most Power Fx hosts. In fact, if you simply write 2*2, it is treated as `Decimal`.

Float is preferred for scientific calculations. A Float can denote numbers in a significantly broader range; it supports values up to 10308. It only gives precision to 15 decimal places. And since the math is done in base 2, it can't represent many common decimal values that might appear precise to humans. As for performance, Float has the edge, so choose it if performance is a concern and precision is not important.

You can learn more about Power Fx data types from the official Microsoft learning docs at:

https://learn.microsoft.com/en-us/power-platform/power-fx/data-types

Understanding the Connectors

Connectors represent powerful tools for the Power Platform ecosystem, supporting the development of applications and workflows that can be easily integrated with cloud services. This is because these connectors act as bridges, incorporating the actual APIs of an application or service to enable data exchange. Over 900 connectors are currently available on the Power Platform. Users can connect to a wide variety of services, including but not limited to: Salesforce, Office 365, Twitter, Dropbox, SharePoint, and SQL Server.

These connectors are developed to transfer data from the Power Platform to the attached services and vice versa. They are input-output mechanisms. The Power Platform provides two types of data sources using these connectors: tabular and function based. Each type is an important method of bringing data into your solutions and as such makes the platform versatile in handling various kinds of data integration scenarios.

Types of Connectors

Power Platform categorizes connectors into three types—standard, premium, and custom.

> **Standard connectors:** These connectors work with any licensing plan. You can use standard connectors in Microsoft Power Platform. Some examples of standard connectors are SharePoint, Outlook, OneDrive, and YouTube.

> **Premium connectors:** These include connectors that involve an additional purchase of a license for your app and the users using it. The main advantage of premium connectors is that you can connect to more services, such as Azure SQL Database, Dynamics 365, and Twitter. See Figure 5-3.

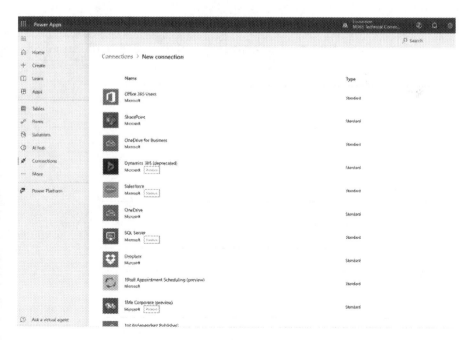

Figure 5-3. *Premium connectors in Power Apps*

Custom connectors: These are wrappers around APIs that let you link your apps to external web services or external data sources like Microsoft Azure. The connectors function by exchanging information through these APIs. A benefit of creating custom connectors is that they can be applied to various platforms, such as Power Apps, Power Automate, and Azure Logic Apps.

Visualizing Data in Power Apps

Now is the perfect moment to explore data visualization in Power Apps, focusing on how Microsoft Copilot integrates with Power Apps. The example in this section uses Microsoft Dataverse as the primary data source, covering everything from basic to advanced concepts and examining how it works in conjunction with Power Apps.

Open the existing project again and expand the left-side menu items. Notice the option named Data, as shown in Figure 5-4.

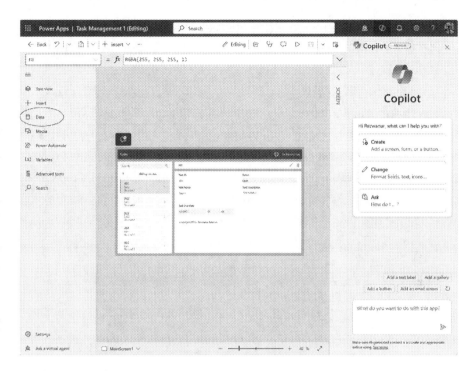

Figure 5-4. *The Data option in Power Apps*

If you opt for Data, you will find an existing database named Tasks, as shown in Figure 5-5. Interestingly, when building this application with Copilot, Copilot creates a default table in Microsoft Dataverse, so you do not need to create the database from scratch.

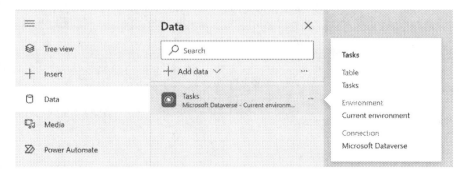

Figure 5-5. *Microsoft Dataverse table that was created by Copilot*

187

First, I explore the Tasks table that was saved in Microsoft Dataverse. Afterward, I create a new table with the help of Microsoft Copilot and compare the two.

To access the Tasks table, click the three dots (...) next to the Tasks option. There, you will find three choices—Edit Data, Refresh, and Remove—as shown in Figure 5-6. When you select Edit Data, you can view the Tasks table and modify the data, as well as add or remove columns and adjust certain table properties. Additionally, after manually inputting some data, clicking Refresh will ensure that the data in the Tasks table is properly synchronized. You also have the option to delete the table from this location and create a new one for your app.

Figure 5-6. *Options to manage the Microsoft Dataverse table*

Click Edit Data to see the table in Figure 5-7.

Figure 5-7. *Microsoft Dataverse table in Edit mode*

Since this is dummy data, you do not need it and can safely delete the rows. However, it is important to remember not to delete any columns. *Removing a column will also eliminate the corresponding field from the app.*

Note the text *+17 more,* shown in Figure 5-8.

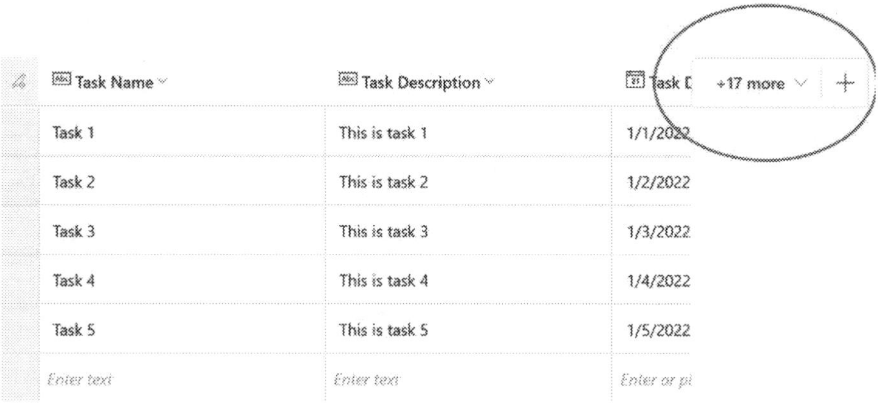

Figure 5-8. *Hidden rows in the Microsoft Dataverse table*

There are 17 other related columns that Copilot made and are now hidden. This is what +17 more means.

When you click the down arrow next to +17 more, you will see the options, as shown in Figure 5-9.

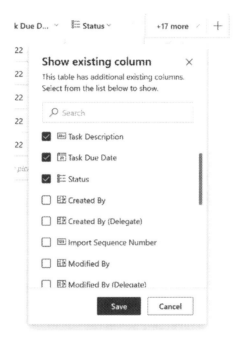

Figure 5-9. *List of columns that are hidden in the Dataverse table*

You can see the columns and add any necessary columns by selecting the checkbox and clicking Save.

In the example app, I added the Modified On, Owning Business Unit, and Status columns, as shown in Figure 5-10.

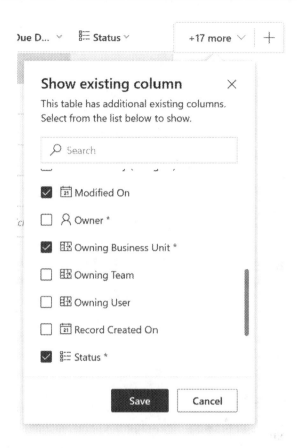

Figure 5-10. *Selecting columns from the hidden column list*

If you did not find your desired column, or the suggested columns do not match your data, you can create a new custom columns. For this example, I create a custom column named Upload Document.

To create a custom column, click the + sign, as shown in Figure 5-11.

Figure 5-11. *Creating a new custom column in Dataverse table*

Then, fill in the form, as shown in Figure 5-12, and click Save.

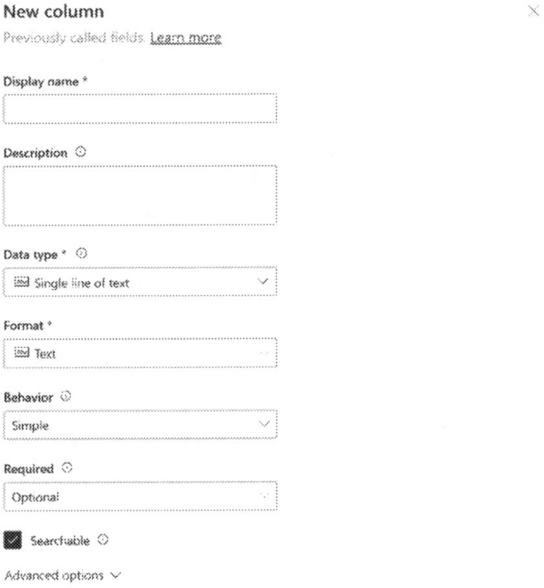

Figure 5-12. *Form to create a new column*

As I am creating an Upload Document column, I need to click Data Type and choose Files, as shown in Figure 5-13.

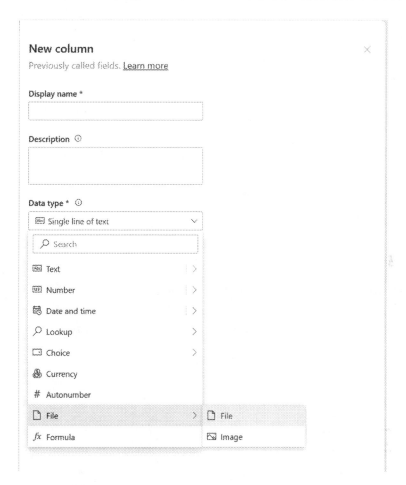

Figure 5-13. *Creating the file upload field*

After selecting the data type, you see the parameters in Figure 5-14.

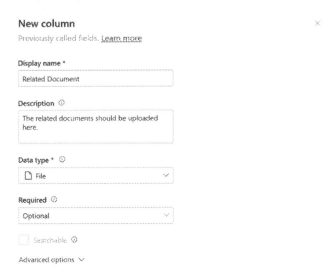

Figure 5-14. *Parameters to create a new column*

Expand the Advanced option to see the advanced features, as shown in Figure 5-15.

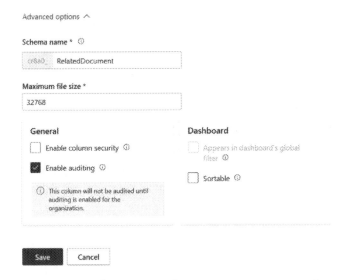

Figure 5-15. *Advanced options when creating a new column*

- **Searchable:** This option will be disabled. You cannot make this field searchable.

- **Schema name:** This is a pre-populated column from the Display name. It includes the Dataverse solution publisher's customization prefix. After you have saved the table, you will not be able to edit it.

- **Maximum file size:** The maximum file size limit is 32768 KB or 32 MB. It is impossible to adjust the maximum file size once it has been saved.

- **Enable column security:** When activated, it restricts access to columns.

- **Enable auditing:** This option will allow tracking user access changes and table record modifications so that you may evaluate the activity later.

- **Sortable:** This determines the setup of the column for interactive dashboards.

Save the column. You can then find a new column named Related Document in the Dataverse table, as shown in Figure 5-16.

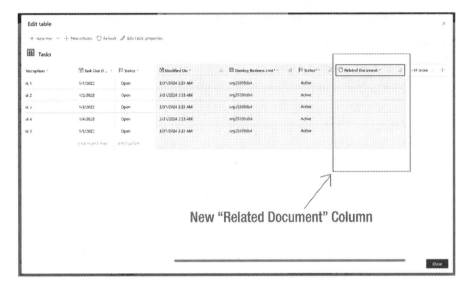

New "Related Document" Column

Figure 5-16. *Newly created column in Dataverse table*

Next, I add the Related Document column to the app.

Adding a column to the table does not automatically make it visible in the app. The app displays only those columns or fields that are relevant and have been added by Copilot.

To add the column to the app, open the MainScreen app and select the Form1 layout, as shown in Figure 5-17.

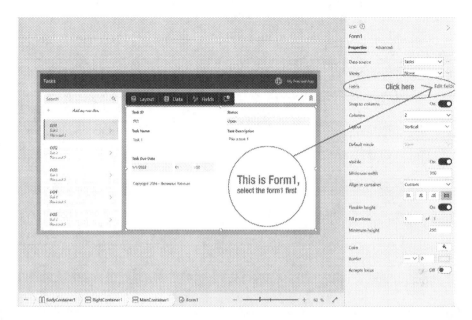

Figure 5-17. *Editing the fields option of MainScreen*

After that, click the Edit Field option to bring columns from the Microsoft Dataverse table to the app. For example, in the app, you will see fields such as Task ID, Status, Task Name, Task Description, and Task Due Date. Their names also indicate where the app gets its field information—from this source.

To add a new field, you need to click +Add Field option, as shown in Figure 5-18.

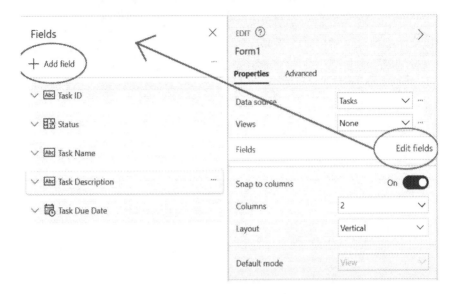

Figure 5-18. *Adding a field in Power Apps screen from Microsoft Dataverse table*

After you click the +Add Field button, a list displaying all the Microsoft Dataverse table fields will appear. From this list, you need to locate and select the newly created column (in this case, Related Document, as shown in Figure 5-19). Finally, click Add.

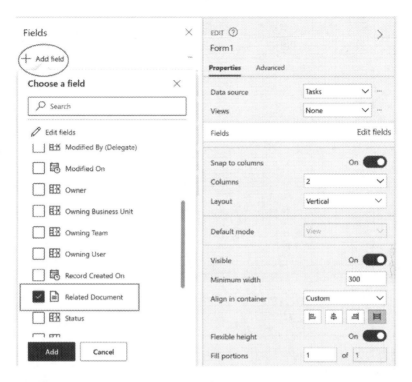

Figure 5-19. *Selecting the column from the Microsoft Dataverse table to show it as a field in Power Apps*

Once you click Add, the Related Document field will become visible in Form1 of the application, as shown in Figure 5-20.

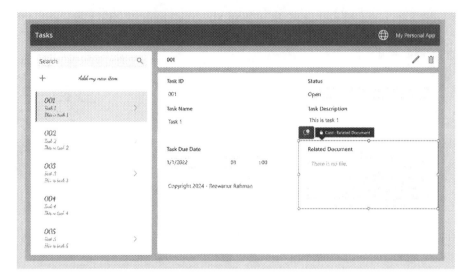

Figure 5-20. *Showing the new custom column in the Power Apps screen*

Working with Connectors

As previously discussed, there are three types of connectors on the Microsoft Power Platform. This section shows you how to integrate several types of connectors in Power Apps.

I will integrate the Office 365 Users connector into the example app, enabling you to access Microsoft 365 users who are part of your tenant. The Office 365 Users connector is a standard connector provided by Microsoft and it's free to use.

To add the Office 365 Users connector, expand the left column ➤ click Data and click +Add Data, as shown in Figure 5-21.

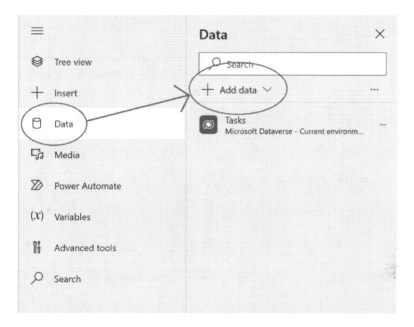

Figure 5-21. *Expanding the Data option in Power Apps to add a connector*

You'll see a list like the one in Figure 5-22. If you navigate to the Connectors section, you can find the Office 365 Users connector. Choose Office 365 Users from the list.

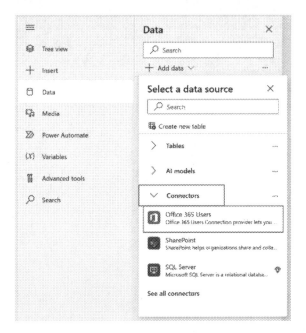

Figure 5-22. *Searching and adding Office 365 Users from the connectors*

If you encounter difficulty finding it, simply use the search bar to look for the connector, and it will appear.

After adding the connector, you can see the connector in the same column of the Tasks table, as shown in Figure 5-23.

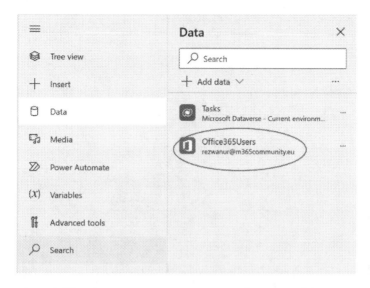

Figure 5-23. *Office 365 Users connector in the Data list*

Next, I show you how to retrieve Office 365 tenant user information within Power Apps. You can retrieve limited information, including user profile pictures, names, manager's names, titles, emails, phone numbers, and so on.

Note   You cannot retrieve sensitive information, such as user's mailbox items, OneDrive files, or Microsoft Teams conversations.

To access Office 365 tenant user information, I add a new column called Assign to Colleague to the Microsoft Dataverse table. This will allow me to populate the column with Office 365 users.

As with the previous steps, navigate to Data, select Edit on the Tasks table, and click the + sign to add a new column. For this column, select Lookup for the Data Type, as shown in Figure 5-24.

Figure 5-24. *Selection of Lookup data type, to retrieve Office 365 user data in Power Apps*

You can learn more about Lookup or other data type from the following Microsoft Learn website: `https://learn.microsoft.com/en-us/power-apps/maker/data-platform/types-of-fields`.

After choosing the Lookup data type, a new field called Related Table will appear. In this field, search for Microsoft Entra ID (previously known as Microsoft Azure AD), as shown in Figure 5-25. This indicates that the Lookup type will directly retrieve users from Microsoft Entra ID.

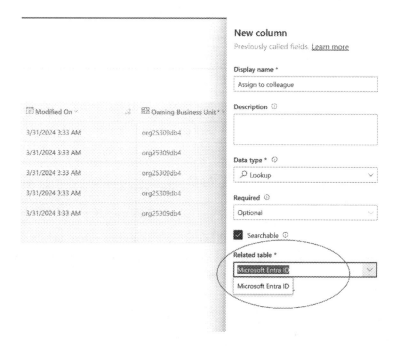

Figure 5-25. *Searching for Microsoft Entra ID in the Lookup column*

After saving the column, you will see a new column named Assign to Colleague, as shown in Figure 5-26.

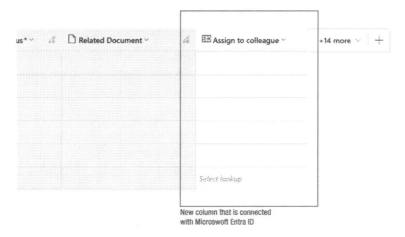

Figure 5-26. *New lookup column that relates to Microsoft Entra ID in Microsoft Dataverse table*

If you double-click any cell in the Assign to Colleague column, a list of users associated with this tenant will be displayed. This indicates that the lookup is connected to Microsoft Entra ID and can access the table, as shown in Figure 5-27.

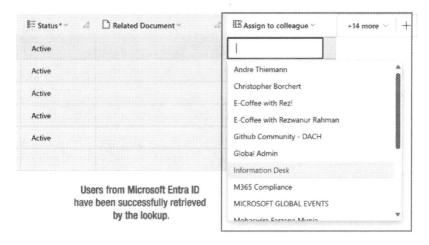

Figure 5-27. *Searching Entra ID users from the lookup column*

To retrieve additional details, such as Email or Role, you must include the respective table in the Related Table option after selecting the Lookup Data Type.

I repeat the same process by adding the column to Form1 as I did previously; refer back to Figure 5-17.

EXERCISE 5-2

Add the Assign to Colleague column to Form1.

Note   Remember to save the project occasionally.

I successfully added the Assign to Colleague column to the project. Now, I run the app by pressing F5 to check how it functions, as shown in Figure 5-28.

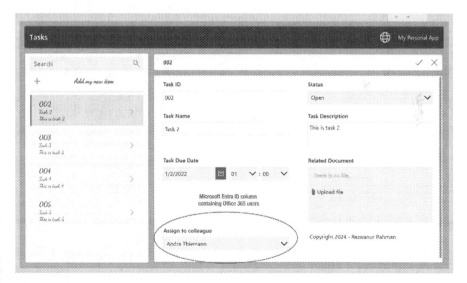

Figure 5-28. *Preview of the app with the newly created lookup field*

Introducing Automation Features

Power Automate, the most practical and interesting instrument of Power Platform by Microsoft, is responsible for setting up automatic workflows between applications and services, such as file synchronization, notification retrieval, and data gathering. In other words, it allows companies and people to automate their daily duties without programming skills. Figure 5-29 show the logos of Power Apps and Power Automate.

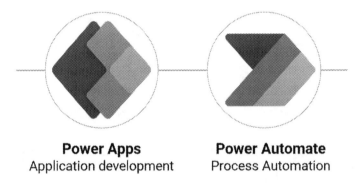

Power Apps
Application development

Power Automate
Process Automation

Figure 5-29. *Logos of Microsoft Power Apps and Power Automate*

Power Automate integrates with various Microsoft services, including SharePoint, Excel, Outlook, and Teams, as well as with other third-party apps like X (formerly Twitter), Dropbox, and Google services. Users can create "flows" using pre-built templates or from scratch. These flows can do things like automatically send emails, update data in a database, or start tasks when specific triggers occur.

The platform supports several types of workflows, including:

- **Automated flows:** Triggered by predefined events, such as receiving an email or updating a record in a database.

- **Button flows:** Execute repetitive tasks conveniently from anywhere, anytime, using a mobile device or desktop.

- **Scheduled flows:** Run tasks at specific times, such as a monthly report generation.

- **Business process flows:** Guide users through a multi-step process in applications like Dynamics 365.

I now show you some basic features of Power Automate in the Microsoft Power Apps platform.

When you select the New Screen option from Tree View, you can search for *Email* to access the Email template, as shown in Figure 5-30.

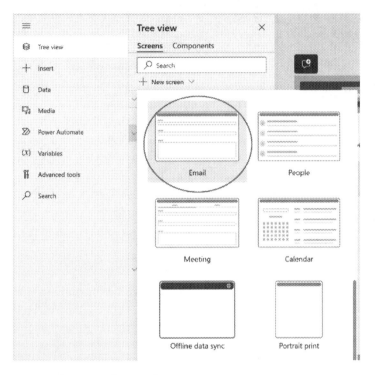

Figure 5-30. *The Email template in Power Apps*

Just add the Email template as a new screen and you can see the preview, as shown in Figure 5-31.

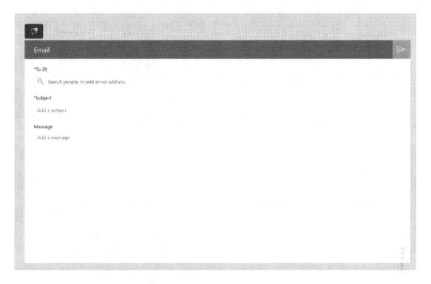

Figure 5-31. *Preview of the Email template*

Now, in the left panel, find the option called Power Automate, as shown in Figure 5-32.

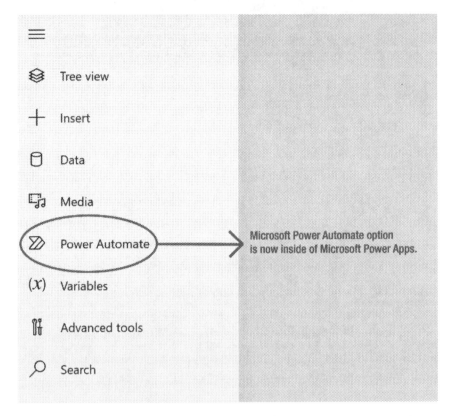

Figure 5-32. *Power Automate option in the Power Apps portal*

If you click the Power Automate option, you will find the Create New Flow or +Add Flow option to create the flow, as shown in Figure 5-33.

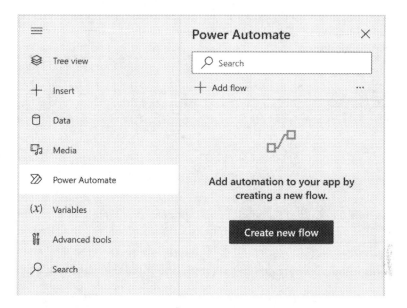

Figure 5-33. *Option to create Power Automate flow*

When you click the Create New Flow button, a new popup will appear with some default flow information provided by Microsoft, as shown in Figure 5-34.

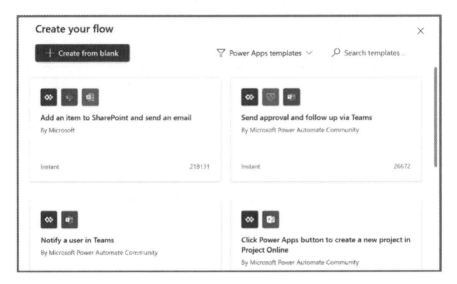

Figure 5-34. *Pre-built automation flow by Microsoft*

This means there is no longer a need to open the Power Apps project separately on the Power Automate site. Power Automate is now fully integrated within Power Apps.

Next, I begin by selecting a default template for the email flow. After setting this up, I explore creating a custom flow so you can fully understand its features and functionality.

In the search bar, type **send email**, and you will get some default email sending flow, as shown in Figure 5-35.

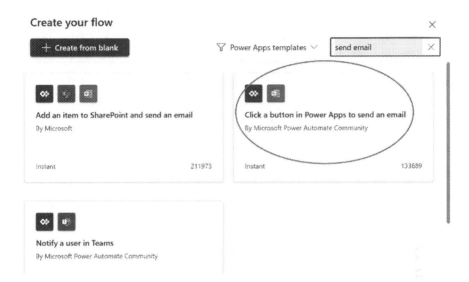

Figure 5-35. *Choosing the correct automation flow to send email*

Choose the Click a Button in Power Apps to Send an Email option. After that, it will ask you to provide a name for the flow, as shown in Figure 5-36.

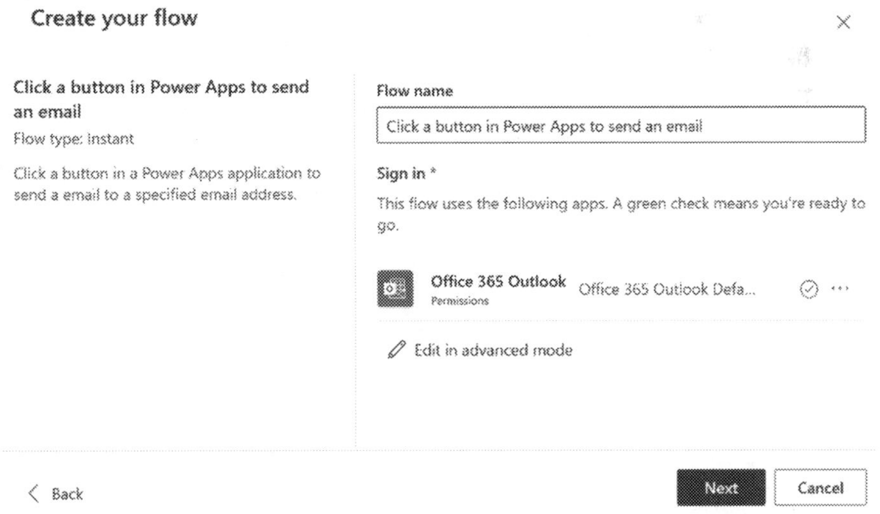

Figure 5-36. *Creating a flow by providing a name*

Click Next to see the option to edit in advanced mode. If you do not need to modify the flow or prefer not to use advanced mode, simply click Create Flow to proceed, as shown in Figure 5-37.

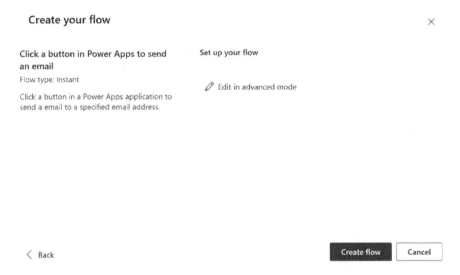

Figure 5-37. *Advanced mode and the Create Flow option*

When you click Create Flow, a new flow will be created and be visible under the Power Automate option, as shown in Figure 5-38.

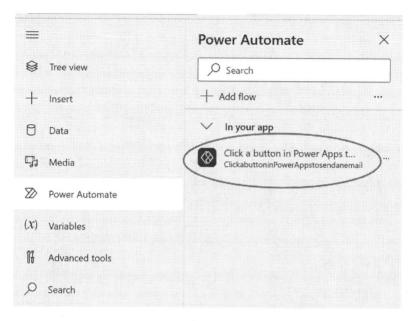

Figure 5-38. *Newly created automation flow is shown in the Power Automate flow list*

Now I need to assign this flow to the send button of an email form. To assign the flow, I first need to add a connector as a data source named Office 365 Outlook, as shown in Figure 5-39.

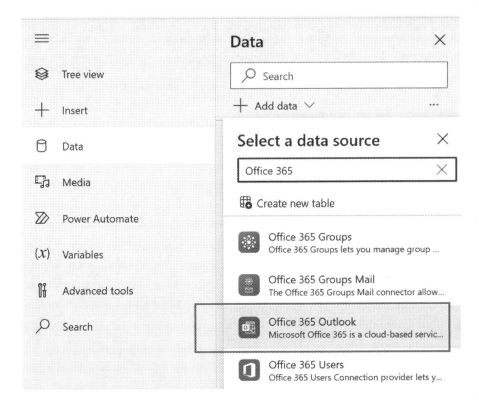

Figure 5-39. *Searching for the Office 365 Outlook connector from the data source list*

Note   When creating a new automated flow in Power Apps, you typically need to specify the data source if the flow will interact with data. However, if you are working with data that's already connected through Power Apps, such as data in Dataverse, you might not need to add a new data source each time.

After adding the Office 365 Outlook connector to the data source, click the send button of email template, as shown in Figure 5-40.

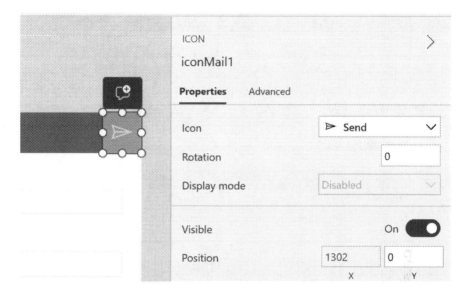

Figure 5-40. *Selecting a send button for the email template*

Then go to the function bar, select OnSelected, and include the following command. Refer to Figure 5-41.

```
ClickabuttoninPowerAppstosendanemail.Run(Title2.Text,
TextEmailSubject1.Text, TextEmailMessage1.Text);
```

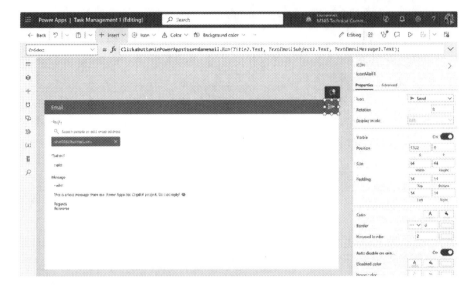

Figure 5-41. *Adding a command to the OnSelect property to send email*

Let's explore this command in detail:

```
ClickabuttoninPowerAppstosendanemail.Run(TextSearchBox1.Text,
TextEmailSubject1.Text, TextEmailMessage1.Text);
```

- **ClickabuttoninPowerAppstosendanemail**: This is the Power Automate flow created for sending emails.

- **Run()**: Use this function to initiate the email-sending process.

- **Title2.text**: Parameter for the To field, it contains the recipient's email address.

- **TextEmailSubject1.text**: Parameter for setting the email's subject line.

- **TextEmailMessage1.text**: Parameter for the email's body content.

To evaluate the email form, just run the app, fill in the form, and click the send button, as shown in Figure 5-42.

Figure 5-42. *Evaluate the email template*

I got a response in a personal email, as shown in Figure 5-43.

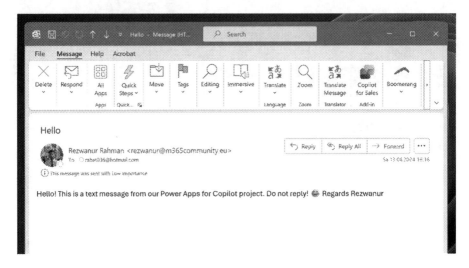

Figure 5-43. *Email received from the Power Apps application through automation*

Power Automation with Copilot

This section explores how to use Copilot to create automated commands in Power Apps. It is important to understand how Copilot integrates with the Power Automate platform, as this helps you grasp its capabilities and limitations in Power Apps. This knowledge is key to effectively using Copilot in your workflows.

So, using Copilot, I create a simple button, which will send a push notification when I click it.

I called this button Notifications, as shown in Figure 5-44.

Figure 5-44. *A new button called Notifications*

In the Copilot prompt, I provide a natural language command like this (also shown in Figure 5-45):

Send a push notification when click on NotificationButton

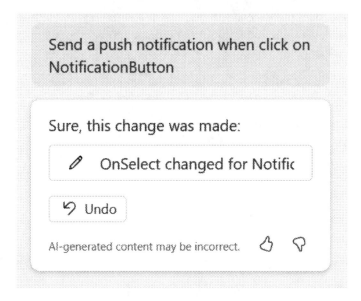

Figure 5-45. *Copilot creates a simple automation to send notifications*

Copilot created an OnSelect method under the button named NotificationButton. If you click the button, you can see the function in the function bar, as shown in Figure 5-46.

Figure 5-46. *The OnSelect function of the Notifications button*

You can see that Copilot created the Notify() function with the PushNotification message. I changed the message to "This is a test push notification", as shown in Figure 5-47.

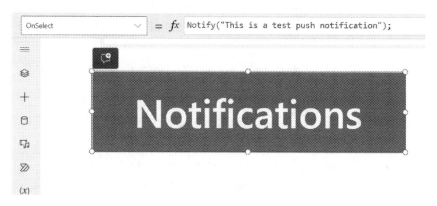

Figure 5-47. *Changing the notification text*

Now run the app and see how it behaves, as shown in Figure 5-48. Press F5 and click the button.

225

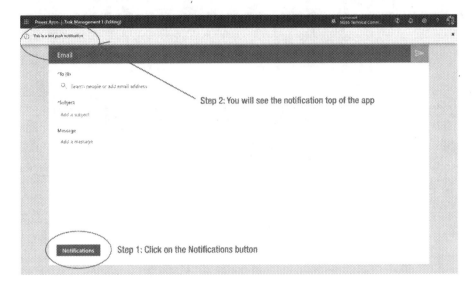

Figure 5-48. *Successfully testing the Notifications button and the function created by Copilot*

You can see that the button has successfully triggered the `Notify()` function, sending a notification in the app.

This is just the basics of automation. You will learn about some advanced customization features in the following chapters.

Summary

This chapter showed you how to dive into advanced customizations and automation within Power Apps, focusing on integrating data sources like Microsoft Dataverse, SQL Server, and Excel. It also explored the capabilities of Power Automate, using natural language commands with Microsoft Copilot to streamline complex tasks. These skills empower you to create dynamic, data-driven applications tailored to your specific business needs.

As you move to the next chapter, the focus shifts to the art of designing exceptional user interfaces and experiences. You'll learn how to refine layouts, optimize the user journey, and enhance accessibility. By mastering the strategic use of color schemes, fonts, and design elements, you'll be able to create applications that are not only powerful but also visually captivating and user-friendly. This next step will elevate your apps, making them a delight for anyone who uses them.

CHAPTER 6

Advanced UI/UX Techniques in Power Apps Development

In the previous chapter, you got hands-on integrating data sources and automating tasks, turning your Power Apps into dynamic, data-driven tools. Now, let's shift gears. This chapter dives into the world of design—where functionality meets aesthetics. It explores how to create interfaces that aren't just functional, but are also visually striking and user-friendly. You'll discover how to optimize layouts, choose the right colors and fonts, and ensure your apps are accessible to everyone. By the end, you'll have the skills to build apps that not only work well but look and feel exceptional, making every interaction a pleasure for your users.

Tailoring Apps: Customization Secrets

When developing applications with Microsoft Power Apps, customization plays a critical role in enhancing functionality and user experience. This section focuses on two crucial aspects: refining user interfaces and dynamically adjusting content. I discuss practical UI/UX best practices aimed at optimizing layout, navigation, and aesthetics to create intuitive

© Rezwanur Rahman 2024
R. Rahman, *Microsoft Copilot for Power Apps*, Inside Copilot,
https://doi.org/10.1007/979-8-8688-0512-7_6

and visually appealing applications. Additionally, I explain how to effectively use variables and formulas to alter app content and appearance in response to user interactions or data changes. These strategies enable developers to tailor applications more closely to specific business needs and user preferences, improving engagement and usability.

Exploring UI/UX Best Practices

This section starts by focusing on creating intuitive interfaces in Power Apps. This involves employing consistent design elements and ensuring the application adapts smoothly across different devices. Making the application accessible to a broad audience is also crucial, as it enhances user satisfaction and overall effectiveness.

Layout Optimization

A clean and organized layout in application design, such as in Power Apps, is essential for enhancing user navigation and accessibility. An effectively designed layout not only makes an application aesthetically pleasing but also increases usability, ensuring users can find the information or functionality they need without confusion or delay.

Importance of Layout Optimization in Power Apps

- **Enhanced user navigation:** A well-structured layout guides users effortlessly through the different parts of the application. This is particularly important in environments where efficiency and speed are valued.

- **Improved accessibility:** Accessibility is crucial in application design, making it easier for people with disabilities to interact with your application. A clean layout with thoughtful spacing and alignment can significantly aid in readability and interaction for users with visual impairments.

- **Increased user engagement:** An organized layout can lead to increased user engagement. When users find the application easy to use and navigate, they are more likely to use it frequently.

- **Professional appearance:** A well-designed application reflects professionalism and attention to detail, enhancing the overall brand perception among users.

Tips for Layout Optimization in Power Apps

I want to share some tips about layout optimization in Power Apps from my experience.

Grid Utilization

A grid system in Power Apps is a framework used to design and align user interface elements systematically across the screens of an application. It provides a structured approach for placing controls like text boxes, labels, and buttons, ensuring that the app's layout is uniform and visually appealing. Grids help make applications responsive, meaning they can adapt smoothly to different screen sizes, from mobile devices to desktops. This adaptability enhances the user experience by maintaining consistency and accessibility across devices. In Power Apps, grids can be implemented using various built-in controls that support flexible and dynamic layouts, facilitating the development of organized and efficient user interfaces.

Why You Need a Grid System

Grids are essential in design and development for several reasons, particularly in digital applications like those created with Power Apps. Here's why grids are so important:

1. **Organizational structure**: Grids provide a coherent structure to lay out elements. Using grids, designers and developers can place UI elements like text, images, and controls in a consistent, aligned manner. This organization makes the interface easier to navigate and interact with, reducing cognitive load for users.

2. **Visual consistency**: Consistency is key in design for creating a smooth, predictable user experience. A grid ensures that elements are uniformly aligned and spaced, which not only enhances the aesthetic appeal but also supports a consistent flow of information, making it easier for users to understand and use the application.

3. **Efficiency in design**: Grids speed up the design process. They serve as a guide that designers can use to quickly add elements to a layout without having to measure and plan each new component from scratch. This can significantly reduce the time spent on adjusting and readjusting elements during the design phase.

4. **Responsiveness and scalability**: With the variety of devices available today, from smartphones to large desktop monitors, designing an interface that works well on all screen sizes is crucial. Grids

facilitate responsive design by allowing elements to resize and rearrange themselves fluidly according to the screen size, maintaining a coherent structure without breaking the layout.

5. **Professional aesthetics**: A grid helps create a polished, professional application. The careful alignment and spacing that a grid imposes results in a cleaner, more orderly design that is visually appealing. This professionalism can affect user trust and satisfaction positively.

6. **Accessibility**: Grids can improve accessibility by creating predictable navigation paths for users. This predictability helps people with visual impairments and those who rely on assistive technologies to better understand and navigate the content.

7. **Facilitate collaboration**: When working in a team, grids provide a common guideline that all designers can adhere to. This uniformity ensures that the work is consistent regardless of who adds to the design, which is crucial in collaborative environments.

Tips for Optimizing the Grid System

Here are some tailored tips for optimizing the grid system in Power Apps:

- **Adaptive dimensions**: Use the Parent.Width and Parent.Height properties to adjust the layout grid to various screen sizes, ensuring a consistent and responsive user experience across different devices. Figures 6-1 and 6-2 demonstrate the adjustments in Height and Weight necessary for optimizing the grid system.

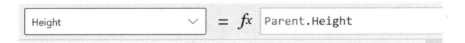

Figure 6-1. *Set the height to optimize the grid system*

Figure 6-2. *Set the weight to optimize the grid system*

- **Uniform spacing**: Implement consistent spacing between elements (*gutters*) and around the perimeter of the screen (*margins*) to maintain visual harmony and enhance readability across the application.

Spacing

In the context of UX/UI design for Power Apps, spacing is a fundamental element that plays a critical role in creating an efficient and visually appealing interface. Proper spacing helps organize the content, improve readability, and enhance the overall user experience.

Importance of Proper Spacing in Power Apps

1. **Clarity and organization**: Spacing can dramatically improve the clarity of your application by defining the relationships between different UI elements. It helps users understand which elements are grouped together and distinguishes between separate sections of the app.

2. **Aesthetic appeal**: Well-spaced elements contribute to a clean and professional look, which can be crucial for business applications built on Power

Apps. It helps in maintaining a balance between the various components on the screen, avoiding a cluttered or overwhelming interface.

3. **Enhanced usability**: Adequate spacing makes interactive elements like buttons and forms easier to use, particularly on touch devices. It reduces the chance of accidental taps and makes the app more accessible, especially for users with motor impairments who may find tightly packed elements challenging to navigate.

Tips for Optimizing Spacing

- **Logical grouping:** Space related items closer together, which helps users quickly associate related functionalities. This can be achieved by using containers in Power Apps to group controls.

- **Adequate padding:** Ensure that there is sufficient space inside each control (padding) to prevent the UI from feeling cramped. This is especially important in forms where users need to enter data.

Alignment

Alignment is, without a doubt, one of the key concepts in UX/UI design. It shapes the look and feel of a design to a great extent. Power Apps is no exception; correct alignment helps design an app that is visually consistent, easy to use, and beautiful. Better alignment not only makes the screen look orderly, but it also establishes flow and thus allows more intuitive navigation, thus enabling the user to perform tasks faster.

Importance of Proper Alignment in Power Apps

1. **Creates visual order**: Alignment helps create a clean, organized interface. This visual order makes it easier for users to process information and understand where to focus their attention.

2. **Enhances readability**: Properly aligned text and controls make content easier to read and scan. This is crucial in business applications where users often need to find information quickly and efficiently.

3. **Improves navigation**: Consistent alignment of elements like buttons, menus, and input fields can significantly enhance the navigation of the app, making it more intuitive for users to move from one task to another.

4. **Creates a professional appearance**: An application with well-aligned elements looks more professional and trustworthy, which is important for business applications designed in Power Apps to reflect the brand's integrity.

Tips to Optimize Alignment

To ensure your designs are effective and aesthetically pleasing, use the following essential tips to optimize alignment.

Use Grid and Layout Containers

Utilizing the grid system and layout containers in Power Apps can help achieve effective alignment. Containers manage the arrangement of child controls and ensure consistent alignment without requiring manual adjustments for each element.

To change the grid alignment, select the container and set properties for alignment within the container (Start, Center, End, and Stretch). See Figure 6-3.

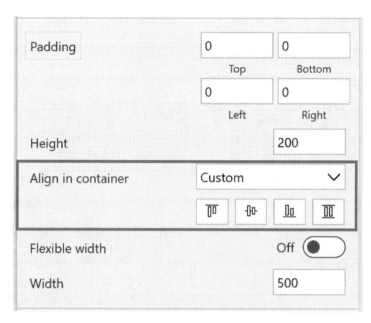

Figure 6-3. *Container alignment options*

Align Text Consistently

Text alignment should be consistent across similar types of content to support readability and create a cohesive look. Typically, the body text is left-aligned, which is easier to read, while titles or headers might be centered or left-aligned, depending on the design.

To change the text alignment, select the text level and choose the text alignment (Left, Center, Right, or Justify). See Figure 6-4.

Figure 6-4. *Text alignment options (Left, Center, Right, or Justify)*

Use Alignment Lines

Power Apps Studio provides alignment lines (smart guides) when moving controls around the canvas, which can help align controls precisely relative to one another. For example, if you drag a control, alignment lines appear when the control aligns with another control's edge or center.

Use Consistent Margins and Padding

Maintaining consistent margins and padding around elements is crucial for alignment. It helps you position elements relative to each other and the overall canvas, providing a balanced and harmonious layout.

To change the margins and padding, select the component, go to the properties, and choose your option. See Figure 6-5.

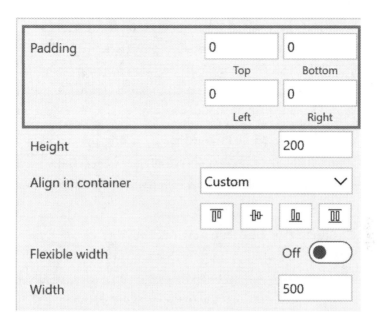

Figure 6-5. *Padding options from the component properties*

Accessibility Considerations

Accessibility in application design is crucial for ensuring that all users, including those with disabilities, can effectively use the software. When designing with Power Apps, it is essential to consider accessibility features that make the app usable for everyone. This includes users with visual impairments, hearing difficulties, motor limitations, and cognitive disabilities. The following sections explain how to implement key accessibility considerations to enhance inclusivity.

Accessibility is important in Power Apps for the following reasons:

- **Legal compliance**: Many regions have legal requirements for digital accessibility (like the ADA in the United States or the AODA in Canada). Ensuring your Power App complies with these standards is not just ethical but also legally prudent.

- **Broader user base**: Designing accessible apps naturally broadens your potential user base, allowing more people to use the app effectively, regardless of their physical abilities.

- **Enhanced user experience**: Accessibility improvements often benefit all users, not just those with disabilities. Features such as clear navigation and readable text improve the overall user experience.

Key Accessibility Considerations for Power Apps

Visual Accessibility

Contrast and colors: Use high contrast colors for text and backgrounds. Avoid color combinations like green and red, which are difficult for colorblind users to distinguish. Power Apps provides properties to customize colors and contrast easily.

To change the Contrast and Colors, select the component, go to the properties, and choose the color. See Figure 6-6.

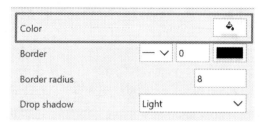

Figure 6-6. *Color option from component properties*

Text Size and Fonts: Ensure that text is resizable without breaking the layout and use legible fonts. Provide functionality within the app to change text sizes if possible. See Figure 6-7.

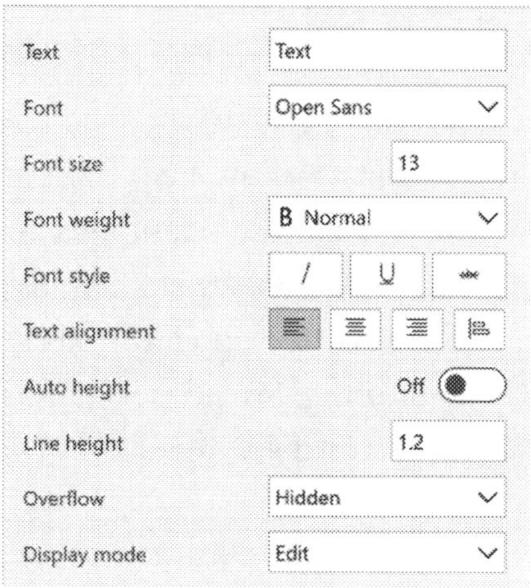

Figure 6-7. *Properties for altering font styles*

Hearing Accessibility

Captions and Subtitles: For multimedia content like videos, include captions and subtitles. If your app integrates such media, ensure these features are accurate and synchronized.

Visual Alerts: Implement visual alerts in addition to auditory ones to notify users about important actions or errors, thereby ensuring that users who are deaf or hard of hearing are also alerted.

Motor Accessibility

Touchable Controls: Make controls large enough to be easily tapped. Power Apps allows you to adjust the size of buttons, drop-downs, and other interactive elements to accommodate users with limited motor skills.

Keyboard Navigation: Ensure the app can be navigated using a keyboard alone. Tab order and keyboard focus should be logical and intuitive.

Gesture Simplification: Avoid complex gestures that might be difficult for users with limited dexterity. Instead, use simple taps or swipes whenever possible.

Cognitive Accessibility

Clear Language: Use plain language to make the content understandable. Avoid technical jargon and complex sentences that can be confusing.

Consistent Layout and Navigation: Maintain a consistent layout and navigation scheme throughout the app to help users with cognitive challenges understand how to use the app more easily.

Feedback and Error Handling: Provide clear, immediate feedback for actions. Error messages should be descriptive and suggest a clear path to resolution.

You can learn more about accessibility controls in Power Apps from here. Scan the QR code in Figure 6-8.

Figure 6-8. *Accessibility controls documentation in Power Apps*

Incorporating Effective Navigation

Designing intuitive navigation within Power Apps is essential to improving the user journey, making the app easier to use and more efficient. Effective navigation helps users find the information they need quickly, complete tasks with fewer clicks, and understand their location within the app at any time. This section explains how to design a simple menu in Power Apps.

Menu Design

This section discusses the design principles for designing a menu. After that, it shows you the process, step-by-step.

- **Simplicity and clarity**: Keep the menu design simple and straightforward. Use clear, descriptive labels for each menu item to ensure users understand their meanings without ambiguity. In Power Apps, you can customize the menu style to fit the app's design and ensure it is easily accessible.

- **Consistent layout**: Place the navigation menu in a consistent location across all pages of the app. Most users expect the main navigation menu either at the top or left side of the screen. Consistency in menu placement helps reduce cognitive load and makes the navigation instinctive.

- **Responsive design**: Ensure that the menu is responsive and works well on different devices and screen sizes. Power Apps allows for adaptive designs that can change layout based on the device, ensuring that the menu remains functional and accessible on mobile and desktop views.

To create a menu, follow the steps:

1. Click the left side menu, select Tree View, click Components, and then choose + New Component. See Figure 6-9.

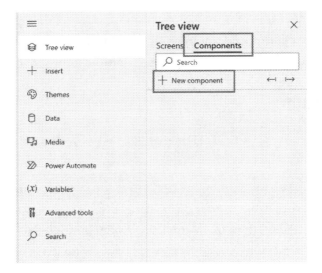

Figure 6-9. *New components create options*

2. You can see a blank component in Figure 6-10.

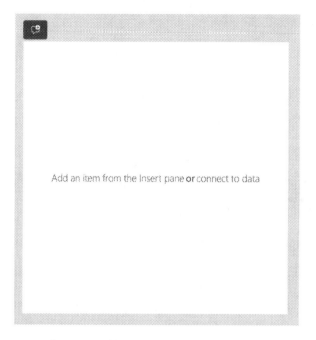

Figure 6-10. *Newly created component*

3. To add the button to this blank component, click
    Insert from the top bar and search for menu. See
    Figure 6-11.

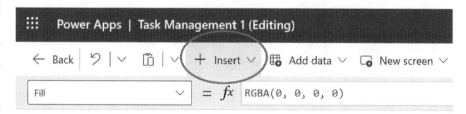

Figure 6-11. *The Insert option in the top bar*

4. If you search for menu, you will get Hamburger
    menu. Select the Hamburger menu and insert it in a
    suitable place in your app. See Figure 6-12.

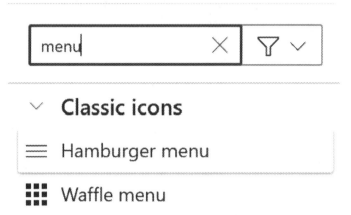

Figure 6-12. *Searching Hamburger menu from the Insert option*

5.   Figure 6-13 shows that I placed the menu in the left
       corner, as this is a common design thinking.

Figure 6-13. *Menu placed in the left corner*

6. Now, search for Flexible Height Gallery from the
   Insert option and choose it, as shown in Figure 6-14.
   This is required because of the scrollable menu. Be
   sure to place it directly below the Hamburger menu.

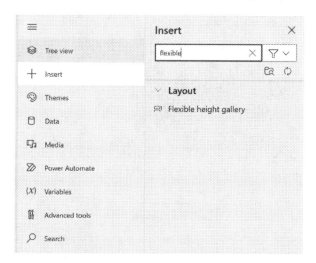

Figure 6-14. *Searching for and adding a Flexible Height Gallery*

7. You can see the blank Flexible Height Gallery in
   Figure 6-15.

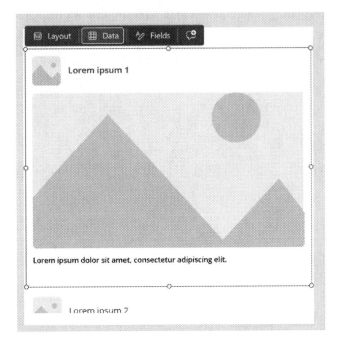

Figure 6-15. *Newly created Flexible Height Gallery*

8. Click the Flexible Height Gallery and select the formula from the top bar. Type Y and write the following code:

    MenuIcon.Height

    This fixes the Y value so that it sits exactly below the Hamburger menu, as shown in Figure 6-16.

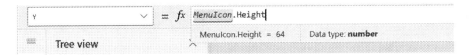

Figure 6-16. *Set the Y value of the Hamburger menu*

Best Practice: Feel free to rename the component as you see fit. This is crucial for clarity when utilizing it in formulas or coding. At this time, I named the icon MenuIcon.

9. You now need to set the flexible height for the component. Select Height from the formula and add the following formula (see Figure 6-17):

```
Parent.Height-MenuIcon.Height
```

Figure 6-17. *Set the flexible height by changing the Height property*

10. You will now create a menu design that helps users recognize their current page location. I add a shape and text level for better understanding. To make the design, you need to add a New Custom Property to the component. Provide a name and select Table as the Data Type. See Figure 6-18.

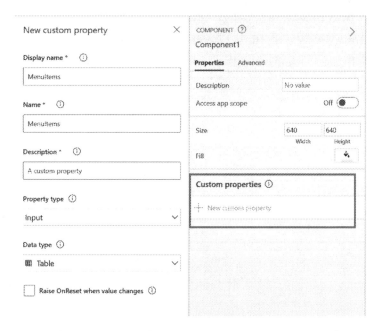

Figure 6-18. *Create a New Custom Property option inside a component*

11. As shown in Figure 6-19, the New Custom Property option is in the right sidebar menu.

Figure 6-19. *The New Custom Property option appears in the Custom Properties list*

12.   As shown in Figure 6-20, click MenuItems to see the
       code in the Formula bar.

Figure 6-20. *MenuItem default formula code*

13.   Click Format Text to simplify the code. See
       Figure 6-21.

Figure 6-21. *Formatting code lines using Format Text option*

14.   Figure 6-22 shows the simplified code.

```
Table(
    {
        SampleStringField: "SampleText",
        SampleNumberField: 10,
        SampleBooleanField: true
    }
)
```

Figure 6-22. *Simplified code after formatting*

15.   You will now customize the table script. You need
       two components and one action for each menu
       item. You need a Menu Label, Menu Icon, and Menu
       Screen Navigation to navigate the menu. I will also
       add something known as the Menu ID.

As shown in Figure 6-23, I change the table as follows:

```
Table(
    {
        MenuLabel: "Home",
        MenuIcon: Icon.Home,
        MenuScreenNavigate: App.ActiveScreen,
        MenuID: 1
    }
)
```

Figure 6-23. Custom script for the Menu table

Note   When you type **Icon** and press the dot (.) in MenuIcon section, you will get a drop-down list with all the related icons. You do not need to add the icons manually.

---

16.   Copy the label and paste it inside the table and separate the labels with commas (,). See Figure 6-24. I create three menu items, named Home, About, and Email. If you want to add more menu items, simply copy and paste the labels, including the {}, and separate them with commas.

```
Table(
    {
        MenuLabel: "Home",
        MenuIcon: Icon.Home,
        MenuScreenNavigate: App.ActiveScreen,
        MenuID: 1
    },
    {
        MenuLabel: "About",
        MenuIcon: Icon.Information,
        MenuScreenNavigate: App.ActiveScreen,
        MenuID: 2
    },
    {
        MenuLabel: "Email",
        MenuIcon: Icon.Mail,
        MenuScreenNavigate: App.ActiveScreen,
        MenuID: 3
    }
)
```

Figure 6-24. *Creating labels for the Hamburger menu*

17. Save the formula and go back to the Container
     page. Select the Flexible Height Gallery. Add a
     new rectangle inside the component, as shown in
     Figure 6-25.

Figure 6-25. *Adding a rectangle for the menu design*

18.   Shrink the width and height (see Figure 6-26).

Figure 6-26. *Shrinking the rectangle's height and weight for beautification*

19. Now, add a + Add icon so that the menu icon can be placed here. Refer to Figure 6-27.

Figure 6-27. *Adding an icon placeholder in the Hamburger menu*

20. As shown in Figure 6-28, you would also add a text label, which will be replaced with the menu name.

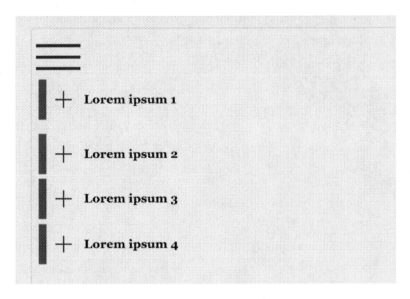

Figure 6-28. *Adding text labels to the Hamburger menu*

21. Select the Flexible Height Gallery, go to the Formula bar on top, and select Items. Type the following formula code to get the menu items (see Figure 6-29):

```
Component1.MenuItems
```

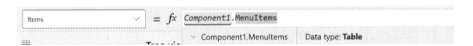

Figure 6-29. *Binding menu items in Flexible Height Gallery*

In this app, the component name is Component1 and the menu item name is MenuItems.

22. As in Figure 6-30, the menu will appear on the app screen, but it will not be formatted correctly. You need to adjust the formatting afterward.

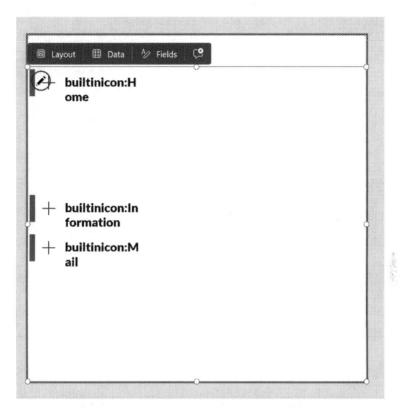

Figure 6-30. *Menu appears with unstructured format*

23. Select the text label, choose the Text formula from the Formula bar, and fix the code so it looks like Figure 6-31.

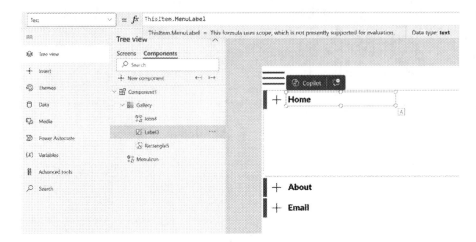

Figure 6-31. *Making a dynamically changeable text label*

I selected the text label, and in the Formula bar, selected the Text formula, then changed the default code from ThisItem.MenuIcon to ThisItem. MenuLabel. I do the same for the icon as well.

24. To change the icon, select it and go to the Properties. Click the Icon option. See Figure 6-32.

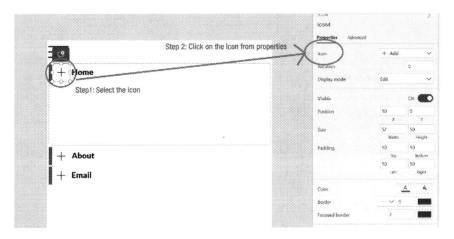

Figure 6-32. *Binding icons in the Flexible Height Gallery*

25. In the Formula bar, under the Icon option, add the following code to fetch the icons that you created before, as shown in Figure 6-33:

```
ThisItem.MenuIcon
```

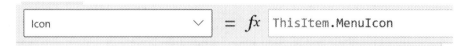

Figure 6-33. *Making a dynamically changeable icon*

26. Figure 6-34 shows that the icons are perfectly set on the app screen.

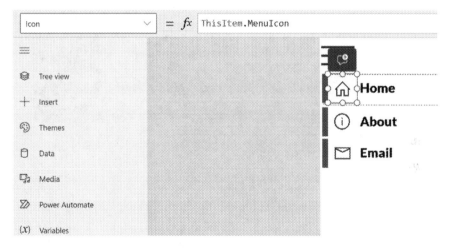

Figure 6-34. *The icons have been successfully fetched on the Hamburger menu*

27. Next, add the menu navigation. As shown in Figure 6-35, select the rectangle. In the Formula bar, select Visible and add the following code:

```
ThisItem.MenuScreenNavigate = App.ActiveScreen
```

Figure 6-35. *Creating a navigation menu*

28. Next, you can add a button, as shown in Figure 6-36. It is important to position the button above the rectangle, icon, and text label so that tapping any of these elements will activate the button, triggering it to change the page or execute an action.

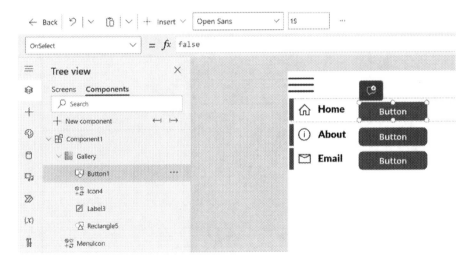

Figure 6-36. *Adding a button to the navigation menu*

29. Change the functions listed in Table 6-1 to make the button transparent and link it with the menu items.

Table 6-1. *Values to Make a Button Transparent and Responsive in Different Devices*

Function	Value
X	0
Y	0
Width	Parent.TemplateWidth
Height	Label3.Height+Label3.Y
Fill	Color.Transparent
Hoverfill	Color.Transparent
PressedFill	Color.Transparent

30. From the Formula bar, select the OnSelect formula and type the following code to connect:

```
Navigate(ThisItem.MenuScreenNavigate,
ScreenTransition.Cover)
```

31. Now, you'll set up a transition to show and hide the Hamburg menu upon clicking or tapping. To set up the transition, create a new variable named showMenu and set it not to show the menu. That means if the value is true, it will become false and if it is false, it will become true. Click in the Hamburg menu icon, select the OnSelect property from the Formula bar, and add the following code (see Figure 6-37):

```
Set(showMenu, !showMenu)
```

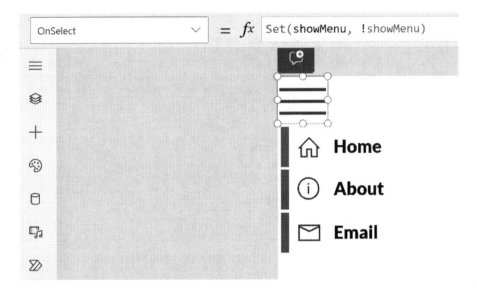

Figure 6-37. Creating a OnSelect condition for the Hamburger menu

32. Now create another new custom property called
ExpandMenu. The data type must be Boolean.
Select the Raise OnReset When Value Changes
option, as shown in Figure 6-38. This option allows
the value changes of this property to trigger the
OnReset of the component. This method is designed
to easily set and reset the default value.

New custom property	×	COMPONENT ⑦	>

Component1

Display name * ⓘ

Expand Menu

Properties Advanced	
Description	No value
Access app scope	Off ⬤

Name * ⓘ

ExpandMenu

Size	640	640
	Width	Height
Fill		🎨

Description * ⓘ

A custom property

Custom properties ⓘ

Property type ⓘ

Input ∨

— New custom property

Menultems	Table

Data type ⓘ

⬭ Boolean ∨

☑ Raise OnReset when value changes ⓘ

Create   Cancel

Figure 6-38. *Creating a new custom property named ExpandMenu*

33.   Click the ExpandMenu property and set it to false, as
      shown in Figure 6-39. It is true by default.

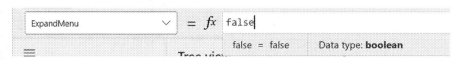

ExpandMenu ∨	= *fx*	false
☰	false = false	Data type: **boolean**

Figure 6-39. *Changing the ExpandMenu value to false*

34. As shown in Figure 6-40, select the Advanced option
of component1 and click the OnReset option.

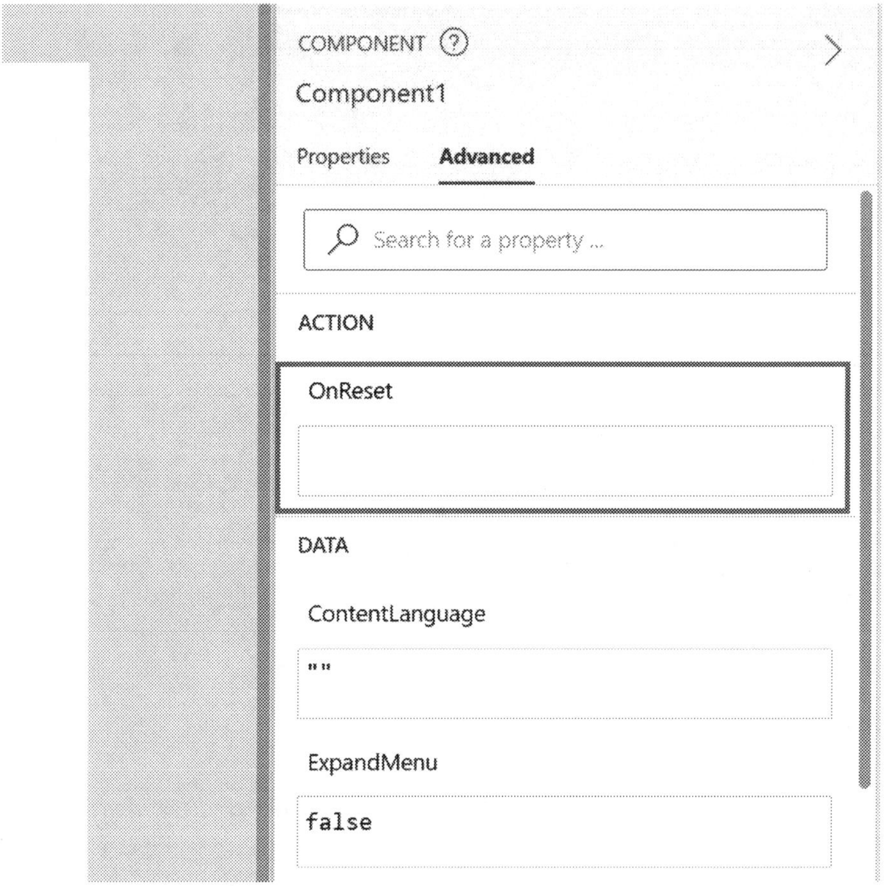

Figure 6-40. *The OnReset option in the advanced component
properties*

35. In the Formula bar, type the following code (also
shown in Figure 6-41):

```
Set(showMenu, Component1.ExpandMenu)
```

Figure 6-41. *Changing the OnReset condition*

36. Select the Flexible Height Gallery. In the Formula
bar, select the Visible formula and write the variable
that you created before showMenu. See Figure 6-42.

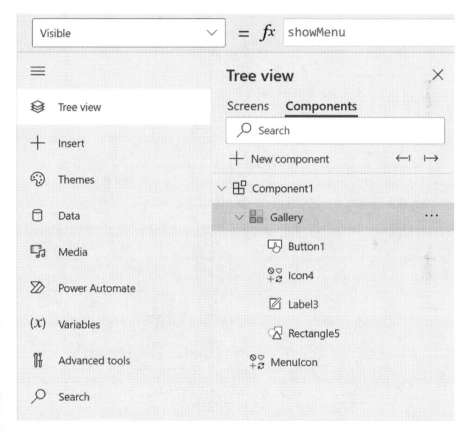

Figure 6-42. *Creating a variable in the Visible formula named*
showMenu

37. The menu is not visible, as shown in Figure 6-43. By holding down the Alt key and clicking the menu, you can make it visible, as shown in Figure 6-44.

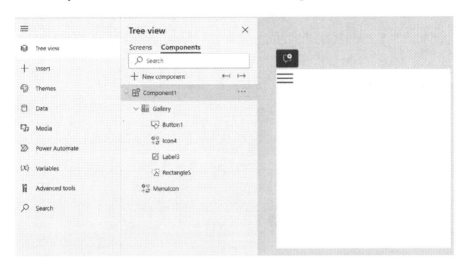

Figure 6-43. *The menu is not visible*

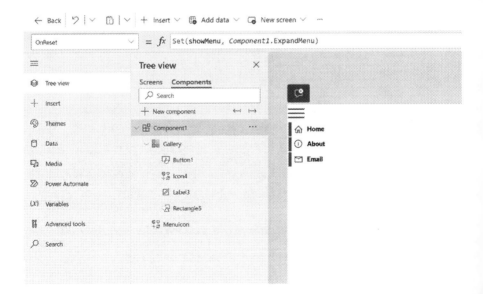

Figure 6-44. *The menu is shown after pressing Alt key and clicking it*

266

38. The menu has been successfully created. Next, you will integrate the menu into the app screen. Select the Email screen as shown in Figure 6-45, which you developed in the previous chapter.

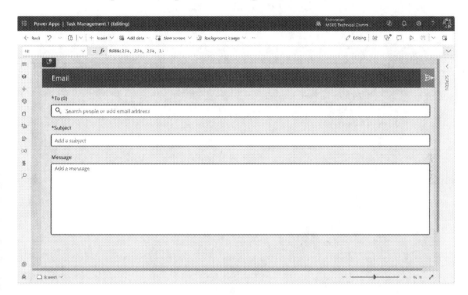

Figure 6-45. *Email screen where the menu will be integrated*

39. Click Insert from the top menu and select
     Component1 under the Custom option, as shown in
     Figure 6-46.

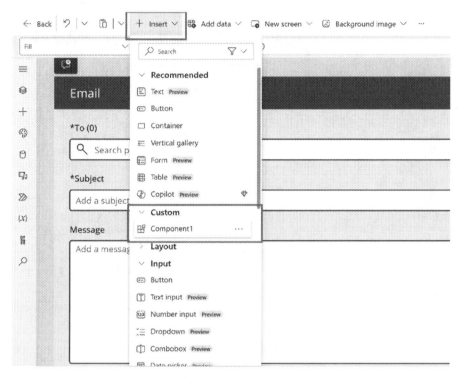

Figure 6-46. *Adding a custom component to the email template*

40.   You will see a preview of the menu, as shown in
      Figure 6-47.

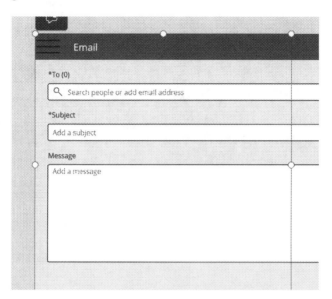

Figure 6-47. *Showing the Hamburger menu in the email template*

41.   Press F5 or run the app as shown in Figure 6-48.
Click the menu to see it.

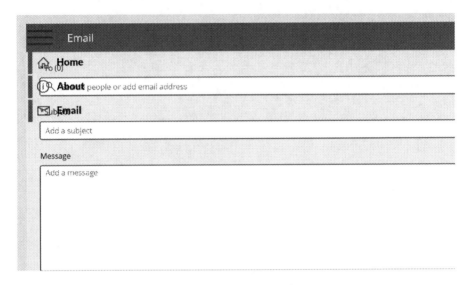

Figure 6-48. *Preview the app and review the menu options*

42.   The menu will be shown as transparent. You need
to add a background so that the user can read the
menu clearly. To change the background color, go
to Component1, select Flexible Height Gallery, and
choose a color from Properties. Follow along in
Figure 6-49.

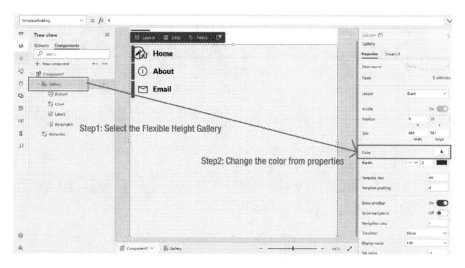

Figure 6-49. *Changing the component background. Select the Flexible Height Gallery and then change the color from Properties*

43. Now go back to the Email screen and run the app by pressing F5, as shown in Figure 6-50.

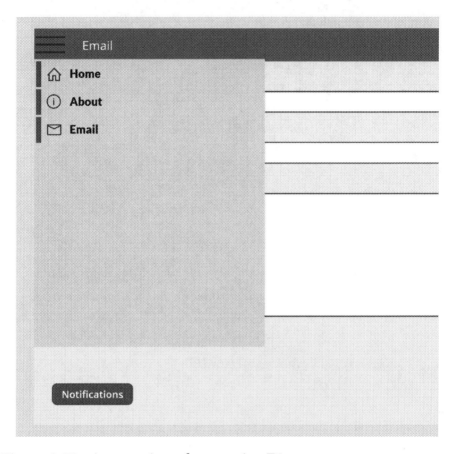

Figure 6-50. *App preview after pressing F5*

This is a simple example of creating a menu in Power Apps. You can explore more advanced features, such as how to connect a button to other pages or create a function, by visiting the following link:

https://techcommunity.microsoft.com/t5/educator-developer-blog/create-a-responsive-menu-navigation-bar-in-canvas-power-apps/ba-p/3796871

Aesthetic Design

Aesthetic design is pivotal in shaping the user experience for Power Apps UX/UI. This section guides you through the selection of color schemes, fonts, and design elements that not only captivate visually but also ensure functional integrity. The choice of specific colors and typefaces carries deep psychological effects, influencing how users feel and interact with the app. Through effective design strategies, you can craft interfaces that are visually pleasing and conducive to a seamless user experience, leading to enhanced user engagement and satisfaction.

Color Schemes

Selecting the perfect color palette for Power Apps is crucial for enhancing the user experience and functionality. Colors do more than beautify; they build a strong connection with your brand and ensure visual consistency across applications, making the user interface intuitive and familiar. They influence mood and behavior, which is essential for apps aimed at specific tasks or emotions. Thoughtful color contrasts enhance readability and accessibility, helping users with visual impairments navigate the app more easily. Strategic use of colors can also highlight essential elements and organize information, facilitating smoother user interactions. A well-chosen color scheme improves the aesthetic appeal of an app and boosts its usability and effectiveness.

Choosing a Color Palette for Power Apps

Based on my experience, I have identified five distinct types of color categories:

- **Primary colors:** These are the central colors of your app, reflecting the brand's identity. They are the most visually dominant. Choose these to set the tone and personality of your application, ensuring they align well with your brand's ethos and the app's purpose.

- **Secondary colors:** These colors are used to support and contrast with the primary palette. Select secondary hues that enhance the visual hierarchy of your interface, helping to clearly distinguish between different UI elements like buttons or notifications, without overpowering the primary colors.

- **Accent colors:** Employed sparingly, accent colors are there to draw attention to critical elements such as call-to-action buttons or active states. These should be distinct and vibrant enough to stand out against primary and secondary colors.

- **Neutral colors:** Utilize shades of white, gray, and black for background, text, and UI components like borders and dividers. These neutrals are essential in creating visual breaks and reducing visual strain, thus contributing to a balanced and cohesive design.

- **Functional colors:** Designated for alerts, indicators, and statuses, choose colors that users universally associate with specific messages and actions, such as caution, error, or success. These should be intuitive enough to instantly communicate the necessary information about the app's processes.

Figure 6-51 shows some examples of different color categories.

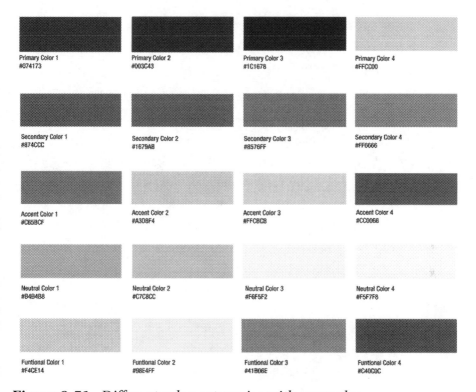

Figure 6-51. *Different color categories with examples*

Tools to Match Color Schemes

Nowadays, you can find many sources to generate or choose color palettes. If you are new to Power Apps environment, check out the following websites, where you can generate and choose free color palettes:

- **Colorhunt** (https://colorhunt.co/): Color Hunt is an online resource that provides a free and open platform for color inspiration, tailored to anyone looking to find or share color combinations. It features thousands of color palettes, making it a popular tool for designers, artists, and anyone involved in creative projects.

The site presents palettes in a straightforward, easy-to-navigate format, allowing you to browse through a variety of schemes quickly.

Each palette on Color Hunt consists of four colors, displayed in a visually pleasing layout, as shown in Figure 6-52. You can easily copy the Hex codes for each color, which you can then use in your digital design projects. Color Hunt is especially useful for discovering trending color schemes, exploring different aesthetic styles, and finding inspiration for Power Apps design, graphic projects, or any other creative work that involves color coordination.

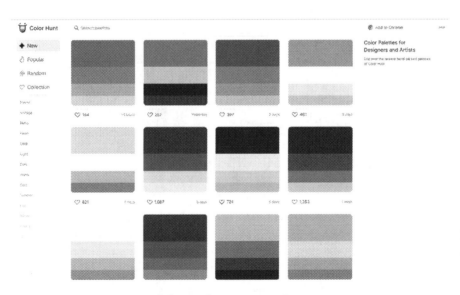

Figure 6-52. *Preview of the Color Hunt website*

- **Coolors** (https://coolors.co/): Coolors is an
  online color scheme generator that is extremely
  helpful for designers and creatives looking to
  develop or refine color palettes for their projects.
  It offers a straightforward interface where you can
  quickly generate, adjust, and explore different color
  combinations, as shown in Figure 6-53. By simply
  pressing a button, you can create a new palette, tailor
  colors to your specific needs using Hex codes, and
  experiment with variations to find the perfect match for
  your design work. Coolors.co is widely appreciated for
  its simplicity and effectiveness in helping users finalize
  their color choices.

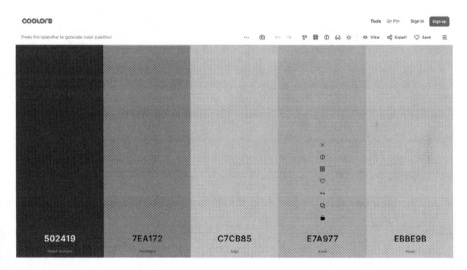

Figure 6-53. *Preview of the Coolors website*

Fonts and Sizes

Selecting the right fonts and font sizes in Power Apps is critical for creating a user-friendly interface. Appropriate fonts enhance readability, allowing users to process information quickly and easily, which is crucial in applications that require frequent interaction or present substantial data. Consistent font usage across the app ensures a cohesive visual experience, reinforcing the app's identity and facilitating intuitive navigation. Well-chosen fonts significantly impact user engagement and satisfaction, emphasizing their importance in the design of Power Apps.

Power Apps supports a variety of standard fonts that are commonly used across many applications for their clarity and compatibility. Here is a list of available fonts in Power Apps:

Arial, Arial Black, Calibri, Cambria, Comic Sans MS, Courier New, Georgia, Helvetica, Lucida Console, Lucida Sans Unicode, Segoe UI, Tahoma, Times New Roman, Trebuchet MS, and Verdana.

These fonts are chosen to ensure optimal readability and consistency across various devices and platforms.

It is common for an app to feature various fonts on the same page. For instance, the header might utilize one style of font, while the body text and footer might use another, shown in Figure 6-54. You can certainly apply multiple fonts in a single Power App. However, it is crucial to ensure that the fonts you choose harmonize with each other. This aspect is not just about aesthetics but also pertains to psychological factors; mismatched fonts can disrupt the user's experience and reduce the overall effectiveness of your app's design.

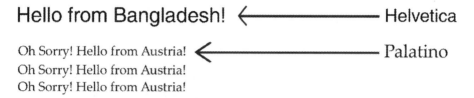

Figure 6-54. *Displaying various text fonts for headers and body text*

Font size is as crucial as selecting the right color or font type. Choosing an incorrect font size can significantly affect the usability and the aesthetics of an app. If the font size is too small, users may struggle to read text without zooming in, which can be especially problematic on mobile devices or for users with visual impairments. Conversely, overly large fonts can also disrupt readability by breaking the natural flow and requiring more scrolling. For instance, I defined five distinct font sizes, which can enhance the reliability, functionality, and uniqueness of an app, as shown in Figure 6-55.

Hello from Bangladesh! (10px)

Hello from Bangladesh! (12px)

Hello from Bangladesh! (14px)

Hello from Bangladesh! (20px)

Hello from Bangladesh! (28px)

Figure 6-55. *Showing different font sizes*

The careful selection of fonts, font sizes, and colors is essential in app design. These choices impact the visual appeal, usability, and accessibility of your application, ensuring a seamless user experience that leads to higher user engagement and satisfaction. Striking the right balance and harmony among these visual components is key to creating an effective and appealing app.

Summary

This chapter explored advanced UI/UX techniques for enhancing your Power Apps, focusing on creating interfaces that are functional and visually compelling. It covered layout optimization, grid systems, spacing, alignment, and accessibility, all aimed at helping you design applications that are professional and user-friendly.

As you move into Chapter 7, the focus turns to making your Power Apps more dynamic and interactive. You'll learn how to use variables, formulas, and responsive design to create adaptable and engaging applications. Additionally, I introduce you to integrating Copilot and chatbot functionalities, allowing your apps to interact intelligently with users in real time. Chapter 7 is about transforming your applications into responsive, intuitive tools that provide a personalized user experience. Let's continue advancing your Power Apps to the next level.

Dynamic Content, Comments, and Copilot Customization in Power Apps

In the previous chapter, you learned how to design Power Apps that are both functional and visually engaging. You focused on optimizing layouts, ensuring accessibility, and creating a seamless user experience. Now, it's time to build on that foundation by introducing dynamic content and AI-driven interactions. This chapter explores how to use variables, formulas, and responsive design techniques to make your apps more adaptable and interactive. Additionally, you'll learn how to integrate Copilot and chatbot features, enabling your apps to deliver intelligent, real-time responses to user inputs. This chapter will transform your Power Apps into powerful, responsive tools that provide a personalized and engaging experience.

© Rezwanur Rahman 2024
R. Rahman, *Microsoft Copilot for Power Apps*, Inside Copilot,
https://doi.org/10.1007/979-8-8688-0512-7_7

Dynamic Content

In applications, the use of variables and formulas enables real-time updates to both content and design, responding to user interactions or data alterations. This strategy empowers developers to build more adaptable and engaging applications by programming them to modify their behavior and appearance based on ongoing user inputs and external data changes. As a result, each user encounter becomes uniquely responsive and personalized, enhancing user engagement and satisfaction.

Using Variables

If you are transitioning from languages like C# or JavaScript to Power Apps, you might initially search for how to handle variables. However, Power Apps approaches this differently, taking cues from Excel's way of handling data.

In traditional programming, you often compute results and store them in variables for future reference. In contrast, both Power Apps and Excel operate on a dynamic formula system, where computations update in real time as input data changes. This minimizes the necessity for manual variable management, streamlining the creation and upkeep of your applications.

Despite this, there are occasions within Power Apps where variables become necessary, particularly due to its enhancement over Excel with behavior formulas. These formulas trigger in response to user interactions, such as clicking a button, where setting a variable can be crucial for facilitating interactivity throughout the application.

In practice, it is wise to rely on variables sparingly. When needed, Power Apps variables are generated implicitly and automatically typed according to how they are employed in setting functions. This method simplifies application development by keeping the focus on real-time data interaction and formula-driven processes, aligning more with functional needs rather than static data storage.

Power Apps has three types of variables, as listed in Table 7-1.

Table 7-1. Variables for Power Apps Development

Variable Type	Scope	Description	Functions That Establish
Global Variable	Application-wide	Accessible across all screens within the app. Useful for information that needs to be accessed or modified globally.	`Set(variableName, value)`: Initializes or updates a global variable, e.g., `Set(CurrentUser, "Munia")`.
Context Variable	Single screen	Located to the screen where they are created. Ideal for managing state within a single screen.	`UpdateContext({variableName: value})`: Creates or updates a context variable, e.g., `UpdateContext({ShowPanel: true})`. `Navigate(ScreenName, Transition, {variableName: value})`: Navigates to another screen and can pass context variables, e.g., `Navigate(ScreenTwo, None, {ShowDetails: true})`.
Collections	Application-wide	Stores tables of data that can be used throughout the app; suitable for data groups like search results.	`Collect(collectionName, item)`: Adds items to a collection, e.g., `Collect(UserTasks, {Task: "Update report", Status: "Pending"})`. `ClearCollect(collectionName, items)`: Clears and readds items to a collection, e.g., `ClearCollect(ProductList, Gallery1.AllItems)`.

Global Variables

Global variables are used to store information that can be accessed and manipulated across different screens and controls within an application. You create and set these variables using the Set() function.

For example, if you want to maintain a consistent theme or color scheme across all screens, you could set a global variable for color as follows:

```
Set(globalColor, "blue")
```

Once this variable is set, you can refer to globalColor in various properties and formulas throughout your app. For instance, you might use it to set the fill color of buttons, backgrounds of screens, or text color of labels, ensuring a uniform look:

```
Fill: globalColor
```

How Do Global Variables Work?

Understanding how global variables function is crucial. I utilized the Set() function to assign a value to the global variable. For instance, Set(globalColor, "blue") configures the global variable globalColor to the value blue. To use the global variable, you simply reference the name assigned to the Set() function. In this scenario, referencing globalColor will yield the value blue. It is important to note that global variables can hold various types of values, including strings, numbers, records, and tables.

Note   *Global variables* are used when data needs to be accessed across multiple screens within an app. This is suitable for storing user preferences or app-wide settings that affect multiple aspects of the application, such as user roles or themes.

Context Variables

In Power Apps, *context variables* are used to store data that is specific to a screen on your app. They are like global variables but have a scope limited to the screen where they are created. Context variables are useful for passing values between screens or for holding data that is temporarily needed while a user is on a particular screen.

You can create and update context variables using the `UpdateContext()` function, which sets the value of one or more context variables for the current screen. For example:

```
UpdateContext({varName: value})
```

You can also pass context variables between screens using the `Navigate()` function:

```
Navigate(TargetScreen, Transition)
```

How Do Context Variables Work?

In Power Apps, context variables store data specific to a screen, starting off as blank when the app launches. They are set using the `UpdateContext()` function in a record syntax, for example, `{x: 1}`. In other programming tools, you commonly use = for assignment, as in `x = 1`. For context variables, use `{x: 1}` instead. You can also pass context variables between screens using the `Navigate()` function, like parameter passing in programming, which helps maintain state across different screens. However, these variables are confined to the screen they are set on and do not persist beyond it unless passed explicitly.

Note   *Context variables* are useful for data that is only relevant to the current screen. They are ideal for managing temporary states like form inputs or control visibility on a specific screen, without impacting memory or performance on other screens.

Collections

Collections in Power Apps are used to store and manage data within an app. Collections are in-memory tables of data that can be used to store temporary data pulled from data sources or generated programmatically during app runtime. They are highly useful in scenarios where offline capabilities are needed, or when data needs to be manipulated and displayed within the app without constant read/write operations to an external database.

In Power Apps, there are two functions available for managing data within collections: Collect() and ClearCollect(). These functions allow for the efficient handling and manipulation of in-memory data collections.

The Collect() function adds one or more records to a collection. If the collection does not exist, it will be created automatically. This function is useful for dynamically adding data to a collection during app usage.

```
Collect(UserData, {Name: "Munia", Age: 27})
```

Here, a new record with the Name set to "Munia" and the Age set to 27 is added to the UserData collection. If UserData does not already exist, this command will create it with this record.

The ClearCollect() function clears all the data in a collection and adds new data to it. This is helpful when you need to completely refresh the data in a collection.

```
ClearCollect(UserData, {Name: "Ruhi", Age: 21}, {Name:
"Gamsjäger", Age: 55})
```

This command clears any existing data in UserData and adds two new records for Ruhi and Gamsjäger, resetting the collection with new data.

Note   Collections are best used when you're dealing with sets of data that require local processing or when you need to perform operations on multiple records, like filtering or sorting. They are also useful for storing data temporarily, especially when working with complex data structures that need to be manipulated or displayed in a gallery control.

Formulas for Dynamic Interaction

In Power Apps, a *formula* is an expression used to calculate values, manipulate data, and control the properties of an app's user interface elements dynamically. Formulas in Power Apps are similar in concept to formulas in spreadsheet applications like Microsoft Excel but are used to drive app logic and user interface behaviors directly.

Formulas can be applied to properties of controls (such as text boxes, labels, buttons, etc.), and they define how these properties should change in response to user inputs, internal state changes, or other dynamic conditions in the app environment. For instance, a formula can set the visibility of a control, change its color, update its text, or even handle more complex logic like filtering data in a gallery based on user input.

Power Apps formulas incorporate a diverse array of functions and operators, including logic, text, math, and table functions. These formulas are essential for several key functions:

- **Data binding:** Formulas enable the display of data within app controls, such as populating galleries or drop-down menus with data from collections or external sources.

- **Interactive responses:** Formulas facilitate modifications to the app's interface in response to user actions, such as clicks or data entries, enhancing interactivity.

- **Logic implementation:** Formulas are crucial for executing app logic, including conditionally formatting data, validating forms, and controlling navigation between screens based on user input or other specified criteria.

Table 7-2 is a complete formula table with descriptions and code examples for your better understanding.

Table 7-2. *A Complete Formula List Available in Power Apps*

Formula	Description	Code Example
Abs	Absolute value of a number.	Abs(-5) returns 5
Acos	Returns the arccosine of a number, in radians.	Acos(0.5) returns 1.047
Acot	Returns the arc cotangent of a number, in radians.	Acot(1) returns 0.785
AddColumns	Returns a table with columns added.	AddColumns(table, "NewCol", 5)
And	Boolean logic AND.	And(true, false) returns false
AIClassify	Classifies text into categories.	AIClassify("Review text")

(*continued*)

Table 7-2. (*continued*)

Formula	Description	Code Example
AIExtract	Extracts specified entities from text.	AIExtract("Contact John at 1234567890")
AIReply	Drafts a reply to the provided message.	AIReply("Your request is noted")
AISentiment	Detects the sentiment of the text.	AISentiment("I love this!") returns positive
AISummarize	Summarizes the text.	AISummarize("Long article text")
AITranslate	Translates text from another language.	AITranslate("Hola", " en")
Asin	Returns the arcsine of a number, in radians.	Asin(0.5) returns 0.524
Assert	Evaluates to true or false in a test.	Assert(5 > 2) returns true
As	Names the current record in gallery.	With({x: 10}, As(x))
AsType	Treats a record reference as a specific table type.	AsType(record, TableType)
Atan	Returns the arctangent of a number, in radians.	Atan(1) returns 0.785
Atan2	Returns the arctangent based on (x,y) coordinates.	Atan2(1,1) returns 0.785

(*continued*)

Table 7-2. (*continued*)

Formula	Description	Code Example
Average	Calculates the average of a set of numbers.	Average(1, 2, 3) returns 2
Back	Displays the previous screen.	Back()
Blank	Returns a blank value, often used to represent NULL.	If(IsBlank(Blank()), "Is Blank")
Boolean	Converts a value to a Boolean.	Boolean(1) returns true
Calendar	Retrieves calendar information for the current locale.	Calendar()
Char	Translates a character code into a string.	Char(65) returns "A"
Choices	Returns a table of values for a lookup column.	Choices(DataTable. LookupColumn)
Clear	Deletes all data from a collection.	Clear(Collection)
ClearCollect	Clears a collection and adds new records.	ClearCollect(Collection, {id:1, name:"John"})
ClearData	Clears data from an app host, like a local device.	ClearData()

(*continued*)

Table 7-2. (*continued*)

Formula	Description	Code Example
Clock	Retrieves clock information for the current locale.	Clock()
Coalesce	Replaces blank values while preserving non-blank ones.	Coalesce(Blank(), "default")
Collect	Creates or adds to a collection.	Collect(NewCollection, {id:2, name:"Jane"})
ColorFade	Fades a color by a specified amount.	ColorFade(Color.Red, 50%)
ColorValue	Translates a CSS color name or Hex code to a color.	ColorValue("#FF5733")
Concat	Concatenates strings in a data source.	Concat(Names, FirstName & " ")
Concatenate	Concatenates two or more strings.	Concatenate("Hello", " ", "World!")
Concurrent	Evaluates multiple formulas at the same time.	Concurrent(Sum(1,2), Average(3,4,5))
Count	Counts the number of numeric entries in a table.	Count(Products.Price)

(*continued*)

Table 7-2. (*continued*)

Formula	Description	Code Example
Cos	Returns the cosine of a specified angle in radians.	Cos(PI()/3) returns 0.5
Cot	Returns the cotangent of a specified angle in radians.	Cot(PI()/4) returns 1
CountRows	Counts the number of rows in a table.	CountRows(Products)
DateAdd	Adds a specified time interval to a date value.	DateAdd(DateValue ("2024-03-01"), 1, Months)
DateDiff	Calculates the difference between two dates.	DateDiff(DateValue ("2024-01-01"), DateValue("2024-01-01"), Years)
DateTimeValue	Converts a date and time string to a date/time value.	DateTimeValue("2024-01-01 12:00")
DateValue	Converts a date-only string to a date/time value.	DateValue("2024-01-01")
Day	Retrieves the day portion from a date/time value.	Day(DateValue("2024-01-01"))

(*continued*)

Table 7-2. (*continued*)

Formula	Description	Code Example
Degrees	Converts an angle in radians to degrees.	Degrees(PI()) returns 180
Distinct	Removes duplicates from a table.	Distinct(Orders, ProductID)
EDate	Adds or subtracts months to a date, keeping the day unchanged.	EDate(DateValue ("2024-10-01"), 2)
EditForm	Resets a form control for editing.	EditForm(Form1)
Enable	Enables a device signal, such as GPS.	Enable(Location)
EncodeHTML	Encodes special characters into HTML format.	EncodeHTML("<tag>") returns <tag>
EncodeUrl	Encodes special characters using URL encoding.	EncodeUrl("name=Rezwanur Rahman")
EndsWith	Checks if a text string ends with another string.	EndsWith("Hello", "lo") returns true
EOMonth	Adds/subtracts months to a date and returns the last day of that month.	EOMonth(DateValue ("2024-10-01"), 1)

(*continued*)

Table 7-2. (*continued*)

Formula	Description	Code Example
Error	Creates or passes through an error.	`Error("Custom error message")`
Errors	Provides error information from a data source.	`Errors(DataSource)`
exactin	Checks if a string or record exactly matches in a table.	`exactin("Text", ["Text", "text"])`
Exit	Exits the app and optionally signs the user out.	`Exit(true)`
Exp	Returns e raised to a specified power.	`Exp(2)` returns `7.389`
Filter	Filters a table based on criteria.	`Filter(Products, Price > 100)`
Find	Finds one string within another and returns the location.	`Find("cat", "concatenate")` returns 4
First	Returns the first record of a table.	`First(Products)`
FirstN	Returns the first N records of a table.	`FirstN(Products, 3)`
ForAll	Performs actions for all records in a table.	`ForAll(Products, Sum(Price))`

(*continued*)

Table 7-2. (*continued*)

Formula	Description	Code Example
GroupBy	Groups records in a table by specified columns.	GroupBy(Orders, "ProductID", "ProductOrders")
GUID	Converts a string to a GUID or creates a new GUID.	GUID("12345")
HashTags	Extracts hashtags from a string.	HashTags("#hello #world") returns ["#hello", "#world"]
Hex2Dec	Converts a hexadecimal string to a decimal number.	Hex2Dec("1A") returns 26
Host	Provides information about the host running the app.	Host().Name
Hour	Returns the hour portion of a date/time value.	Hour(DateTimeValue("2024-02-01T15:45:00")) returns 15
If	Returns one value if a condition is true and another if it's false.	If(5 > 3, "Yes", "No") returns "Yes"
IfError	Provides an alternative value or action if an error is detected.	IfError(1/0, "Error") returns "Error"

(*continued*)

Table 7-2. (*continued*)

Formula	Description	Code Example
in	Checks if a string contains another string, case independently.	"apple" in "Pineapple" returns true
Index	Retrieves a record based on its ordered position in a table.	Index(Products, 2)
Int	Rounds down to the nearest integer.	Int(3.7) returns 3
IsBlank	Checks if a value is blank.	IsBlank("") returns true
IsBlankOrError	Checks for a blank value or an error.	IsBlankOrError(Error ("error")) returns true
IsEmpty	Checks if a table is empty.	IsEmpty([]) returns true
IsError	Checks if a value is an error.	IsError(Error("error")) returns true
IsMatch	Checks if a string matches a pattern using regular expressions.	IsMatch("123", "\d+") returns true
IsNumeric	Checks if a value is numeric.	IsNumeric("123") returns true
ISOWeekNum	Returns the ISO week number of a date.	ISOWeekNum(DateValue ("2024-01-10")) returns 2

(*continued*)

Table 7-2. (*continued*)

Formula	Description	Code Example
IsToday	Checks if a date is today based on the local time zone.	IsToday(Today()) returns true
IsType	Checks if a record refers to a specific table type.	IsType(record, Employees)
IsUTCToday	Checks if a date is today in UTC.	IsUTCToday(UTCNow()) returns true
JSON	Generates a JSON string from a table, record, or value.	JSON({name:"John", age:30})
Language	Returns the language tag of the current user.	Language() returns "en-US"
Last	Returns the last record of a table.	Last(Products)
LastN	Returns the last N records of a table.	LastN(Products, 3)
Launch	Launches a web page or app.	Launch("http://example.com")
Left	Returns the left-most portion of a string.	Left("Hello World", 5) returns "Hello"
Len	Returns the length of a string.	Len("Hello") returns 5
Ln	Returns the natural logarithm of a number.	Ln(7.389) returns 2

(*continued*)

Table 7-2. (*continued*)

Formula	Description	Code Example
LoadData	Loads a collection from local storage.	LoadData("LocalData")
Location	Returns the current location as a map coordinate.	Location()
Log	Calculates the logarithm of a number in any specified base.	Log(100, 10) returns 2
LookUp	Looks up a single record in a table based on criteria.	LookUp(Users, ID = 123)
Lower	Converts all letters in a text string to lowercase.	Lower("Hello World") returns "hello world"
Match	Extracts a substring based on a regular expression pattern.	Match("abc123", "\d+").Value returns "123"
MatchAll	Extracts multiple substrings based on a pattern. Regular expressions can be used.	MatchAll("abc123 def456", "\d+").Value

(*continued*)

Table 7-2. (*continued*)

Formula	Description	Code Example
Max	Returns the maximum value from a set of arguments or table column.	Max(1, 2, 3) returns 3
Mid	Returns the middle portion of a string.	Mid("Hello", 2, 2) returns "el"
Min	Returns the minimum value from a set of arguments or table column.	Min(1, 2, 3) returns 1
Minute	Retrieves the minute portion of a date/time value.	Minute(Time(14, 30, 0)) returns 30
Mod	Returns the remainder of a division.	Mod(5, 3) returns 2
Month	Retrieves the month portion of a date/time value.	Month(DateValue ("2024-04-01")) returns 4
Navigate	Changes the displayed screen in an app.	Navigate(Screen2)
NewForm	Resets a form control for the creation of an item.	NewForm(Form1)

(*continued*)

Table 7-2. (*continued*)

Formula	Description	Code Example
Not	Returns true if its argument is false and false if it's true.	Not(false) returns true
Notify	Displays a banner message to the user.	Notify("Hello World")
Now	Returns the current date and time in the user's time zone.	Now()
Or	Boolean OR logic; true if any argument is true.	Or(true, false) returns true
Param	Accesses parameters passed to a Canvas app upon launch.	Param("id")
Parent	Accesses the properties of a container control.	Parent().Width
ParseJSON	Converts a JSON text to an object.	ParseJSON('{"name":"Ruhi"}')
Patch	Modifies or creates a record in a data source.	Patch(Contacts, Contact1, {Name: "Munia"})
PDF	Exports the current screen contents to a PDF object.	PDF(Screen1)

(*continued*)

Table 7-2. (*continued*)

Formula	Description	Code Example
Pi	Returns the mathematical constant π.	Pi() returns 3.141592653589793
PlainText	Removes HTML and XML tags from a string.	PlainText("\Hello\") returns "Hello"
Power	Returns a number raised to a specified power.	Power(2, 3) returns 8
Proper	Capitalizes the first letter of each word in a string.	Proper("hello world") returns "Hello World"
Radians	Converts degrees to radians.	Radians(180) returns π
Rand	Returns a pseudo-random number between 0 and 1.	Rand()
RandBetween	Returns a pseudo-random number between two specified numbers.	RandBetween(1, 10)
ReadNFC	Reads a Near Field Communication (NFC) tag.	ReadNFC()

(*continued*)

Table 7-2. (*continued*)

Formula	Description	Code Example
RecordInfo	Provides information about a record of a data source.	RecordInfo(Contact)
Refresh	Refreshes the records of a data source.	Refresh(DataSource)
Relate	Relates records of two tables through a relationship.	Relate(Customers, Orders)
Remove	Removes specific records from a data source.	Remove(Products, SelectedProduct)
RemoveIf	Removes records from a data source based on a condition.	RemoveIf(Products, Price < 10)
RenameColumns	Renames columns of a table.	RenameColumns(Products, "OldName", "NewName")
Replace	Replaces part of a string starting at a specific position.	Replace("Hello", 1, 2, "a") returns "Hallo"
RequestHide	Hides a SharePoint form.	RequestHide()
Reset	Resets an input control to its default value.	Reset(TextInput1)

(*continued*)

Table 7-2. (*continued*)

Formula	Description	Code Example
ResetForm	Resets a form control for editing of an existing item.	ResetForm(Form1)
Revert	Reloads and clears errors for the records of a data source.	Revert(DataSource)
RGBA	Returns a color value for red, green, blue, and alpha components.	RGBA(255, 0, 0, 0.5)
Right	Returns the right-most portion of a string.	Right("Hello World", 5) returns "World"
Round	Rounds to the nearest number.	Round(3.2) returns 3
RoundDown	Rounds down to the nearest lower integer.	RoundDown(3.7) returns 3
RoundUp	Rounds up to the nearest higher integer.	RoundUp(3.3) returns 4
SaveData	Saves a collection to local device storage.	SaveData(LocalData, "SavedData")
Search	Finds records containing a specified string in their columns.	Search(Products, "apple", "Name")
Second	Retrieves the second portion of a date/time value.	Second(Time(14, 30, 25)) returns 25

(*continued*)

Table 7-2. (*continued*)

Formula	Description	Code Example
Select	Simulates a Select action on a control.	Select(Button1)
Self	Provides access to the properties of the current control.	Self().Width
Sequence	Generates a table of sequential numbers.	Sequence(5)
SendApp Notification	Sends an in-app notification.	SendAppNotification(User(), "Message")
Set	Sets the value of a global variable.	Set(GlobalVar, 10)
SetFocus	Moves input focus to a specific control.	SetFocus(TextInput1)
SetProperty	Simulates interactions with input controls.	SetProperty(Button1, "Text", "Click Me")
ShowColumns	Returns a table with only selected columns.	ShowColumns(Products, "Name", "Price")
ShowHostInfo	Displays host information in the app.	ShowHostInfo()
Shuffle	Randomly reorders the records of a table.	Shuffle(Products)
Sin	Returns the sine of an angle in radians.	Sin(Radians(30)) returns 0.5
Sort	Sorts a table based on a formula.	Sort(Products, Price)

(*continued*)

Table 7-2. (*continued*)

Formula	Description	Code Example
SortByColumns	Sorts a table based on one or more columns.	SortByColumns(Products, "Name", Ascending)
Split	Splits a text string into a table of substrings.	Split("apple, banana, cherry", ", ")
Sqrt	Returns the square root of a number.	Sqrt(16) returns 4
StartsWith	Checks if a text string starts with another text string.	StartsWith("Hello World", "Hello") returns true
StdevP	Returns the standard deviation of its arguments.	StdevP(1, 2, 3, 4, 5)
Substitute	Replaces part of a string with another by matching strings.	Substitute("Hello World", "World", "There")
SubmitForm	Saves the item in a form control to the data source.	SubmitForm(Form1)
Sum	Calculates the sum of a set of arguments or a table expression.	Sum(1, 2, 3) returns 6
Switch	Matches a set of values and evaluates a corresponding formula.	Switch(Status, "Open", 1, "Closed", 2, 0)

(*continued*)

Table 7-2. (*continued*)

Formula	Description	Code Example
Table	Creates a temporary table.	Table({Name: "Rahat", Age: 31}, {Name: "Munia", Age: 27})
Tan	Returns the tangent of an angle specified in radians.	Tan(Pi()/4) returns 1
Text	Converts any value and formats it to a string of text.	Text(12345, "$#,###") returns $12,345
ThisItem	Returns the record for the current item in a gallery or form.	ThisItem.Name
ThisRecord	Returns the record for the current item in a record scope function.	With({x: 10, y: 20}, ThisRecord.x + ThisRecord.y)
Time	Returns a date/time value based on hour, minute, and second values.	Time(14, 30, 0)
TimeValue	Converts a time-only string to a date/time value.	TimeValue("14:30:00")
TimeZoneOffset	Returns the difference between UTC and the user's local time in minutes.	TimeZoneOffset()

(*continued*)

Table 7-2. (*continued*)

Formula	Description	Code Example
Today	Returns the current date-only value.	`Today()`
Trace	Provides additional information in your test results.	`Trace("Testing", Trace Severity.Information)`
Trim	Removes extra spaces from the ends and interior of a string.	`Trim(" Hello World ") returns "Hello World"`
TrimEnds	Removes extra spaces from the ends of a string only.	`TrimEnds(" Hello World ") returns "Hello World"`
Trunc	Truncates the number to the integer portion.	`Trunc(8.9) returns 8`
Ungroup	Removes grouping from a grouped table.	`Ungroup(Groups, "Children")`
UniChar	Translates a Unicode code into a string.	`UniChar(65) returns "A"`
Unrelate	Unrelates records of two tables from a relationship.	`Unrelate(Orders, Products)`
Update	Replaces a record in a data source.	`Update(Contacts, {Name: "John"})`

(continued)

Table 7-2. (*continued*)

Formula	Description	Code Example
UpdateContext	Sets the value of one or more context variables of the current screen.	UpdateContext({varName: 10})
UpdateIf	Modifies a set of records based on a condition.	UpdateIf(Products, Price < 100, {Price: 99.99})
Upper	Converts all letters in a text string to uppercase.	Upper("hello world") returns "HELLO WORLD"
User	Returns information about the current user.	User().FullName
UTCNow	Returns the current UTC date/time value.	UTCNow()
UTCToday	Returns the current UTC date-only value.	UTCToday()
Validate	Checks if a value is valid for a data source.	Validate(Contacts, {Name: "Rezwanur", Email: "rezwanur@m365community.eu"})
Value	Converts a string to a number.	Value("123") returns 123
VarP	Returns the variance of its arguments.	VarP(1, 2, 3, 4, 5)

(*continued*)

Table 7-2. (*continued*)

Formula	Description	Code Example
ViewForm	Resets a form control for viewing an existing item.	ViewForm(Form1)
Weekday	Retrieves the weekday portion of a date/time value.	Weekday(Today())
WeekNum	Returns the week number of a date/time value.	WeekNum(Today())
With	Performs actions for a single record, including inline records.	With({x: 10}, x + 20)
Year	Retrieves the year portion of a date/time value.	Year(Today()) returns the current year

Responsive Design Techniques

Responsive design is essential in app development to ensure that applications deliver a seamless viewing experience on various devices and screen sizes. For developers working with Microsoft Power Apps, numerous techniques and strategies are available to ensure that apps adapt effectively to changes in device size and orientation.

Why Should You Build a Responsive App?

Building responsive apps is essential because end users may access your application from a variety of devices, including smartphones, tablets, laptops, and desktops, each with different screen sizes and pixel densities. To guarantee an optimal user experience and usability across all these form factors, it is crucial to implement responsive design principles in your app development. This is true even if the app is primarily designed for use on web browsers or mobile phones, as screen sizes can still vary widely within those categories. Adopting responsive design ensures that the app functions well and looks great on any device.

Responsive Design Principle

Before beginning the UI design for your app, you should consider several key factors:

- Identify which form factors or devices your app will support.

- Determine how the app should appear on each form factor.

- Decide which elements of the app should be scalable or resizable.

- Consider whether any elements should be hidden in certain form factors.

- Evaluate if the app's behavior should vary across different form factors.

After gathering these requirements, you should begin considering how to implement these varied UI layouts within a single application using the responsive design tools available in Power Apps.

310

The following steps are required before you can use the responsive layouts:

1. Open Power Apps from `https://make.powerapps.com` and open your project where you want to use responsive layout.

2. Click Settings from the top bar and choose Display, as shown in Figure 7-1.

Figure 7-1. Configuring Power Apps settings for responsive design

3. Disable Scale to Fit, Lock Aspect Ratio, and Lock Orientation, and then select Apply.

Let's explore what these settings mean:

• **Scale to Fit**: This setting, when enabled, automatically adjusts the size of the app's screen to fit the display area of the device being used. It scales the entire app to ensure that all elements are visible without the need to scroll horizontally or vertically, regardless of the device's screen size.

311

- **Lock Aspect Ratio**: When this feature is activated, it maintains the aspect ratio (the ratio of the width to the height) of the app screen as it was designed. This prevents distortion that can occur when the app is viewed on screens with different aspect ratios. It ensures that the proportions of the app's UI remain consistent, which can be crucial for maintaining the layout's intended design.

- **Lock Orientation**: This setting allows the designer to fix the app's orientation to portrait or landscape mode. When this setting is enabled, the app will not rotate its orientation in response to the device being turned. This is useful for apps that are optimized for or require a specific orientation due to their design or functionality.

Responsive Layouts

Power Apps provides responsive layouts that display optimally on phones, tablets, and laptops.

Note   The new responsive layouts are available for app formats, but the new screen templates are exclusively available for the *tablet* format.

Figure 7-2 shows some example layouts that are deemed responsive.

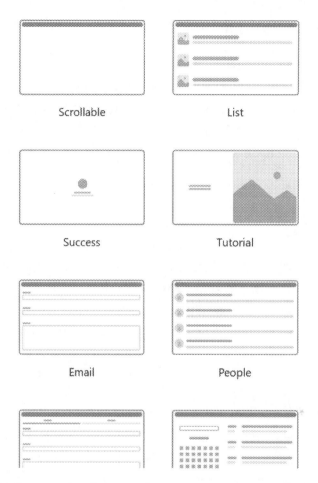

Figure 7-2. *Responsive layouts that you can use to make responsive Power Apps*

The next section discusses two important layouts for developing Power Apps: *split-screen* and *sidebar*. Understanding these layouts is key to effective app design.

The Split-Screen Layout

The *split-screen* layout divides the screen into two sections, each occupying half of the screen width when viewed on desktops. This layout is particularly useful for applications that need to display two categories of information side-by-side, such as comparing two datasets, showing detail alongside a list, or having a form on one side and descriptive content on the other.

The Sidebar Layout

The *sidebar* layout features a fixed-width sidebar typically placed on the left side of the screen. This sidebar can house navigation links, filters, or other tools that the user might need to access frequently. The main body of the layout includes a fixed height header and a main section that takes up the remainder of the screen width, accommodating the primary interactive or content area of the app.

Working with Containers

Containers are essential building blocks for responsive design in app development. They can be configured as *auto-layout containers,* which organize their contents in a vertical or horizontal arrangement, or as *fixed-layout containers,* which will eventually support constraints. When building your app's UI, always place UI elements that collectively form a table within a container. This strategy allows each container to maintain its own responsive properties and settings, enabling appropriate resizing and repositioning across different screen sizes. Additionally, you can modify how child components are arranged within the container to improve responsiveness. Depending on your design requirements, you can choose between manual layout and auto-layout (horizontal or vertical) for each container's layout mode.

Auto-Layout Containers

In app design, the *horizontal* and *vertical* containers serve as powerful tools for effortlessly organizing child components. These containers eliminate the need to manually adjust the X and Y coordinates of elements within them. Instead, they automatically determine the optimal placement of each component, efficiently distributing space according to predefined settings. Furthermore, these containers also take charge of aligning components, ensuring proper vertical and horizontal alignment, which simplifies the layout process and enhances the overall aesthetic of the app.

Auto-layout containers are particularly useful in a variety of scenarios:

- Adapting the user interface to accommodate different screen sizes or device types.

- Dynamically resizing or repositioning multiple child components based on changes in screen size or device form factor.

- Arranging elements in a vertical or horizontal stack, regardless of their individual dimensions.

- Evenly distributing elements across the display area.

Creating a Demo

This section shows you how to create a quick demo of responsive layout:

1. Create a blank Canvas app in Power Apps. See Figure 7-3.

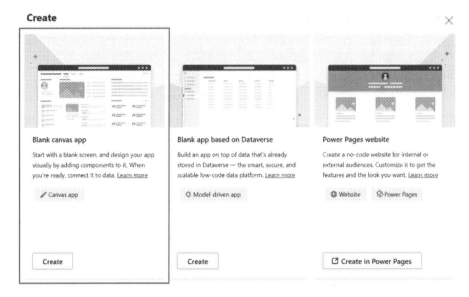

Figure 7-3. *Create a blank Canvas app in Power Apps*

2. Provide an app name and select the Tablet layout, as shown in Figure 7-4.

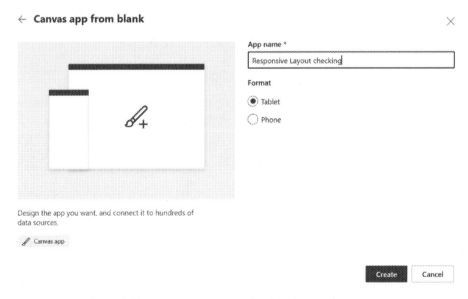

Figure 7-4. *Providing app name and selecting a format*

316

3. Go to Settings from the top bar and choose Display.
   Disable Scale to Fit, Lock Aspect Ratio, and Lock
   Orientation, and then select Apply. Refer to
   Figure 7-1 to check the complete process.

4. From the Insert panel in the left sidebar, under
   Layout, find Horizontal Container and Vertical
   Container, as shown in Figure 7-5. Choose
   Horizontal Container.

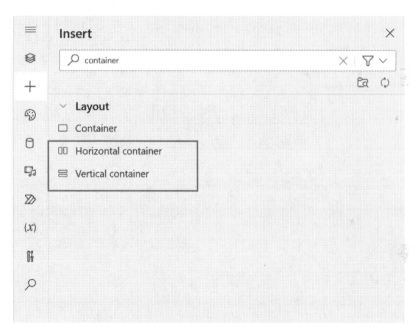

Figure 7-5. *Choose Horizontal Container here*

5. The primary container should expand to occupy the entire space, adjusting its size to match the screen as it resizes. Change the properties to the following values:

```
X = 0
Y = 0
Width = Parent.Width
Height = Parent.Height
```

6. Insert a new Copilot control in the container and link it to a data source, like what you did in the previous chapter. See the example in Figure 7-6.

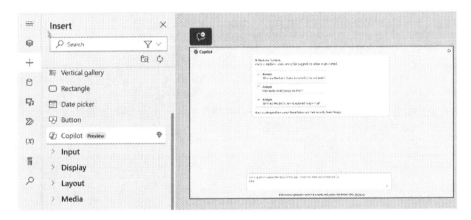

Figure 7-6. *Adding Copilot to the Power Apps container*

7. Run the app by pressing F5, as shown in Figure 7-7.
    Select Canvas size first.

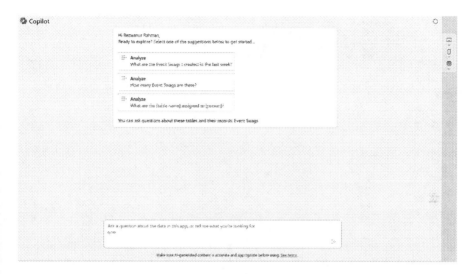

Figure 7-7. *Verifying the responsive app in Canvas size*

Now change the device from Canvas size to any phone device size, as shown in Figure 7-8, and check the design's responsiveness.

Figure 7-8. *Verifying the responsive app in a phone device*

Change the mode from Phone to Tablet. Choose any tablet you want. For example, I chose Apple iPad Pro 12.9, as shown in Figure 7-9.

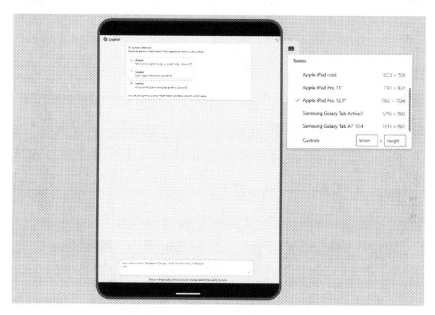

Figure 7-9. *Verifying the responsive app on a tablet device*

The same control in the container adjusts its size to fit the screen when you turn the device. For example, I rotated the iPad, as shown in Figure 7-10, for better understanding.

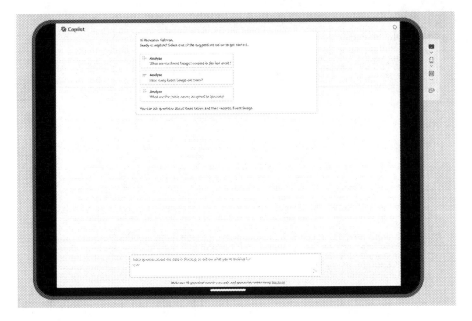

Figure 7-10. *App responsiveness check in landscape mode*

Copilot Components and Conditional Formatting in Power Apps

This section explores the Copilot components available in Power Apps. It covers both Copilot Studio and Copilot Chatbot, teaching you how to enhance and personalize Copilot's functionality. You will learn to adjust response styles, integrate various data sources, and utilize advanced features such as custom workflows and plugins. You will also learn how conditional formatting works, and how it relates to Copilot.

As you progress, the section transitions into practical applications, offering examples and best practices that you can immediately implement in your projects. This shift from theoretical to practical is designed to equip you with the necessary tools and knowledge to make your interactions with Copilot more dynamic and efficient.

The Copilot Control

The Copilot control represents a sophisticated AI assistant specifically tailored for integration into Canvas applications. It provides a dynamic, AI-powered chat interface that allows users to interact and derive insights from application data via natural language conversations. This innovative feature empowers users to ask questions and receive information directly related to the app's data in an intuitive, conversational format.

App developers have the flexibility to implement this control within any Canvas app, enabling a seamless and interactive user experience. They can configure the control to access specific datasets within the app, ensuring that Copilot can deliver accurate and relevant answers based on the available data. This customization capability allows developers to tailor the AI's responses to the unique needs and contexts of their applications, enhancing the overall functionality and user engagement of the app.

Consider this important information about Copilot control:

- Your environment must be in the US region to utilize this capability.

- Enabling data movement across regions is essential for using Copilot features in Power Apps, especially if your organization's environment is in a different region. For more details, refer to the documentation at `https://learn.microsoft.com/en-us/power-platform/admin/geographical-availability-copilot#enable-data-movement-across-regions`.

- This feature is driven by the Azure OpenAI Service.

- Using this capability may be limited or subject to throttling.

- Environments with *customer-managed keys* (CMKs)
  or those using Lockbox do not support the Copilot
  control.

Activate the Copilot Control

To activate the Copilot control, it is necessary to enable the Copilot
option from the Power Platform Admin Center, where it is set to disabled
by default. It is important to verify whether this option has already been
activated.

To verify the Copilot settings from the Power Platform Admin Center,
follow these steps:

1. As shown in Figure 7-11, visit `https://admin.`
   `powerplatform.microsoft.com/`.

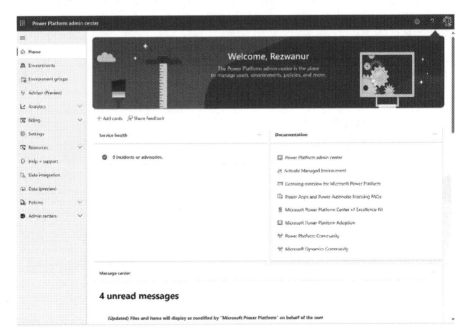

Figure 7-11. *Power Platform Admin Center preview*

2. Click Environments and select your environment
    from the list, as shown in Figure 7-12.

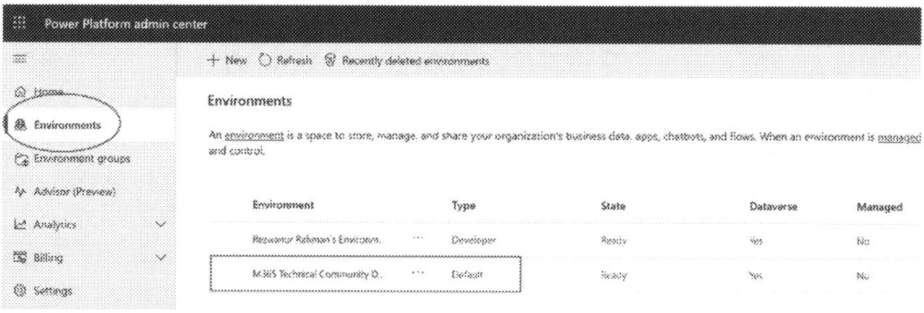

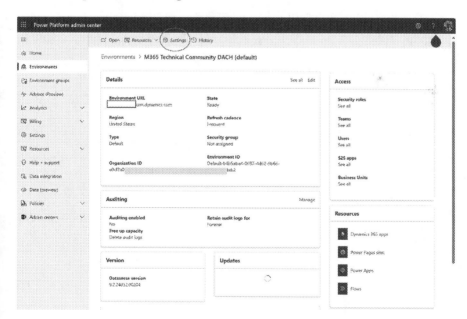

Figure 7-12. *Selecting Environments in Power Platform*
admin center

3. After selecting Environments, click Settings on the
    top border. See Figure 7-13.

Figure 7-13. **The** *Settings option of the Power Platform*
Admin Center

4.   After selecting Settings, expand the Product option and select Features. See Figure 7-14.

Figure 7-14.   *The Features option in the Product area*

5.   As shown in Figure 7-15, make sure Copilot is turned on.

Environments > M365 Technical Community DACH (default) > Settings > **Features**

Learn more about Features ⊏

Copilot   [Ⓐ Preview]

Enable new AI-powered Copilot features for people who make apps. In addition, enable the AI prompts feature. Learn more ⊏

⬤ On

Allow users to analyze data using an AI-powered chat experience in canvas ⊏ and model-driven apps ⊏. Learn more ⊏ Requires Copilot licensing ⊏

[Default   ⌄]

Figure 7-15.   *Copilot option in Power Apps feature settings*

Enable the Copilot Component for a Canvas App

1. To activate the Copilot component for a Canvas app, go to `https://make.powerapps.com/` and open an existing project or create a new one. As you are working on a common project, open that project, as shown in Figure 7-16.

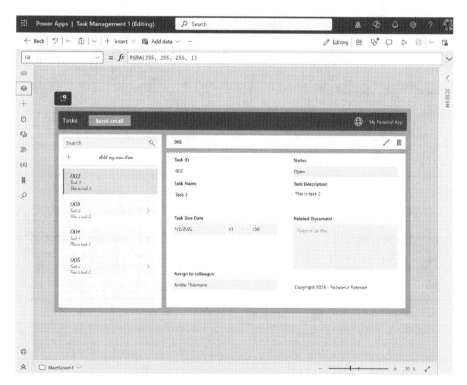

Figure 7-16. *Open the project in Power Apps*

2.   Click Settings in the top bar, as shown in Figure 7-17.

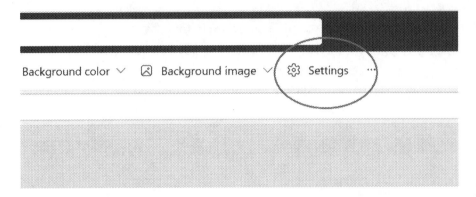

Figure 7-17. Settings of Power Apps

3.   Click Upcoming Features and make sure the Copilot
     component is turned on. See Figure 7-18. You must
     do this so Power Apps will recognize the Copilot
     component in this project.

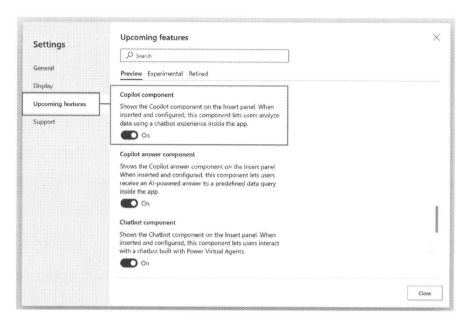

Figure 7-18. Enable the Copilot component option in Power Apps settings

---

Note   Your browser language must be set to English (United States).

You are now done checking your requirements. Next, you learn how to add Copilot to your app so that you can chat with your data.

Add the Copilot Control to a Canvas App

To add Copilot to a Canvas app, go back to the project and follow these instructions:

1.   Create a new screen and select your favorite template. I am choosing the Header and Footer template, as this example creates a chat window, as shown in Figure 7-19.

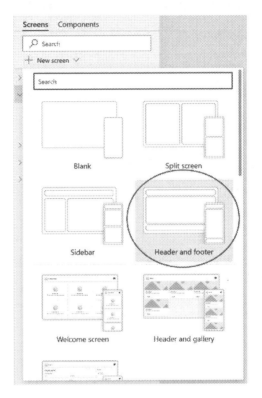

Figure 7-19. *Adding a new template in a new screen*

You can make your own screen manually. This example uses the template to save time and to show the capabilities of Power Apps templates.

This is not mandatory to create new screens. You can use the Copilot component on the same page or existing page if you want.

2.   After clicking Header and Footer, you will see an empty screen, as shown in Figure 7-20.

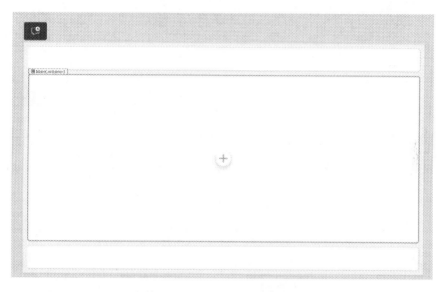

Figure 7-20. *New Header and Footer template in a Power Apps window*

3. Next, you add the Copilot component. To add it,
   click the + icon and select Copilot, as shown in
   Figure 7-21.

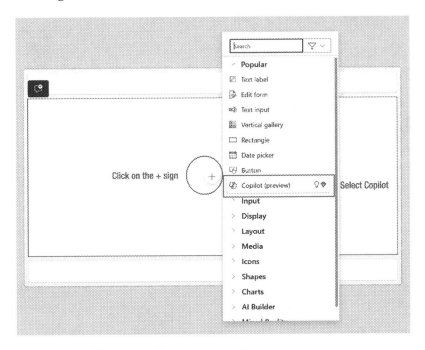

Figure 7-21. *Adding Copilot to Power Apps*

4. As shown in Figure 7-22, you now need to add the data source.

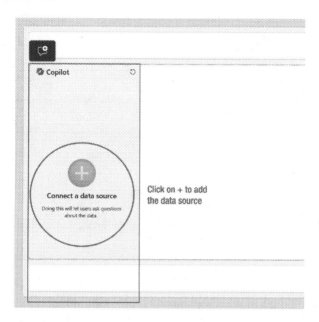

Figure 7-22. *Adding a data source to Copilot*

5. To add the data source, click + and select the data source, as shown in Figure 7-23. This example selects the default table as the data source, which is called *Tasks*.

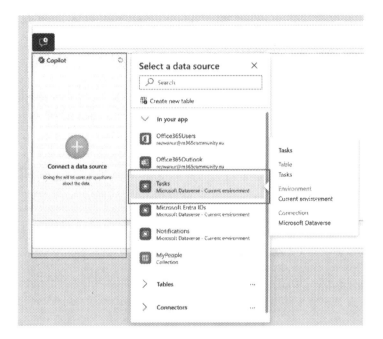

Figure 7-23. *Adding a data source to Copilot*

6. You should see that the Copilot Chat has been added successfully, as shown in Figure 7-24.

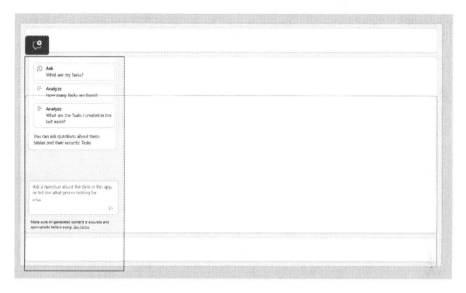

Figure 7-24. *Successful data source connection*

7.   Initially, this will appear as a small box, as illustrated
in Figure 7-24. You will need to manually adjust its
design. To modify the width, height, and alignment,
select the Copilot component and access Properties,
as shown in Figure 7-25.

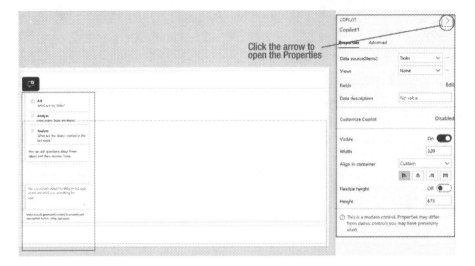

Figure 7-25. *Copilot properties to change the height and width*

8.   Change the Align in Container from Start to Stretch and set the Height to 555, as shown in Figure 7-26.

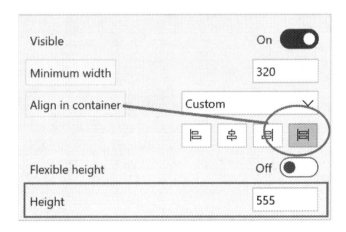

Figure 7-26. *Settings for changing width and height*

You might be wondering why I did not opt for
Flexible Height in this case. The reason is that using
Flexible Height would cause Copilot to extend below
the footer, obscuring the text field and preventing
users from engaging in conversation.

9. The final Copilot Chat window, after these
    customizations, is shown in Figure 7-27.

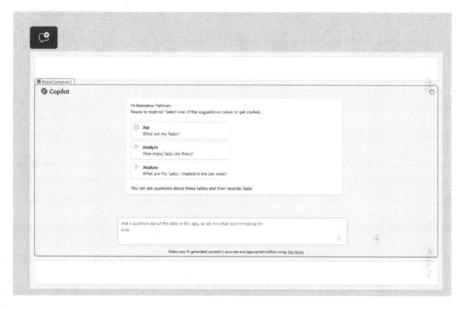

Figure 7-27. *Final Copilot control in a container after fixing the
height and width*

10. Run the app to see how Copilot responds to the
     natural language command. I sent the simple
     command shown in Figure 7-28.

Figure 7-28. *Conversation with Copilot based on the data table*

I asked Copilot for the name of Task ID 003, and
Copilot responded that the name is Task 3. You can
confirm this response with the data source.

If you open the Dataverse table named Tasks, it
shows that the task name for Task ID 003 is Task 3.
See Figure 7-29.

Tasks

Task ID	Created On	Task Name	Task Description
002	3/31/2024 3:33 AM	Task 2	This is task 2
003	3/31/2024 3:33 AM	Task 3	This is task 3
004	3/31/2024 3:33 AM	Task 4	This is task 4
005	3/31/2024 3:33 AM	Task 5	This is task 5
Enter text		Enter text	Enter text

Figure 7-29. *Verifying Copilot's response with the Microsoft
Dataverse table*

As you can see, Task ID 003 is in the same row as the name of Task 3.

11. You can also add dummy data to the Tasks table and check Copilot Chat for the result. For example, I added dummy data to the Dataverse table, as shown in Figure 7-30.

| 010203 | 4/15/2024 5:23 PM | Writing a book | Writing a book is not a easy thing. |
| 040506 | 4/15/2024 5:24 PM | Traveling to USA | Sumon will travel to USA nd I will ... |

Figure 7-30. *Adding dummy data to the Microsoft Dataverse table to verify Copilot's response*

12. Next, verify the dummy data via a Copilot conversation. See Figure 7-31.

Figure 7-31. *Verifying Microsoft Dataverse data via a Copilot conversation*

Copilot successfully read the data; it accurately retrieved the due date for Task ID 010203, which I set for April 25, 2024, at 8:00 PM. When I asked, "What is the due date for Task ID 010203?" it provided the correct answer.

Note   Copilot is designed to read data from a single data source. If you want to interact with different data sources, you must create a new Copilot component for each source. It is not possible to use the same Copilot component for multiple data sources.

The Copilot Answer Control

The *Copilot Answer* control for Power Apps is a new feature that allows users to add generative AI to their Canvas apps, providing quick answers to predefined prompts. This control is part of a suite of Copilot controls in Power Apps, which includes user controls for natural language interaction and data summarization. Copilot in Power Apps can answer queries related to app development, code, formulas, and specific technical terms, and it can be used to style apps and deploy them into production. This feature makes technology more accessible to citizen developers and enhances the functionality and accessibility of Power Apps.

You will now see how to implement Copilot Answer in Power Apps. To add the control to your app, follow the steps:

1. Go to your preferred page and click Insert. Then search for the Copilot Answer component. You can also add the component by clicking the + sign of any empty container. Refer to Figure 7-32 to learn more.

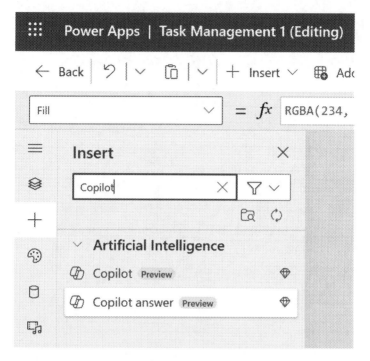

Figure 7-32. *Adding Copilot Answer to Power Apps*

2. Select Copilot Answer. It will ask you to add the data
    source as before, as shown in Figure 7-33.

Figure 7-33. *Data source selection for Copilot Answer*

3.   Select the Tasks data source, as this is your default
     data source for the example app. Feel free to select a
     different data source if needed.

4.   Click the Properties area of Copilot Answer, as
     shown in Figure 7-34.

Figure 7-34. *Properties of Copilot Answer*

Here, you must define the Title and the Question for Copilot. As this is a predefined control, you cannot change the value or question after debugging it.

I changed the Title to Status Overview and the Question for Copilot to Summarize Total Status, as shown in Figure 7-35.

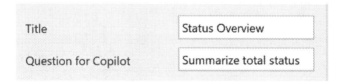

Figure 7-35. *Changing the title and question for Copilot*

5. Run the app and click the generate button, as shown in Figure 7-36. You can see the total status count, as shown in Figure 7-37.

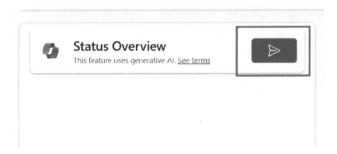

Figure 7-36. *Copilot Answer button to trigger the Copilot question*

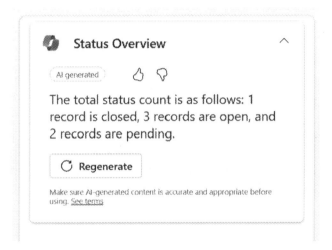

Figure 7-37. *Generated answer in Copilot Answer*

Copilot Customization with Copilot Studio

You can enhance the Copilot (preview) control using Copilot Studio, which allows you to add more topics, plugin actions, and various other capabilities. Before starting with Copilot customization, you need to learn about Copilot Studio.

Copilot Studio is a development platform designed by Microsoft to help users create and manage conversational AI agents, often referred to as Copilot. These AI agents are built using large language models and can be integrated with various data sources to provide enriched, interactive experiences. The platform typically allows users to customize their AI agents without the need for deep technical expertise in AI or programming, making it accessible to a wider range of users, including those without a background in data science or development.

Copilot Studio may include tools for defining the AI's responses, training the model on specific data, and setting up integrations with various communication channels, such as websites, mobile apps, and popular communication platforms like Microsoft Teams and Facebook. This enables organizations to deploy AI copilots for a variety of purposes, from customer service and support to employee interaction and information dissemination.

Versions of Copilot Studio

Copilot Studio is accessible as a standalone web application and as an integrated app in Teams. The two versions share most functionalities, and the choice between them may depend on specific user needs and how they plan to use Copilot Studio.

The standalone web application of Copilot Studio can be accessed from any browser on any operating system at `https://copilotstudio.microsoft.com`. The web application is particularly useful for various users, including IT administrators who want to create Copilot components for customer service, individuals familiar with Copilot services looking to trial or test Copilot Studio, and users interested in exploring advanced Copilot concepts, such as entities and variables to develop more complex Copilot components.

To use the Copilot Studio app in Microsoft Teams, simply log in with your licensed credentials, search for Copilot Studio in the Microsoft Teams app store, and add it to your workspace, as shown in Figure 7-38.

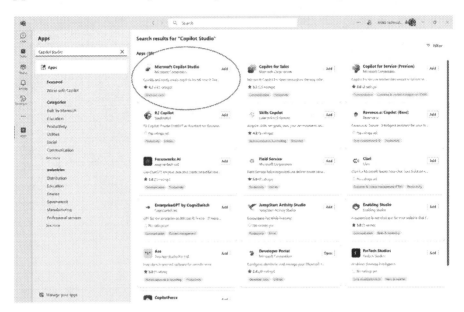

Figure 7-38. *Microsoft Copilot Studio in the Microsoft Teams apps store*

This integration is ideal for various applications, such as an organization member who wants to deploy Copilot to address frequent employee inquiries. It is also suitable for those looking to implement advanced concepts like entities and variables for an internally accessible Copilot within Teams. Additionally, this setup is perfect for anyone aiming to create and distribute Copilot as quickly as possible.

You can also go to this URL if you cannot find the Copilot Studio app in Microsoft Teams: `https://aka.ms/PVATeamsApp?azure-portal=true`. When you visit the URL, the Microsoft Teams app will open Microsoft Copilot Studio, as shown Figure 7-39.

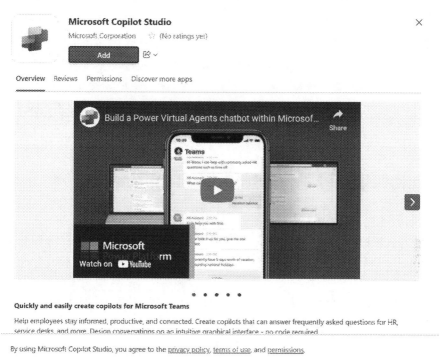

Figure 7-39. *The Microsoft Copilot Studio app in Microsoft Teams*

IMPORTANT NOTE FROM MICROSOFT

Microsoft Copilot Studio is *not*:

- A medical device intended for medical use, including diagnosis, treatment, or prevention of diseases, nor should it be integrated into clinical products.

- A substitute for professional medical advice, diagnosis, or treatment. It should not be used to replace medical judgment or in emergency situations.

- Capable of handling emergency calls or supporting emergency services.

Any Copilot component created with Microsoft Copilot Studio is entirely your product or service. You are fully responsible for its design, development, and implementation, including providing necessary warnings and disclaimers about its use. You also bear sole responsibility for any personal injuries or deaths that may result from the use of your Copilot component or Microsoft Copilot Studio.

Copilot Studio Licensing Information

Unfortunately, an additional license is required to use Copilot Studio. While this is not necessary for th0078Ce current project or for this book, I am mentioning it to inform advanced or enterprise users who may need this information.

As of the writing of this chapter, the price was $200.00 USD, which included 25,000 messages/month, as shown in Figure 7-40. Visit the official Microsoft Copilot Studio website at https://www.microsoft.com/en-us/microsoft-copilot/microsoft-copilot-studio to check for any updated pricing information.

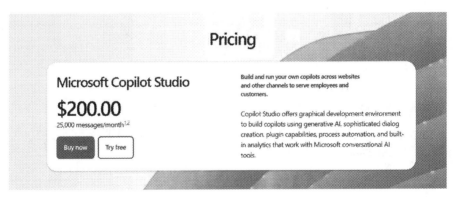

Figure 7-40. *Microsoft Copilot Studio pricing on the Microsoft website*

The Copilot Chatbot

You can incorporate the Chatbot control into your Canvas apps to enhance user interaction by embedding a Microsoft Copilot Studio Chatbot. This integration allows the chatbot to assist users with a variety of requests, ranging from simple queries to complex problem resolutions. Additionally, the Chatbot control is compatible with custom pages in model-driven apps and supports Teams-authenticated bots from Microsoft Copilot Studio. An intuitive bot picker feature simplifies the process by listing all available bots within the same app environment, ensuring seamless integration and management.

This functionality is vital for improving the efficiency and responsiveness of your applications, providing users with immediate assistance, and enriching the overall user experience.

You have two dynamic options for enhancing user interactions using AI bots:

> **AI Chatbots:** You can build an extensive answer tree to support your users efficiently. For more details and steps, follow the official Microsoft Docs at `https://learn.microsoft.com/en-us/microsoft-copilot-studio/fundamentals-get-started`.

> **AI Boosted Conversations:** You can equip your Microsoft Copilot Studio bot with advanced response capabilities using prompts or generating responses from a designated "fallback" website. This website can host internal documents or be a publicly accessible site. Visit this link to learn more: `https://learn.microsoft.com/en-us/microsoft-copilot-studio/nlu-gpt-overview`.

Additionally, you can customize the Chatbot control by naming it, adjusting the control window size, and positioning it anywhere on your screen for optimal integration and user experience.

Prerequisites for Using the Chatbot Component

The following prerequisites must be met to use the Chatbot component:

- Create and publish a bot on the Microsoft Copilot Studio web app. Options include an AI bot or a new generative AI-enriched Microsoft Copilot Studio bot.

- View all your Microsoft Copilot Studio bots (published and unpublished) in the Chatbot control list when connecting a bot.

- Only add published bots to the Chatbot control. Unpublished bots will appear grayed out and cannot be added.

Creating a Bot Using a Chatbot Component

Follow these steps to create a chatbot:

1. To integrate the chatbot into Power Apps, start by creating a new screen in the app and choosing the Split Screen layout, as shown in Figure 7-41. (Although feel free to select any layout that suits your needs.)

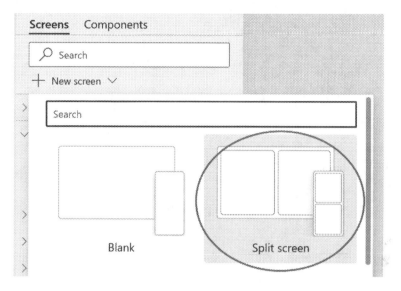

Figure 7-41. *Selecting Split Screen to create a Copilot Chatbot*

2. Click the + sign and search for Chatbot. You will get
    the Chatbot option, shown in Figure 7-42.

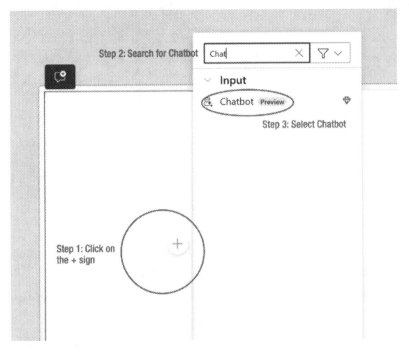

Figure 7-42. *Searching and adding the Copilot Chatbot*

3. After selecting the Chatbot, it will ask you to add a
   data source, as shown in Figure 7-43.

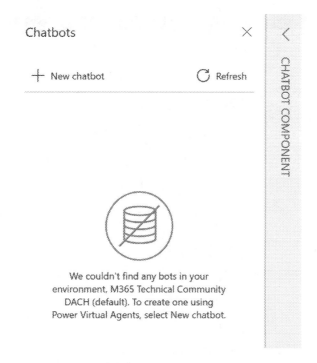

Figure 7-43. *Option to add a data source to the chatbot*

However, you will notice a message indicating that
Power Apps could not find a bot in the environment.
As mentioned, the bot must be published in
Microsoft Copilot Studio. Now, you will create a
bot in Microsoft Copilot Studio and link it to your
chatbot in Power Apps.

4. Click + New Chatbot, as shown in Figure 7-43. A new
    tab will open, directing you to Microsoft Copilot
    Studio. If you are not already signed in, you will be
    prompted to enter your credentials. Figure 7-44
    shows the Microsoft Copilot Studio portal.

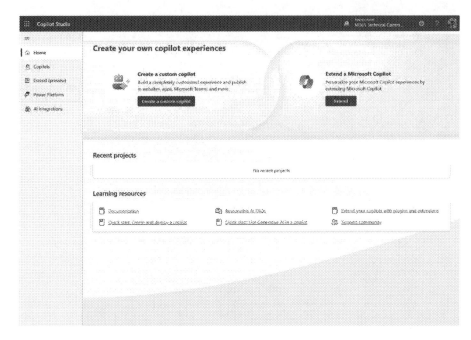

Figure 7-44. *Microsoft Copilot Studio portal*

5.   As shown in Figure 7-45, select Copilots from the left
panel and click + New Copilot.

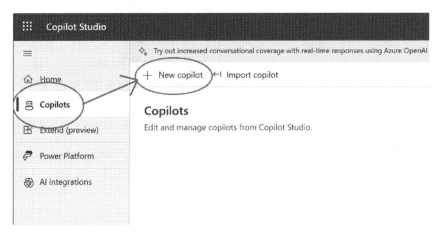

Figure 7-45. *Creating a new Copilot component in Microsoft*
Copilot Studio

354

6. After clicking the + New Copilot option, it will ask you three questions, as shown in Figure 7-46.

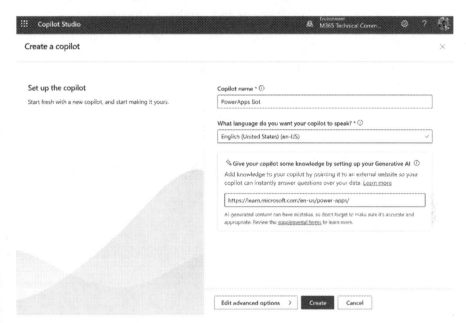

Figure 7-46. *Creating a Copilot component in Microsoft Copilot Studio*

a. **Copilot name:** Provide the name of the Copilot. For this project, I named it Power Apps Bot.

b. **Language:** Choose the language for communicating with Copilot. I selected English (United States) (en-US).

c. **URL:** To enhance interactions using AI-generated responses, insert a URL in the Give Your Copilot Some Knowledge by Setting Up Your Generative AI field. I provided the Microsoft Learn documentation for Power Apps: `https://learn.microsoft.com/en-us/power-apps/`

You can edit the Copilot icon or the Schema name
by clicking the Edit Advanced option. However,
these changes are optional and can be made later if
preferred.

Click Create after filling out the information. It will
take a few seconds to minutes to set up Copilot.

7. After a few seconds, you will see that Copilot has
been successfully created, as shown in Figure 7-47.

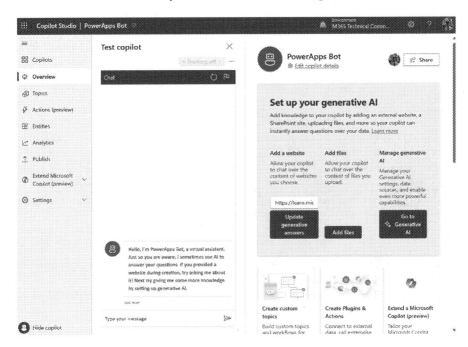

Figure 7-47. *Copilot has been successfully created in the Microsoft*
Copilot Studio portal

8. You should test Copilot before publishing. You do
this by asking Copilot Chat some questions and
checking the response; see Figure 7-48.

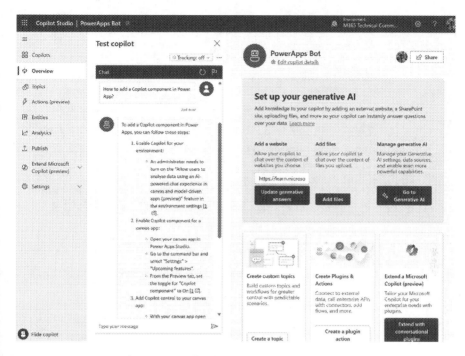

Figure 7-48. *Verifying Copilot before publishing*

As you can see, I asked Copilot "How to add a
Copilot component in Power App?" and Copilot
replied the correct information from the official
Microsoft documentation. Figure 7-49 shows
another question.

357

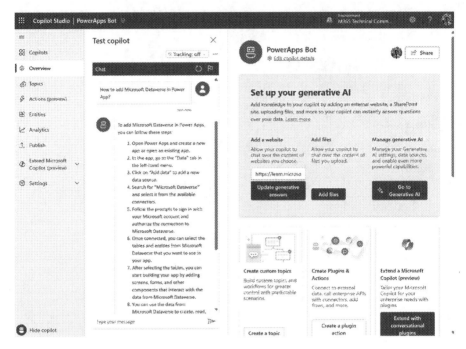

Figure 7-49. *Verifying Copilot with complex questions from Microsoft Copilot Studio*

This time I asked Copilot chat, "How to add Microsoft Dataverse in Power App?" and Copilot responded with the correct steps and the documentation link.

9. You can also conduct tests to see how it responds to questions that exceed its capabilities. See Figure 7-50.

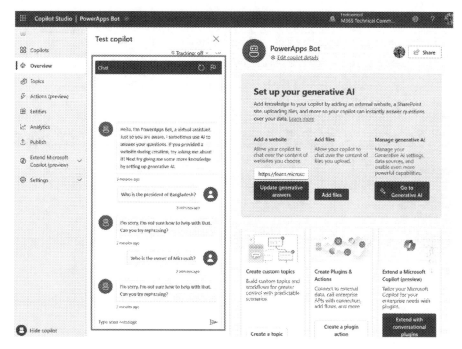

Figure 7-50. *Verifying Copilot with out-of-scope questions*

I tested Copilot by asking questions unrelated
to its training, such as "Who is the president of
Bangladesh?" and "Who is the owner of Microsoft?"
Each time, the response was, "I am sorry, I'm not
sure how to help with that. Can you try rephrasing?"

This indicates that Copilot can only access and
respond to information from the URL provided
and lacks the ability to retrieve data from external
sources.

10. After testing the bot, you have to publish it. If you don't publish the bot, you cannot use it in Power Apps. To publish the bot, scroll down the Copilot page and find the Go to Publish link, as shown in Figure 7-51.

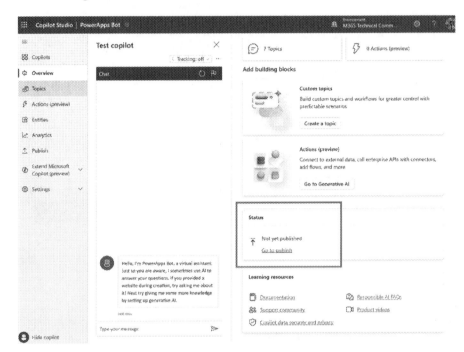

Figure 7-51. *Publishing Copilot in Power Apps*

11. On the next page, you will see the Publish button, as shown in Figure 7-52.

Publish

Excited to go live with your copilot and Microsoft Copilot plugins? Publish both in one go. Then, try out your copilot on a website and configure channels to meet your users where they are. Learn more

Figure 7-52. *The Publish button of Copilot in Microsoft Copilot Studio*

12. Shortly after, as shown in Figure 7-53, you will be directed to a confirmation page indicating that the publishing process is complete.

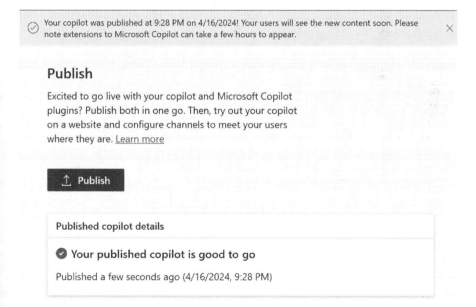

Figure 7-53. *Confirmation of successful publishing of Copilot*

13. Go back to the Power Apps window and refresh the
     chatbot properties. You will see the new bot in the
     list that you created a few minutes ago, as shown in
     Figure 7-54.

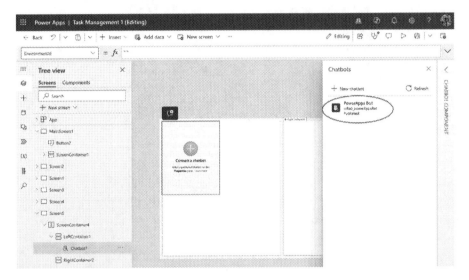

Figure 7-54. *Showing the newly published Copilot in Power Apps*

14. Select the Power Apps Bot. The bot will be saved in
the container, as shown in Figure 7-55.

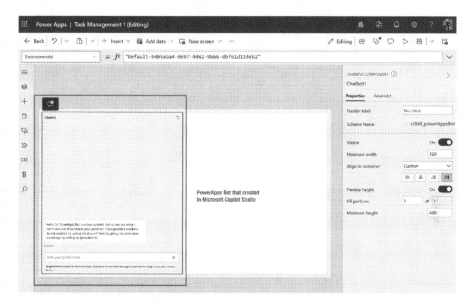

Figure 7-55. *Added the published Copilot component to*
Copilot Chat

15.   Press F5 or execute the project to see if Copilot is
functioning correctly. See Figure 7-56.

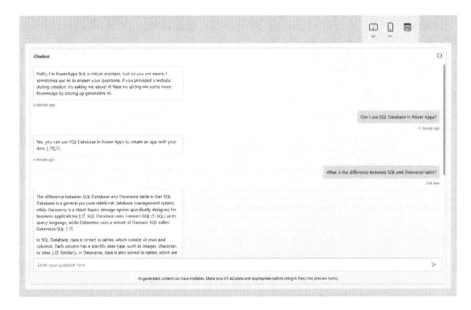

Figure 7-56. *Preview of Copilot Chatbot in Power Apps*

I posed two different questions to Copilot: "Can I use SQL Database
in Power Apps?" and "What is the difference between SQL and Dataverse
table?" The responses were accurate. Therefore, you can conclude that
Copilot is operating correctly.

Most Common Power Apps Design Component

This section explores the integration of Copilot chat in Power Apps,
focusing on how to create intuitive and interactive interfaces. By
incorporating elements such as tables, media galleries, forms, lists, and
charts, Copilot chat not only enriches the visual appeal of applications but

also enhances their functionality. Each component can be customized to meet specific user needs, enabling more personalized interactions. This approach streamlines workflows and improves user satisfaction by making applications more responsive and easier to navigate. I provide practical insights and strategies to help developers effectively utilize these tools, fostering a highly customized and user-focused application environment. So, let's start from here!

Adding Comments

When building a Canvas app in Power Apps Studio, it's beneficial to add comments to aid in team review and feedback, or to offer insights into the implementation details of your app. To enable other creators to contribute comments, ensure that you share the app with them. This facilitates collaboration and communication within your development team.

You can add comments to different components or pages, as shown in Figure 7-57.

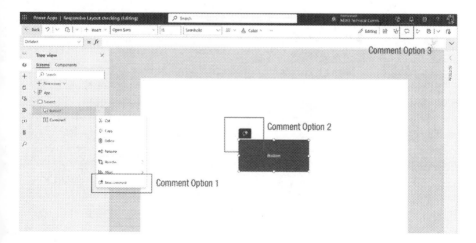

Figure 7-57. *Different ways to add comments*

There are several ways to add comments in Power Apps:

- **Tree view**: Select a screen from the Tree view and right-click to add a new comment. See Figure 7-58.

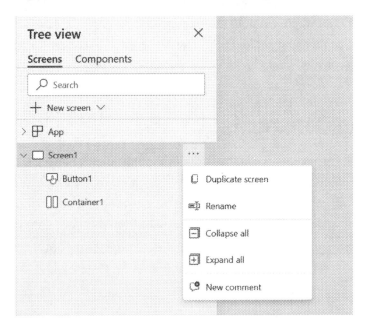

Figure 7-58. *Adding a comment from Tree view*

- **Component**: In the canvas area, right-click a component to add a new comment. See Figure 7-59.

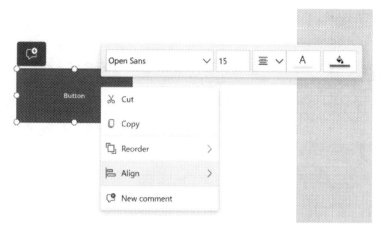

Figure 7-59. *Adding a comment from the component properties*

- **Component with Copilot**: In the canvas area, click the component. You will get the icon shown in Figure 7-60, which allows you to add a comment.

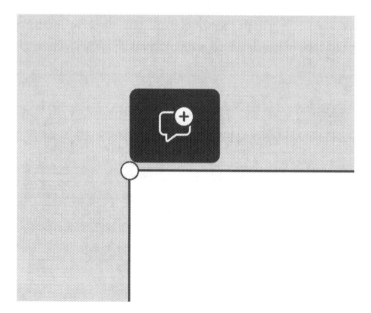

Figure 7-60. *Adding a comment from a Copilot tooltip*

- **App actions**: Select Comments ➤ New and then add your comments. See Figure 7-61.

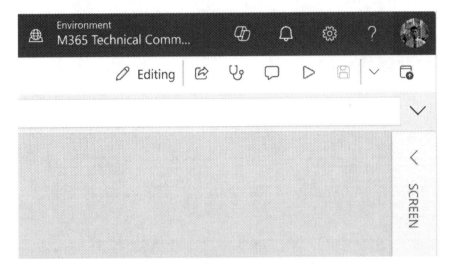

Figure 7-61. *Adding a comment from the app's action bar*

After you select any of the comment options, the Comments option will appear in the right sidebar, as shown in Figure 7-62.

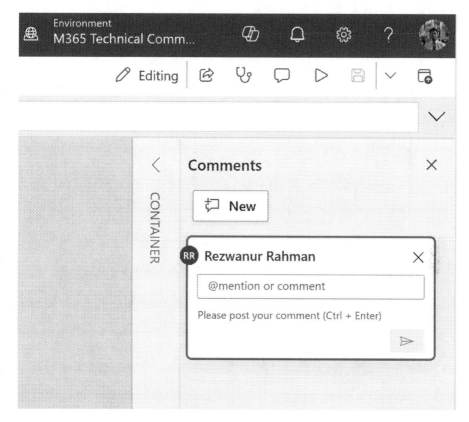

Figure 7-62. *Comments option after selecting it*

Commenting is important for teamwork. When you are part of a team and you want to collaborate with your team members, you can comment on their task, and you can tag them by their name or email.

Mention or Tag Someone in Power Apps

In your Power Apps project, you can mention a user by using the @ symbol followed by their username, like tagging someone on social media. Each time you tag a user, they will receive an email notification. I demonstrate this feature with a demo.

1. Select the Comment option and enter @ to see the user list, as shown in Figure 7-63.

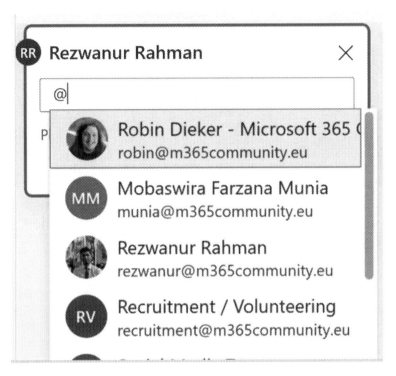

Figure 7-63. *People suggestions after entering @ in the Comments option*

You cannot invite someone outside of your organization using @. You must first add the user to your Microsoft Entra ID (previously known as Azure Active Directory). Visit this site to learn how to add a user to your Microsoft Entra ID:

```
https://learn.microsoft.com/en-us/entra/
external-id/b2b-quickstart-add-guest-
users-portal
```

2. Choose the user and click Send. You can add more information to the comments, as shown in Figure 7-64.

Figure 7-64. *Choosing a user and sharing feedback in the Comment section*

3. Power Apps will show a popup for confirmation, as shown in Figure 7-65.

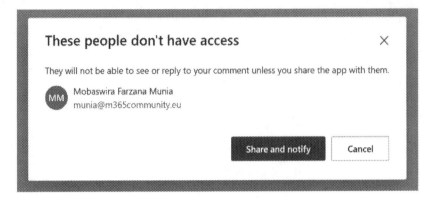

Figure 7-65. *Warning notification before sharing your comment with others*

4. The mentioned user will get the email, as shown in Figure 7-66.

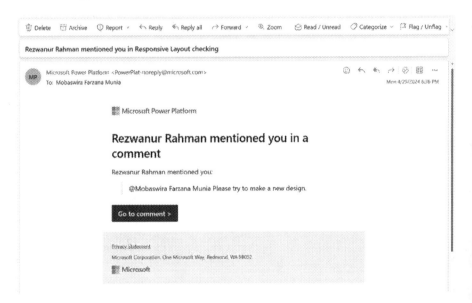

Figure 7-66. *The user will get a notification email*

Power Apps Comment Limitations

Here are a few notable limitations regarding comments in Power Apps:

- Power Apps Studio imposes a limit on the number of users who can edit an app simultaneously. If you tag someone while the app is open, they will be notified via email; however, they must wait until you close the app to view and address the comment.

- When working on an app through Git, comments are not supported.

- The @mention feature is not available for custom Power Apps on SharePoint.

Summary

This chapter explained how to make your Power Apps more dynamic and interactive by using variables, formulas, and responsive design techniques. It also explored how to integrate AI-driven features like Copilot and chatbots, enhancing the user experience with real-time, intelligent responses. Additionally, I demonstrated how to incorporate comments for better collaboration and customization within your apps.

As you move to Chapter 8, I build on these foundations by focusing on integrating diverse data sources, such as Microsoft Dataverse, SharePoint, and Azure SQL. I teach you how to design custom tables, manage multimedia elements, and seamlessly connect your Power Apps to various data repositories, further enhancing your app's functionality and data management capabilities.

CHAPTER 8

Integrating Diverse Data Sources and Media in Power Apps

The previous chapter explored how to create dynamic and interactive Power Apps by incorporating variables, formulas, and AI-driven features like Copilot and chatbots. These elements help elevate the user experience, making your apps more responsive and intelligent.

This chapter shifts focus to integrating various data sources into your Power Apps, such as Microsoft Dataverse, SharePoint, and Azure SQL. You'll learn how to design custom tables, manage multimedia content, and connect your app to external data repositories. This will enable you to create more robust and data-driven applications that meet the specific needs of your users.

Table Designer

In the previous chapter, you learned that when Copilot creates a project, it automatically includes a Microsoft Dataverse table in the data source. This section focuses on the detailed process of creating a custom Dataverse table. This section guides you through each step of designing and

© Rezwanur Rahman 2024
R. Rahman, *Microsoft Copilot for Power Apps*, Inside Copilot,
https://doi.org/10.1007/979-8-8688-0512-7_8

implementing a tailored Dataverse table to meet the specific needs of your application, enhancing data management and functionality in your Power Apps projects.

To create a custom Dataverse table, follow these steps:

1. To begin, open your browser and navigate to the Power Apps portal at `https://make.powerapps.com/`. From there, you can either continue working on the Power Apps project you started earlier or choose to start a new project. This will set the stage for you to dive into creating custom Dataverse tables. This example uses the previous project.

2. Click Data in the left sidebar. Select +Add Data and then select Create New Table, as shown in Figure 8-1.

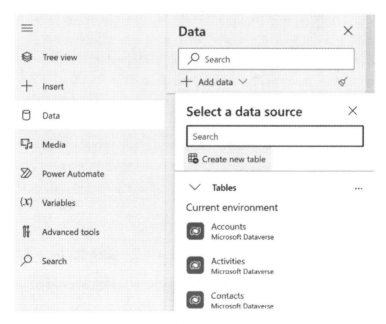

Figure 8-1. *Creating a new table in the Power Apps project*

3. The next page will ask you in which way you want to create the table, as shown in Figure 8-2.

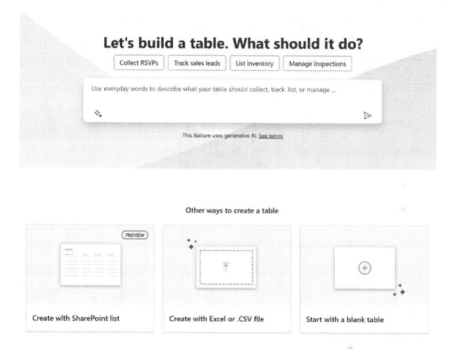

Figure 8-2. *Select your preferred method for creating the table*

I will begin with an empty table this time. Unlike previously, I will not be using Copilot, as you have already seen how it can automatically generate a table for this project.

4. After choosing Start with a Blank Table, you will be taken to a page displaying a completely blank table. Unlike previous instances, you will not find any prepopulated or recommended columns. This setup allows you to customize the table from scratch according to your specific requirements. See Figure 8-3.

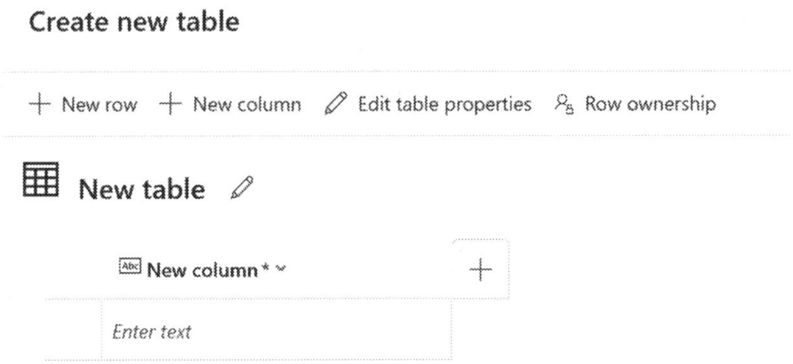

Create new table

Figure 8-3. Option to create a table, row, and column

5. You need to name this table. Click Edit Table Properties and you will get the option to edit the table name, as shown in Figure 8-4.

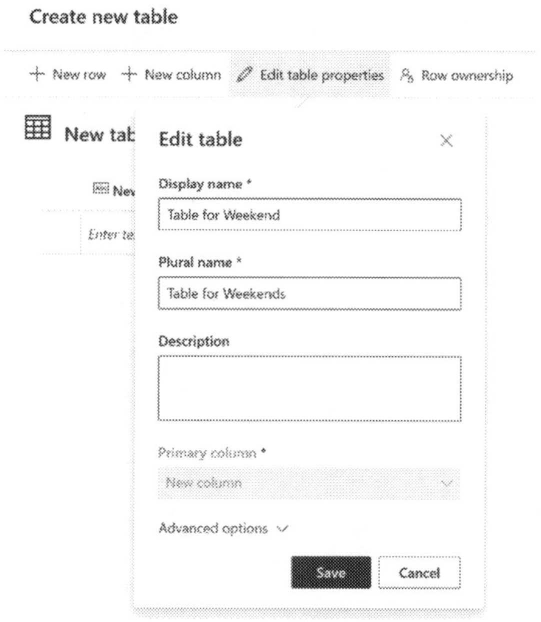

Create new table

Figure 8-4. *Change the table properties*

6. I named the table Table for Weekend. Next, you
    will insert some dummy data and attempt to display
    it on a new screen, as shown in Figure 8-5.

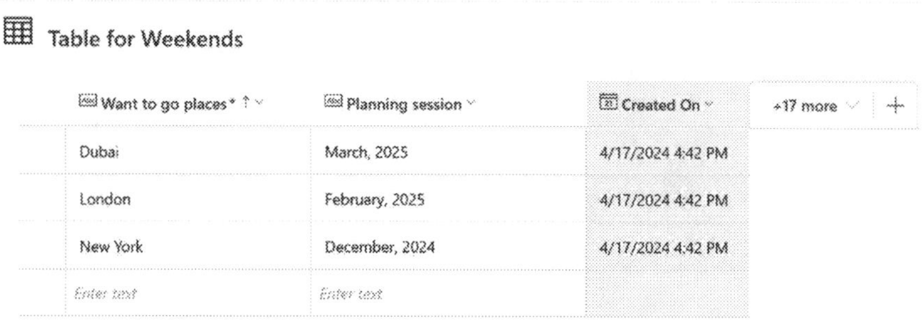

Figure 8-5. *Creating a row and dummy data inside*

7. Create a new screen. Click the + icon and search for Data Table, as shown in Figure 8-6.

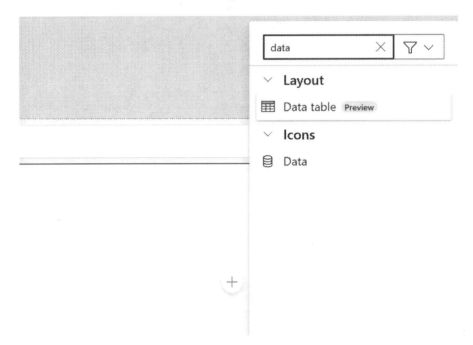

Figure 8-6. *Searching for Data Table to fetch new table data*

8. Add the Data Table to the screen and select Table for Weekend as the data source. You will see the data in the table, as shown in Figure 8-7.

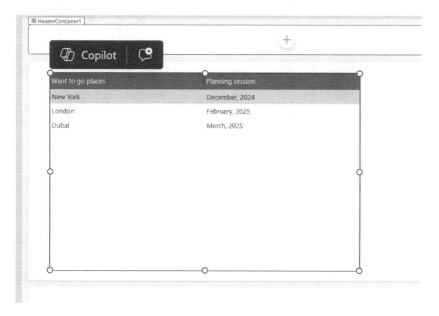

Figure 8-7. *Fetching data from a newly created table*

9. Now you will design the table for the best look. Resize the table using your mouse to fit it in the screen, as shown in Figure 8-8.

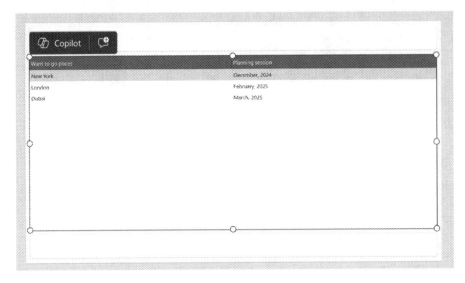

Figure 8-8. *Fixing the table size*

10. You can modify the table's design in various ways. In the previous chapter, you learned how to use Copilot Chat to change the color or text of a table. Now, you will see how to use default themes in a table.

    In the top bar, when you select the Data Table, there is an option named Theme, as shown in Figure 8-9.

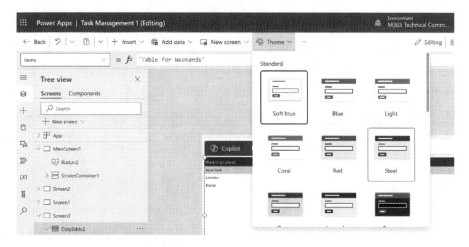

Figure 8-9. *Selecting Theme from the top bar*

11. Select a theme and it will be changed accordingly.
    See Figure 8-10.

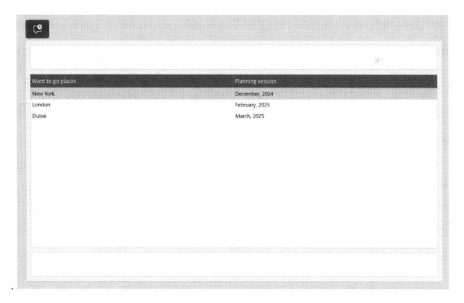

Figure 8-10. *Changing the theme color after manually selecting Theme from the top bar*

12. You can also change the font name, size, and style. Remember, you must select the Data Table component first to access these options. See Figure 8-11.

Figure 8-11. *Options to change the text family, size, and style*

13. For example, I changed the font from Segoe UI to Dancing Script, the font size from 13 to 17, and the font style from Normal to Bold. You can see this table style in Figure 8-12.

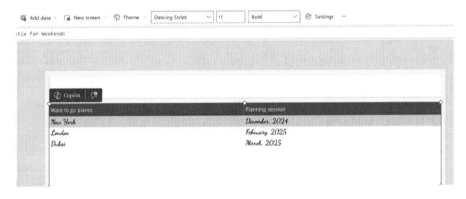

Figure 8-12. *Changing the font family, size, and style*

14. Next, you will explore another method for modifying component properties. While the previous chapter covered using Copilot Chat for this purpose, and you utilized the top bar options, you will now learn how to directly alter parameters through the component's Properties panel.

Select the Data Table control and click Properties on
the right side, as shown in Figure 8-13.

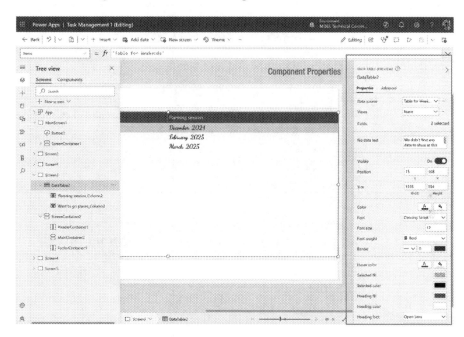

Figure 8-13. *Properties of the Data Table control*

15. Let's change the background color from here. You
     will find two options in Color—one for the font and
     another for the visual background color. Select the
     visual background option and choose any color you
     want, as shown in Figure 8-14.

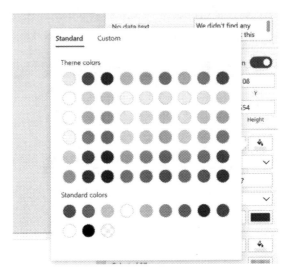

Figure 8-14. *Selecting the visual background color from Properties*

16. You will see the updated color after changing the option. See Figure 8-15.

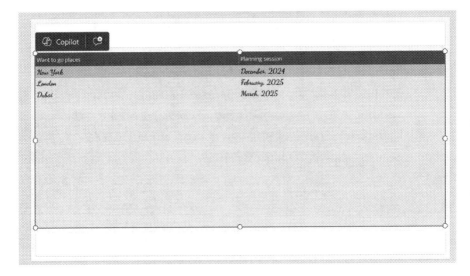

Figure 8-15. *Changed the background color*

You learned about three different ways to change the component properties:

1. Change with a Copilot conversation.

2. Change from the top bar options (limited change).

3. Change from the component's properties.

Permissions and Limitations of Table Creation in Dataverse

To create a table in Dataverse, it is essential that a Dataverse database already be provisioned in the environment. Additionally, you need to hold either system customizer or system administrator permissions in the specific environment where you intend to construct a table. If these prerequisites are not fulfilled, the Create New Table button will be disabled.

It is important to note that you can only create and edit tables within the current Dataverse environment. Should you switch your Dataverse environment using the environment picker, the options to Create New Table and Edit Table will be disabled.

Image and Video

The Media and Gallery panes in Power Apps provide a user-friendly way to incorporate multimedia into your apps, enhancing the user experience and data presentation. Customizable and easy-to-use, these features allow for quick creation and deployment of visually appealing and engaging apps, improving communication and productivity.

You will now see how to work with multimedia in Power Apps.

Add Images, Audio, or Video Using the Media Pane

Adding media, whether it is images, audio, video, or any other format, follows a similar process. As an example, this section shows how to add a video to the app.

To add media to your app using Copilot, follow these steps:

1. To start, navigate to your project and choose the screen where you want to incorporate the media. In this case, since this app is for learning purposes, first create a new screen to accommodate the media content. See Figure 8-16.

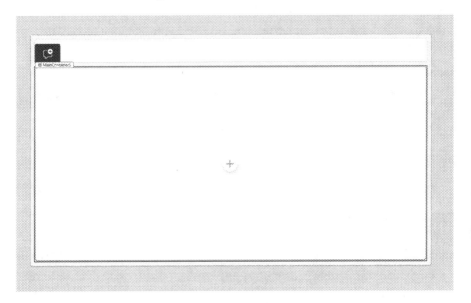

Figure 8-16. *Creating a new screen to see how adding media works*

2. Click Insert from the left sidebar and choose Media.
    You can add any of the following media to Power
    Apps, as shown in Figure 8-17.

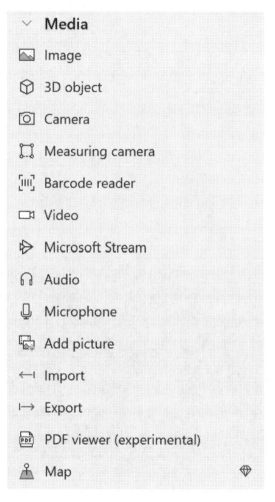

Figure 8-17. *Available media controls in Power Apps*

Note You cannot directly use Copilot to add media to Power Apps. Instead, you need to manually add the appropriate media type control to your app. Additionally, you have to upload the media files within Power Apps manually, as Copilot cannot access your device data for this purpose. Copilot's capabilities are limited to assisting with internal designs, text, data, formulas, and code adjustments within the app interface.

3. I select the Video control so that I can add a video to the app. See Figure 8-18.

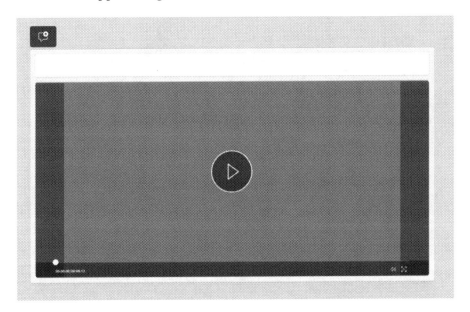

Figure 8-18. *Adding a Video control in Power Apps*

4. I have successfully added the Video component to
    the app, but I have not linked the video yet. Before
    proceeding, you need to upload a video file to the
    app, after which you can establish the link with this
    component.

    Click Media in the left sidebar, select +Add Media,
    and choose Upload, as shown in Figure 8-19.

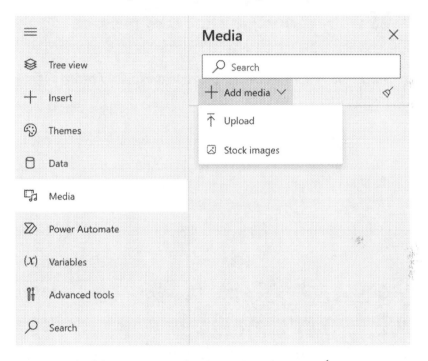

Figure 8-19. *Adding new media to Power Apps*

5. Select and upload your video. You will then see the
    video in the list, as shown in Figure 8-20.

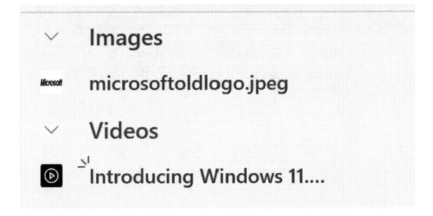

Figure 8-20. *Successfully adding new media to the Power Apps project*

6. Select the Video control and then select Properties from the right side, as shown in Figure 8-21.

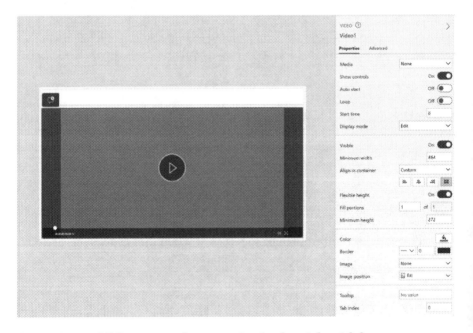

Figure 8-21. *Video control properties in the right sidebar*

7. As shown in Figure 8-22, from Properties, click
    Media and choose the video that you just uploaded.

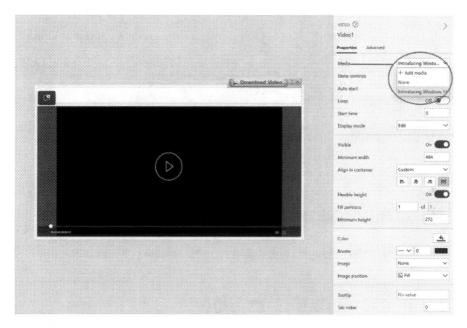

Figure 8-22. *Choosing the media to add in the control*

8. Press F5 or run the app to check the video, as shown
    in Figure 8-23.

Figure 8-23. *Checking the video in app preview*

Add Media from URL or Cloud

You can also add media from the cloud or an URL (example, YouTube). When adding media files by URL, you need to consider the following:

- Use HTTPS to ensure compatibility with modern browsers.

- Ensure the URL is accessible anonymously without any authentication. Try to enter the URL in private browsing mode to verify that it is accessible without signing in.

Follow these steps to add media from an URL:

1. Add an image control in Power Apps, as shown in Figure 8-24.

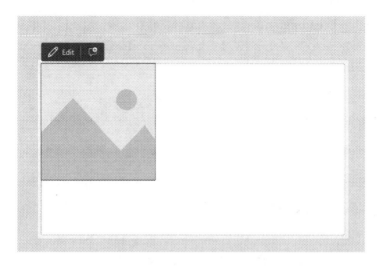

Figure 8-24. *Added image control in Power Apps*

2. Select the control from screen, select Image from
   the Formula bar, and then add the URL of the image
   that is publicly available, as shown in Figure 8-25.

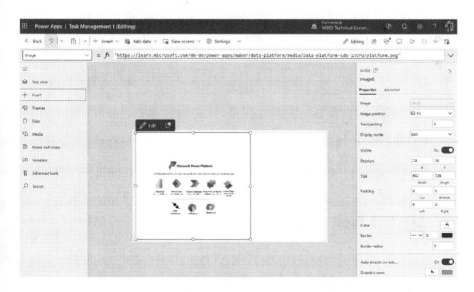

Figure 8-25. *Adding an image from an URL*

Note that the image must be uploaded as public and accessible from the app. Be sure to add the URL in quotation marks ("URL"), as shown in Figure 8-26.

```
"https://learn.microsoft.com/de-de/power-apps/maker/data-
platform/media/data-platform-cds-intro/platform.png"
```

Figure 8-26. *Example of an image URL*

Known Limitations of Power Apps Media

Here are some identified limitations concerning the media capabilities within Power Apps:

- To enable better performance while loading an app, the following size restrictions apply:

  - The total size of all media files uploaded to an app cannot exceed 200MB.

  - The maximum size of an individual media file in an app cannot exceed 64MB.

- Supported media file types include `.jpg`, `.jpeg`, `.gif`, `.png`, `.bmp`, `.tif`, `.tiff`, `.svg`, `.wav`, `.mp3`, and `.mp4`.

Pen Input Control

The Pen input control in Power Apps is a versatile tool designed for capturing handwritten input and signatures within an app. This control allows users to draw or write directly on the screen using their finger or a stylus, making it ideal for applications requiring signature capture or freehand drawing tasks. The data captured by the Pen input control is stored as an image, which can be saved into a data source or used in the app for further processing. This feature enhances the functionality of Power Apps by enabling a more interactive user experience, particularly useful in scenarios like form completion, artistic applications, or any situation where manual input is preferred over traditional keyboard entries.

To add the Pen input control in Power Apps, follow these steps:

1. Open your project in Power Apps. Click Insert and choose the Pen Input control, as shown in Figure 8-27.

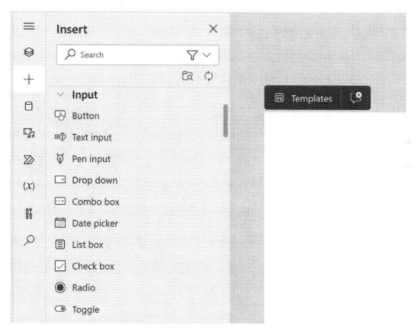

Figure 8-27. *Selecting the Pen input in Power Apps*

2. Adjust the size for the screen, as shown in Figure 8-28.

Figure 8-28. *Changing the size of the Pen input*

3. Press F5 and check the app by writing on it, as
    shown in Figure 8-29.

Figure 8-29. *Preview of the Pen input*

You can learn more about the Pen input control from Microsoft's official learning website at `https://learn.microsoft.com/en-us/power-apps/maker/canvas-apps/controls/control-pen-input`.

Known Limitation of the Power Apps Pen Control

Drawing with a mouse or a touch input in the Windows app might not work well with the Pen control. Strokes can be broken. For better drawing, use a pen or open the app in a browser.

Integration Diverse Data Sources

Integrating diverse data sources, such as SQL databases, Dynamics 365, Microsoft Excel, or third-party APIs is essential for creating comprehensive business insights. This section outlines various methods and tools for extracting, transforming, and loading data from these sources into a unified system. By implementing robust data integration practices, organizations can enhance their decision-making processes and achieve a more holistic view of their operations.

Adding a SharePoint Data Source from Microsoft List

This section explains how to add a SharePoint data source in Power Apps, aimed at beginners. This section guides you through creating a blank list in SharePoint and connecting it to Power Apps. If you are already familiar with SharePoint lists, feel free to skip this section. This exercise is an excellent starting point for those new to these tools.

To create a list in SharePoint, follow these steps:

1. Go to `https://portal.office.com` from your browser, click Apps, and select SharePoint. See Figure 8-30.

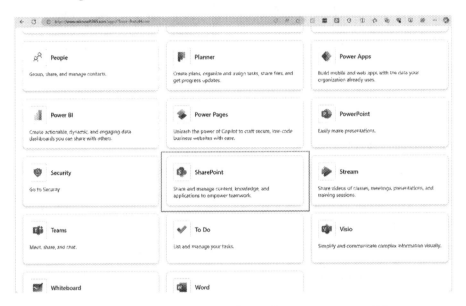

Figure 8-30. *Selecting SharePoint from the Apps page of the Microsoft 365 Portal*

2. You can also access SharePoint by clicking the nine-dot grid icon located in the top-left corner of any Microsoft application. See Figure 8-31.

Figure 8-31. *You can select SharePoint from the nine-dot grid*

3. Once you open the SharePoint portal, click the
    My List option in the left sidebar. You will see the
    available list in your SharePoint environment, as
    shown in Figure 8-32. In my environment, I have
    a list called Microsoft Test Environment. If you do
    not have any lists, do not worry! I show you how to
    create one.

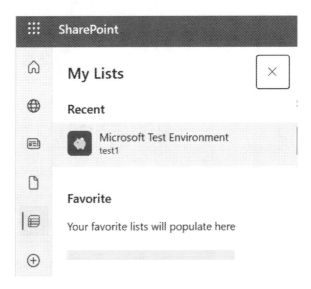

Figure 8-32. *My Lists option in the Microsoft SharePoint Portal*

4. I select the list called Microsoft Test Environment. It
    will open, as shown in Figure 8-33.

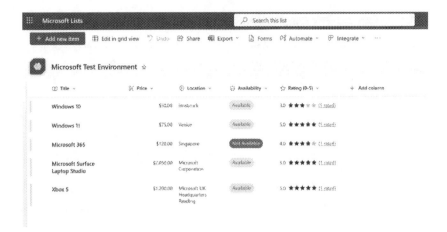

Figure 8-33. *Data that is saved in a Microsoft list*

You might be confused about SharePoint Lists versus Microsoft Lists. I will make this clear by the end of these steps! Do not worry!

5. You need to create an app with the data source. There are two ways to create an app in Power Apps.

   1. **From a Microsoft List**: From the list that you opened, choose Integrate ➤ Power Apps ➤ Create an App, as shown in Figure 8-34.

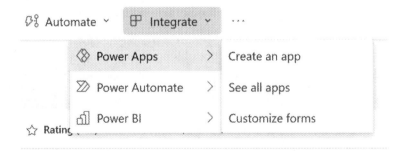

Figure 8-34. *Creating Power Apps from a Microsoft List*

2. **From Power Apps**: Create an app or open your
    existing app, click Data in the left sidebar, and then
    choose SharePoint under the Connector option, as
    shown in Figure 8-35.

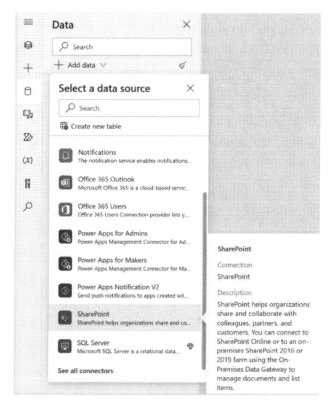

Figure 8-35. SharePoint connector in Power Apps

6. Since you are already on the Microsoft List page,
    let's use this method to create the app. Click the
    Create an App option (see Figure 8-34). It will
    redirect you to another tab and will take a few
    seconds to create an app.

7. After that, you will see the app in the Power Apps window, as shown in Figure 8-36.

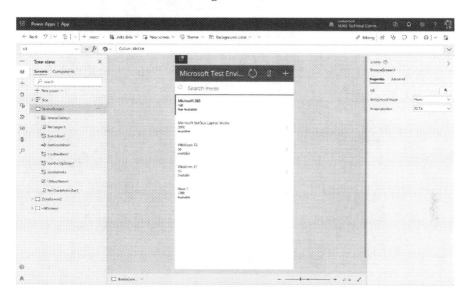

Figure 8-36. *The Microsoft List data in Power Apps*

8. Run the app by pressing F5 for a better understanding. See Figure 8-37.

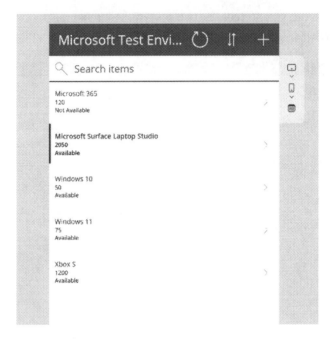

Figure 8-37. *Preview of Power App and fetching data from Microsoft List*

Adding SharePoint Data Source from Power Apps Studio

In this section, you learn how to connect SharePoint to Power Apps using Power Apps Studio. To set up a connection between SharePoint and Power Apps, either start a new Canvas project in Power Apps or open an existing project where you want to include the SharePoint data source.

As I showed in multiple projects in this book, I am not creating a new project, I am opening an existing one. Follow these steps:

1. Open the project and click Data in the left sidebar. Then choose SharePoint under the Connector option, as shown in Figure 8-38.

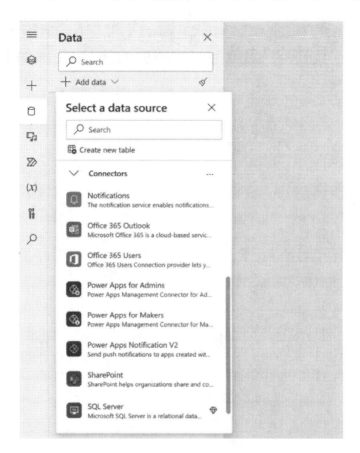

Figure 8-38. *SharePoint connector in data source*

2. After clicking SharePoint, a sidebar will open on the right, asking you to connect to the SharePoint site, as shown in Figure 8-39.

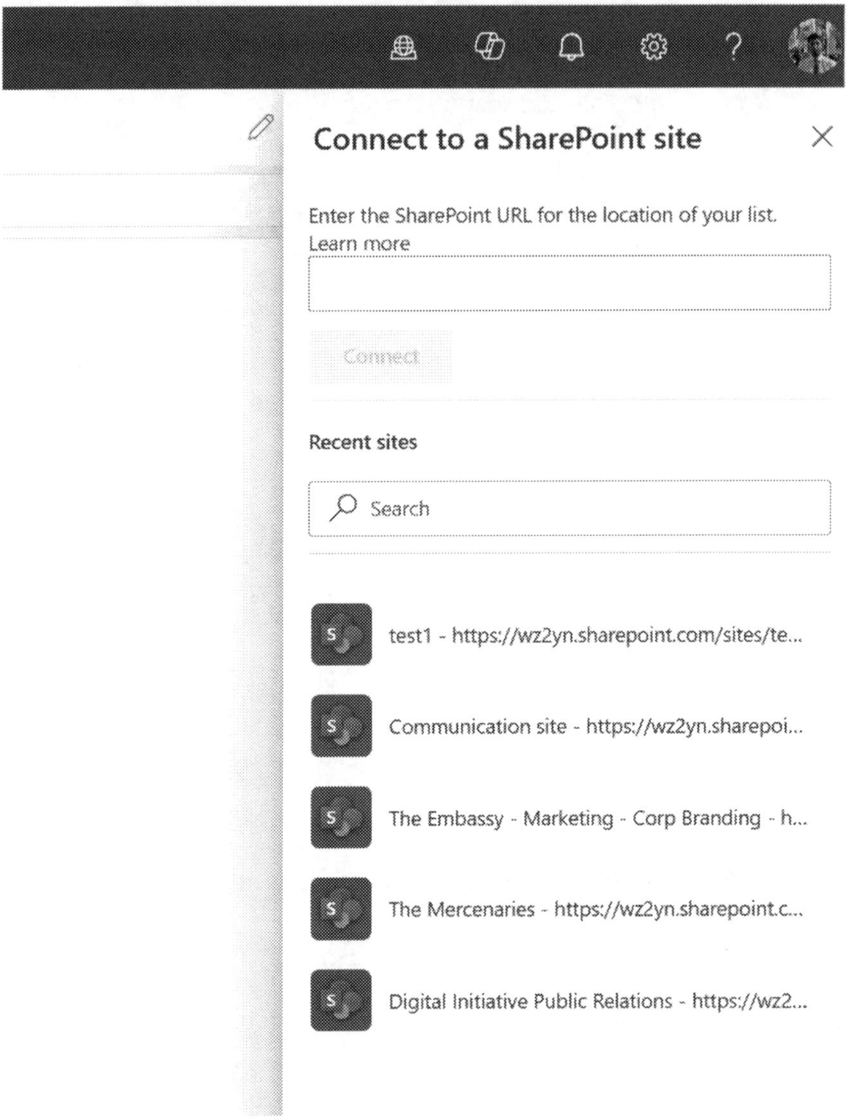

Figure 8-39. *SharePoint site list in Power Apps*

3. As shown in Figure 8-40, select the SharePoint site
    where your list is saved, choose the list, and click
    Connect.

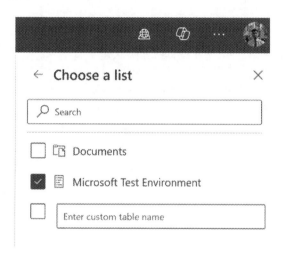

Figure 8-40. *Choosing the list in from the SharePoint
connector option*

4. It will take a few moments to connect. After a
    successful connection, you will see the SharePoint
    data source listed in the Data option, as shown in
    Figure 8-41.

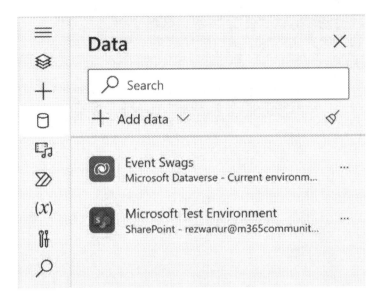

Figure 8-41. *Showing the SharePoint list in the Data source option*

5. Now, add a Data Table using the Insert option, as shown in Figure 8-42.

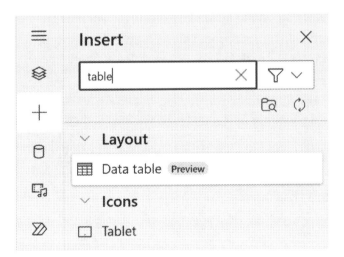

Figure 8-42. *Adding a Data Table to fetch data*

6. You will now see a page where Power Apps asks you
    to connect the data source. As shown in Figure 8-43,
    choose the SharePoint Data Source that you added a
    few minutes before.

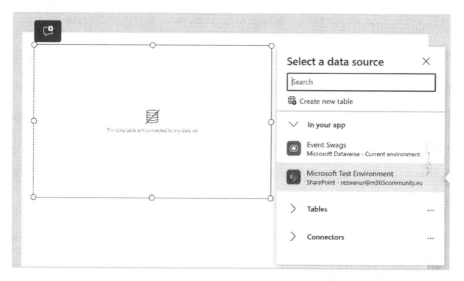

Figure 8-43. *Adding a SharePoint data source to the Data Table*

7. Next, you will see the SharePoint table displayed in
    Power Apps. See Figure 8-44.

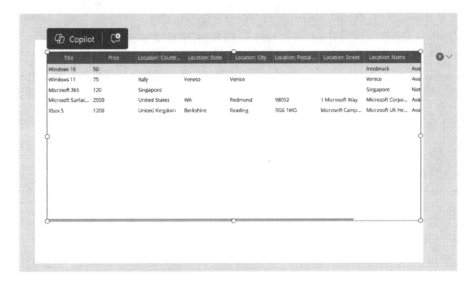

Figure 8-44. *Showing SharePoint data in the Data Table*

The Difference Between Microsoft List and SharePoint List

Microsoft Lists and SharePoint Lists are both integral components of the Microsoft 365 ecosystem, although they serve slightly different purposes and offer distinct user experiences:

- **Microsoft Lists** is an evolution of SharePoint Lists, designed as a versatile app within Microsoft 365. It supports task management and information tracking with a modern interface, providing advanced templates and customization options suitable for diverse organizational needs.

- **SharePoint Lists**, traditionally embedded in SharePoint sites, focus on data management and storage. While functional, they feature a more conventional interface and offer basic templates compared to the enhanced, user-centric capabilities of Microsoft Lists.

By default, when you create a list in Microsoft SharePoint, it will open in Microsoft List. Also, if you create a list in Microsoft List, you can directly create a Power Apps from the Integrate option.

Note   Power Apps does not support all types of SharePoint data. Learn more here: `https://learn.microsoft.com/en-us/power-apps/maker/canvas-apps/connections/connection-sharepoint-online#known-issues`

Adding an Azure SQL Data Source

You will now see how to connect an Azure SQL database in Power Apps. But before proceeding with the Azure SQL database, you need to meet the following prerequisites:

- Enable pop-ups in your browser settings.

- An Azure subscription is required. If you do not have one, you can create a free account. Follow this link to create an account: `https://azure.microsoft.com/free/`.

- Access to an existing SQL database is necessary. If you do not have access, you need to create a new database. I show you how to create a SQL database in Microsoft Azure.

- Modify your firewall settings to allow Azure services access to your SQL Database server.

- Ensure that your SQL database table includes at least one column with a text data type.

Note   If you are a valid student, you can claim $100 Azure credit free from Microsoft. Check it out from here: `https://azure.microsoft.com/en-us/free/students/`. No credit or debit card is required to get the Azure student account.

Let's explore this process:

1. To access Azure Portal, navigate to `https://portal.azure.com/`. Once you're there, use the tenant admin credentials that are also used for Power Apps to sign in.

2. Click Azure Services, select Database from the Category located in the left sidebar, and choose SQL Database under the Azure SQL option, as shown in Figure 8-45.

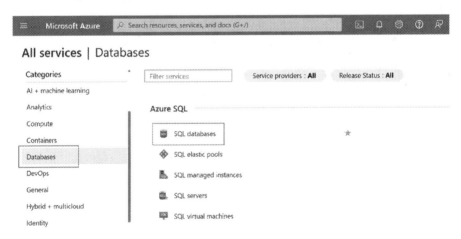

Figure 8-45. *Creating an Azure SQL database in the Azure Portal*

3. Click Create in the top bar to create an Azure SQL
    database, as shown in Figure 8-46.

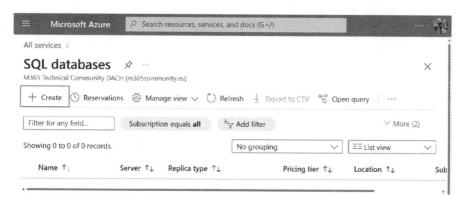

Figure 8-46. *Creating an Azure SQL database*

4. When you select the Create option, a form will
    appear with several important fields, as shown in
    Figure 8-47.

Figure 8-47. *Information that is needed to create Azure SQL database*

Here is the description of the entries on that form:

a. **Subscription**: If you have multiple Azure subscriptions, choose your Azure subscription from here. If you have one subscription, choose that one.

b. **Resource Group**: A resource group in Azure is a container that holds related resources for an Azure solution. This grouping helps organize and manage assets as a single unit based on project, service, or lifecycle. If you do not have a resource group, click Create New and provide a name to create a new Resource Group.

c. **Database name**: Provide a name of your database.

d. **Server**: To deploy a database for any solution in Azure or another cloud service, you must first select a server that will host and run the solution. If you do not have a server, click Create New. The page shown in Figure 8-48 will open.

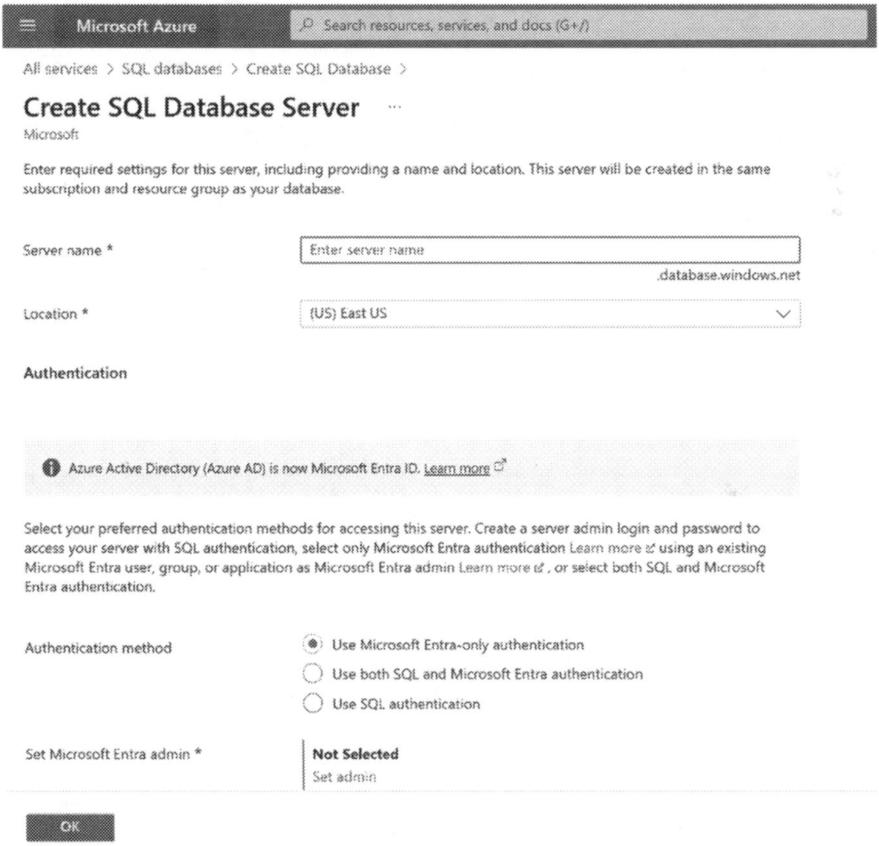

Figure 8-48. *Creating SQL database server*

Provide a server name and choose the location. Choose the Use Microsoft Entra-Only Authentication method. Also, select an admin responsible for managing the server.

5. Next, the Networking page will appear. On this page, enable the Add Current Client IP Address option, as shown in Figure 8-49.

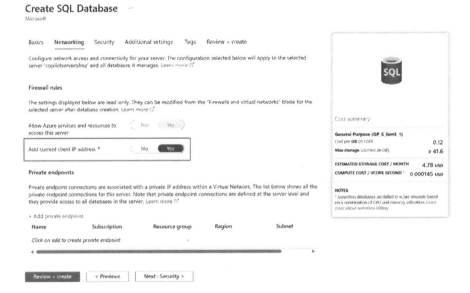

Figure 8-49. *Configuring the network option in the Azure SQL database*

6. Choose your required settings from Security, Additional Settings, and Tags, after that, click Review + Create.

It will display the monthly cost required for this Azure SQL database, as shown in Figure 8-50.

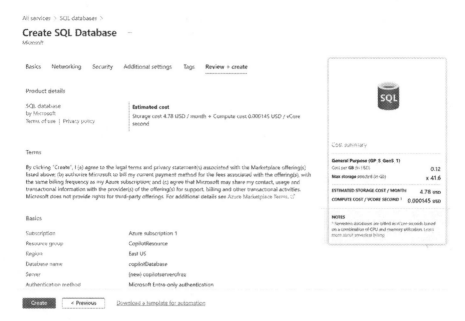

Figure 8-50. *Review + Create page of SQL database, where you can see how much you'll pay every month*

7. It will take a few minutes to create the database in Azure SQL, as shown in Figure 8-51.

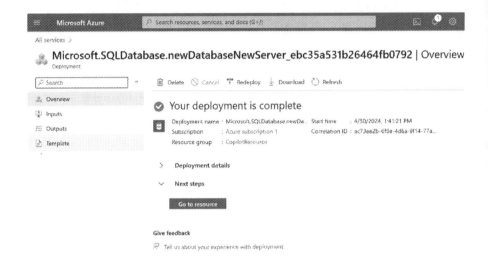

Figure 8-51. *Azure SQL Database deployment confirmation page*

8. This step requires you to create a new table and
    populate it with data. Since Power Apps relies on
    tables and data for display within the app, you can
    create a table and add some sample data by clicking
    the Query Editor in the left panel, as shown in
    Figure 8-52.

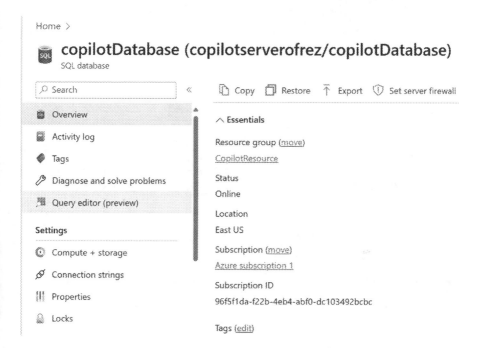

Figure 8-52. *Select the Query Editor to edit the Azure SQL database*

9. You will be prompted to log in using either a
    SQL Server Authentication or Microsoft Entra
    Authentication, as shown in Figure 8-53. I use the
    Microsoft Entra Authentication since I am already
    logged in with that user.

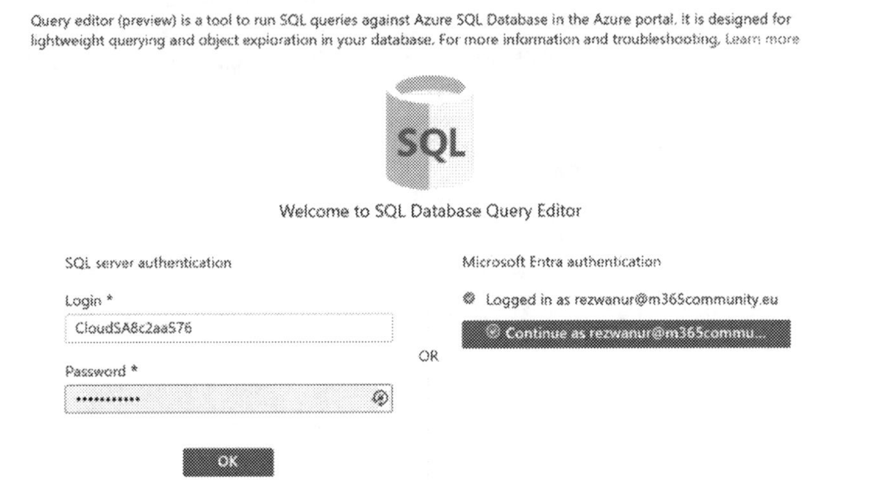

Query editor (preview) is a tool to run SQL queries against Azure SQL Database in the Azure portal. It is designed for lightweight querying and object exploration in your database. For more information and troubleshooting, Learn more

Welcome to SQL Database Query Editor

SQL server authentication

Login *

CloudSA8c2aa576

Password *

••••••••••••

OK

Microsoft Entra authentication

Logged in as rezwanur@m365community.eu

Continue as rezwanur@m365commu...

OR

Figure 8-53. *Choose the authentication method to access SQL database Query Editor*

10. You need to run a SQL query to create a table and add data. After login, a page will pop up where you must run the SQL query, as shown in Figure 8-54.

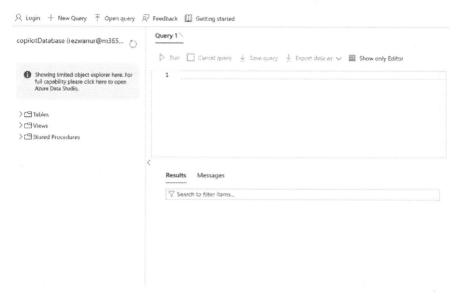

Figure 8-54. *Field to run the SQL query in the Query Editor*

11. In the Query 1 box, run the following SQL command
     to create a table named MicrosoftCopilotBook
     with three columns named Users, Location and
     DateofBirth, as shown in Figure 8-55.

```
CREATE TABLE MicrosoftCopilotBook (
    Users VARCHAR(255),
    Location VARCHAR(255),
    DateofBirth DATE
);
```

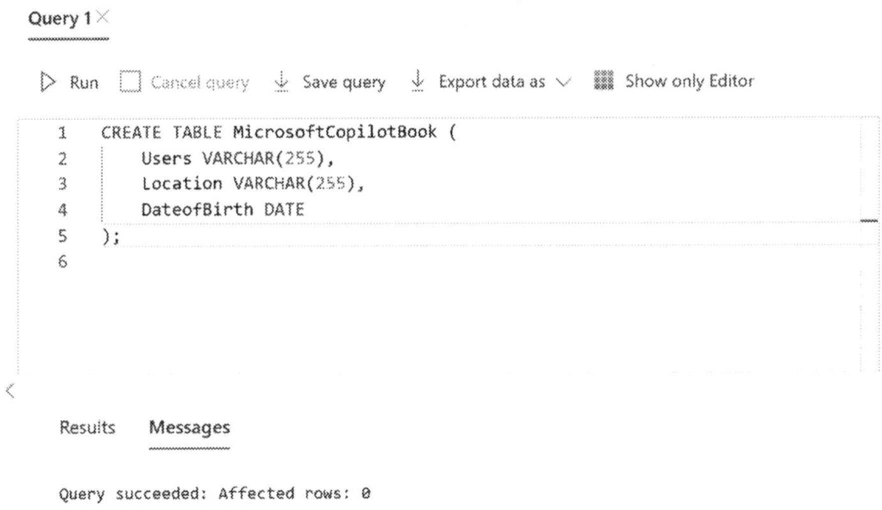

Query 1 ✕

▷ Run   ☐ Cancel query   ↓ Save query   ↓ Export data as ∨   ▦ Show only Editor

```
1    CREATE TABLE MicrosoftCopilotBook (
2        Users VARCHAR(255),
3        Location VARCHAR(255),
4        DateofBirth DATE
5    );
6
```

Results   Messages

Query succeeded: Affected rows: 0

Figure 8-55. *Query to create a table named MicrosoftCopilotBook with the Users, Location, and DateofBirth columns*

If you want to learn more about SQL query, see the Microsoft official documentation at https:// learn.microsoft.com/en-us/azure/azure-sql/ database/connect-query-portal?view=azuresql.

12. You can also run a query in your natural language to Copilot web (https://copilot.microsoft.com), as shown in Figure 8-56.

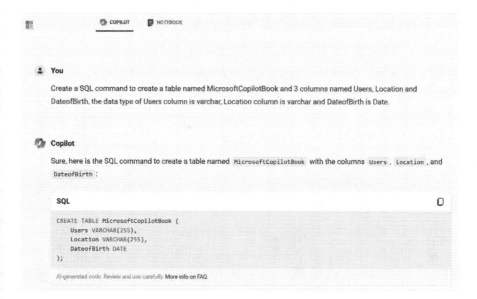

Figure 8-56. *Asking Copilot to create a SQL query*

13. After executing the command, as shown in Figure 8-57, you will see that the table and its columns have been created.

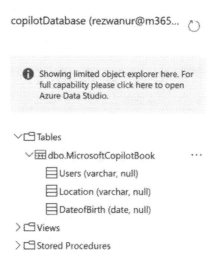

Figure 8-57. *The table and columns have been successfully created*

425

14. Add some data to the table, as shown in Figure 8-58.
    To add data, use this command:

```
INSERT INTO MicrosoftCopilotBook
(Users, Location, DateofBirth)
VALUES
        ('Rahat', 'Innsbruck', '1993-10-23'),
        ('Munia', 'New York', '1996-06-12'),
        ('Ruhi', 'Dhaka', '2003-03-13'),
        ('Sonia', 'London', '1996-06-12');
```

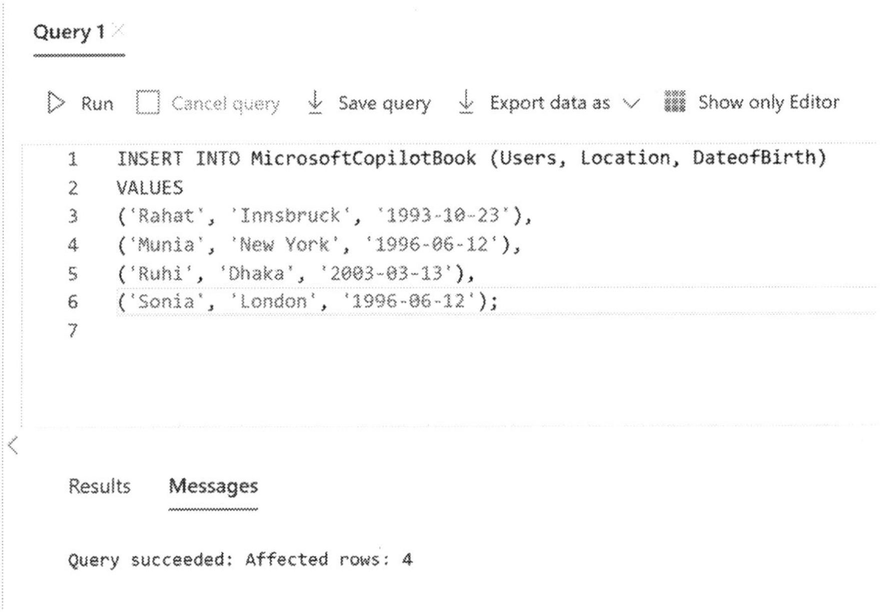

Query 1 ×

▷ Run   ☐ Cancel query   ↓ Save query   ↓ Export data as ∨   ▦ Show only Editor

```
1    INSERT INTO MicrosoftCopilotBook (Users, Location, DateofBirth)
2    VALUES
3    ('Rahat', 'Innsbruck', '1993-10-23'),
4    ('Munia', 'New York', '1996-06-12'),
5    ('Ruhi', 'Dhaka', '2003-03-13'),
6    ('Sonia', 'London', '1996-06-12');
7
```

‹

Results   **Messages**

Query succeeded: Affected rows: 4

Figure 8-58. *SQL query to add data to a table*

15. Next, check if the data was successfully saved in the
    table, as shown in Figure 8-59. To verify this, run the
    following command:

```
SELECT * FROM MicrosoftCopilotBook;
```

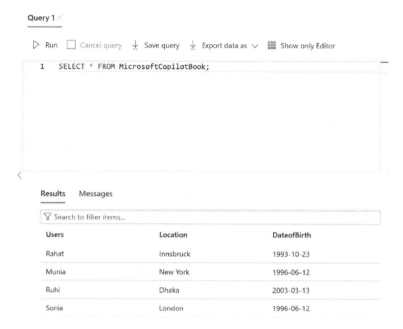

Figure 8-59. *Verifying table data*

The data is displaying correctly as per the command, confirming that the command functioned perfectly. Next, you will integrate this table with dummy data into Power Apps.

16. Go to https://make.powerapps.com/ and create a new Canvas app.

17. Click Data in the left sidebar and connect SQL Database from Connector, as shown in Figure 8-60.

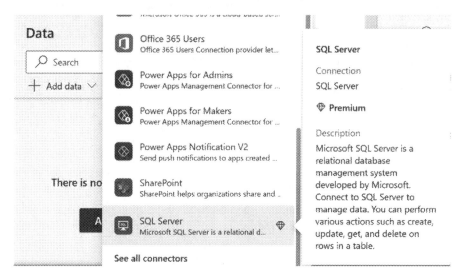

Figure 8-60. *Select SQL Server from Connector to get the Azure SQL database in Power Apps*

Note   SQL Server is considered a premium connector within Power Apps, requiring a premium license to utilize this feature. The cost of the license may vary by country. For more details on the Power Apps premium license, visit the official Microsoft website at `https://powerapps.microsoft.com/en-us/pricing/`

---

18.   As shown in Figure 8-61, click Add a Connection.

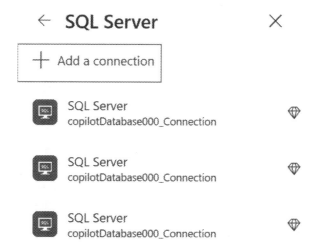

Figure 8-61. *Adding a SQL Server connection in Power Apps*

19. Choose Microsoft Entra ID Integrated from
     Authentication Type, as shown in Figure 8-62. Click
     Next after selecting the authentication type.

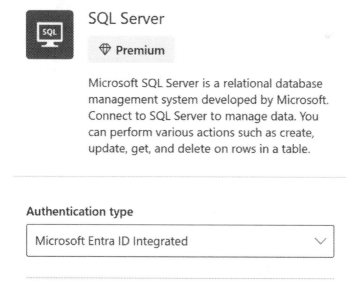

Figure 8-62. *Selecting the authentication type in SQL Server*

20. In the next part, provide the SQL Server Name and the SQL Database Name, as shown in Figure 8-63. You can get the information from the Azure SQL database overview page, as shown in Figure 8-64.

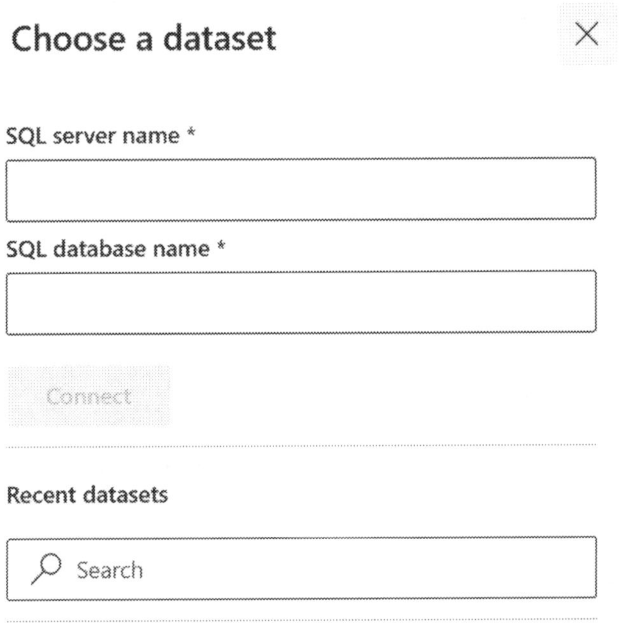

Figure 8-63. *Provide the SQL Server name and SQL database name to connect SQL Server with Power Apps*

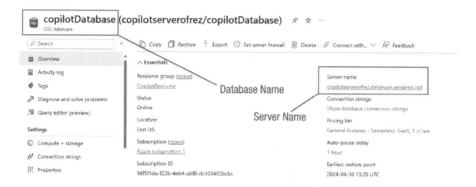

Figure 8-64. *Find your SQL Server name and SQL Database name from the Azure SQL Database overview page*

21. After providing the SQL Database Name and the SQL Server Name, you will be asked to select a table from those available on your server, as shown in Figure 8-65.

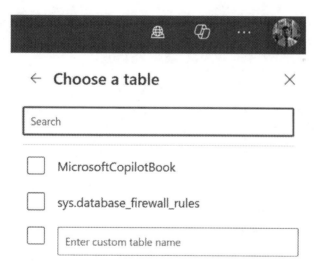

Figure 8-65. *Select the table that you want to connect with your Power Apps*

22. Select the table and click Connect.

23. After that, you can see the SQL Database in the Data list, as shown in Figure 8-66.

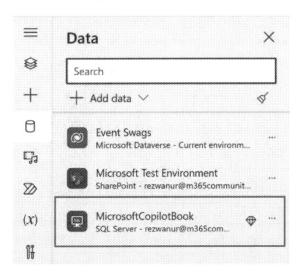

Figure 8-66. Showing Azure SQL Database list in the Data source option

24. Add a Data Table control using the Insert option to the screen and connect the SQL Server as the data source. You will see the data coming from Azure SQL database, as shown in Figure 8-67.

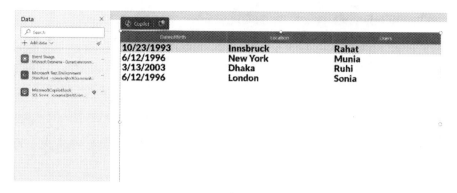

Figure 8-67. *Successfully fetching data from the Azure SQL database*

25. You might have noticed that there is an option in
     the Azure SQL Database portal to connect SQL
     Database to Power Apps, as shown in Figure 8-68.
     Let me explain to you why I did not use this option.

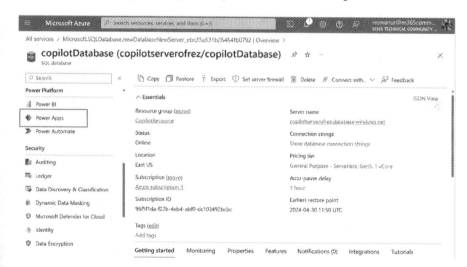

Figure 8-68. *Power Apps option in the Azure SQL database*

26. If you click Power Apps, in the next page, you will be
     asked for some essential information, as shown in
     Figure 8-69.

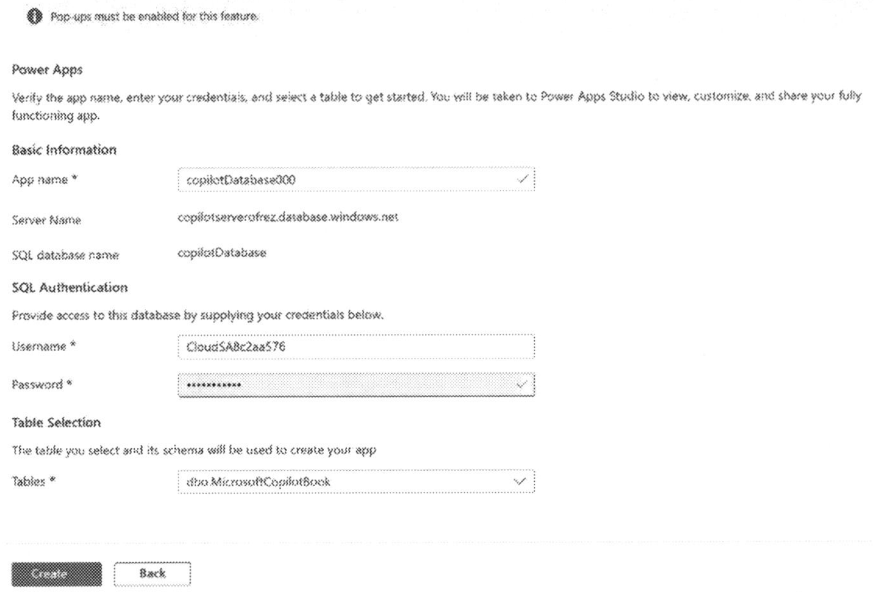

Figure 8-69. *Information needed to create Power Apps from the*
Azure Portal

As you used Microsoft Entra authentication previously (see
Figure 8-69), you do not have the SQL authentication username and
password. To learn more, see the Microsoft documentation at https://
learn.microsoft.com/en-us/power-apps/maker/canvas-apps/app-
from-azure-sql-database.

Note   To utilize Microsoft Entra Integrated authentication with
an Azure SQL database rather than SQL authentication, consider
creating an app through Power Apps and employing the SQL Server
connector.

Summary

This chapter explored how to integrate diverse data sources and multimedia into Power Apps. I showed you how to create and customize Dataverse tables, connect Power Apps to external data sources like SharePoint and Azure SQL, and add multimedia elements like images, videos, and pen input controls. These skills will help you make your apps more dynamic, data-driven, and engaging for users.

As you move to Chapter 9, I introduce you to the powerful capabilities of AI Builder in Power Apps. You will learn how to enhance your apps with AI, automate tasks, and extract valuable insights from your data. Chapter 9 will help you create smarter, more proactive applications that can significantly improve business processes and decision-making.

CHAPTER 9

Introducing AI Builder in Power Apps

In the previous chapter, you gained hands-on experience in integrating various data sources and multimedia elements into your Power Apps, allowing you to build more interactive and data-driven applications. This foundation of connecting external data sources and managing custom tables sets the stage for creating robust, user-centric apps.

This chapter takes you a step further by introducing AI Builder in Power Apps. You'll discover how to harness the power of artificial intelligence to automate processes, predict outcomes, and extract meaningful insights from your data—all without needing any specialized AI knowledge. By the end of this chapter, you'll be equipped to add intelligent features to your apps, making them not just functional, but also proactive and insightful tools for your users.

AI Builder: Enhancing Power Apps with AI Capabilities

Moving from the advanced customization techniques of the previous chapter, this chapter introduces AI Builder—a transformative addition within Power Apps that makes artificial intelligence accessible to every app developer. AI Builder is a robust tool that seamlessly integrates with

R. Rahman, *Microsoft Copilot for Power Apps*, Inside Copilot,
https://doi.org/10.1007/979-8-8688-0512-7_9

Power Apps and the broader Microsoft ecosystem. It enables you to automate processes, predict outcomes, and extract actionable insights from data without needing deep technical expertise in AI.

Imagine a Power App that manages customer data, predicts purchasing trends, automates responses based on customer behavior, and streamlines operations—all powered by AI. This capability is not just about enhancing functionality; it's about transforming business operations, making them more responsive, efficient, and ahead of the curve.

In this section, I explore how AI Builder acts as a bridge between complex AI algorithms and the practical needs of business applications, empowering you to build smarter and more proactive apps. This tool revolutionizes your approach to app development by making advanced AI functionalities accessible and actionable.

AI Builder Overview

AI Builder in Power Apps is a key feature that enables users to easily add artificial intelligence to their applications. It offers a straightforward, no-code interface that simplifies the integration of AI capabilities. With AI Builder, users can automate routine tasks, analyze data more effectively, and make smarter decisions more quickly. The tool is equipped to handle a variety of common business needs, such as processing forms, detecting objects, and predicting outcomes, making sophisticated AI functionalities accessible to users who may not have a technical background. This not only makes creating AI models simpler but also ensures they can be easily trained and improved, right within Power Apps.

Types of AI Models Available

Power Apps provides a broad range of AI models that enhance the automation and intelligence of applications. This includes pre-built AI models that are ready-to-use for tasks like text recognition, extracting information from text, and classifying categories. For solutions tailored to specific needs, users can develop custom AI models using tools from AI Builder and Azure Machine Learning. This flexibility enables businesses to automate simple data entry tasks or undertake complex predictive analytics, allowing them to deploy AI solutions that align precisely with their operational needs and strategic objectives. Now, as you move forward, you'll learn about the unique characteristics and potential applications of pre-built and custom AI models and explore how each can be strategically utilized to reshape and energize your business processes.

In AI Builder, you have access to various model types that cater to different business needs. Here are a few examples:

- To detect specific products in images, you can customize and train an AI Builder *object detection model* to recognize the items you are interested in.

- To streamline your expense management, you can employ a pre-built AI Builder model designed for scanning and processing business receipts, enabling immediate productivity enhancements.

- To create a marketing campaign that leverages insights from past trends, you can develop a *custom prediction model* that utilizes your historical data to forecast future patterns.

These examples represent just a few of the numerous possibilities for incorporating intelligence into your business workflows using AI Builder.

Note   To continue using your AI models in AI Builder, you must purchase an AI Builder add-on license. Additionally, an administrator is required to allocate AI Builder capacity to any environment in which you intend to use AI Builder. Without a license, you can't create or modify AI Builder models, and no new inferences are possible after the trial period expires.

Model Types

Table 9-1 outlines the different data types, model types, and build types available.

> **Data type:** This specifies the kind of AI each model utilizes, such as documents, text, structured data, or images.
>
> **Build type:** This category shows whether a model is customizable—requiring you to build, train, and publish it according to your specific needs— or whether it's a pre-built model that's ready for immediate use. Generally, custom AI Builder models are ideal for unique business-specific data, while pre-built models are better suited for common scenarios across various industries.

Table 9-1. *List of Data Types, Model Types, and Build Types in AI Builder*

Data Type	Model Type	AI Template Table UniqueName mapping	Build Type
Documents	Business card reader	BusinessCard	Pre-built
Documents	Document processing	DocumentScanning, (DocumentLayoutAnalysis is used during training)	Custom
Documents	Text recognition	TextRecognition	Pre-built
Documents	Receipt processing	ReceiptScanning	Pre-built
Documents	Invoice processing	InvoiceProcessing	Pre-built
Documents	ID reader	IdentityDocument	Pre-built
Text	Text generation (preview)	GptPowerPrompt, (GptPromptEngineering was used during Preview)	Pre-built
Text	Category classification	TextClassificationV2	Pre-built (preview) and custom
Text	Entity extraction	EntityExtraction	Pre-built and custom

(*continued*)

Table 9-1. (*continued*)

Data Type	Model Type	AI Template Table UniqueName mapping	Build Type
Text	Key phrase extraction	KeyPhraseExtraction	Pre-built
Text	Language detection	LanguageDetection	Pre-built
Text	Sentiment analysis	SentimentAnalysis	Pre-built
Text	Text translation	TextTranslation	Pre-built
Structured data	Prediction	BinaryPrediction, GenericPrediction	Custom
Images	Object detection	ObjectDetection, (ObjectDetectionProposal is used during training)	Custom
Images	Image Description	ImageDescription	Pre-built (preview)
Images	Text Recognition	TextRecognition	Pre-built
Images	Preview version of App Copilot	CopilotSidePanePredict	Pre-built (preview)

Follow these steps to get the full list of AI models, as shown in
Figure 9-1:

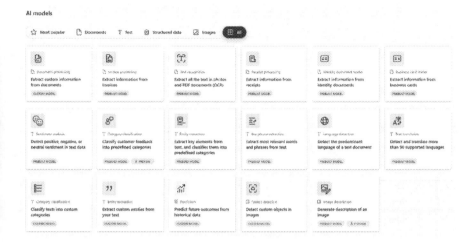

Figure 9-1. *List of pre-built and custom models in the Microsoft
Power Apps AI Hub*

1. Visit `https://make.powerapps.com` and log in with
   your credentials.

2. Select AI Hub from the left sidebar, as shown in
   Figure 9-2.

Figure 9-2. *Selecting AI Hub from the left sidebar*

3. Select AI Models from the screen shown in
   Figure 9-3.

Figure 9-3. *AI models from the AI Hub*

Common Business Scenarios

AI Builder offers a variety of AI model types that equip you with extensive
AI functionalities without requiring deep coding skills or data expertise.
Table 9-2 explores some typical business situations and the ideal AI model
types to handle them.

Table 9-2. *Common Business Scenarios with Preferred Model Types*

Business Scenario	Model Type
Automate customer application processing	Document processing
Automate expense reports	Receipt processing
Categorize user feedback based on their focus	Category classification
Extract insights from product reviews	Entity extraction
Identify language of text	Language detection
Identify and classify customer feedback	Sentiment analysis
Translate support requests into your language	Text translation
Identify fraudulent transactions	Prediction
Get alerted to social media posts referencing your brand	Key phrase extraction
Automate contact list	Business card reader
Automate inventory taking	Object detection
Take a photo of text and save it to a database	Text recognition
Automate customer application processing	Document processing

Pre-Built AI Models

Pre-built AI models in Power Apps offer a ready-to-use solution for businesses looking to integrate artificial intelligence quickly and efficiently. These models cover a wide range of common business scenarios, such as text and image recognition, sentiment analysis, and form processing. Designed to be user-friendly, they require no prior coding or deep data science knowledge, making it easier for users of all skill levels to enhance their applications with AI capabilities. By using pre-built models, organizations can accelerate their digital transformation, improve accuracy in data handling and streamline operations, all while saving time and resources on model development and training.

Pre-built models can be accessed within Power Automate and Power Apps. Table 9-3 lists the models currently available through AI Builder.

Table 9-3. *Pre-Built AI Models with Uses*

Pre-Built AI Model	Description of Use
Invoice Processing	Automates the extraction and processing of data from invoices for quicker financial workflows.
Text Recognition	Converts images of text into editable, searchable data.
Sentiment Analysis	Analyzes text to determine the tone and sentiment, useful for customer feedback and social media analysis.
Receipt Processing	Simplifies the extraction of information from receipts, aiding in expense management.
Entity Extraction	Identifies and categorizes entities within text, useful for data organization and retrieval.
ID Reader	Extracts data from identification documents to automate data entry and verification processes.

(continued)

Table 9-3. (*continued*)

Pre-Built AI Model	Description of Use
Key Phrase Extraction	Pulls out important phrases from text to highlight main ideas or concepts, enhancing content analysis.
Business Card Reader	Digitizes contact information from business cards into a manageable format.
Category Classification	Automatically classifies text into predefined categories, streamlining content sorting and management.
Text Generation (Preview) (Deprecated)	Generates text based on input prompts; no longer recommended for new deployments due to deprecation.
Language Detection	Identifies the language of the given text, enabling multi-lingual support and analysis.
Text Translation	Translates text from one language to another, facilitating communication across different languages.
Image Description (Preview)	Generates descriptions for images, enhancing accessibility and content understanding.

To learn more about pre-built AI models, scan the QR code shown in Figure 9-4 or visit `https://learn.microsoft.com/en-us/ai-builder/prebuilt-overview`.

Figure 9-4. Learn more about pre-built AI models

Custom AI Models

Custom AI models in Power Apps allow businesses to tailor artificial intelligence solutions specifically to their unique requirements. Unlike pre-built models, these custom models enable users to leverage their own data to create, train, and publish AI functionalities that are perfectly aligned with their specific operational needs. This capability is particularly valuable for addressing complex or niche tasks that standard models cannot handle. By using Azure Machine Learning alongside AI Builder, organizations can develop sophisticated AI models that enhance decision-making, automate intricate workflows, and provide deeper insights into their data, thereby driving innovation and competitive advantage in their respective industries.

Table 9-4 lists the custom models that are currently available in AI Builder.

Table 9-4. *Custom AI Models with Uses*

Custom Model	Description of Use
Document Processing	Extracts custom information from various types of documents to streamline data capture and analysis.
Category Classification	Classifies texts into user-defined categories, enhancing content organization and management.
Entity Extraction	Extracts user-specified entities from text; useful for detailed content analysis and customization.
Prediction	Uses historical data to predict future outcomes, aiding in data-driven decision-making.
Object Detection	Identifies and locates user-defined objects within images for detailed visual analysis.
Azure Machine Learning Models	Integrates custom models developed in Azure Machine Learning for specific analytical tasks.

To learn more about custom AI models, scan the QR code shown in Figure 9-5 or visit `https://learn.microsoft.com/en-us/ai-builder/custom-overview`.

Figure 9-5. *Learn more about custom AI models*

In-Depth Exploration of AI Builder

This section explains the key components of AI Builder, including how to use its components. It also includes examples of custom AI models.

Key Components of AI Builder

In Microsoft Power Apps, you can utilize AI Builder two main ways, based on the specific model you choose to deploy. These include:

1. Integrating AI models directly within the Formula bar.

2. Incorporating AI Builder components into your applications.

Each method offers a tailored way to enhance your applications with artificial intelligence, allowing for seamless integration and functionality enhancement.

Integrating AI Models in the Formula Bar

You can access the AI Builder models listed in Table 9-5 directly through the Formula bar in Power Apps.

Table 9-5. *AI Models Available from the Formula Bar in Power Apps*

AI Model	Model Type	Build Type
Business Card Reader	Text Extraction	Pre-built
Category Classification	Text Classification	Pre-built and custom
Entity Extraction	Text Analysis	Pre-built and custom
Identity Document Reader	Text Extraction	Pre-built
Image Description	Image Analysis	Pre-built
Invoice Processing	Text Extraction	Custom
Key Phrase Extraction	Text Analysis	Pre-built
Language Detection	Text Analysis	Pre-built
Receipt Processing	Text Extraction	Custom
Sentiment Analysis	Text Analysis	Pre-built
Text Recognition	Text Extraction	Pre-built
Text Translation	Text Translation	Pre-built
AI Reply	Text Generation	Custom
AI Classify	Text Classification	Custom
Empty Dynamic Prompt	Text Generation	Custom
AI Sentiment	Sentiment Analysis	Custom
AI Summarize	Text Summarization	Custom
AI Extract	Text Extraction	Custom

You can find all the AI models in Power Apps Studio. Open a project and select Data ➤ Add Data ➤ AI Models, as shown in Figure 9-6.

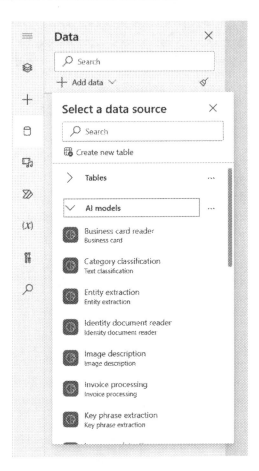

Figure 9-6. AI models in the data source list

Using Power Fx, you can create more dynamic and flexible integrations of AI models in Power App. AI model prediction formulas can be seamlessly linked to any control within a Canvas app. For example, you can detect the language of text entered in a text input control and display the results in a label control. Or you can get text from an image.

Requirements

To utilize Power Fx in AI Builder models, the following are required:

- Access to a Microsoft Power Platform environment that includes a database.

- AI Builder license, either trial or paid.

Demo

This section takes you through a quick demo to learn how to use AI Model directly from the Formula bar. To get started, follow these steps:

1. Create a new Canvas app or open your existing Canvas app project in `https://make.powerapps.com`, as shown in Figure 9-7.

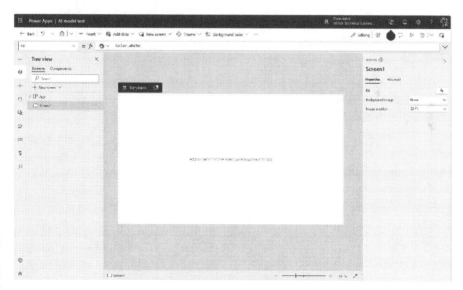

Figure 9-7.   *New Canvas app created in Power Apps Studio*

2. Choose Language Detection from Data ➤ Add
    Data ➤ AI Models, as shown in Figure 9-8.

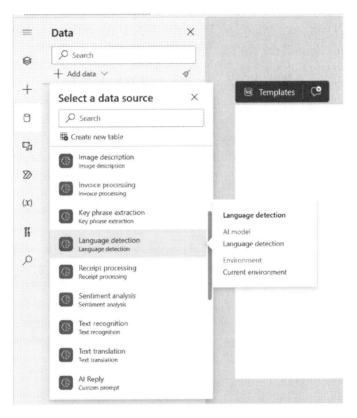

Figure 9-8. *Choosing Language Detection from the AI Model*

3. Click Insert, then choose Text Input and Text Label, as shown in Figure 9-9.

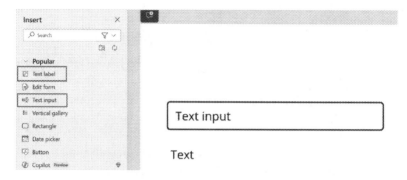

Figure 9-9. *Adding a text label and text input to your app*

4. Add another text label named Language, as shown in Figure 9-10.

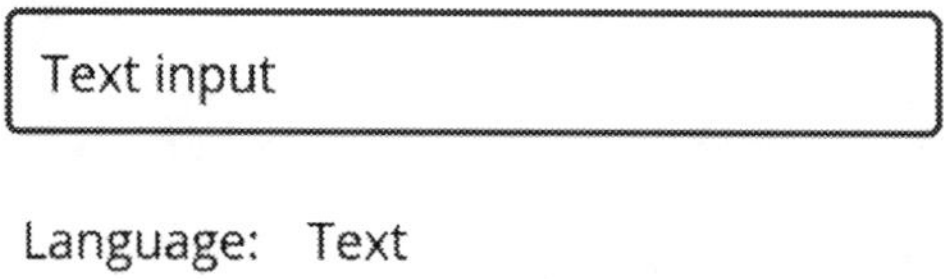

Text input

Language: Text

Figure 9-10. *Adding a new text label named Language*

5. Select the text and then select the Formula bar, as shown in Figure 9-11.

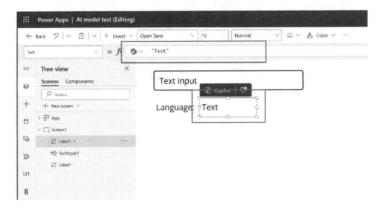

Figure 9-11. *Select the Text label and the Formula bar*

6. Write the following code in the Formula bar (also
    shown in Figure 9-12):

    ```
    'Language detection'.Predict(TextInput1.Text).Language
    ```

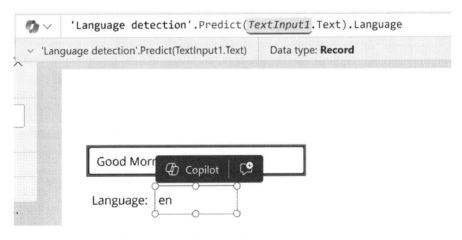

Figure 9-12. *Code to detect the text language*

7. Run the app by pressing F5. Type something in a
    different language and check the result, as shown in
    Figure 9-13.

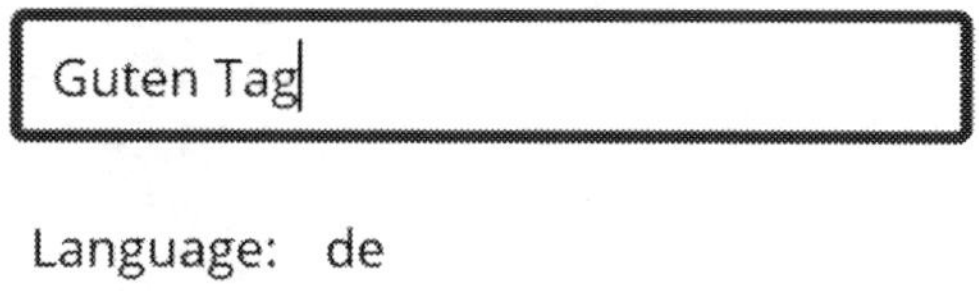

```
Guten Tag|
```

Language: de

Figure 9-13. *The language detector detected "Guten Tag" as Deutsch (German)*

If you type something in another language, you will see a different result, as shown in Figure 9-14.

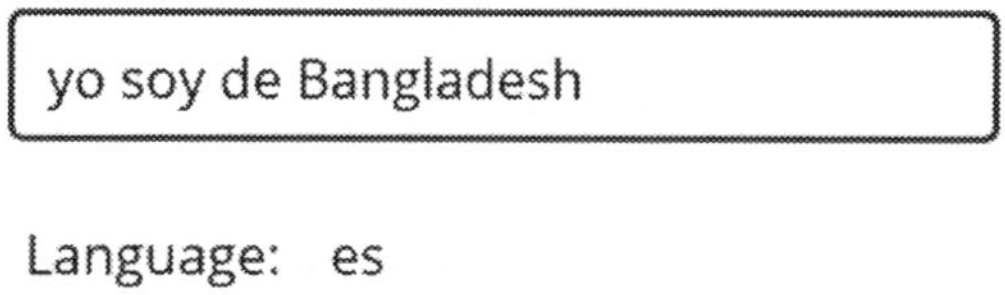

```
yo soy de Bangladesh
```

Language: es

Figure 9-14. *Language detection recognizes the Spanish sentence*

Use AI Builder Components

This section demonstrates how to utilize AI Builder components within Power Apps. AI Builder offers two types of components for Power Apps. Select the component that aligns with the models you intend to use.

1. The components that use pre-built AI models are ready to use now. For example, the Business Card Reader, Invoice Processor, and Text Recognizer.

2. You'll need to build and train the components that use custom AI models. For example, the form processor or object detector.

This chapter explains both types of models.

You can see the AI Builder components from the Power Apps project. Open the Power Apps project in Power Apps Studio, click Insert, and then expand the AI Builder, as shown in Figure 9-15.

457

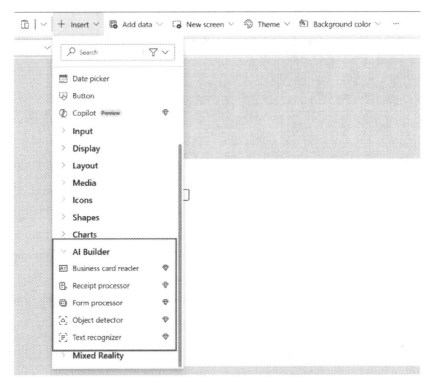

Figure 9-15. *AI Builder components in Power Apps*

Example Uses of AI Builder Models and Components

This section explores the AI Builder models and components.

Business Card Reader Component

You can use the AI Builder Business Card Reader component to effortlessly detect and pull details from business cards. You can take pictures directly from the component or upload a previously captured image. If you are going to capture or extract information from a business card, you can get the information listed in Table 9-6.

Table 9-6. *Properties That Can Be Read by the Business Card Reader Component*

Property	Definition
AddressCity	City
AddressCountry	Country
AddressPostalCode	Postal code
AddressPostOfficeBox	Post office box
AddressState	State address
AddressStreet	Street address
BusinessPhone	The first phone or fax number
CompanyName	Company name
Department	Organization department
Email	The contact's email address if any
Fax	The third phone or fax number
FirstName	The contact's first name
FullAddress	The contact's full address
FullName	The contact's full name
JobTitle	The contact's job title
LastName	The contact's last name
MobilePhone	Second phone or fax number
OriginalImage	The original image, before processing
Website	The contact's website

Demo

You can use the Business Card Reader component in Canvas or any model-driven app. This example shows how to use the Business Card Reader component in a Canvas app.

To add the Business Card Reader component to Power Apps, follow these steps:

1. Open your Canvas project in `https://make.powerapps.com`.

2. Add the Business Card Reader component from the Insert option, as shown in Figure 9-16.

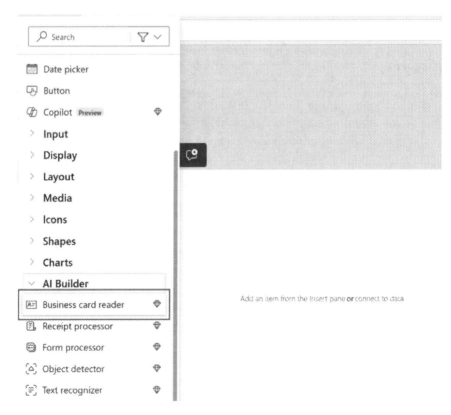

Figure 9-16. *Adding the Business Card Reader component to Power Apps*

3. Once you've added it, you can see the component in the screen, as shown in Figure 9-17.

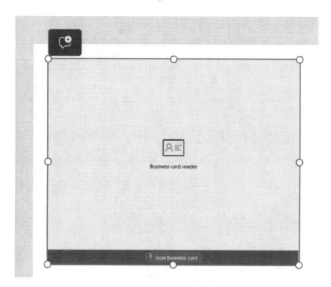

Figure 9-17. *The Business Card Reader component shown in the Power App screen*

4. Next, you'll create two sets of text labels for each piece of information: Name, Job Title, Email, Phone Number, and Website. One set will serve to label and identify the fields, and the other will display the data extracted from the Business Card Reader component, as shown in Figure 9-18.

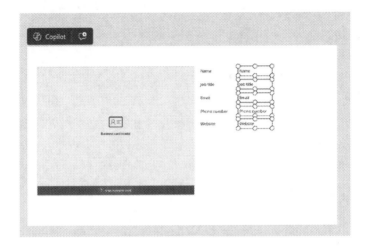

Figure 9-18. *Creating labels to extract data from Business Card Reader*

5. Add some code to each label. For example, I select Name (see Figure 9-19) and, in the Formula bar, I add the following code:

```
BusinessCardReader1.Fullname
```

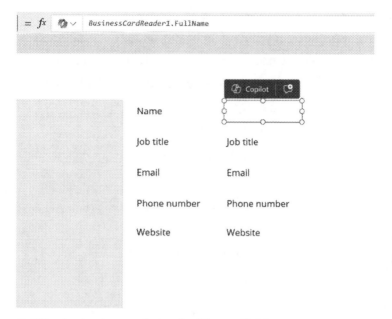

Figure 9-19. *Assigning code to the Name field*

Note   When you assign code to a text label, the previous text becomes invisible because the label is now linked to the Full Name component of the Business Card Reader.

---

6. Do the same for Job Title, Email, Phone Number, and Website. Select the label. Then, in the Formula bar, type **BusinessCardReader1** and then . (period). Then select or type the property name. You can get the property name from Table 9-6.

Note   The name of my Business Card Reader component is
BusinessCardReader1, which is typically the default. However,
be sure to verify the component's name before beginning the
assignment.

7.   Now it's preview time. Press F5 or run the app, as
shown in Figure 9-20.

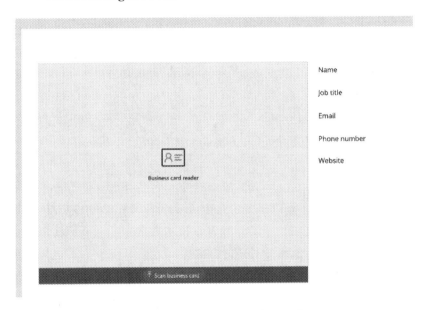

Figure 9-20. Preview of the Business Card Reader component

8.   You can now upload a business card to the app.
Click the Scan Business Card button and upload a
business card, as shown in Figure 9-21.

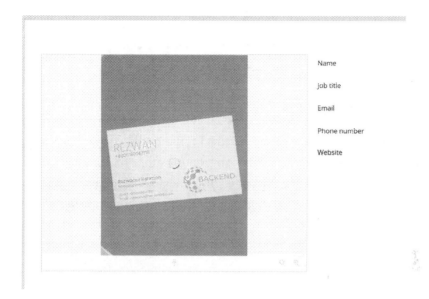

Figure 9-21. *Uploading a business card to Power Apps*

9. After a few minutes, you will see the information in
    the labels, as shown in Figure 9-22.

Figure 9-22. *Extracting information from a business card using the*
Business Card Reader component

In this image, the website field is missing, indicating that the Business Card Reader was unable to retrieve it. This is likely because the website was not present on the front side of the business card.

The Receipt Processor Component

The Receipt Processor component in AI Builder efficiently scans and captures data from receipts. This component supports direct photo capture and the uploading of preexisting images for processing. This example demonstrates how to integrate and use this component in a Canvas app on Power Apps.

When you capture or extract information from the Receipt Processor component, you can capture the information listed in Table 9-7.

Table 9-7. *Properties That Can Be Read by the Receipt Processor Component*

Property	Definition
MerchantName	Merchant name
MerchantAddress	Merchant address
MerchantPhone	Merchant phone number
TransactionDate	Transaction date
TransactionTime	Transaction time
PurchasedItems	The list of purchased items
	Name: Name of the purchased item
	Price: Price of the purchased item
	Quantity: Quantity of the purchased item
	TotalPrice: Total price of the purchased item

(continued)

Table 9-7. (*continued*)

Property	Definition
Subtotal	Subtotal
Tax	Tax
Tip	Tip
Total	Total

Requirements

The Receipt Processor component performs optimally with sales receipts, such as those from restaurants, gas stations, and retailers. It can recognize printed and handwritten text.

Currently, only English receipts from the United States are supported. For best results, ensure that each receipt is provided as a clear photo or scan.

- Accepted formats include JPEG, PNG, and PDF.

- The file size must be under 20MB.

- Image dimensions should range from 50x50 pixels to 10,000x10,000 pixels.

- PDF dimensions should not exceed 17x17 inches, which corresponds to legal or A3 paper sizes and smaller.

- For PDF files, only the first 200 pages are processed.

Demo

Let's start with a demo. To start working with the Receipt Processor, follow these instructions:

1. Open your project where you want to add the Receipt Processor component or create a new one from `https://make.powerapps.com`. For my demo, I created a new Canvas app in the phone format, as shown in Figure 9-23.

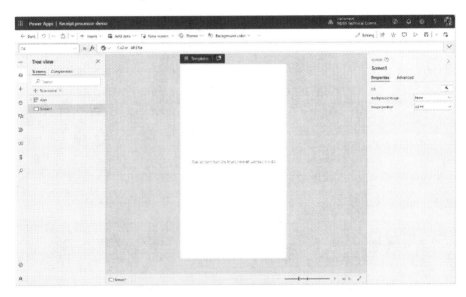

Figure 9-23. *Created a new Canvas app in the phone format for the Receipt Processor demo*

2. Add Receipt Processor from the Insert option in the
    screen and fix the margin, as shown in Figure 9-24.
    Ensure there is adequate space below the Receipt
    Processor component to accommodate a button.

Figure 9-24. *Adding a Receipt Processor control from the*
Insert option

3. Add the next arrow button under the Receipt Processor control, as shown in Figure 9-25. It will help to go to the next page, where I place the text label controls to fetch the receipt information.

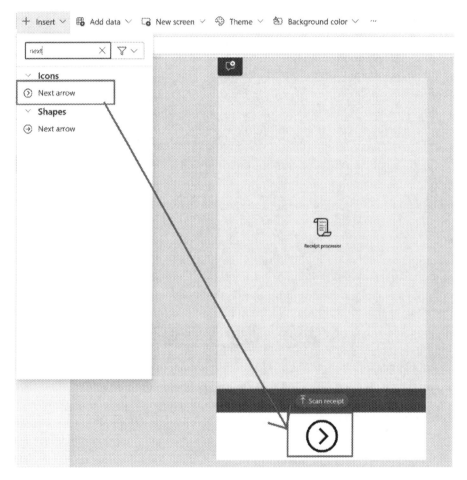

Figure 9-25. *Added next arrow next to the Receipt Processor*

4. Run the app and upload a receipt to the Receipt
   Processor control, as shown in Figure 9-26.

Figure 9-26. *Uploading a receipt to the Receipt Processor*

5. Create a new screen and add the Vertical Gallery
    component from Insert option, as shown in
    Figure 9-27.

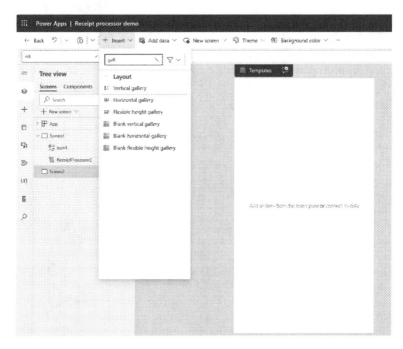

Figure 9-27. *Creating a new screen and adding a vertical gallery*

6. When you select Vertical Gallery, the Formula
   bar will show that the Items option is bound to
   CustomGallerySample, as shown in Figure 9-28.

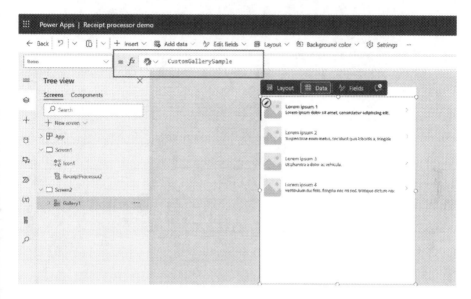

Figure 9-28. *Vertical gallery items data source*

7. In the Formula bar (see Figure 9-29), remove
   CustomGallerySample and include the receipt
   component name then a period (.). Then include
   PurchasedItems:

   ReceiptProcessor2.PurchasedItems

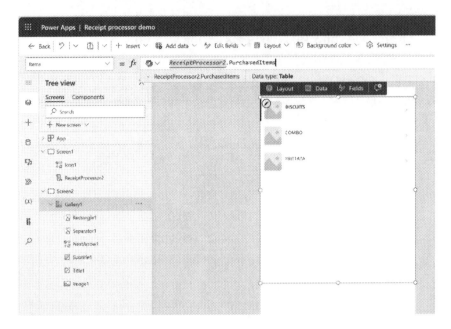

Figure 9-29. *Changing the items list source to the Receipt Processor data*

In the vertical gallery, you will see the item names sourced from the receipt. In my case, the Receipt Processor name is ReceiptProcessor2. Be sure to check the name of the component before proceeding.

8. Change the gallery list. I removed everything except the separator, as shown in Figure 9-30.

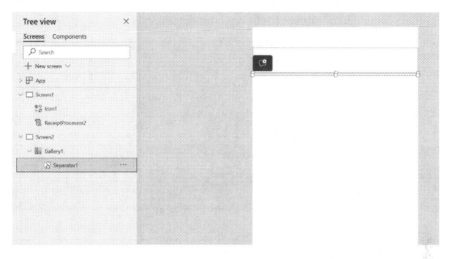

Figure 9-30. *Removing all the components from the vertical gallery except separator*

9. Add some labels using the formula code listed in Table 9-8.

Table 9-8. *Labels Created to Fetch Information from the Receipt Processor*

Label Name	Formula Code
NameLabel	"Item name"
ItemName	ThisItem.Name
QuantityLabel	"Item Quantity"
ItemQuantity	ThisItem.Quantity
PriceLabel	"Item Price"
ItemPrice	ThisItem.TotalPrice

Figure 9-31 shows the labels that I created for fetching information.

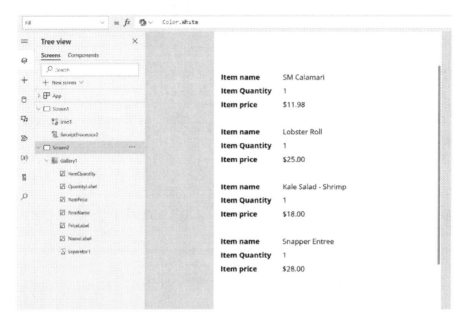

Figure 9-31. *Preview after creating the labels and changing the formula code*

10. Now add the merchant's name, address, date and time, and the total bill to the app. I added the labels listed in Table 9-9.

Table 9-9. *Labels Created to Fetch Merchant Information, Address, Date and Time, and Total Bill*

Label Name	Formula Code
MerchantNameLabel	"Merchant Name"
MerchantName	ReceiptProcessor2.MerchantName
MerchantAddressLabel	"Merchant Address"
MerchantAddress	ReceiptProcessor2.MerchantAddress
TotalBillLabel	"Total Bill"
TotalBill	ReceiptProcessor2.Total
PurchasedDateLabel	"Purchased Date"
PurchasedDate	ReceiptProcessor2.TransactionDate
PurchasedTimeLabel	"Purchased Time"
PurchasedTime	ReceiptProcessor2.TransactionTime

Figure 9-32 shows all the information that I tried to fetch from the receipt, including the merchant's name, address, date and time, list of items, quantity, price by item, and total price.

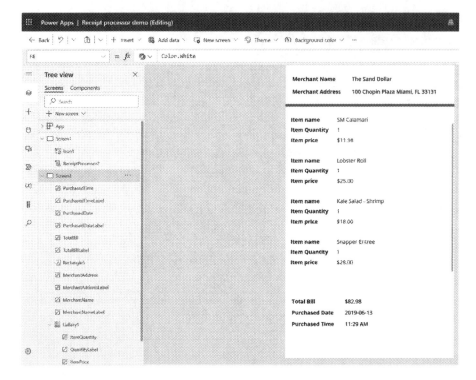

Figure 9-32. *All the important information from the Receipt Processor component*

11. Go to the main page and connect the next arrow button with this details screen using Copilot. In Copilot, write the following prompt (also shown in Figure 9-33):

```
Connect icon1 with screen2
```

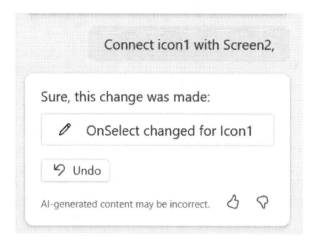

Figure 9-33. *The Copilot prompt to connect the next arrow to the next page*

> My next arrow name is `icon1` and the details screen page is called `Screen2`. Do not forgot to verify the name of the components before proceeding.

12. At this stage, run the app from the main screen, upload another receipt, and click the Next button. See Figures 9-34 and 9-35.

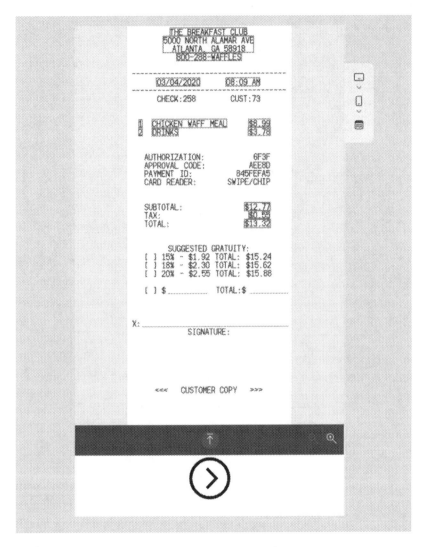

Figure 9-34. *Uploading the new receipt to the Receipt Processor component*

After clicking the next arrow, the next page will appear with all the details, as shown in Figure 9-35.

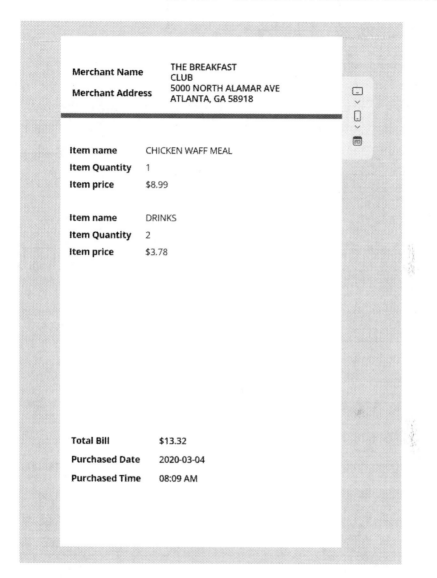

Figure 9-35. *Information from the newly uploaded receipt*

In this section, you learned that the Receipt Processor component can process any kind of receipt.

Text Recognizer Component

The Text Recognizer component in Power Apps AI Builder uses advanced AI to seamlessly extract and interpret text from images and documents. It supports various use cases, including digitizing handwritten notes, processing printed receipts, and automating data entry from forms. By integrating this component into your applications, you can enhance efficiency and accuracy in handling text-based information.

Demo

In this section, you explore the Text Recognizer component with a hands-on demo. To start using the Text Recognizer component, follow these steps:

1. Open your project and create a new screen. Or create a new project in `https://make.powerapps.com`.

2. From a new screen, add Text Recognizer from the Insert option, as shown in Figure 9-36.

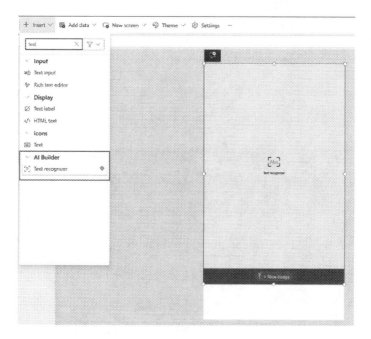

Figure 9-36. *Adding Text Recognizer using the Insert option*

3. Run the app and upload an image of your choice.
   See Figure 9-37.

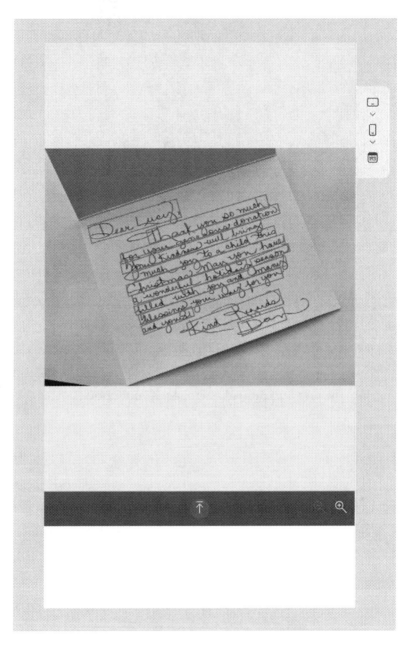

Figure 9-37. *Uploading a handwritten letter in Text Recognizer as a sample image*

4. Add a new next arrow icon next to the Text
   Recognizer control. Then create a new screen and
   connect the icon to the new screen, as shown in
   Figure 9-38.

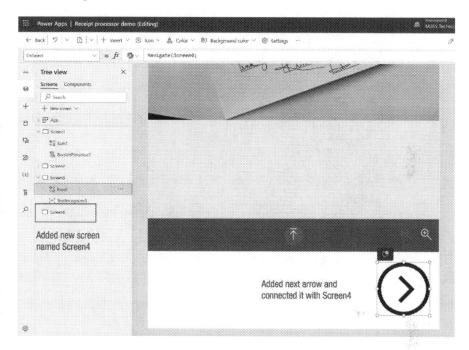

Figure 9-38. Adding a new screen and a next arrow icon

5. To the new screen (called Screen4 in this example),
    add a new text label. In the properties of the text
    label, change the font size from 21 to 15, and change
    the Overflow option from Hidden to Scroll. See
    Figure 9-39.

Figure 9-39. *Changing the text label font size and Overflow option*

6. Enlarge the text label by selecting it and adjusting the size, ensuring that the text retrieved from Text Recognizer fits perfectly, as shown in Figure 9-40.

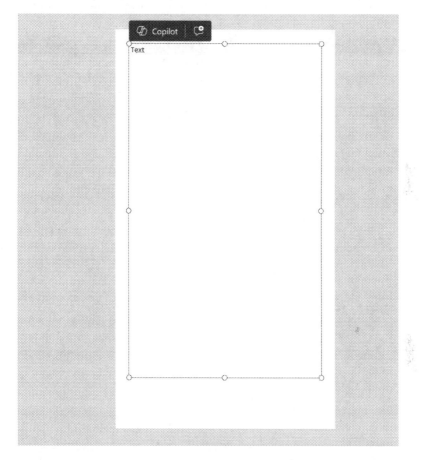

Figure 9-40. *Selecting the text label and resizing it*

7. Now, in the Formula bar, type the following code by selecting the text label (also shown in Figure 9-41):

```
Concat(TextRecognizer3.Results, Text & Char(13))
```

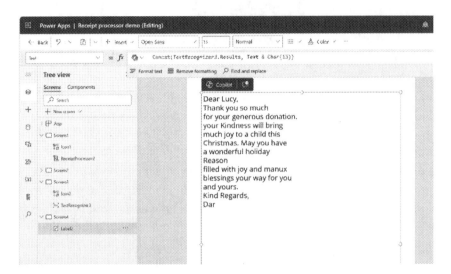

Figure 9-41. *Connect the Text Recognizer result to the text label*

8. Run the app from the screen where you added the Text Recognizer component. Upload a new image to verify the process, as shown in Figure 9-42.

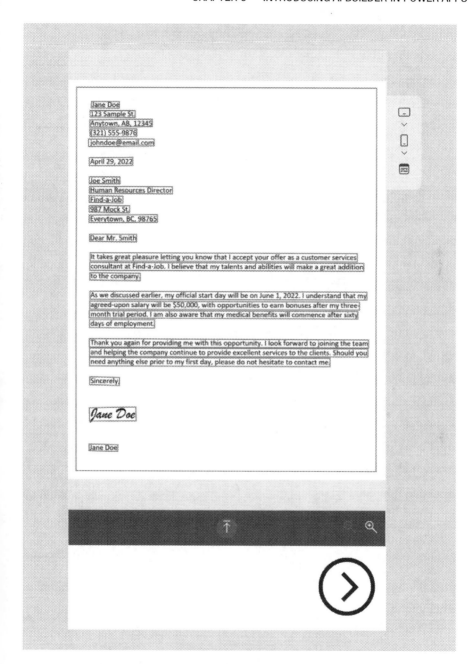

Figure 9-42. *Adding a new image to test the Text Recognizer*

9. Click the next arrow to view the text recognized by the Text Recognizer, as shown in Figure 9-43.

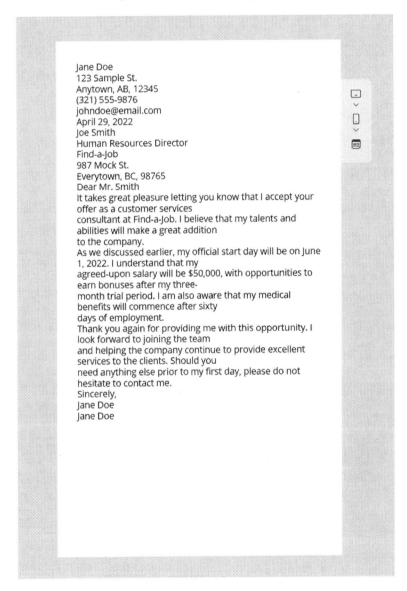

Figure 9-43. *Text recognized by the Text Recognizer component*

Pre-Built AI Builder Models

This section explains some important pre-built AI Builder components that are not available as components in Canvas apps. You have two options to utilize these components:

1. **Create the app from AI models:** Go to Power Apps Studio ➤ AI Hub ➤ AI Models (as shown in Figure 9-44) and choose the model, then create an app. This method automatically generates a default app with the necessary formulas, eliminating the need for manual coding.

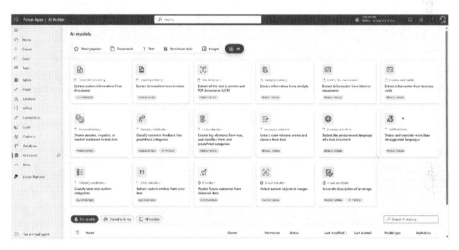

Figure 9-44. *Pre-built and custom AI models in Power Apps*

2. **Add the AI model to a new or existing app:** Create a new app or select an existing one, then add the AI model via Add Data ➤ AI Models (as shown in Figure 9-45). In this case, you need to manually write the formula code for each label.

491

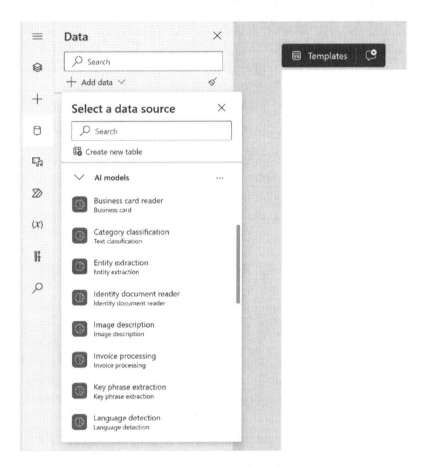

Figure 9-45. *AI models that can be used as data sources*

The next section discusses some important AI models with demos.

The Invoice Processing Pre-Built Model

The Invoice Processing AI model in Power Apps uses advanced machine learning to automate the extraction and processing of invoice data. This model can accurately capture key information such as invoice numbers, dates, totals, and line items from various invoice formats, streamlining accounts payable workflows. By integrating this AI model into your

Power Apps, you can reduce manual data entry, minimize errors, and significantly increase processing efficiency. This pre-built solution is ideal for businesses looking to enhance their financial operations with minimal development effort.

Demo

This demos shows you two ways to use the Invoice Processing model. You can access and use the model directly from the AI model page, or you can manually add the Invoice Processing model from the app page as a data source.

Create the Invoice Processing app from the AI model page

To use the Invoice Processing model, follow these steps:

1. Visit https://make.powerapps.com. Click the AI Hub from the left sidebar, and then select AI Models, as shown in Figure 9-46.

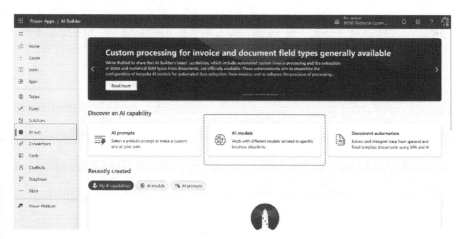

Figure 9-46. *Choosing AI models from the AI Hub*

2. Select Documents or All from the upper filter, and
    choose Extract Information from Invoices, as shown
    in Figure 9-47.

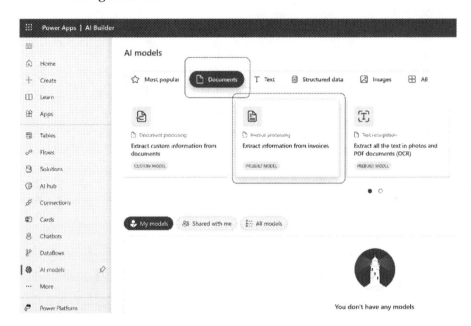

Figure 9-47. *Choose the Extract Information from Invoices pre-built*
model from the AI Models list

3. After choosing the Extract Information from
    Invoices model, you will see the page in Figure 9-48.

Figure 9-48. *Inside of Extract Information from Invoice model*

Figure 9-48 shows how the AI model can extract information from an invoice, including details such as invoice numbers, dates, totals, and line items.

4. There are two options here: one is to use a pre-built model, and the other is to create a custom model. If you choose to use the pre-built model, you can immediately start utilizing its capabilities without additional setup. However, if you choose to create a custom model, you will need to design the model to fit your specific needs and train it with relevant data to ensure accuracy and effectiveness. This process involves defining the data structure, labeling the data, and running training iterations to optimize the model's performance.

For this demo, I chose Use Prebuilt Model and selected Use in an App, as shown in Figure 9-49.

495

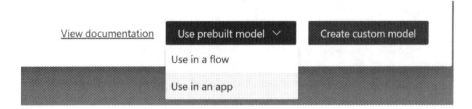

Figure 9-49. *Creating an app from an AI model*

5. When you click Use in an App, you will be redirected
    to another page where you can see a default app
    created by Power Apps, as shown in Figure 9-50.

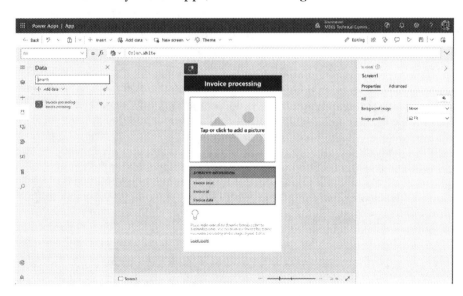

Figure 9-50. *Invoice Processing app created by Power Apps*

6. Run the app and upload an invoice to see the processed result, as shown in Figure 9-51.

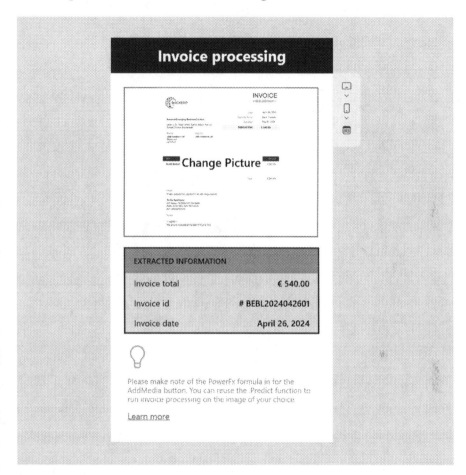

Figure 9-51. *Invoice Processing app test that was created by Power Apps*

As you can see, the Invoice Processing model can read the information from the invoice. When you create an app from AI model, it will only create a phone format app, which can extract limited information. The next section explains how to create an Invoice Processing app manually in Tablet format.

Create an Invoice Processing app manually

To create an Invoice Processing app manually, follow these steps:

1. Create an app in Power Apps Studio (https://make. powerapps.com) in Tablet format.

2. Add the Invoice Processing model by choosing the Data ➤ Add Data ➤ AI Models option, as shown in Figure 9-52.

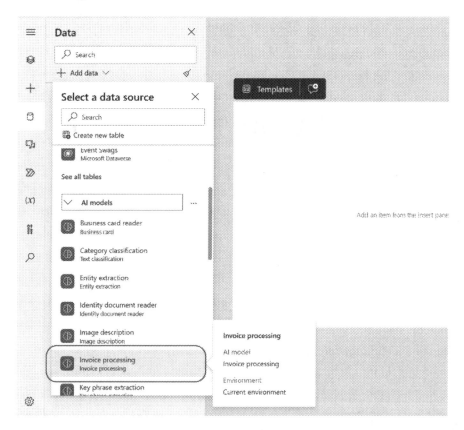

Figure 9-52. *Selecting Invoice Processing from the AI models*

3. After adding the Invoice Processing AI model,
    choose the Add Picture component under the
    Media category from the Insert option, as shown in
    Figure 9-53.

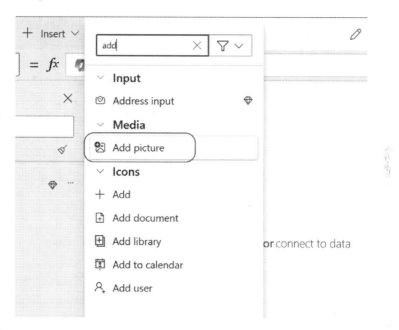

Figure 9-53. *Selecting the Add Picture component from the
Insert option*

4. If you extend the tree view, you can see inside
    the Add Picture component. There are two more
    components there—AddMediaButton1 and
    UploadedImage1—as shown in Figure 9-54.

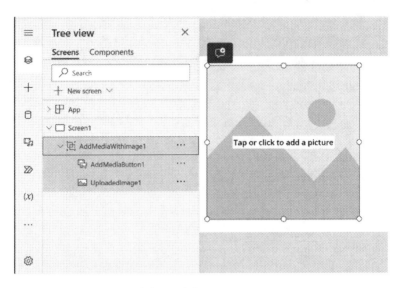

Figure 9-54. *Tree view of the Add Picture component,*

5. Select AddMediaButton1 from the tree view (see
   Figure 9-55) and add the following code to the
   Formula bar by selecting the OnChange property:

```
Set(PredictionResult, 'Invoice processing'.
Predict(UploadedImage1.Image));
IfError(PredictionResult, Notify(FirstError.
Message,NotificationType.Error))
```

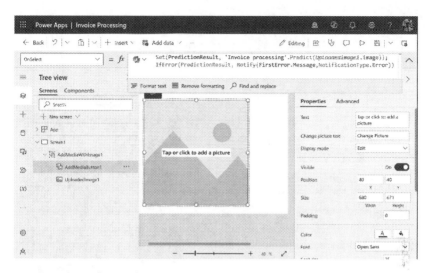

Figure 9-55. *Adding code to the OnSelect property from the Formula bar*

6. Run the app and upload the invoice, as shown in Figure 9-56.

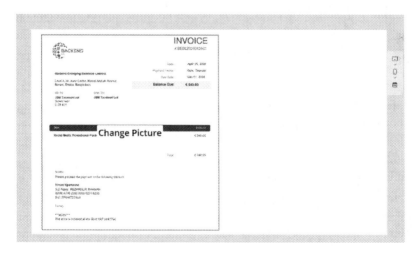

Figure 9-56. *Uploading an invoice to the app*

7. Create some labels to get the extracted information from the invoice, as I showed you in the previous demo. See Figure 9-57.

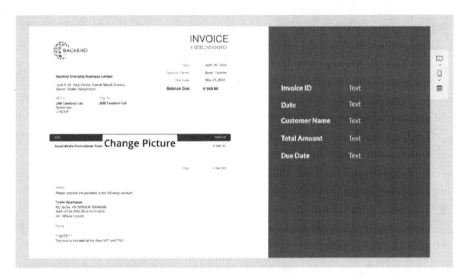

Figure 9-57. *New labels have been created to get the extracted information from the Invoice Processing AI model*

8. After creating the labels, you need to assign a formula to each label. Let's start with Invoice ID.

   Select the right label of Invoice ID and add the following code to the Formula bar (also shown in Figure 9-58):

   ```
   If(!IsBlank(PredictionResult.Fields.InvoiceId),
   PredictionResult.Fields.InvoiceId.Value.Text, "")
   ```

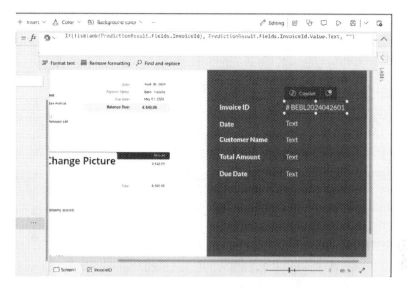

Figure 9-58. *Changing the Invoice ID with prediction result of Invoice Processing AI model*

The invoice ID has been changed. Do this for every label that you want to show. Table 9-10 shows the code used to get the information from the Invoice Processing AI model.

Table 9-10. *Formula Code of All Labels That Save Extracted Information*

Property Name	Formula Code
Date	If(!IsBlank(PredictionResult.Fields.InvoiceDate), PredictionResult.Fields.InvoiceDate.Value.Text, "")
Customer Name	If(!IsBlank(PredictionResult.Fields.CustomerName), PredictionResult.Fields.CustomerName.Value.Text, "")

(continued)

503

Table 9-10. (*continued*)

Property Name	Formula Code
Total Amount	If(!IsBlank(PredictionResult.Fields.InvoiceTotal), PredictionResult.Fields.InvoiceTotal.Value.Text, "")
Due Date	If(!IsBlank(PredictionResult.Fields.DueDate), PredictionResult.Fields.DueDate.Value.Text, "")

9. Run the app and upload a new invoice to test the Invoice Processing model. See Figure 9-59.

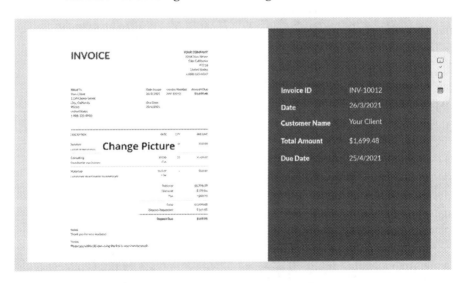

Figure 9-59. *Uploading a new invoice to test the AI model*

As you can see, the Invoice Processing model read the invoice successfully, extracted the information from the invoice, and placed it in the text labels.

Pre-Built Model Image Description

The pre-built model for generating descriptions of images in Power Apps utilizes advanced AI to analyze and interpret visual content, automatically producing accurate and meaningful descriptions. This model can identify and describe various elements within an image, such as objects, scenes, and activities, making it a valuable tool for applications requiring image recognition and interpretation. By integrating this model into Power Apps, users can enhance accessibility, streamline content management, and improve user engagement without needing extensive coding or data science expertise. This pre-built solution simplifies the integration of sophisticated image analysis into custom applications. If you navigate to Power Apps Studio ➤ AI Hub ➤ AI Models ➤ Images ➤ Generate Description of an Image, you will find a built-in demo that allows you to check any image you want, as shown in Figure 9-60.

Figure 9-60. *The Generate Description of an Image model provides a description of any image*

The next section explains how to create an app manually in Power Apps, not using the pre-built model.

Demo

To start with the demo, follow these instructions:

1. Create an app in Power Apps Studio or open your existing app with a new screen. For my demo, I created a new app in the Tablet format.

2. Choose Data ➤ Add Data ➤ AI Models ➤ Image Description, as shown in Figure 9-61.

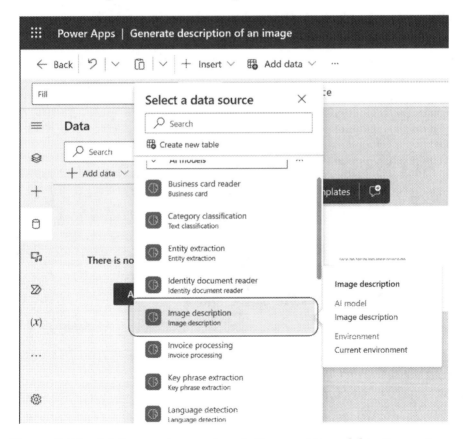

Figure 9-61. *Adding an image description an AI model in Power Apps*

506

3. Add the Add Picture component from the Insert
    option, as shown in Figure 9-62.

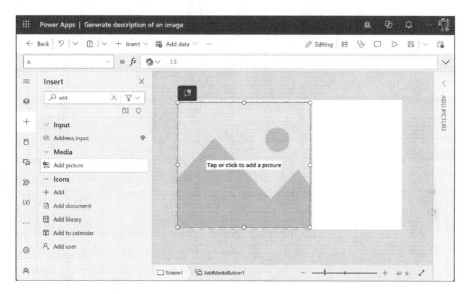

Figure 9-62. *Adding the Add Picture component from the Insert option*

4. From the tree view, select AddMediaButton1 and add
    the following code to the OnSelect properties from
    the Formula bar (also shown in Figure 9-63):

```
Set(PredictionResult, 'Image description'.Predict
(UploadedImage1.Image));
IfError(PredictionResult, Notify(FirstError.Message,
NotificationType.Error))
```

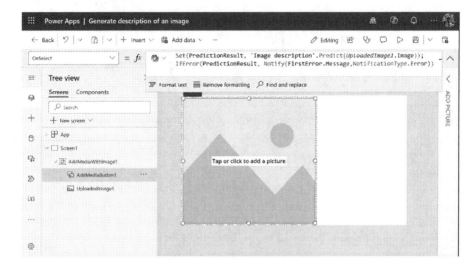

Figure 9-63. *Adding the formula code to the OnSelect properties*

5. Add the labels as before to save the extracted information. See Figure 9-64. Check out the previous demo to see how to add the labels.

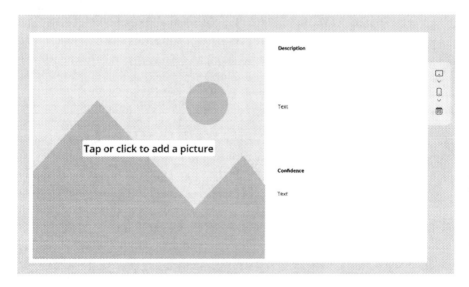

Figure 9-64. *Adding the text labels to show the extracted information*

6. Add the code in Table 9-11 to the text properties of the text labels.

Table 9-11. *Formula Code to Get the Image Description and Confidence Level*

Property Name	Formula Code
Description	`If(IsBlank(PredictionResult), "", PredictionResult.Description)`
Confidence	`If(IsBlank(PredictionResult), "", $"{Int(PredictionResult. DescriptionConfidence * 100)} % ")`

7. After adding the code, run the app and upload an image. You will see the description and confidence level, as shown in Figure 9-65.

Figure 9-65. *Uploading an image to test the Image Description AI model*

To use the Image Description AI model, keep in mind the following requirements: accepted image formats are .JPG, .JPEG, .PNG, and .BMP; the maximum image size is 4MB; and the image dimensions must be greater than 50x50 pixels.

Pre-Built Model Sentiment Analysis

The pre-built model for Sentiment Analysis in Power Apps uses advanced natural language processing to evaluate and classify the sentiment of text data. This model can determine whether the expressed sentiment is positive, negative, or neutral, making it an invaluable tool for businesses seeking to understand customer feedback, social media interactions, and other text-based communications. By integrating this model into your applications, you can gain valuable insights into customer opinions and trends without needing extensive coding or data science expertise. This pre-built solution simplifies the process of incorporating sophisticated sentiment analysis into your custom apps. If you visit Power Apps Studio ➤ AI Hub ➤ AI Models ➤ Text ➤ Detect Positive, Negative, or Neutral Sentiment in Text Data, you will find a built-in demo that allows you to check any paragraph or dialogue for sentiment analysis, as shown in Figure 9-66.

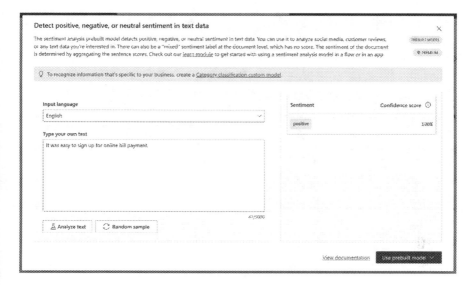

Figure 9-66. *Built-in demo for detecting text sentiment*

The next section explains how to use the AI model in your Power Apps.

Demo

To start with the demo, follow these instructions:

1. Open your Power Apps project or create a new Canvas apps from Power Apps Studio (`https://make.powerapps.com`).

2. Choose Data ➤ Add Data ➤ AI Models ➤ Sentiment Analysis to add the Sentiment Analysis AI model, as shown in Figure 9-67.

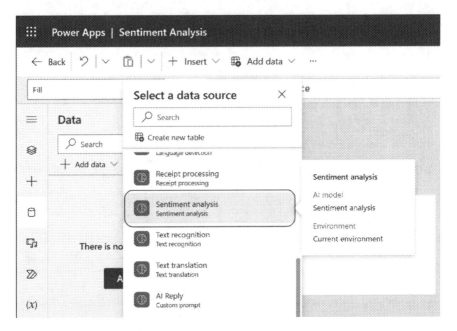

Figure 9-67. *Adding the Sentiment Analysis AI model to the Power Apps project*

3. This example added a text field to receive input from the keyboard, a button for submission, and four text labels, as shown in Figure 9-68. Two labels identify the purpose of the other labels, while the remaining two display information from the Sentiment Analysis model.

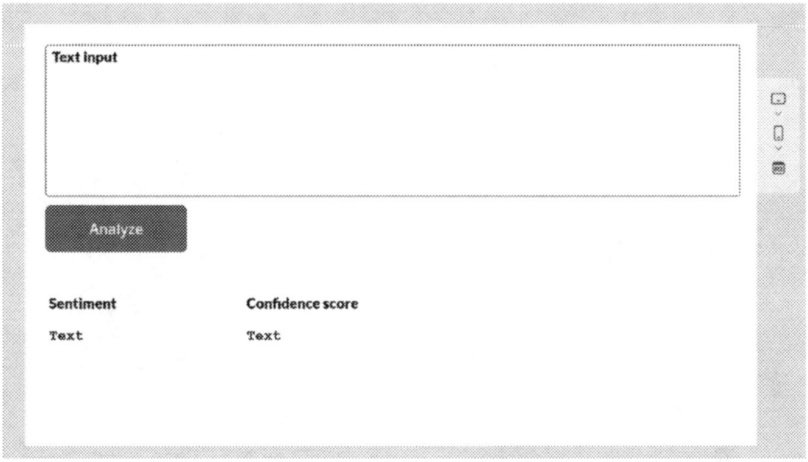

Figure 9-68. *Adding a text field, button, and text labels to communicate with the Sentiment Analysis model*

4. Do not add a formula to the text field, but instead start with the button. Call the button Analyze and add the following code to the Formula bar of the OnSelect property, as shown in Figure 9-69.

```
Set(TextInputSentiment, 'Sentiment analysis'.
Predict(TextInput1.Text).Document.TopSentiment);
IfError(TextInputSentiment, Notify(FirstError.
Message,NotificationType.Error))
```

Figure 9-69. *Adding the code to the OnSelect property of the button*

5. Add the code in Table 9-12 to the text properties of
    the Sentiment and Confidence Score labels.

Table 9-12. *Formula Code to Use in the Text Properties of the Sentiment and Confidence Score Text Labels*

Property Name	Formula Code
Sentiment	TextInputSentiment.Name
Confidence Score	TextInputSentiment.Confidence * 100 & " % "

6. Run the app. Write something in the textbox and
    click Analyze. One potential result is shown in
    Figure 9-70.

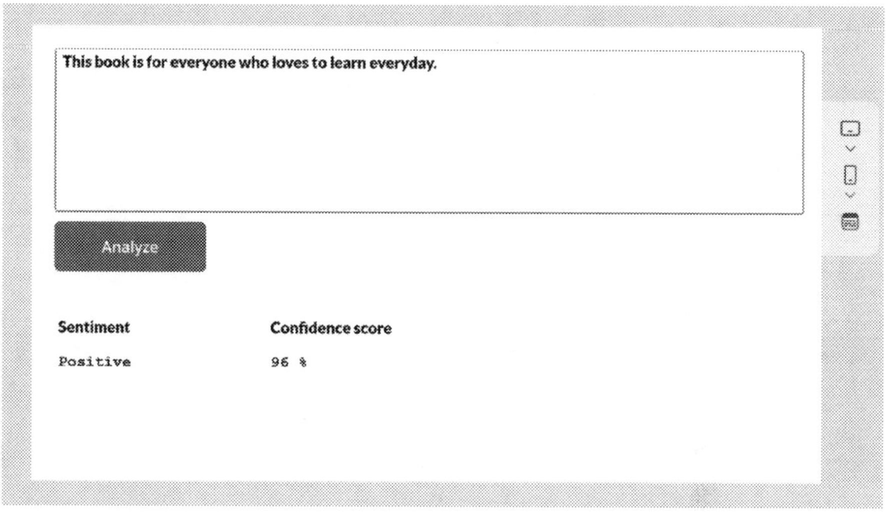

Figure 9-70. Preview of the Sentiment Analysis model

Summary

This chapter introduced AI Builder in Power Apps, guiding you through the process of integrating AI capabilities into your applications. You learned how to leverage pre-built and custom AI models to add intelligent features like text recognition, sentiment analysis, and invoice processing, all without needing extensive technical knowledge. This chapter aimed to empower you to create smarter, more proactive, and data-driven apps.

As you transition into Chapter 10, I take you further by exploring advanced techniques with AI Builder, including the creation of custom AI prompts and mastering conditional formatting. These skills will enable you to design even more dynamic and responsive applications, enhancing both functionality and the user experience.

Advanced Techniques with AI Builder and Conditional Formatting

In the last chapter, I showed you how to leverage AI Builder to integrate advanced AI capabilities into your Power Apps. Together, we explored various AI models, enabling you to enhance your applications with features like text recognition, sentiment analysis, and predictive analytics—all without needing extensive technical expertise.

This chapter guides you through more advanced techniques to further refine and expand your use of AI Builder. You'll learn how to create custom AI prompts tailored to your specific needs, and I also introduce you to the powerful tool of conditional formatting. These skills will help you make your apps not only intelligent but also highly responsive and visually engaging, ensuring they meet the complex needs of your users.

© Rezwanur Rahman 2024
R. Rahman, *Microsoft Copilot for Power Apps*, Inside Copilot,
https://doi.org/10.1007/979-8-8688-0512-7_10

Using AI Prompts

AI prompts in Power Apps represent a significant advancement in the way applications are developed. By harnessing the power of natural language processing, these prompts guide users through the process of building complex app functionalities without requiring deep technical knowledge. This innovation is particularly valuable to non-developers, as it opens the app development landscape to a broader audience, encouraging creativity and collaboration across different skill levels.

Overview of AI Prompts

AI prompts in Power Apps streamline app development by using natural language processing, making it easy for users to create complex formulas, automate tasks, and integrate AI features with minimal coding. This increases accessibility, allowing more people to participate in app creation and boosting overall productivity. The main benefits include faster development times and the creation of smarter, more efficient applications. This innovative approach empowers users to meet dynamic business needs effectively.

If you navigate to Power Apps Studio ➤ AI Hub ➤ AI Prompts, you will see the pre-built AI prompts and the option to create your own prompt, as shown in Figure 10-1.

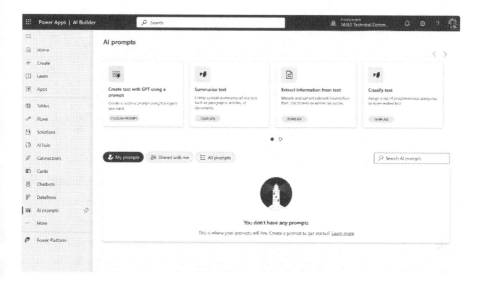

Figure 10-1. *AI prompt page in Power Apps Studio*

Utilizing Pre-built AI Prompts for Generative AI Capabilities

This section shows you how to use the pre-built AI prompts in Power Apps. If you navigate to Power Apps Studio ➤ AI Hub ➤ AI Prompts ➤ All Prompts, you will see the list of pre-built prompts that you can use in your Power Apps, as shown in Figure 10-2.

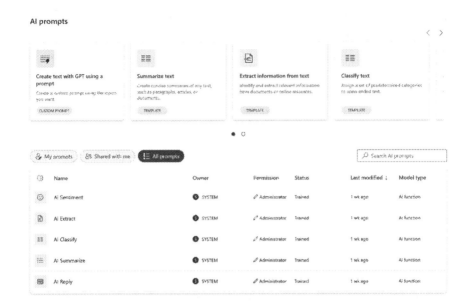

Figure 10-2. *List of pre-built AI prompt templates on the AI prompt page*

Like all AI models, AI prompts can be utilized in two ways. You can either select a prompt from the AI prompts list (as shown in Figure 10-2) and choose the Use in App option, or you can create the app first and then add the AI prompts by navigating to Data ➤ AI Models and configuring the app. For this demo, I demonstrate both methods and show one specific prompt: AI Summarize.

AI Prompt: AI Summarize

The AI Summarize prompt in Power Apps is a powerful tool designed to condense lengthy text into concise summaries, making it easier to digest large amounts of information quickly. By integrating this prompt, users can enhance their apps with automated summarization capabilities, improving efficiency and productivity. Whether summarizing reports, articles, or user-generated content, AI Summarize ensures that the key points are captured and presented clearly. This feature is particularly useful for applications that handle extensive data and require streamlined, accessible insights for decision-making.

Using AI Summarize from the AI Prompts Option

To use AI Summarize from the AI prompts option, follow these steps:

1. Open Power Apps Studio (`https://make.powerapps.com`) and navigate to AI Hub ➤ AI Prompts ➤ All Prompts, as shown in Figure 10-2.

2. Choose AI Summarize from the list. You will see AI Summarize pop up, as shown in Figure 10-3.

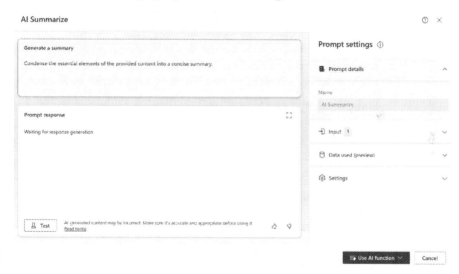

Figure 10-3. *AI Summarize*

3. In Figure 10-3, note that there is a panel on the right side. The full panel is shown in Figure 10-4.

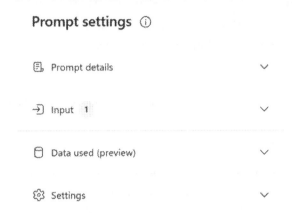

Figure 10-4. *Prompt Settings options*

From this area, you can change the settings of this prompt. The following options are available:

- **Prompt details:** You can see the name of the prompt, AI Summarize. The option to edit the name is disabled by default since this is a pre-built template, as shown in Figure 10-5.

Prompt details   ∧

Name

AI Summarize

Figure 10-5. *Prompt details of AI Summarize prompt*

- **Input:** In the Input section, you can add text or a paragraph to test the prompt before incorporating the prompt into your app. See Figure 10-6.

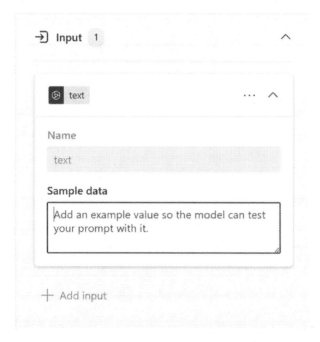

Figure 10-6. *Input settings of the AI Summarize prompt*

- **Data used (preview):** In this section, you can add your own data source, allowing AI Summarize to provide answers tailored to your business needs. See Figure 10-7.

Figure 10-7. *Data used (preview) option for the AI Summarize prompt*

Settings: In the Settings section, you can change the GPT model used to generate responses. By default, it is set to GPT-3.5, but you can switch it to GPT-4 (preview). Additionally, you can adjust the temperature of AI Summarize. The *temperature* controls the creativity of the responses; a lower temperature yields more predictable results, while a higher temperature produces more diverse and creative responses. See Figure 10-8.

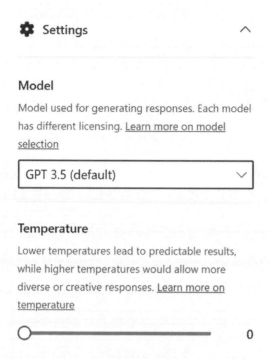

Figure 10-8. Settings option of the AI Summarize prompt

4. Add some text to the Input section and click the Test
    button, as shown in Figure 10-9.

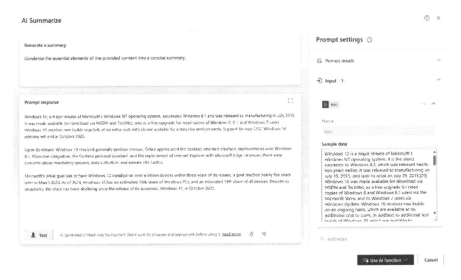

Figure 10-9. *Testing articles in AI Summarize*

5.   You can see that AI Summarize works perfectly. Now
     click the Use AI Function button and choose Use in
     App, as shown in Figure 10-10.

Figure 10-10. *Creating an app with the AI Summarize prompt*

6.   You will be redirected to another tab, where a
     new mobile app will be created, as shown in
     Figure 10-11.

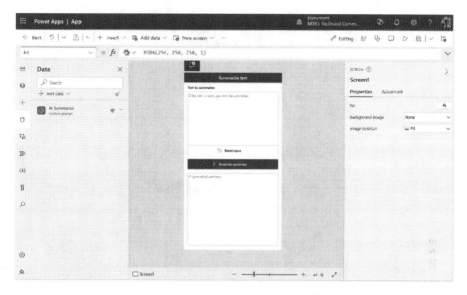

Figure 10-11. *The AI Summarize app created by Power Apps*

7. Run the app, add some text to the Summarize
    option, and click Generate Summary to see the
    summary of the text, as shown in Figure 10-12.

Figure 10-12. *AI Summarize prompt check in the newly created Power Apps*

Use AI Summarize in a New or Existing App

To use AI Summarize in an existing app or a newly created Power App, follow these steps:

1. Create a new app in Power Apps Studio (`https://make.powerapps.com`) or open an existing app.

2. From the left sidebar, navigate to Data ➤ Add Data, then add AI Summarize under the AI model, as shown in Figure 10-13.

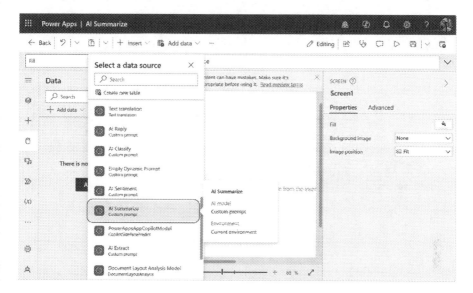

Figure 10-13. *Adding AI Summarize in Power Apps*

3. On the screen, add two text fields (one for inputting
    text and the other for displaying the generated
    response), two buttons (one for triggering the
    generate action and another for resetting the text
    fields), and two text labels to identify the text fields,
    as shown in Figure 10-14.

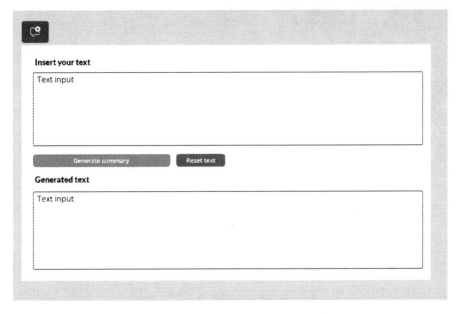

Figure 10-14. *Designing an app to generate a summary with AI Summarize*

4. Select the Reset Text button, and in the formula bar, change the code of the OnSelect property to the following (also shown in Figure 10-15):

    Reset(TextInput1)

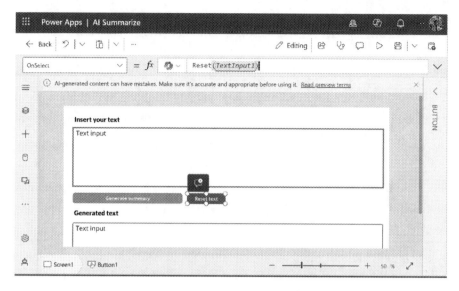

Figure 10-15. *Configuring the Reset Text button*

5. Select the Generate Summary button, and in the
    formula bar, add the following code for the OnSelect
    property. See Figure 10-16.

```
Set(
    SummarizeResult,
    'AI Summarize'.Predict(TextInput1.Text)
)
```

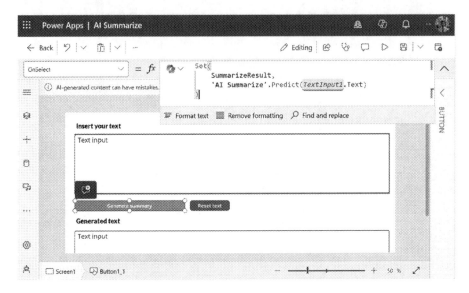

Figure 10-16. *Configuring the Generate Summary button*

6. Next, choose the Text Field below the Generate
    Text label, where the response will appear. In the
    formula bar, choose the Default property and add
    the following code; also shown in Figure 10-17.

```
SummarizeResult.Text
```

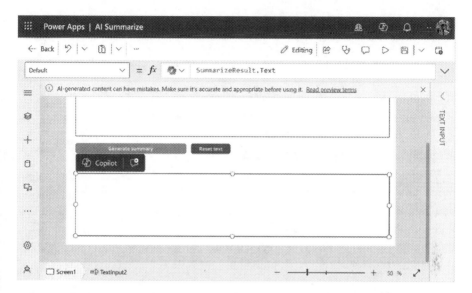

Figure 10-17. *Configuring a text field to get a response from AI Summarize*

7.   Run the app and test AI Summarize. Figure 10-18
shows that AI Summarize is working perfectly.

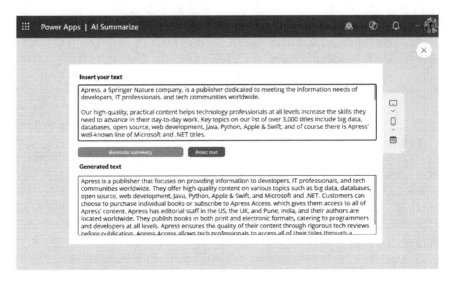

Figure 10-18. *Checking AI Summarize by creating the app manually.*

You can create apps using other pre-built AI prompts in this same manner.

Using Custom AI Prompts

Custom AI prompts for Power Apps let you add smart features to your apps, making them better at handling tasks and talking to users. You can set up these prompts to do specific jobs, such as sorting data or automating repetitive tasks, all in a way that feels natural and easy for users. This makes your apps not only smarter but also more helpful and efficient for everyone using them. It is a great way to make your apps do more, without making them overly complicated.

If you navigate to Power Apps Studio ➤ AI Hub ➤ AI Prompts, you will see the custom prompt option named Create Text with GPT Using a Prompt, as shown in Figure 10-19. This feature allows you to create custom prompts within the Power Platform.

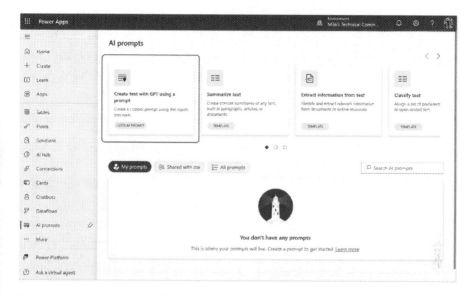

Figure 10-19. *Custom prompt option on the AI prompt page*

This section explains how to create a custom prompt and manually integrate it into Power Apps.

Creating a Custom Prompt

To create a custom prompt, follow these instructions:

1. Open the Power Apps Studio (https://make. powerapps.com), navigate to AI Hub ➤ AI Prompts, and select Create Text with GPT Using a Prompt.

2. After selecting the Create Text with GPT Using a Prompt option, you will see the screen in Figure 10-20.

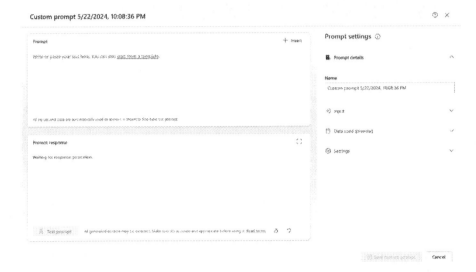

Figure 10-20. *Initial screen of a custom prompt*

Just like pre-built AI prompts, you can find the same options in the Prompt settings on the left sidebar. However, with custom AI prompts, you have the flexibility to adjust and customize the settings as much as you need.

3. Create a custom prompt. You can write the prompt based on your own preferences or specific business needs. Additionally, you can find some AI prompt examples on the Microsoft Adoption website by visiting https://aka.ms/power-prompts.

4. After visiting the provided URL, you will see many samples for creating AI prompts, as shown in Figure 10-21.

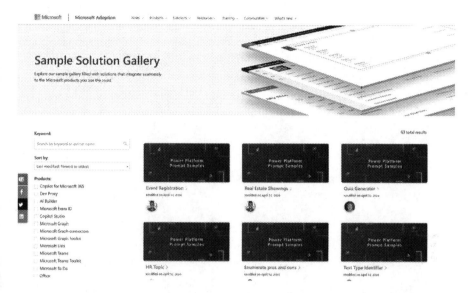

Figure 10-21. *AI prompt samples on the Microsoft Adoption website*

5. For this demo, I wrote the following prompt:

Act as a programmer. You should know the object-oriented programming languages, like Python, JavaScript, SQL, PSQL, R, C, C++. You should know how to solve the complex programming problem, suggest the code by reading natural language. You should use your Data Structure, Algorithm, Database, Artificial Intelligence, Machine Learning knowledge. Try to avoid too many technical details but use them when necessary. I want you to reply with the solution, not write any explanations. My question is

6. Copy this prompt and add it to the Prompt section, as shown in Figure 10-22.

Figure 10-22. *Adding the prompt to the Prompt section of the Custom Prompt modal box*

7. Let's change the name of this custom prompt. Go to the Prompt Details option on the right sidebar and edit the default name, as shown in Figure 10-23.

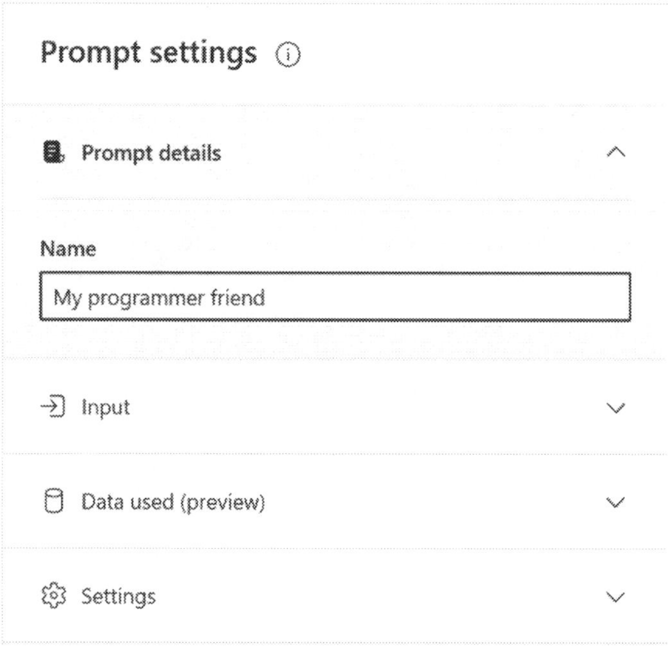

Prompt settings ⓘ

🗐 Prompt details   ⌃

Name

My programmer friend

→] Input   ⌄

🗍 Data used (preview)   ⌄

⚙ Settings   ⌄

Figure 10-23. *Changing the name of the custom prompt*

8. Create a dynamic value. A dynamic value when
    creating a custom prompt refers to a variable or
    placeholder that can change based on user input
    or other data sources. It allows the prompt to be
    flexible and adapt to different scenarios, making
    the AI's response more relevant and personalized.
    For example, in a customer service app, a dynamic
    value could be the customer's name or the specific
    issue they are facing, which the AI uses to provide a
    tailored response.

    To create a dynamic value, click the Input option
    and select Add Input, as shown in Figure 10-24.

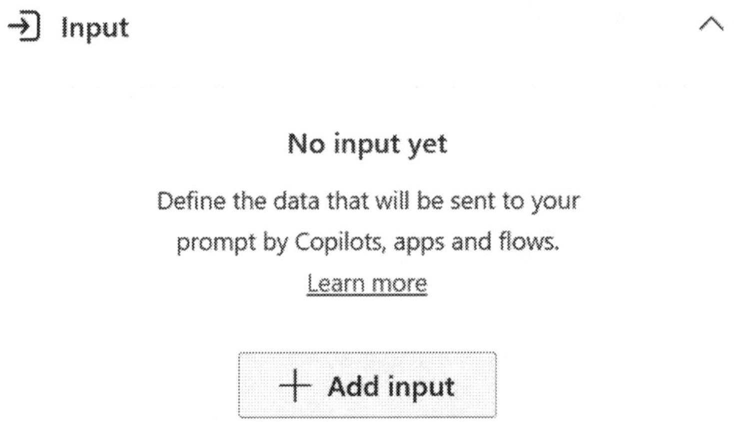

→] Input   ⌃

No input yet

Define the data that will be sent to your
prompt by Copilots, apps and flows.
Learn more

+ Add input

Figure 10-24. Creating a dynamic value by adding an Input option

9. After clicking the Add Input option, Copilot will ask
    you to provide a name for your dynamic value, as
    shown in Figure 10-25.

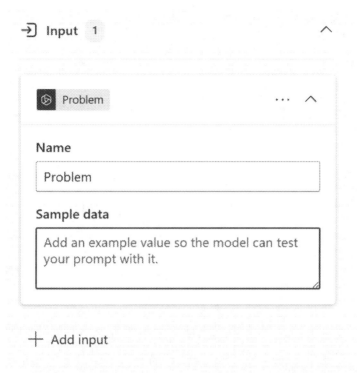

Figure 10-25. *Creating a dynamic value from the Input option*

10.   I named mine `Problem`. Return to the prompt, click
      Insert, select the value, and insert it into the prompt.
      Ensure you add it after the phrase My question is, or
      in any other location you want to trigger, as shown
      in Figures 10-26 and 10-27.

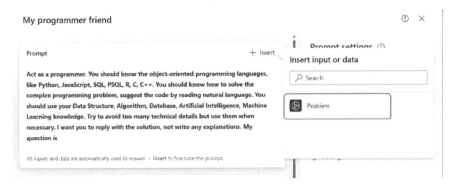

Figure 10-26. *Choosing the dynamic value to add a prompt*

My programmer friend

Prompt ＋ Insert

Act as a programmer. You should know the object-oriented programming languages, like Python, JavaScript, SQL, PSQL, R, C, C++. You should know how to solve the complex programming problem, suggest the code by reading natural language. You should use your Data Structure, Algorithm, Database, Artificial Intelligence, Machine Learning knowledge. Try to avoid too many technical details but use them when necessary. I want you to reply with the solution, not write any explanations. My question is ⬡ Problem ✕

All inputs and data are automatically used to answer. + Insert to fine tune the prompt.

Figure 10-27. *The dynamic value is added to the prompt*

You can add multiple dynamic inputs if you want, using this same process. Go to the Input option, create a new input, and add it to the prompt.

11. You can skip the Data Used option. If you have business data, you can use it as the source of data. I am skipping the Data Used option for this demo.

12. Next, from the Settings option, choose your preferable AI model. For this demo, I use GPT 4 (preview), as shown in Figure 10-28. By default, the model is set to GPT-3.5.

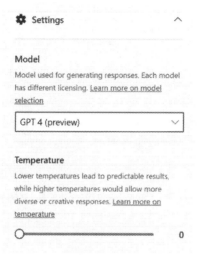

Figure 10-28. *Choosing a GPT model from the Settings option*

13. You need to test the prompt before saving or adding it to Power Apps.

    To test the prompt, go back to the Input option and provide a prompt like this one:

    ```
    Write a Python program to create a calculator.
    ```

    Figure 10-29 shows where to write this input.

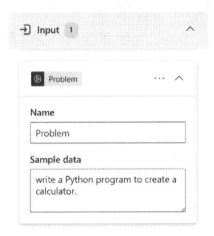

Figure 10-29. *Writing input as a dynamic value*

14. Click the Test Prompt button to see the result of this
prompt, as shown in Figure 10-30.

Figure 10-30. *Testing the custom prompt*

15. Figure 10-31 shows the result of this custom prompt.

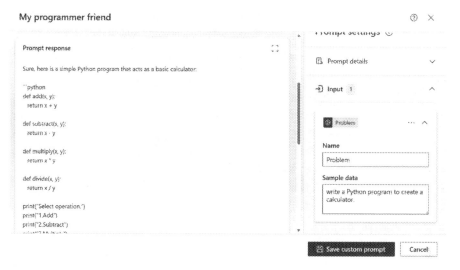

Figure 10-31. *Response from the prompt*

You can see that the prompt created the Python code to create a calculator.

16. Click the Save Custom Prompt button. You will get the confirmation shown in Figure 10-32.

Figure 10-32. *Confirmation of saving the custom prompt*

17. You can create an app from here or create a custom app and add the prompt, as I showed you in Figure 10-13.

Visit `https://aka.ms/promptguide` or scan the QR code in Figure 10-33 to learn more about how to create efficient and accurate GPT prompts.

Figure 10-33. *Prompt engineering guide*

Conditional Formatting

Conditional formatting is an essential feature of Microsoft Power Apps that enables you to modify the appearance of app components based on defined criteria. This functionality allows you to emphasize key data points, enhance the clarity of information, and create a more engaging and responsive user interface. By applying rules that adjust colors, text styles, and visibility, conditional formatting ensures that critical information stands out, improving the overall usability and visual appeal of your app. It empowers you to design applications that are not only functional but also visually intuitive and user-friendly.

Overview of Conditional Formatting with Copilot

Copilot in Microsoft Power Apps takes conditional formatting to the next level by offering AI-driven support and suggestions. Copilot helps you seamlessly set up conditional rules that modify the appearance of app controls in real-time, based on data changes or user interactions. This capability is invaluable for highlighting key information and enhancing user engagement. With Copilot, you can effortlessly implement complex formatting rules without extensive coding knowledge, making it an accessible tool for developers at all levels to improve the overall effectiveness and usability of their applications.

Using Copilot for Conditional Formatting

This section shows a quick demo of how to use Copilot for conditional formatting. In the next chapter, I show you conditional formatting with a practical demo.

To use conditional formatting with Copilot, follow these steps:

1. Open your Power Apps project or create a new project from Power Apps Studio.

2. Add a new text label. You will notice a Copilot button at the top of the label. Click this button to access the conditional formatting options, as shown in Figure 10-34.

Figure 10-34. *The Conditional Formatting option in the text label, powered by Copilot*

3. Once you click the Conditional Formatting option, a list of ideas or suggestions provided by Copilot will appear, as shown Figure 10-35.

547

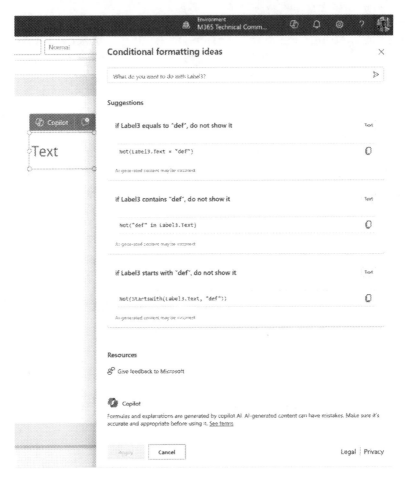

Figure 10-35. *Conditional formatting ideas and suggestions provided by Power Apps*

Let's look at this page in detail:

At the top of this block, you will see a textbox where you can write your idea in natural language, as shown in Figure 10-36. Copilot will then create the condition for you based on your input.

Conditional formatting ideas   ✕

What do you want to do with Label3?   ⊳

Figure 10-36. *Option to input ideas using natural language to get conditional formatting code from Copilot*

In the middle of the block, you will find some suggestions provided by Copilot, as shown in Figure 10-37. You can use these suggestions if they meet your criteria.

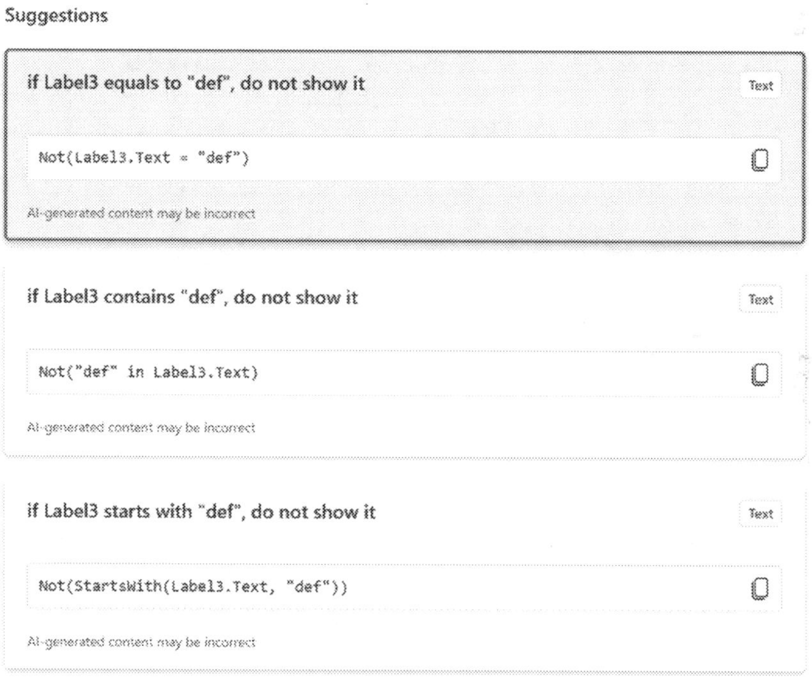

Suggestions

if Label3 equals to "def", do not show it   Text

```
Not(Label3.Text = "def")
```
                                                                               ⟐

Al-generated content may be incorrect

if Label3 contains "def", do not show it   Text

```
Not("def" in Label3.Text)
```
                                                                               ⟐

Al-generated content may be incorrect

if Label3 starts with "def", do not show it   Text

```
Not(StartsWith(Label3.Text, "def"))
```
                                                                               ⟐

Al-generated content may be incorrect

Figure 10-37. *Copilot suggestions to use for conditional formatting*

4. In the Idea option, enter your idea in natural language and press Enter. For this demo, I use the following idea (also shown in Figure 10-38):

    ```
    If the value is less than 1, set the text color to red;
    otherwise, use a different color (e.g., green)
    ```

Conditional formatting ideas   ✕

If the value is less than 1, set the text color to red; otherwise, use a different color (e.g., green)   ▷

Suggestions

if the numeric value of the text in Label3 < 1, show Red, otherwise show Green   Color

```
If(Value(Label3.Text) < 1, Color.Red, Color.Green)
```

AI-generated content may be incorrect

Resources

⅋ Give feedback to Microsoft

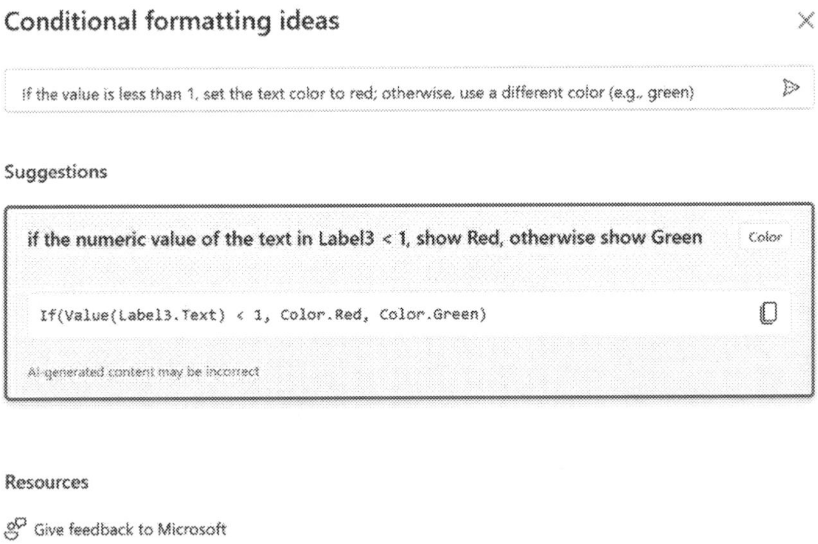

Figure 10-38. *Inputting an idea into Copilot to create conditional formatting*

5. Select the condition and apply it. Note that there may be more suggestions on the list, and you need to understand which one is best for you.

6. I add two text fields (TextInput1 and TextInput2) and a button to make a calculation, as shown in Figure 10-39. To the button's OnSelect property, I add the following code:

    UpdateContext({ Result: Value(TextInput1.Text) + Value(TextInput2.**Text) })**

Select the label where you added conditional formatting code, choose the Text property, and add the following code (see Figure 10-39):

```
Text(Result)
```

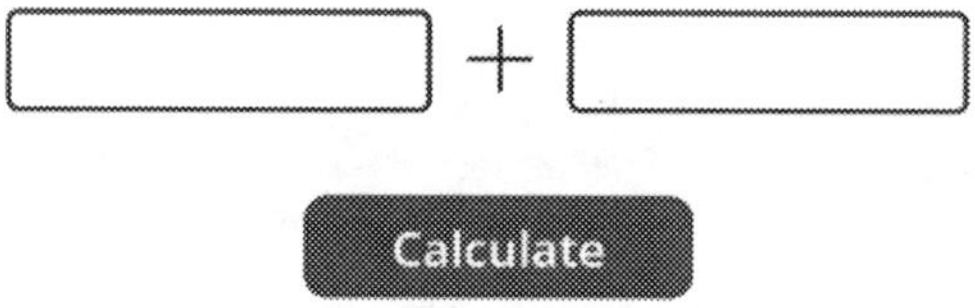

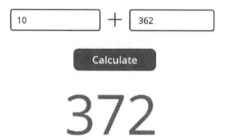

Figure 10-39. *Added two new text fields and a button to calculate numbers*

7. Run the app and calculate a result using two positive values, as shown in Figure 10-40.

Figure 10-40. *Testing conditional formatting with positive values*

8. Check the result when you use negative values, as shown in Figure 10-41.

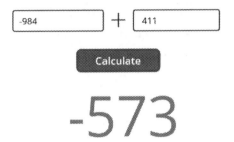

Figure 10-41. *Testing conditional formatting with negative values*

If the value is less than 1, the text color will be red; otherwise, it will be green. After testing the app, you can see that this is working perfectly.

Using Copilot in the Formula Bar

As previously discussed, Copilot in Power Apps has revolutionized conversation creation. Microsoft has recently enhanced this by integrating a Copilot button directly into the formula bar. This new feature provides increased efficiency, productivity, and a better understanding of its functionalities.

To utilize this feature, you must first enable it from the Power Apps settings. Open your project and go to Settings ➤ Upcoming Features, where you will find an option labeled Power Fx Formula Bar under the Preview tab. Activate this feature to use the Copilot in the formula bar, as shown in Figure 10-42.

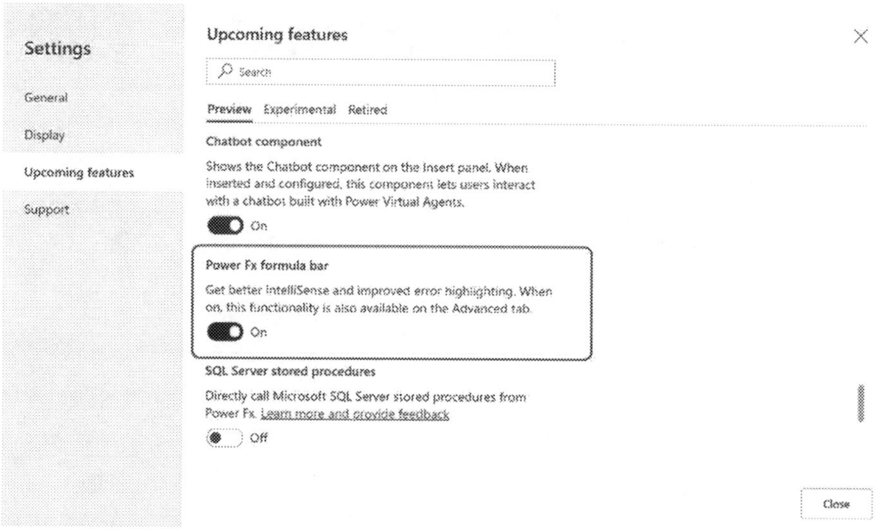

Figure 10-42. *Option to activate Copilot in the formula bar*

Overview of Copilot in the Formula Bar

Copilot now offers direct explanations of formula code within the formula bar. This update is particularly useful when you're dealing with complex formulas, picking up a project that someone else started, or working with projects generated from AI models or prompts. It's also an excellent resource for newcomers to the Power Platform, making it easier for them to understand and use the platform effectively.

If you open your project, you can see the Copilot button in the formula bar, as shown in Figure 10-43.

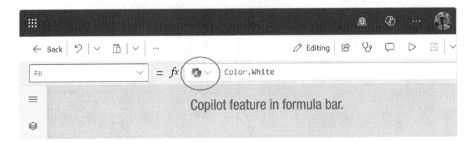

Figure 10-43. *The Copilot button in the formula bar*

Formula Explanation

When you select a component, the formula code appears in the formula bar. When you click the Copilot option, you will find a feature named Explain This Formula, as shown in Figure 10-44.

Figure 10-44. *Option to explain a formula in Copilot*

When you click the feature, you will see the explanation of the formula, as shown in Figure 10-45.

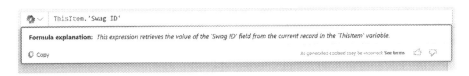

Figure 10-45. *Explanation of the formula provided by Copilot*

Summary

This chapter explained advanced techniques in Power Apps, focusing on AI Builder and conditional formatting. You learned how to create custom AI prompts and integrate them into your apps to enhance their intelligence and responsiveness. You also learned how to use conditional formatting to make your apps more visually engaging and user-friendly.

As you move into Chapter 11, I help you take these skills further by using Microsoft Copilot to transform the user interface (UI) of Power Apps. In the next chapter, I walk you through a complete project, demonstrating how to create a modern, dynamic UI with features like theme switching and collapsible menus, all powered by Copilot. Get ready to elevate your Power Apps design and functionality to the next level.

Revolutionizing Power Apps UI with Microsoft Copilot: A Complete Project

Building on the foundations of AI Builder and conditional formatting, you've already explored how to add intelligence and visual appeal to your Power Apps. Now, it's time to take a significant step forward in app design.

This chapter introduces you to the powerful capabilities of Microsoft Copilot for transforming the user interface of your Power Apps. You'll work through a complete project that showcases how to create a modern, dynamic UI, including features like theme switching and collapsible menus. This chapter will equip you with the skills to design apps that are not only functional but also visually striking and user-friendly. Let's dive in and elevate your Power Apps to new heights.

© Rezwanur Rahman 2024
R. Rahman, *Microsoft Copilot for Power Apps*, Inside Copilot,
https://doi.org/10.1007/979-8-8688-0512-7_11

Project Demo

This section designs a simple app with Copilot and Power Fx (Formula). Additionally, it demonstrates how to implement a feature that allows users to switch between light and dark themes using a toggle button. Follow along with the instructions to start the demo. Let's start!

Creating a Modern Menu

First, you will create a dynamic menu for the project. Then, you will learn how to expand the menu and add a theme switcher, allowing users to toggle between light and dark themes. To make the dynamic menu, follow these steps:

1. Create a new Canvas app in tablet format from `https://make.powerapps.com`, as shown in Figure 11-1.

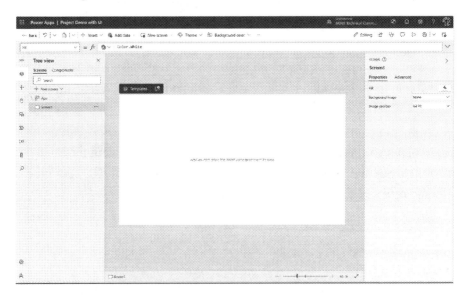

Figure 11-1. *Creating a new app for the project demo*

2. Next, create a collapsible side menu in the app.
   I showed you in the previous chapter how to create
   a basic menu in Power Apps. Now I will show you
   how to create an attractive, dynamic and responsive
   side menu with an advanced formula. To create the
   collapsible menu, create a new component named
   CollapsibleMenu from the Tree View option, as
   shown in Figure 11-2.

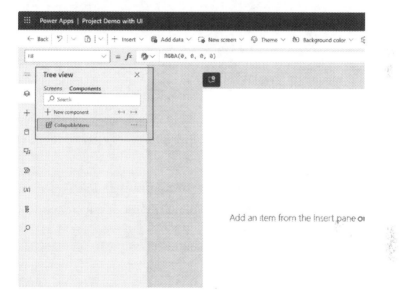

Figure 11-2. *Creating a new component for a collapsible side menu*

3. Adjust the size of the component to a width of
    70 and a height of 768, as shown in Figure 11-3.

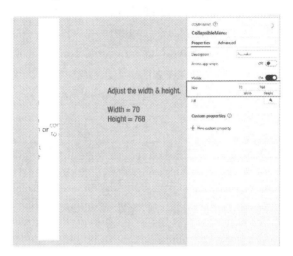

Figure 11-3. *Adjusting the width and height*

4. Add a vertical container to the component and
    change the settings to the following parameters:

X = 0
Y = 0
Width = 70
Height = 768
Border Radius = 0
Drop Shadow = None

I adjusted the vertical container to match the size of
the component, as shown in Figure 11-4.

Figure 11-4. *Adjusting the vertical container properties*

5. Create a new custom property and change the
    parameters as follows:

Display name = NavigationBackground
Name = NavigationBackground
Description = CustomNavigationBG
Property type = Input
Data Type = Color

561

You can see the property in the Custom Properties list shown in Figure 11-5.

Custom properties ⓘ

╀ New custom property

NavigationBackground   Color

Figure 11-5. *The custom property has been created*

6. Select the NavigationBackground custom property
    and change the background color from the Formula
    bar as the following code:

    RGBA(244, 244, 244, 1)

    Figure 11-6 shows where you need to change
    the code.

Figure 11-6. *Changing the RGBA color of the NavigationBackground custom property*

7. Select the vertical container that you added. Choose the Fill properties and add the following code:

CollapsibleMenu.NavigationBackground

Here, CollapsibleMenu is the name of the component and NavigationBackground is the custom property that I created before. Figure 11-7 shows this step.

Figure 11-7. *Fill in the vertical container with the NavigationBackground custom property*

8. Adjust the padding of the vertical container with the following parameters:

Top = 20
Bottom = 20
Left = 10
Right = 10

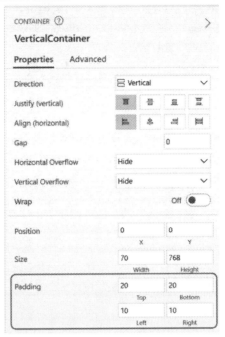

Figure 11-8. *Adjusting the padding of the vertical container*

9. Add an image to the container from the Insert menu
    and set the following parameters:

    Align in container = Justify
    Minimum width = 0
    Height = 30
    Name = LogoImage

    Figure 11-9 shows the changes to the image
    component properties.

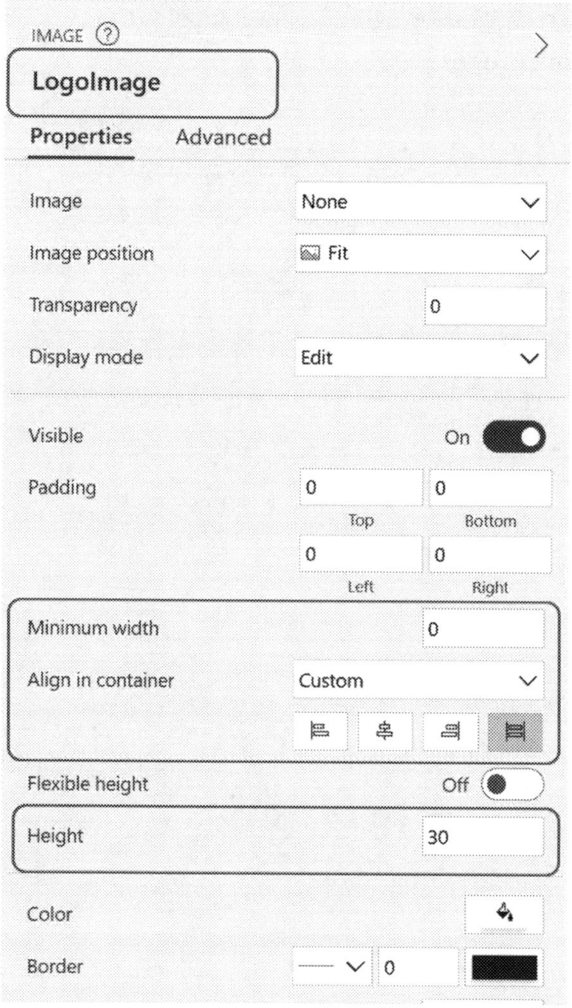

Figure 11-9. *Setting the image containers parameters*

10. Create another custom property with the following
parameters:

Name = Logo_compact
Data Type = Image

Figure 11-10 shows the parameters of the new
custom property.

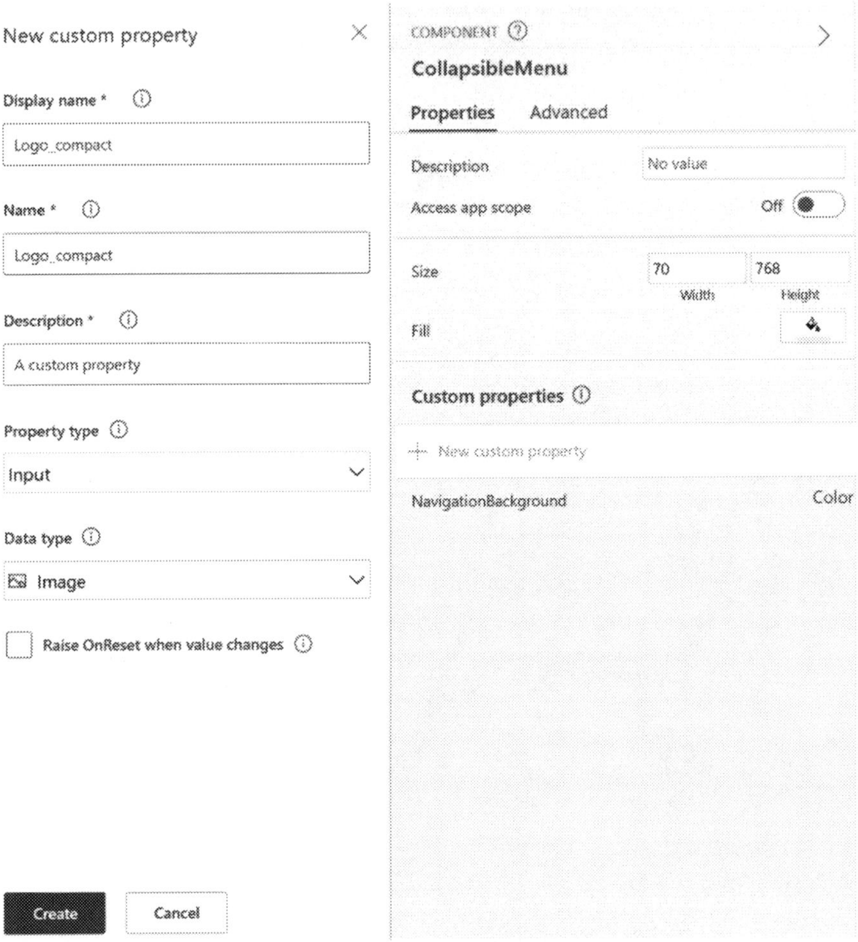

Figure 11-10. *The new custom property named Logo_compact*

11. From the Media ➤ Add Media option, add your logo file, as shown in Figure 11-11.

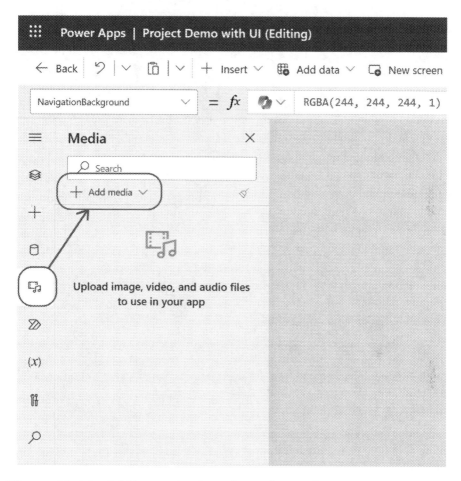

Figure 11-11. *Adding a new logo from the Media option*

12. Bo back to the container, select the image component, and in the Formula bar, add the image by its name. For example, my image is called Backend Logo and I am writing the logo name in the Formula bar, as shown in Figure 11-12.

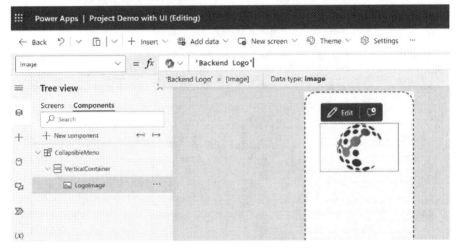

Figure 11-12. *Adding an image from the Formula bar*

13. Create another custom property named
    Logo_padding with the following parameters:

    Name = Logo_padding
    Data Type = Number

You can see these parameters in Figure 11-13.

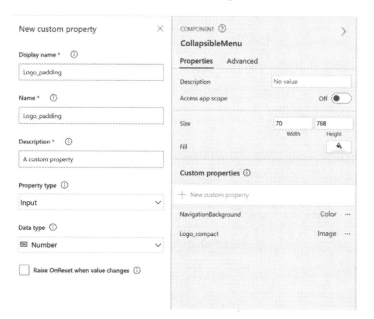

Figure 11-13. *Properties of new custom property named Logo_padding*

14. Select the Logo_padding property and set the percentage to 20%, as shown in Figure 11-14.

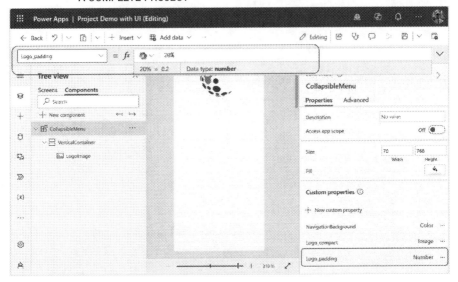

Figure 11-14. *Setting the Logo_padding custom properties value to 20%*

15. Select the image. Then, from the Formula bar, select the PaddingTop property and add the following code:

Self.Height * CollapsibleMenu.Logo_padding

Figure 11-15 shows the formula code for the PaddingTop property.

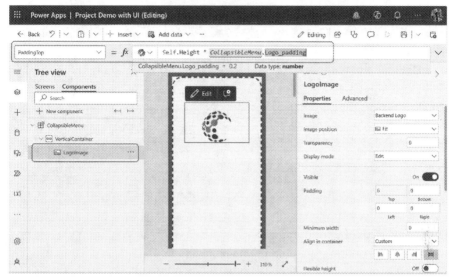

Figure 11-15. *Changing the padding of the logo image from the Formula bar*

16. Do the same for `PaddingBottom` property, using the same code.

17. Next, you'll add some icons to the menu. Before adding the icon, you need to add a blank vertical gallery, where you can set the icons. To add the vertical gallery, go to Insert and choose Blank Vertical Gallery, as shown in Figure 11-16.

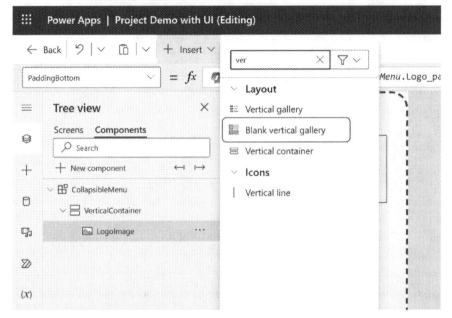

Figure 11-16. Adding a blank vertical gallery to the container

18. Change the following parameters of the vertical
gallery:

Minimum width = 0
Template size = 50
Template padding = 0

From the Formula bar, select the Height properties
and add the following code:

**Self.AllItemsCount * (Self.TemplateHeight+
Self.TemplatePadding)**

This code ensures that the gallery's height is
always based on the height of its items, while also
accounting for padding.

Figure 11-17 shows the parameters and formula
code for the vertical gallery.

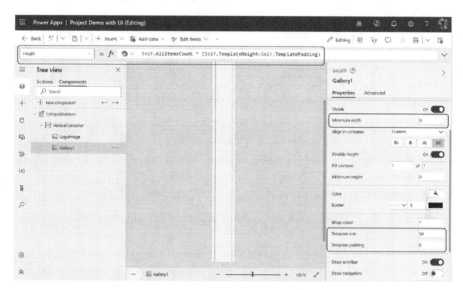

Figure 11-17. *Changing parameters for the vertical gallery*

19.   Create another custom property named
MenuContents with the following parameters (see
Figure 11-18):

Name = MenuContents

Data type = Table

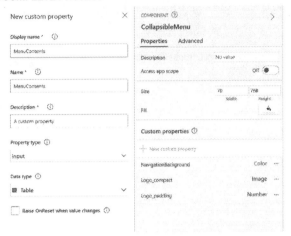

Figure 11-18. *Parameters for new custom property named MenuContents*

20. You can now add icons to the menu. You can either search for icons using the Insert option or upload custom icons from your device. This example shows you how to add icons from external resources.

    To add icons, go to `https://getbootstrap.com/` in another tab of your browser, and you will see the bootstrap website, as shown in Figure 11-19.

Figure 11-19. *Bootstrap website to get icons*

21. Click the Icons option from the menu, and you will
    see the page in Figure 11-20.

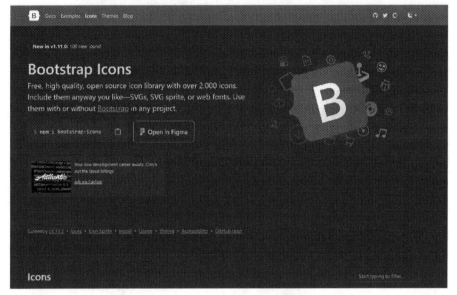

Figure 11-20. *Bootstrap Icons page to get free icons*

The Bootstrap icons are free, open source, and easy to
use. You can visit `https://icons.getbootstrap.com/`
to get these icons.

22.   Search for an icon. Because I am building an office
management app, I search for a badge icon and
copy the HTML code that contains the SVG file, as
shown in Figure 11-21.

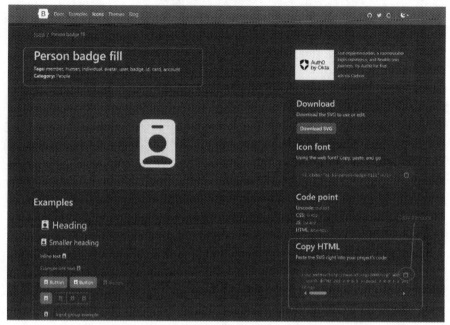

Figure 11-21. *Searching for an icon and copying the HTML code*

23.   Go back to the Power Apps project and click
      MenuContents. In the Formula bar, select the
      MenuContents property, and you will see the code in
      Figure 11-22.

Figure 11-22. *Sample table design code after creating a new custom property*

24.   Remove the sample code and create a menu item by
adding the following code:

```
Table(
    {
        MenuIcon: "<svg xmlns='http://www.w3.org/2000/
        svg' width='16' height='16' fill='currentColor'
        class='bi bi-person-
        badge-fill' viewBox='0 0 16 16'>
         <path d='M2 2a2 2 0 0 1 2-2h8a2 2 0 0 1 2
         2v12a2 2 0 0 1-2 2H4a2 2 0 0 1-2-2zm4.5 0a.5.5
         0 0 0 0 1h3a.5.5 0 0 0 0-1zM8 11a3 3 0 1 0 0-6
         3 3 0 0 0 0 6m5 2.755C12.146 12.825 10.623 12 8
         12s-4.146.826-5 1.755V14a1 1 0 0 0 1 1h8a1 1 0
         0 0 1-1z'/>
         </svg>",
        MenuID: 1,
        MenuName: "Employee Board",
        Page: App.ActiveScreen
    }
)
```

Let's look at this code first before moving to the
next step:

- MenuIcon: This is the HTML code that I got from
  Bootstrap. Ensure you enclose the code in double
  quotes ("HTML Code"). If you encapsulate the
  code in double quotes, it will lead to errors due to
  existing double quotes within the code. Replace
  these internal double quotes with single quotes.

- MenuID: This unique ID is assigned to this menu
  item. As you add more items to the menu, each will
  gets its own unique ID.

- MenuName: This is the name of the menu item. For
  instance, you can label it "Home" or "Contact"
  depending on the button you want to include in
  your menu.

- Page: This refers to the page that will open when
  the button is clicked or tapped.

This code creates one menu item, so I will add two
more menu items by separating the code using
commas (,). You can add the code as follows:

```
Table(
    {
        MenuIcon: "<svg xmlns='http://www.w3.org/2000/
        svg' width='16' height='16' fill='currentColor'
        class='bi bi-person-
        badge-fill' viewBox='0 0 16 16'>
                    <path d='M2 2a2 2 0 0 1 2-2h8a2 2 0
                    0 1 2 2v12a2 2 0 0 1-2 2H4a2 2 0 0
                    1-2-2zm4.5 0a.5.5 0 0 0 0 1h3a.5.5
```

```
                        0 0 0 0-1zM8 11a3 3 0 1 0 0-6 3 3 0
                        0 0 0 6m5 2.755C12.146 12.825 10.623
                        12 8 12s-4.146.826-5 1.755V14a1 1 0
                        0 0 1 1h8a1 1 0 0 0 1-1z'/>
                        </svg>",
     MenuID: 1,
     MenuName: "Employee Board",
     Page: App.ActiveScreen
},
{
     MenuIcon: "<svg xmlns='http://www.w3.org/2000/
     svg' width='16' height='16' fill='currentColor'
     class='bi bi-file-text-fill' viewBox='0
     0 16 16'>
                        <path d='M12 0H4a2 2 0 0 0-2 2v12a2 2
                        0 0 0 2 2h8a2 2 0 0 0 2-2V2a2 2 0 0
                        0-2-2M5 4h6a.5.5 0 0 1 0 1H5a.5.5 0 0
                        1 0-1m-.5 2.5A.5.5 0 0 1 5 6h6a.5.5 0
                        0 1 0 1H5a.5.5 0 0 1-.5-.5M5 8h6a.5.5
                        0 0 1 0 1H5a.5.5 0 0 1 0-1m0 2h3a.5.5
                        0 0 1 0 1H5a.5.5 0 0 1 0-1'/>
                        </svg>",
     MenuID: 2,
     MenuName: "Received Application",
     Page: App.ActiveScreen
},
{
     MenuIcon: "<svg xmlns='http://www.w3.org/2000/
     svg' width='16' height='16' fill='currentColor'
     class='bi bi-check-circle-fill' viewBox='0
     0 16 16'>
```

```
<path d='M16 8A8 8 0 1 1 0 8a8
8 0 0 1 16 0m-3.911-3.03a.75.75
0 0 0-1.08.022L7.477 9.417
5.384 7.323a.75.75 0 0 0-1.06
1.06L6.97 11.03a.75.75 0 0 0
1.079-.02l3.992-4.99a.75.75 0 0
0-.01-1.05z'/>
</svg>",
    MenuID: 3,
    MenuName: "Status",
    Page: App.ActiveScreen
  }
)
```

Figure 11-23 shows the actual code in the Power
Apps application.

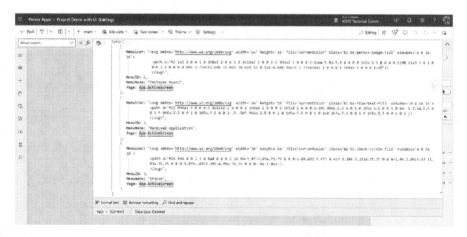

Figure 11-23. *Menu configuration displaying three menu items with
SVG icons, names, and links to the active screen*

I don't have another screen at this moment, so I simply link the active screen in every menu item. I will add new screens to this demo later, at which time I will show you how to change the page navigation.

25. Go back to the Power Apps Studio, select the gallery, and in the Items property, add the following code:

CollapsibleMenu.MenuContents

Figure 11-24 shows the formula code in the Items property of the gallery.

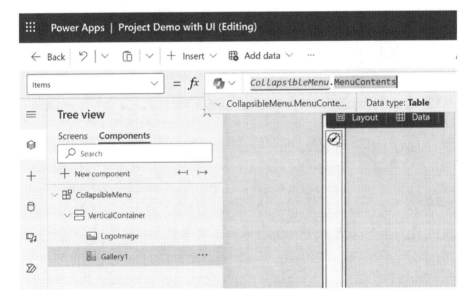

Figure 11-24. *The formula code in the Items property of the gallery*

26. Also, turn off the Flexible Height option in the gallery, as shown in Figure 11-25.

Figure 11-25. *Turning off the flexible height option*

27. Click the Gallery Edit icon (the pen symbol) and
     add a container inside the gallery, as shown in
     Figure 11-26. Change the following parameters from
     the Formula bar:

X = 0
Y = 0
Width = Parent.TemplateWidth
Height = Parent.TemplateHeight

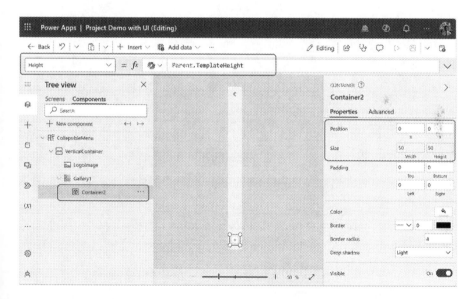

Figure 11-26. *Adding a new component inside the gallery*

28. This time, add another container inside this
     container, as shown in Figure 11-27, and set the
     following parameters from the Formula bar.

     X = (Parent.Width - Self.Width)/2
     Y = (Parent.Height - Self.Height)/2
     Width = Self.Height
     Height = Parent.Height * 70%
     Border radius = 10
     Drop shadow = None

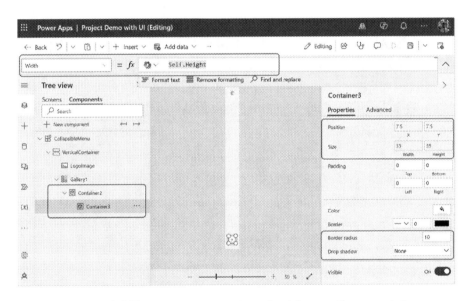

Figure 11-27. *Adding a new container inside another container*

29. This time, I add a new image inside the new
     container that I created and set the following
     parameters from the Formula bar.

     X = 0
     Y = 0

Width = Parent.Width

Height = Parent.Height

PaddingTop = 8

PaddingBottom = 8

Image = "data:image/svg+xml;utf8, " &
EncodeUrl (ThisItem.MenuIcon)

You will see the logos in the menu bar after adding
the formula code shown in Figure 11-28.

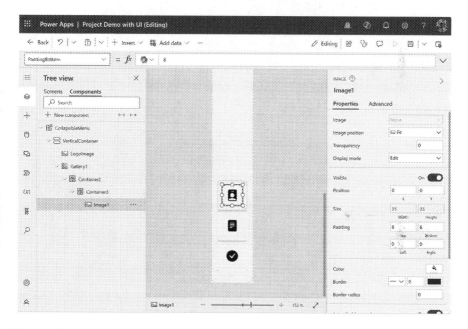

Figure 11-28. *Adding icons to the menu*

30. I now add a button in the same container that holds
    the image. This is necessary because the image
    needs to be interactive, allowing users to tap or click
    it. Just add a button from the Insert option and set
    the following parameters from the Formula bar:

Text = _BLANK_ (DO NOT ADD ANYTHING)

X = 0

Y = 0

Width = Parent.Width

Height = Parent.Height

PaddingTop = 8

PaddingBottom = 8

Border = None

Color = Transparent

31. Create two new custom properties named
HoverFilled and PressedFill, both with the
data type set to color, as shown in Figures 11-29
and 11-30.

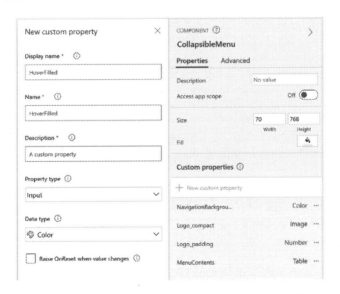

Figure 11-29. *Creating a new custom property named HoverFilled*

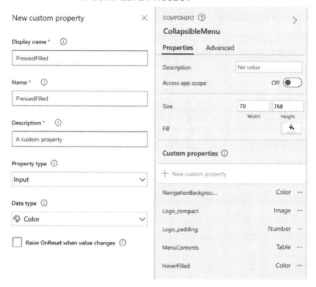

Figure 11-30. *Creating a new custom property named PressedFilled*

32. Click the HoverFilled property and change the
     color code from the Formula bar from RGBA(0,
     0, 0, 1) to RGBA(0, 0, 0, 0.1), as shown in
     Figure 11-31.

Figure 11-31. *RGBA value changes from (0,0,0,1) to (0,0,0,0.1) for
the HoverFilled custom property*

33. Click the `PressedFilled` property and change the
color code from the Formula bar from RGBA(0,
0, 0, 1) to RGBA(0, 0, 0, 0.2), as shown in
Figure 11-32.

Figure 11-32. *RGBA value changes from (0,0,0,1) to (0,0,0,0.2) for
the PressedFilled custom property*

34. Click the button created in the same container as
the image, select the `PressedFill` property from
the Formula bar, and enter the following code, also
shown in Figure 11-33.

CollapsibleMenu.PressedFilled

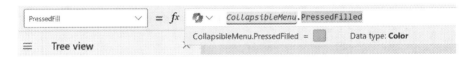

Figure 11-33. *Adding formula code to the PressedFill property for the
button component*

Note   `CollapsibleMenu` is the component name of this project.
Be sure to replace `CollapsibleMenu` with the component name
used in your project.

---

35. Select the HoverFill property for the button and
add the following code, as shown in Figure 11-34.

CollapsibleMenu.HoverFilled

Figure 11-34. *Adding formula code to the HoverFill property for the button component*

36. Now, select the OnSelect property and add the
following code, also shown in Figure 11-35.

Navigate(ThisItem.Page)

Figure 11-35. *Configuring navigation on the button through the OnSelect property*

This formula navigates to the screen specified by the
Page property value of the current item, as outlined
in the MenuContents formula code.

37. After that, create a new custom component named
CurrentMenuID, which will track which menu item
is active. Set the data type of this component to
Number. Refer to Figure 11-36.

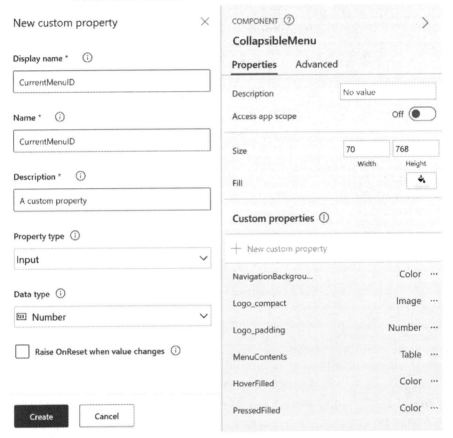

Figure 11-36. *Creating a custom property with the Number data type*

38. Set the default value to 1 for this custom property, as
shown in Figure 11-37.

Figure 11-37. *Setting the default value of CurrentMenuID to 1*

39. Select the container where you create the image
     and the button. In this demo, the container name is
     Container3, as shown in Figure 11-38.

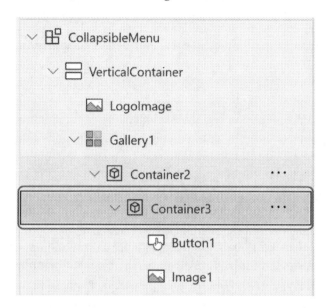

Figure 11-38. *Selecting the container where you add the image and
the button*

40. After selecting the container, select the Fill
     property from the Formula bar and add the
     following code:

```
If(
CollapsibleMenu.CurrentMenuID =
ThisItem.MenuID,
Color.White,
    RGBA(0,0,0,0)
    )
```

This formula determines if `CurrentMenuID`
of `CollapsibleMenu` is equal to `MenuID` of the
current item. If it is true, it returns the color white.
Otherwise, it returns a transparent color.

Figure 11-39 shows the code in the `Fill` property.

Figure 11-39. *The Fill property of Container3*

41. Because the plan is to implement both light and
    dark modes for this application, the current formula
    won't function correctly in dark mode. Therefore,
    you must create another custom property to adjust
    the container's color in dark mode.

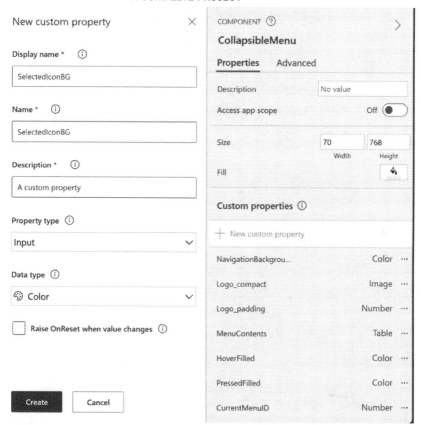

Figure 11-40.   *Creating a new custom property named*
SelectedIconBG

42.   Choose the default value RGBA(255, 255, 255, 1),
which is white, as shown in Figure 11-41.

Figure 11-41.   *Choosing the default value of white (RGBA (255,*
255, 255,1))

43. Link it to `Container3` by changing the code as follows:

```
If(
    CollapsibleMenu.CurrentMenuID = ThisItem.MenuID,
    CollapsibleMenu.SelectedIconBG,
    RGBA(0,0,0,0)
)
```

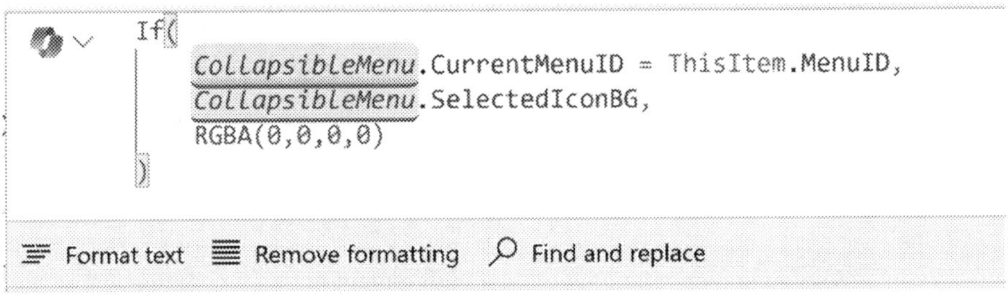

Figure 11-42. *Updated formula code for the Fill property of Container3*

44. Let's move to the icon color. If the menu is active, the color will be Teal; otherwise, the color will be gray. To control this, you need to create custom properties for both active and inactive menus.

45. For the active menu, create two custom properties named `ActiveIcon` and `ActiveIcon_Text`. The data type of `ActiveIcon` will be `Color`, and the data type of `ActiveIcon_Text` will be `Text`, as shown in Figures 11-43 and 11-44, respectively.

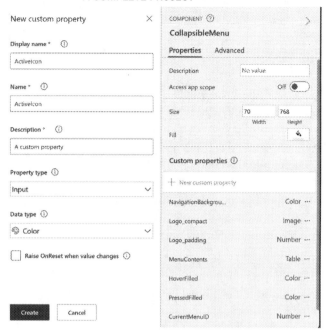

Figure 11-43. *Creating a custom property named ActiveIcon*

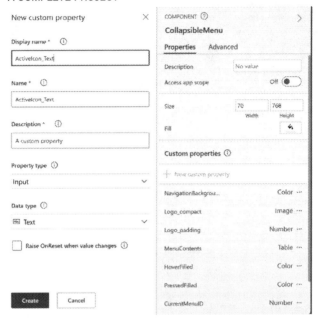

Figure 11-44. *Creating a custom property named ActiveIcon_Text*

46. Select the `ActiveIcon` custom property and change
the default value from the Formula bar as follows:

RGBA(0, 215, 218, 0.99)

Figure 11-45 shows the actual change to the
`ActiveIcon` property.

Figure 11-45. *Changing the default value of ActiveIcon property*

47. Select the ActiveIcon_Text custom property, and
change the default value from the Formula bar to
the following code:

"RGBA(0, 215, 218, 0.99)"

Figure 11-46 shows the change to the ActiveIcon_
Text property.

Figure 11-46. *Changing the default value of the ActiveIcon_Text*
property

Note   Because this color is used in an SVG, you also need a
text version. That's why I created the custom property named
ActiveIcon_Text.

---

48. Now do the same for the inactive menu. Create
two custom properties named InactiveIcon and
InactiveIcon_Text. The data type of InactiveIcon
will be Color, and the data type of InactiveIcon_
Text will be Text, as shown in Figures 11-47 and
11-48, respectively.

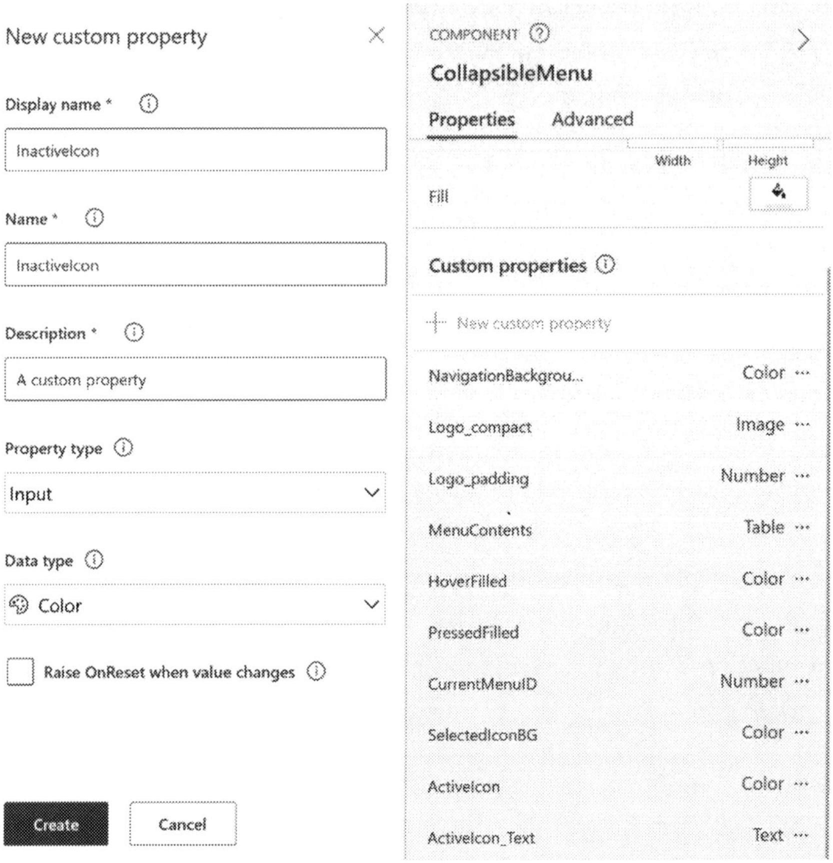

New custom property   ×

Display name *   ⓘ

Inactiveicon

Name *   ⓘ

Inactiveicon

Description *   ⓘ

A custom property

Property type   ⓘ

Input   ⌄

Data type   ⓘ

🎨 Color   ⌄

☐ Raise OnReset when value changes   ⓘ

Create   Cancel

COMPONENT ⓘ   >

CollapsibleMenu

Properties   Advanced

                                Width   Height

Fill   🎨

Custom properties ⓘ

── New custom property

NavigationBackgrou...   Color ···

Logo_compact   Image ···

Logo_padding   Number ···

MenuContents   Table ···

HoverFilled   Color ···

PressedFilled   Color ···

CurrentMenuID   Number ···

SelectedIconBG   Color ···

Activeicon   Color ···

Activeicon_Text   Text ···

Figure 11-47. *Creating a custom property named InactiveIcon*

New custom property   ×

Display name *   ⓘ

Inactivelcon_Text

Name *   ⓘ

Inactivelcon_Text

Description *   ⓘ

A custom property

Property type   ⓘ

Input   ⌄

Data type   ⓘ

Ⓐᵇᶜ Text   ⌄

☐ Raise OnReset when value changes   ⓘ

Create   Cancel

COMPONENT ⓘ   ＞

CollapsibleMenu

Properties   Advanced

	Width	Height
Fill		🖌

Custom properties ⓘ

─┼─ New custom property

NavigationBackgrou...	Color ···
Logo_compact	Image ···
Logo_padding	Number ···
MenuContents	Table ···
HoverFilled	Color ···
PressedFilled	Color ···
CurrentMenuID	Number ···
SelectedIconBG	Color ···
Activelcon	Color ···
Activelcon_Text	Text ···

Figure 11-48. *Creating a custom property named InactiveIcon_Text*

49. Select the InactiveIcon custom property and
     change the default value to the following RGBA
     color code:

RGBA(200, 200, 200, 0.99)

Figure 11-49 shows the actual change to the
InactiveIcon property.

Figure 11-49. Adding an RGBA color to the InactiveIcon property

50. As before, change the default value of the
    InactiveIcon_Text property to the color code
    added to the InactiveIcon property.

    "RGBA(200, 200, 200, 0.99)"

    Figure 11-50 shows the changes to the
    InactiveIcon_Text property.

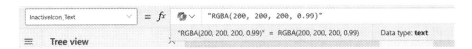

Figure 11-50. Changing the default value of the InactiveIcon_Text property

51. Apply the color to the icons. I am using icons from
    Bootstrap. In the Property Settings, Bootstrap uses
    the CurrentColor attribute in the Fill property
    for all Bootstrap icons. You can substitute that by
    replacing it with an active icon color or an inactive
    icon color, depending on whether the menu item
    is active. To achieve it, select image1 from the Tree
    View and add the following code:

    ```
    "data:image/svg+xml;utf8, " & EncodeUrl (
        Substitute(
            ThisItem.MenuIcon,
            "currentColor",
    ```

```
If(
    CollapsibleMenu.CurrentMenuID =
    ThisItem.MenuID,
    CollapsibleMenu.ActiveIcon_Text,
    CollapsibleMenu.InactiveIcon_Text
    )
  )
)
```

Figure 11-51 shows the substitute function used in the formula.

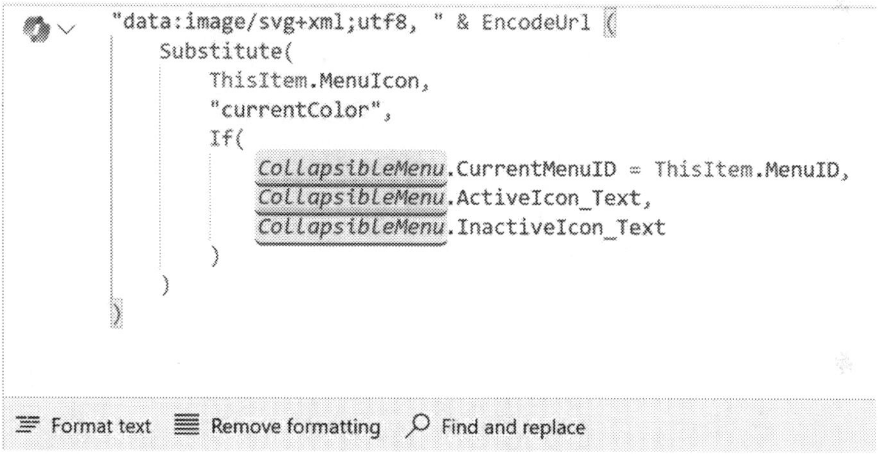

```
"data:image/svg+xml;utf8, " & EncodeUrl (
    Substitute(
        ThisItem.MenuIcon,
        "currentColor",
        If(
            CollapsibleMenu.CurrentMenuID = ThisItem.MenuID,
            CollapsibleMenu.ActiveIcon_Text,
            CollapsibleMenu.InactiveIcon_Text
        )
    )
)
```

≡ Format text   ≡ Remove formatting   ⌕ Find and replace

Figure 11-51. *Substitute function in the Image formula to change the icon color based on whether it is active or inactive*

52. At this point, I create something unique. I have used filled icons throughout the menu. Now, I add the same icons again from Bootstrap, but the normal one. This way, when someone clicks an icon, the filled icon will be replaced with the non-filled icon, making it distinct and helping users recognize that the menu item is selected.

For example, I used the People Badge icon, as
shown in Figure 11-52.

Person badge fill

Tags: member, human, individual, avatar, user, badge, id, card, account
Category: People

Figure 11-52. *People icon is used in the menu from Bootstrap*

Next, I add the People Badge icon that is not filled,
as shown in Figure 11-53.

Person badge

Tags: member, human, individual, avatar, user, badge, id, card, account, profile
Category: People

Figure 11-53. *People icon that will be used to indicate selection*

53. Copy the icons that are unfilled and use them as filled in the app.

- People badge (used as the icon for Employee Board in the menu item):

```
<svg xmlns="http://www.w3.org/2000/svg" width="16"
height="16" fill="currentColor" class="bi
bi-person-badge" viewBox="0 0 16 16">
    <path d="M6.5 2a.5.5 0 0 0 0 1h3a.5.5 0 0 0
    0-1zM11 8a3 3 0 1 1-6 0 3 3 0 0 1 6 0"/>
    <path d="M4.5 0A2.5 2.5 0 0 0 2 2.5V14a2 2 0 0
    0 2 2h8a2 2 0 0 0 2-2V2.5A2.5 2.5 0 0 0 11.5
    0zM3 2.5A1.5 1.5 0 0 1 4.5 1h7A1.5 1.5 0 0 1 13
    2.5v10.795a4.2 4.2 0 0 0-.776-.492C11.392 12.387
    10.063 12 8 12s-3.392.3811-4.224.803a4.2 4.2 0 0
    0-.776.492z"/>
</svg>
```

- File badge (used as the icon for Received Application in the menu item):

```
<svg xmlns="http://www.w3.org/2000/svg" width="16"
height="16" fill="currentColor" class="bi bi-file-
text" viewBox="0 0 16 16">
    <path d="M5 4a.5.5 0 0 0 0 1h6a.5.5 0 0 0 0-1zm-
    .5 2.5A.5.5 0 0 1 5 6h6a.5.5 0 0 1 0 1H5a.5.5 0
    0 1-.5-.5M5 8a.5.5 0 0 0 0 1h6a.5.5 0 0 0 0-1zm0
    2a.5.5 0 0 0 0 1h3a.5.5 0 0 0 0-1z"/>
    <path d="M2 2a2 2 0 0 1 2-2h8a2 2 0 0 1 2 2v12a2
    2 0 0 1-2 2H4a2 2 0 0 1-2-2zm10-1H4a1 1 0 0 0-1
    1v12a1 1 0 0 0 1 1h8a1 1 0 0 0 1-1V2a1 1 0 0
    0-1-1"/>
</svg>
```

- Check circle badge (used as the icon for Status in the menu item):

```
<svg xmlns="http://www.w3.org/2000/svg" width="16"
height="16" fill="currentColor" class="bi bi-check-
circle" viewBox="0 0 16 16">

    <path d="M8 15A7 7 0 1 1 8 1a7 7 0 0 1 0 14m0 1A8
    8 0 1 0 8 0a8 8 0 0 0 0 16"/>

    <path d="m10.97 4.911-.02.022-3.473
    4.425-2.093-2.094a.75.75 0 0 0-1.06 1.06L6.97
    11.03a.75.75 0 0 0 1.079-.02l3.992-4.99a.75.75 0
    0 0-1.071-1.05"/>

</svg>
```

54. Select MenuContents and under the Table tag, create
    a new column named MenuSelected, and paste the
    HTML code for each menu item, as I showed you
    before. Figure 11-54 shows the new column under
    the Table tag.

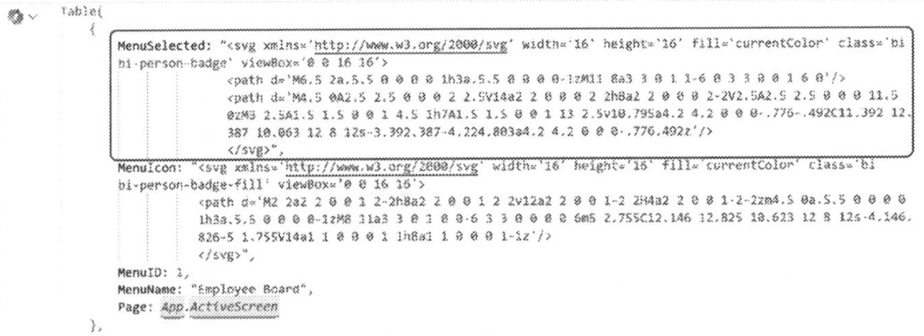

Figure 11-54. *Adding a new column named MenuSelected under the Table tag*

Here is the full formula code:

```
Table(
    {
        MenuSelected: "<svg xmlns='http://www.w3.org/
        2000/svg' width='16' height='16' fill='current
        Color' class='bi bi-person-badge' viewBox='0
        0 16 16'>
                        <path d='M6.5 2a.5.5 0 0 0 0
                        1h3a.5.5 0 0 0 0-1zM11 8a3 3
                        0 1 1-6 0 3 3 0 0 1 6 0'/>
                        <path d='M4.5 0A2.5 2.5 0 0
                        0 2 2.5V14a2 2 0 0 0 2 2h8a2
                        2 0 0 0 2-2V2.5A2.5 2.5 0 0
                        0 11.5 0zM3 2.5A1.5 1.5 0 0
                        1 4.5 1h7A1.5 1.5 0 0 1 13
                        2.5v10.795a4.2 4.2 0 0 0-.776-
                        .492C11.392 12.387 10.063 12 8
                        12s-3.392.3811-4.224.803a4.2 4.2
                        0 0 0-.776.492z'/>
                        </svg>",
        MenuIcon: "<svg xmlns='http://www.w3.org/2000/
        svg' width='16' height='16' fill='currentColor'
        class='bi bi-person-badge-fill' viewBox='0
        0 16 16'>
                        <path d='M2 2a2 2 0 0 1 2-2h8a2 2 0
                        0 1 2 2v12a2 2 0 0 1-2 2H4a2 2 0 0
                        1-2-2zm4.5 0a.5.5 0 0 0 0 1h3a.5.5 0
                        0 0 0-1zM8 11a3 3 0 1 0 0-6 3 3 0 0
                        0 0 6m5 2.755C12.146 12.825 10.623
                        12 8 12s-4.146.826-5 1.755V14a1 1 0
                        0 0 1 1h8a1 1 0 0 0 1-1z'/>
```

```
                        </svg>",
        MenuID: 1,
        MenuName: "Employee Board",
        Page: App.ActiveScreen
    },

    {

        MenuSelected: "<svg xmlns='http://www.w3.org/
        2000/svg' width='16' height='16' fill='current
        Color' class='bi bi-file-text' viewBox='0
        0 16 16'>
                        <path d='M5 4a.5.5 0 0 0 0
                        1h6a.5.5 0 0 0 0-1zm-.5 2.5A.5.5
                        0 0 1 5 6h6a.5.5 0 0 1 0
                        1H5a.5.5 0 0 1-.5-.5M5 8a.5.5
                        0 0 0 1h6a.5.5 0 0 0 0-1zm0
                        2a.5.5 0 0 0 0 1h3a.5.5 0 0
                        0 0-1z'/>
                        <path d='M2 2a2 2 0 0 1 2-2h8a2
                        2 0 0 1 2 2v12a2 2 0 0 1-2 2H4a2
                        2 0 0 1-2-2zm10-1H4a1 1 0 0 0-1
                        1v12a1 1 0 0 0 1 1h8a1 1 0 0 0
                        1-1V2a1 1 0 0 0-1-1'/>
                        </svg>",
        MenuIcon: "<svg xmlns='http://www.w3.org/2000/
        svg' width='16' height='16' fill='currentColor'
        class='bi bi-file-text-fill' viewBox='0
        0 16 16'>
                        <path d='M12 0H4a2 2 0 0 0-2 2v12a2 2
                        0 0 0 2 2h8a2 2 0 0 0 2-2V2a2 2 0 0
                        0-2-2M5 4h6a.5.5 0 0 1 0 1H5a.5.5 0 0
                        1 0-1m-.5 2.5A.5.5 0 0 1 5 6h6a.5.5 0
```

```
                    0 1 0 1H5a.5.5 0 0 1-.5-.5M5 8h6a.5.5
                    0 0 1 0 1H5a.5.5 0 0 1 0-1m0 2h3a.5.5
                    0 0 1 0 1H5a.5.5 0 0 1 0-1'/>
                    </svg>",
        MenuID: 2,
        MenuName: "Received Application",
        Page: App.ActiveScreen
    },

    {
        MenuSelected: "<svg xmlns='http://www.w3.org/
        2000/svg' width='16' height='16'
        fill='currentColor' class='bi bi-check-
        circle' viewBox='0 0 16 16'>
                    <path d='M8 15A7 7 0 1 1 8 1a7 7
                    0 0 1 0 14m0 1A8 8 0 1 0 8 0a8 8
                    0 0 0 0 16'/>
                    <path d='m10.97
                    4.911-.02.022-3.473
                    4.425-2.093-2.094a.75.75 0 0
                    0-1.06 1.06L6.97 11.03a.75.75 0
                    0 0 1.079-.02l3.992-4.99a.75.75
                    0 0 0-1.071-1.05'/>
                    </svg>",
        MenuIcon: "<svg xmlns='http://www.w3.org/2000/
        svg' width='16' height='16' fill='currentColor'
        class='bi bi-check-circle-fill' viewBox='0
        0 16 16'>
                    <path d='M16 8A8 8 0 1 1 0 8a8
                    8 0 0 1 16 0m-3.911-3.03a.75.75
                    0 0 0-1.08.022L7.477 9.417
                    5.384 7.323a.75.75 0 0 0-1.06
```

```
                    1.06L6.97 11.03a.75.75 0 0 0
                    1.079-.02l3.992-4.99a.75.75 0 0
                    0-.01-1.05z'/>
                    </svg>",
            MenuID: 3,
            MenuName: "Status",
            Page: App.ActiveScreen
        }
    )
```

55. Lastly, select the Image component, and in the
     formula code, make the following changes:

```
"data:image/svg+xml;utf8, " & EncodeUrl (
    Substitute(
        If(
            CollapsibleMenu.CurrentMenuID = ThisItem.
            MenuID,
            ThisItem.MenuSelected,
            ThisItem.MenuIcon
        ),
        "currentColor",
        If(
            CollapsibleMenu.CurrentMenuID = ThisItem.
            MenuID,
                CollapsibleMenu.ActiveIcon_Text,
                CollapsibleMenu.InactiveIcon_Text
        )
    )
)
```

Figure 11-55 shows the actual code that changed in the Image component.

```
"data:image/svg+xml;utf8, " & EncodeUrl(
    Substitute(
        If(
            CollapsibleMenu.CurrentMenuID = ThisItem.MenuID,
            ThisItem.MenuSelected,
            ThisItem.MenuIcon
        ),
        "currentColor",
        If(
            CollapsibleMenu.CurrentMenuID = ThisItem.MenuID,
            CollapsibleMenu.ActiveIcon_Text,
            CollapsibleMenu.InactiveIcon_Text
        )
    )
)
```

≡ Format text   ≡ Remove formatting   ⌕ Find and replace

Figure 11-55. *Formula code in the Image component that switches the icon between active and inactive modes*

56.   The menu creation process is finished. But it is not collapsible yet. You need to add it to the screen and then I will show how to make it collapsible.

Go to the screen and add a horizontal container, as shown in Figure 11-56.

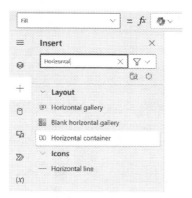

Figure 11-56. *Adding a horizontal container to the main screen*

57. Change the following parameters for this horizontal
    container:

    Width = Parent.Width
    Height = Parent.Height
    Border radius = 10
    Drop shadow = None

58. Add a new container under the horizontal container
    and set the following parameters:

    Align in Container = Stretch
    Minimum height = 0
    Flexible width = Off
    Width = 70
    Border radius = 0
    Drop shadow = None

    Figure 11-57 shows the parameters of the container.

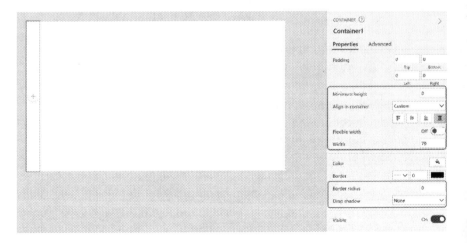

Figure 11-57. *Changing the properties of the container*

59. Now, under this container, add a new vertical
     container and set the following parameters:

Border radius = 0

Drop shadow = None

Figure 11-58 shows the newly added vertical
container.

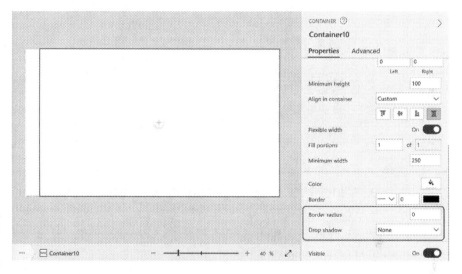

Figure 11-58. *Adding a new vertical container to the screen*

60. Click the + sign from the left container named
     Container1 and choose CollapsibleMenu under the
     Custom category, as shown in Figure 11-59.

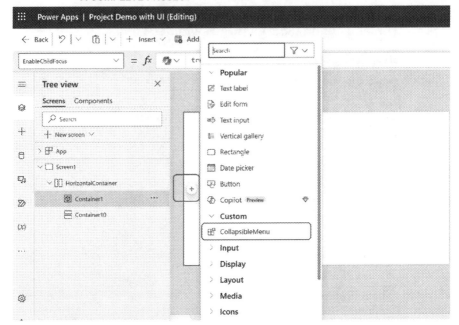

Figure 11-59. *Choosing CollapsibleMenu to integrate the menu bar*

You will see the side menu after choosing the `CollapsibleMenu` component, as shown in Figure 11-60.

Figure 11-60. *Successfully adding the modern menu to Power Apps*

Creating the Menu Collapsible with Mode Switcher

Great! The last section demonstrated how to create a dynamic menu in Power Apps. This section shows you how to make the menu collapsible and add a mode switcher. These are essential features of a modern app and greatly enhance the user experience.

To get started, open the demo again!

1. To make this menu collapsible, go to the Components option and duplicate the CollapsibleMenu component. Rename it CollapsibleMenu_Activate, as shown in Figures 11-61 and 11-62.

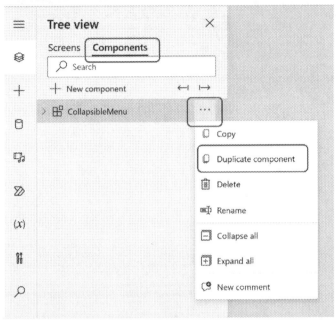

Figure 11-61. *Duplicating the CollapsibleMenu component*

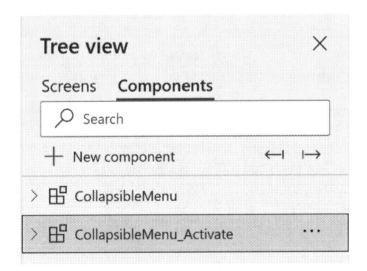

Figure 11-62. *Renaming CollapsibleMenu_1 to CollapsibleMenu_*
Activate

2. The width of the menu I created, as shown in
   Figure 11-57, was initially set at 70. Let's increase
   the width to 150 when it expands. To achieve this,
   add a new container in between LogoImage_1 and
   Gallery1_1 and name it ContainerExpand, as
   shown in Figure 11-63.

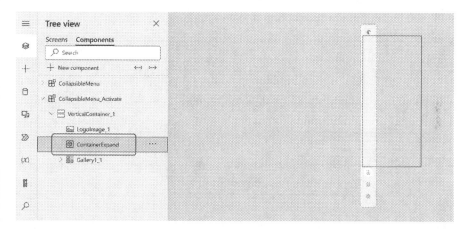

Figure 11-63. *Adding a new container between LogoImage1 and
Gallery1_1*

3. Change the following parameters of
   ContainerExpand.

   Align in Container = Center
   Flexible width = Off
   Width = 35
   Height = 35
   Border radius = 10
   Drop shadow = None

   Figure 11-64 shows the ContainerExpand
   parameters.

Figure 11-64. *Changing the parameters of ContainerExpand*

4. Inside this container, add a new image control and change the parameters as follows:

Width = Parent.Width
Height = Parent.Height
X = 0
Y = 0

Figure 11-65 shows the image control parameters.

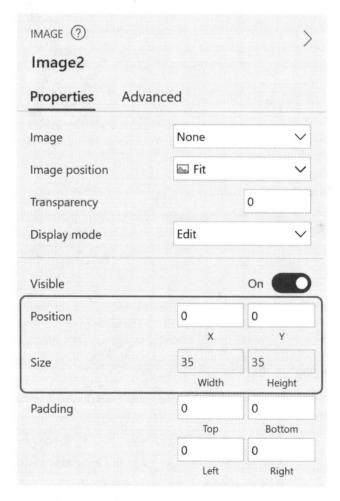

Figure 11-65. *Changing the image control properties*

5. Go to Bootstrap and search for the hamburger
    menu. Copy the HTML code, as shown in
    Figure 11-66.

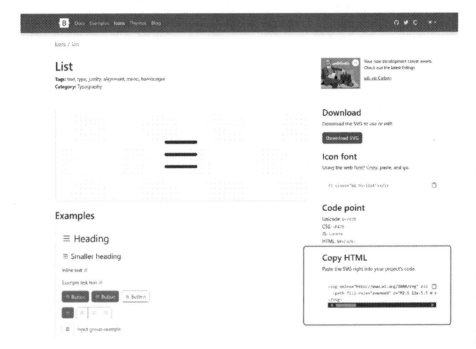

Figure 11-66. *Choosing the hamburger menu icon and copying the
HTML code*

6. Replace the double quotations with single
    quotations and add the following code to the default
    image property from the Formula bar.

```
"data:image/svg+xml;utf8, " & EncodeUrl (
    Substitute(
        "<svg xmlns='http://www.w3.org/2000/svg'
        width='16' height='16' fill='currentColor'
        class='bi bi-list' viewBox='0 0 16 16'>
```

```
<path fill-rule='evenodd' d='M2.5 12a.5.5 0 0 1 .5-
.5h10a.5.5 0 0 1 0 1H3a.5.5 0 0 1-.5-.5m0-4a.5.5 0 0
1 .5-.5h10a.5.5 0 0 1 0 1H3a.5.5 0 0 1-.5-.5m0-4a.5.5
0 0 1 .5-.5h10a.5.5 0 0 1 0 1H3a.5.5 0 0 1-.5-.5'/>
</svg>",
        "currentColor",
        CollapsibleMenu_Activate.InactiveIcon_Text
    )
)
```

Figure 11-67 shows the formula code for the Image property.

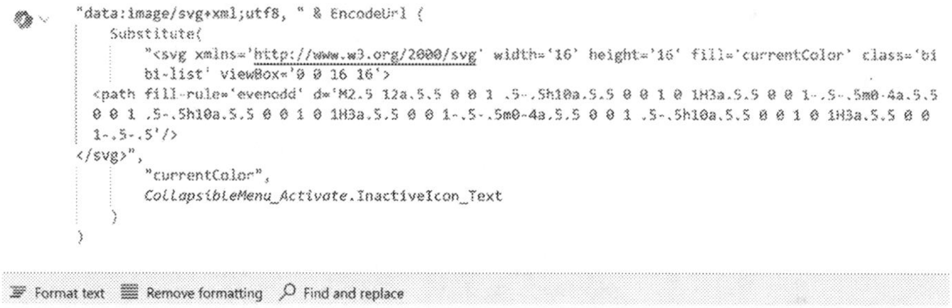

Figure 11-67. *Formula code for adding a hamburger menu to the Image property*

7. Now, add a button inside the ContainerExpand container and change the following parameters in the Formula bar (also shown in Figure 11-68):

Text = ""
X = 0
Y = 0
Height = Parent.Height
Width = Parent.Width

Fill = Color.Transparent

Border style = BorderStyle.None

PressedFill = *CollapsibleMenu_Activate*.PressedFilled

HoverFill = *CollapsibleMenu_Activate*.HoverFilled

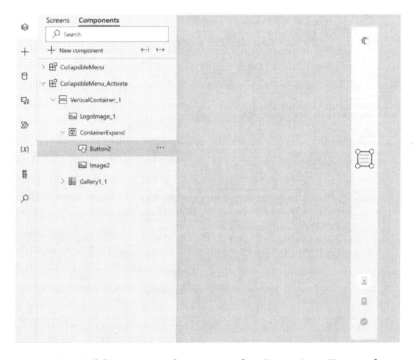

Figure 11-68. *Adding a new button to the ContainerExpand*
container

8. Before proceeding to the next move, position
    the component items first. Select the
    VerticalContainer_1 and change the following
    parameters, also shown in Figure 11-69.

    Justify (vertical) = Start

    Gap = 10

Figure 11-69. Positioning VerticalComponent_1

9. Now, select Gallery1_1 and change the following parameters, as shown in Figure 11-70.

Flexible Height = On
Minimum Height = 0

Figure 11-70. Changing the parameters of Gallery1_1

10. Now you'll make the component expandable. Select the hamburger icon button, which is named `Button2`, and add the following code to the `OnSelect` property (also shown in Figure 11-71):

Set (varMenuExpanded,!varMenuExpanded)

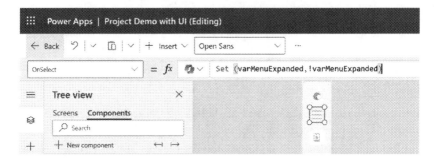

Figure 11-71. *Adding the formula code to the hamburger menu button*

This code will create a Boolean variable named `varMenuExpanded`, which toggles the icon on and off.

11. Now, create a custom property named `MenuExpanded` with the following parameters:

Property type = Output
Data type = Boolean

Figure 11-72 shows the parameters of this customer property named `MenuExpanded`.

New custom property   ×   COMPONENT ⑦   >

                                                CollapsibleMenu_Activate

Display name * ⓘ   Properties   Advanced

MenuExpanded   Description   No value

                                                Access app scope   Off ⬤
Name * ⓘ

MenuExpanded   Size   70   768
                                                                        Width   Height

Description * ⓘ   Fill   🎨

A custom property
                                                Custom properties ⓘ

Property type ⓘ
                                                ╬ New custom property
Output   ⌄

                                                NavigationBackgrou...   Color ···
Data type ⓘ
                                                Logo_compact   Image ···
⬭ Boolean   ⌄
                                                Logo_padding   Number ···

☐ Raise OnReset when value changes ⓘ   MenuContents   Table ···

                                                HoverFilled   Color ···

                                                PressedFilled   Color ···

   Create   Cancel
                                                CurrentMenuID   Number ···

Figure 11-72. *Creating a custom property named MenuExpanded and configuring the parameters*

12. Select the newly created custom property named
     MenuExpanded and change the default value (true)
     to varMenuExpanded, as shown in Figure 11-73.

MenuExpanded	⌄	= *fx*	🐵⌄	varMenuExpanded
		varMenuExpanded = true		Data type: **boolean**

≡   Tree view

Figure 11-73. *Adding formula code to the MenuExpanded custom property*

13. Now create a new custom property called Logo_
Expanded. This property will display the full logo
whenever the menu is expanded. Use the following
parameters:

Property type = Input
Data type = Image

Figure 11-74 shows the new custom property named
Logo_Expanded with the parameters.

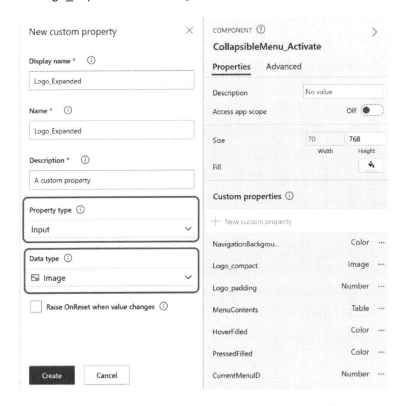

Figure 11-74. *Creating a new custom property named Logo_*
Expanded

14. Add the full logo in Media and set the full logo as the default value of the custom property, as shown in Figure 11-75.

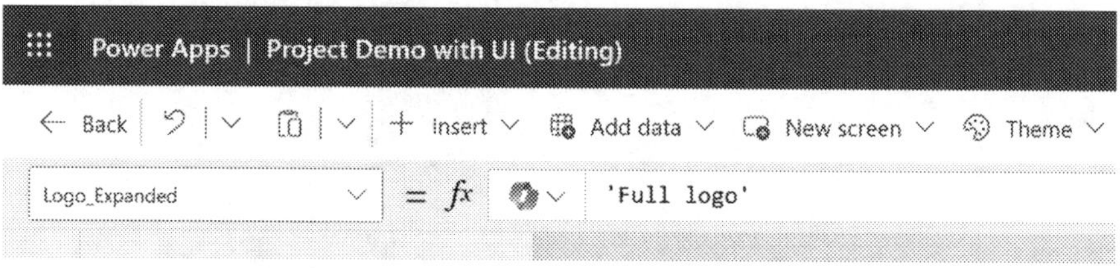

Figure 11-75. *Adding the full logo as a default value for Logo_ Expanded property*

15. Select the LogoImage1 control, choose the Image property, and add the following code:

```
If(
    CollapsibleMenu_Activate.MenuExpanded,
    CollapsibleMenu_Activate.Logo_Expanded,
    CollapsibleMenu_Activate
    .Logo_compact
)
```

Figure 11-76 shows the formula code that changes the logo when it is expanded.

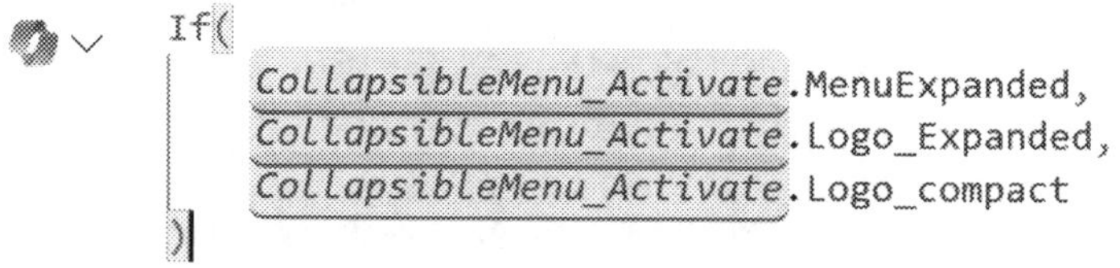

Figure 11-76. *Formula code that changes the logo when expanded*

16.   Adjust the alignment of the menu items. As shown
in Figure 11-77, the items are currently centered
when the menu is expanded. To better adhere to
design principles, I suggest shifting the position of
the menu items to the left.

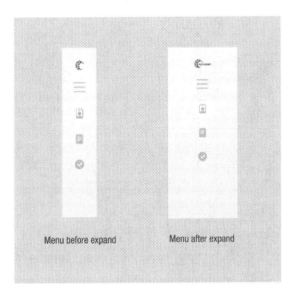

Figure 11-77. *Menu items before and after the menu expands*

17.   To do this, select the ContainerExpand container
(which you created to put the hamburger icon
image and button) and place the following formula
code in the AlignInContainer property.

```
If(
    CollapsibleMenu_Activate.MenuExpanded,
    AlignInContainer.Start,
    AlignInContainer.Center
)
```

Figure 11-78 shows the formula code that changes
the alignment position of the menu items.

```
If(
    CollapsibleMenu_Activate.MenuExpanded,
    AlignInContainer.Start,
    AlignInContainer.Center
)
```

Figure 11-78. *Formula code that changes the alignment position of
the menu items*

18. Modify the alignments of the menu icons. To do this,
     expand the Gallery1_1 component. Inside, you
     will find two containers. Select the last container,
     which holds the Image and Button, to adjust their
     alignment positions, as shown in Figure 11-79.

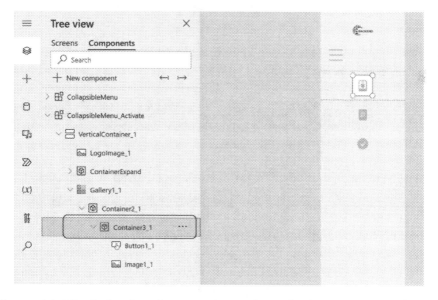

Figure 11-79. *Selecting the container where the icons are saved*

627

19. Choose the Width for the container and add the
following formula code:

If(

    CollapsibleMenu_Activate.MenuExpanded,

    Parent.Width,

    Self.Height

)

Figure 11-80 shows the formula code for changing
the width of the container.

```
If(
    CollapsibleMenu_Activate.MenuExpanded,
    Parent.Width,
    Self.Height
)
```

Figure 11-80. *Formula code for changing the width of the container*

20. Select Image1_1 (which is carrying the icons) and set
the width to Self.Height, as shown in Figure 11-81.

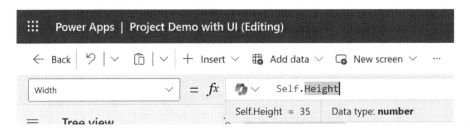

Figure 11-81. *Set the width of the image container for the
menu icons*

21. At this stage, you should add a name to the menu.
To do this, insert a text label within the container,
ensuring that it is positioned after the button. This
placement will make the text label clickable, as
shown in Figure 11-82.

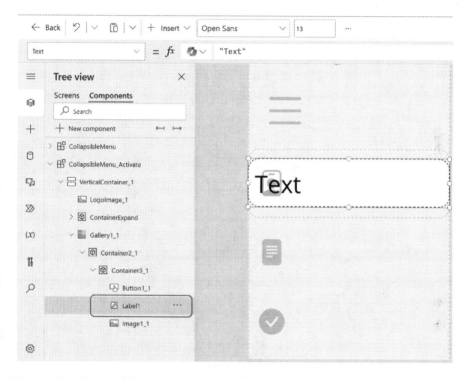

Figure 11-82. *Adding a new text label to show the menu name*

22. Set the following parameters of this text label:

X = Image1_1.Width
Width = Parent.Width - Self.X
Height = Parent.Height

Note The X value specifies that the text within the text label will begin immediately following Image1_1, which is the menu icon.

Figure 11-83 shows the preview after these parameters have been set.

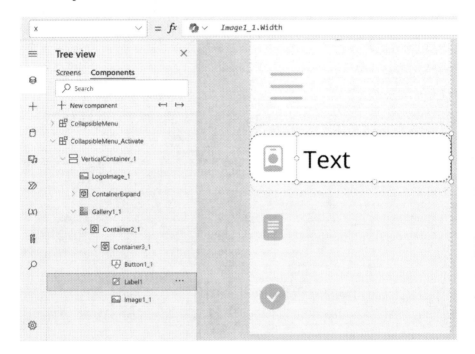

Figure 11-83. *Preview of the menu after adding the text label*

23. As part of the plan to implement a light mode and dark mode, it is essential to adjust the text colors. To facilitate this process, create a new custom property called TextColor using the Color data type.

24. Set the default value of the TextColor custom
    property as follows:

RGBA (50, 68, 125, 1)

Figure 11-84 shows the formula code for the
TextColor property.

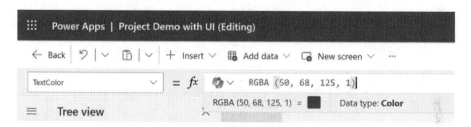

Figure 11-84. *Setting the text color for the light mode*

25. Change the label color with the custom property
    that you just created, using the following code:

CollapsibleMenu_Activate.TextColor

Figure 11-85 shows the formula code and the
preview after changing the color.

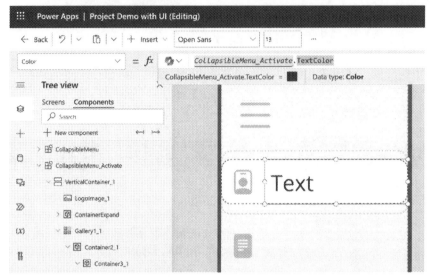

Figure 11-85. *Changing the text label color with the custom property*

26.   Select the label, choose the text property from the
       Formula bar, and add the following formula code:

ThisItem.MenuName

Figure 11-86 shows the code in the Formula bar with
the preview.

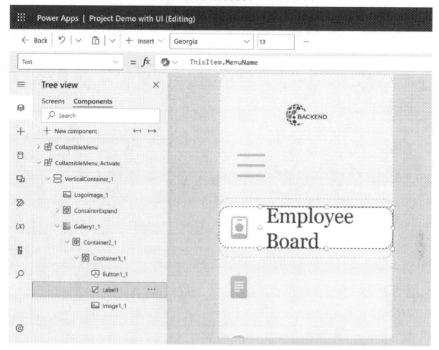

Figure 11-86. *Preview after adding the menu name to the text label*

27. You can see that the font size is too big and not
    perfectly set inside the container. To fix this, change
    the font size from the Label properties, as shown in
    Figure 11-87.

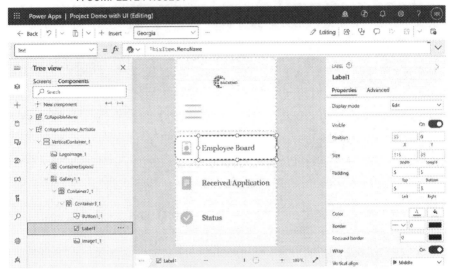

Figure 11-87. *Changing the font size to set the menu name inside the container*

28. Set up a condition to ensure that the menu name is only visible when the menu is expanded. To do this, select label1 (the text label where you just fetch the menu name), choose the Visible property from the Formula bar, and add the following code:

CollapsibleMenu_Activate.MenuExpanded

Figure 11-88 shows the formula code for the visible property of label1.

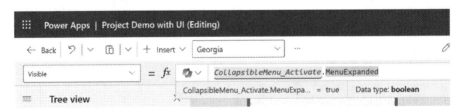

Figure 11-88. *Formula code for showing the menu name when the menu is expanded*

634

29.   The collapsible menu is done! Figure 11-89 shows
the menu before and after expanding.

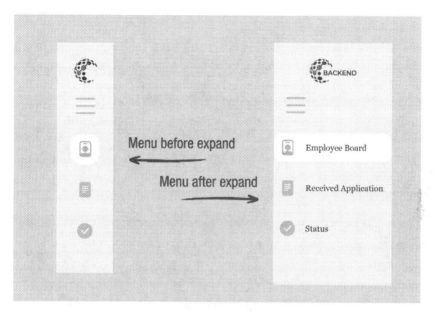

Figure 11-89. *Menu before and after expanding*

Just a note: If the logo appears too small, consider reducing the
percentage set in the Logo_Padding custom component. I initially set it to
20%. If you reduce it, the logo will appear larger, as shown in Figure 11-90.

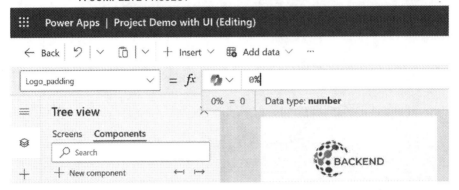

Figure 11-90. *Making the logo larger from the Logo_Padding custom property*

The next example shows you how to add a crucial feature called a *theme switcher,* which is commonly seen in modern applications. This feature includes a toggle option that allows users to switch between light and dark themes.

To create the theme switcher, follow these steps:

1. In your `CollapsibleMenu_Activate` component, create a new custom property named `AppColorMode` with the `Text` data type, as shown in Figure 11-91.

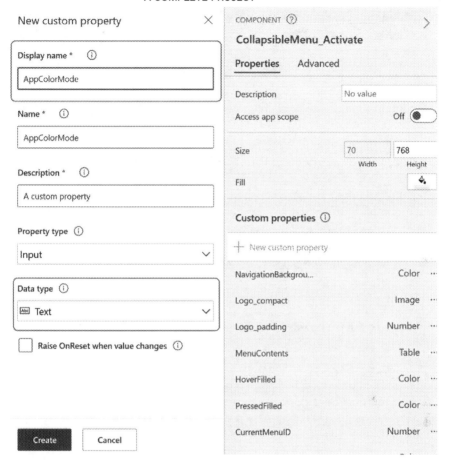

Figure 11-91. *Creating new custom property named AppColorMode*

2. Set the default value of AppColorMode to "Light", as
    shown in Figure 11-92.

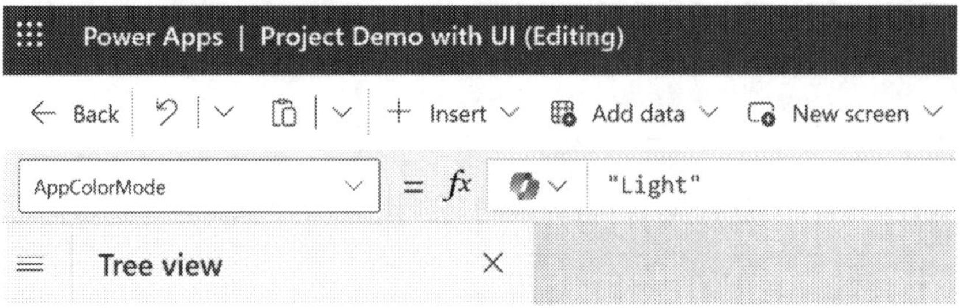

Power Apps | Project Demo with UI (Editing)

← Back   ↺ | ∨   ⬚ | ∨   + Insert ∨   ⊞ Add data ∨   ⬚ New screen ∨

| AppColorMode ∨ | = ƒx | ⬤ ∨ | "Light" |

≡   Tree view   ✕

Figure 11-92. Setting the default value of AppColorMode

3. Add a container to the CollapsibleMenu_Activate
   component and set the following parameters:

   Align in Container = *Center*
   Width = 60
   Height = 60
   Flexible Height = *Off*
   Border Radius = 0
   Drop Shadow = *None*

   Figure 11-93 shows the container named
   AppThemeSwitcherContainer with its parameters.

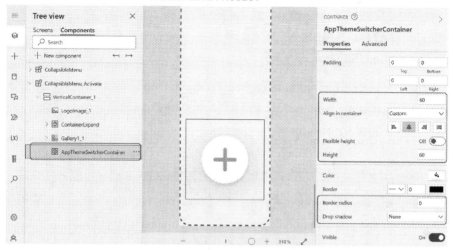

Figure 11-93. *Adding a new container named*
AppThemeSwitcherContainer

4. Add a vertical container inside the
    AppThemeSwitcherContainer, rename it
    AppThemeSwitcher, and set the following
    parameters:

    X = 0
    Y = 0
    Width = 60
    Height = 60
    Border Radius = 0
    Drop Shadow = *None*

5. Add a new non-responsive container, rename it to
    SwitchContainer, and set the following parameters:

    Align in Container = *Stretch*
    Minimum Width = 0
    Minimum Height = 0

Flexible Height = *On*

Border Radius = 0

Drop Shadow = *None*

6. Add an image inside the SwitchContainer
    container, rename it to LightIcon, and set the
    following parameters:

    X = 0

    Y = 0

    Width = Parent.Width

    Height = Parent.Height

    Figure 11-94 shows the LightIcon image
    component inside the SwitchContainer container.

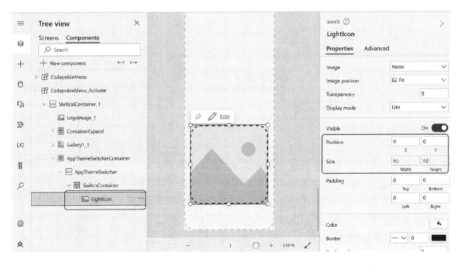

Figure 11-94. *Adding a new image component named LightIcon
inside SwitchContainer*

7. Go to `https://icons.getbootstrap.com` and search for the Light icon. For example, I chose the icon shown in Figure 11-95.

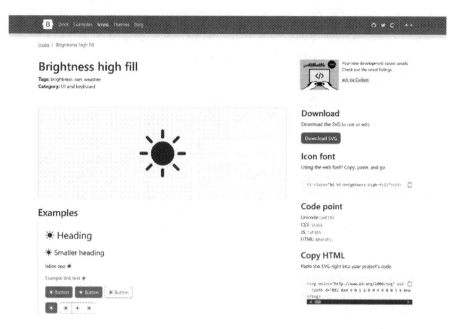

Figure 11-95. *Choosing an icon from Bootstrap for a light theme*

8. Copy the HTML code, replace the double quotes with single quotes, and paste the code in the `LightIcon` Image property from the Formula bar.

```
"data:image/svg+xml;utf8, " & EncodeUrl (

    "<svg xmlns='http://www.w3.org/2000/svg'
    width='16' height='16' fill='currentColor'
    class='bi bi-brightness-high-fill' viewBox='0
    0 16 16'>
```

```
<path d='M12 8a4 4 0 1 1-8 0 4 4 0 0 1 8 0M8 0a.5.5
0 0 1 .5.5v2a.5.5 0 0 1-1 0v-2A.5.5 0 0 1 8 0m0
13a.5.5 0 0 1 .5.5v2a.5.5 0 0 1-1 0v-2A.5.5 0 0 1 8
13m8-5a.5.5 0 0 1-.5.5h-2a.5.5 0 0 1 0-1h2a.5.5 0 0
1 .5.5M3 8a.5.5 0 0 1-.5.5h-2a.5.5 0 0 1 0-1h2A.5.5
0 0 1 3 8m10.6511-5.657a.5.5 0 0 1 0 .707l-1.414
1.415a.5.5 0 1 1-.7011-.708l1.414-1.414a.5.5 0
0 1 .707 0m-9.193 9.193a.5.5 0 0 1 0 .707L3.05
13.657a.5.5 0 0 1-.7011-.707l1.414-1.414a.5.5
0 0 1 .707 0m9.193 2.121a.5.5 0 0 1-.707
0l-1.414-1.414a.5.5 0 0 1 .7011-.707l1.414 1.414a.5.5
0 0 1 0 .707M4.464 4.465a.5.5 0 0 1-.707 0L2.343
3.05a.5.5 0 1 1 .7011-.707l1.414 1.414a.5.5 0 0 1
0 .708'/>
</svg>"
)
```

Figure 11-96 shows the code in the Formula bar and
the preview after adding the code.

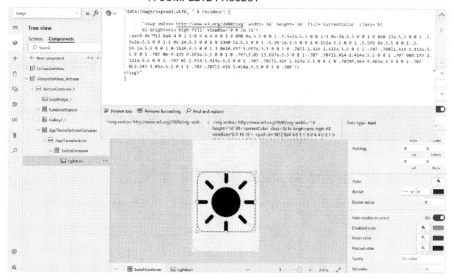

Figure 11-96. *Adding an icon to the LightIcon image*

Make sure to replace the double quotes with single quotes and add the `data:image/svg+xml;utf8` prefix, followed by `EncodeUrl`, before adding the URL. For more detailed information, refer to the official Microsoft documentation provided in the link or scan the QR code shown in Figure 11-97.

```
https://powerusers.microsoft.com/t5/Power-Apps-
Community-Blog/Custom-SVG-Icons-using-Formulas/
ba-p/2595770
```

Figure 11-97. *Microsoft documentation to learn about custom SGV icons in a formula*

9. This theme switcher will switch from a dark theme to a light one and vice versa, so you need to implement a condition in the Image property that changes the color from dark to light when the theme is switched.

    Change the formula code that you added in the image as follows:

```
"data:image/svg+xml;utf8, " & EncodeUrl (
Substitute(
        "<svg xmlns='http://www.w3.org/2000/svg'
        width='16' height='16' fill='currentColor'
        class='bi bi-brightness-high-fill' viewBox='0
        0 16 16'>
<path d='M12 8a4 4 0 1 1-8 0 4 4 0 0 1 8 0M8 0a.5.5
0 0 1 .5.5v2a.5.5 0 0 1-1 0v-2A.5.5 0 0 1 8 0mo
13a.5.5 0 0 1 .5.5v2a.5.5 0 0 1-1 0v-2A.5.5 0 0 1 8
13m8-5a.5.5 0 0 1-.5.5h-2a.5.5 0 0 1 0-1h2a.5.5 0 0
1 .5.5M3 8a.5.5 0 0 1-.5.5h-2a.5.5 0 0 1 0-1h2A.5.5
```

```
0 0 1 3 8m10.6511-5.657a.5.5 0 0 1 0 .7071-1.414
1.415a.5.5 0 1 1-.7011-.70811.414-1.414a.5.5 0
0 1 .707 0m-9.193 9.193a.5.5 0 0 1 0 .707L3.05
13.657a.5.5 0 0 1-.7011-.70711.414-1.414a.5.5
0 0 1 .707 0m9.193 2.121a.5.5 0 0 1-.707
01-1.414-1.414a.5.5 0 0 1 .7011-.70711.414 1.414a.5.5
0 0 1 0 .707M4.464 4.465a.5.5 0 0 1-.707 0L2.343
3.05a.5.5 0 1 1 .7011-.70711.414 1.414a.5.5 0 0 1
0 .708'/>
</svg>",
"currentColor", If(CollapsibleMenu_Activate.
AppColorMode = "Light","White", CollapsibleMenu_
Activate.InactiveIcon_Text)
)
 )
```

This code dynamically adjusts the SVG icon's
color based on the app theme, toggling between
light and dark modes. It embeds the icon into a
URL, using the Substitute() function to replace
the currentColor attribute based on the theme
setting—white for Light and another color for other
settings. The EncodeUrl() function ensures that the
SVG is properly formatted for web compatibility.
This technique enhances UI consistency and
aesthetics by adapting icon visibility to different
backgrounds. Figure 11-98 shows the formula code
and its resulting output, demonstrating how the
icon changes color from black to white.

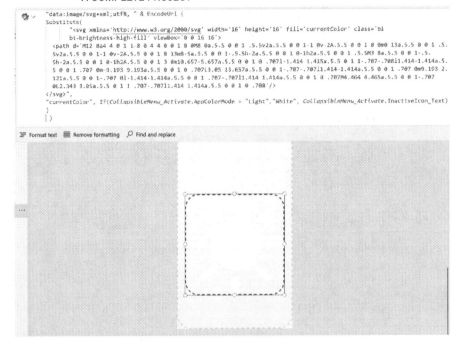

Figure 11-98. *Formula code for changing the theme icon based on the application mode*

Adjust the `PaddingTop` and `PaddingBottom` values from 0 to 8, to ensure that the icon is properly positioned within the frame.

10. Select `SwitchContainer`, choose its fill property from the Formula bar, and add the following code:

```
If(
    CollapsibleMenu_Activate.AppColorMode = "Light",
    CollapsibleMenu_Activate.InactiveIcon,
    RGBA(0,0,0,0)
)
```

Figure 11-99 displays the formula code used in the `Fill` property of `SwitchContainer`.

```
If{
    CollapsibleMenu_Activate.AppColorMode = "Light",
    CollapsibleMenu_Activate.InactiveIcon,
    RGBA(0,0,0,0)
}
```

≡ Format text   ≡ Remove formatting   🔍 Find and replace

Figure 11-99. *Code to change the color*

11. After that, duplicate the SwitchContainer container and rename it SwitchContainer_Dark.

12. Choose a moon icon from Bootstrap and paste the HTML code inside the Image property of the SwitchContainer_Dark container, as shown in Figures 11-100 and 11-101.

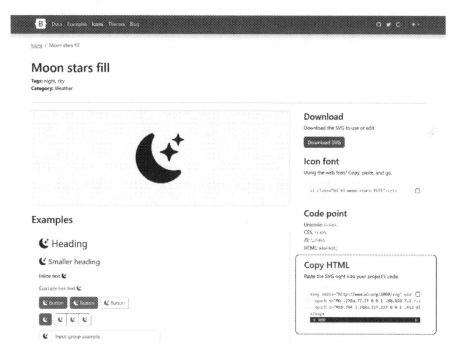

Figure 11-100. *Choosing the night theme icon from Bootstrap*

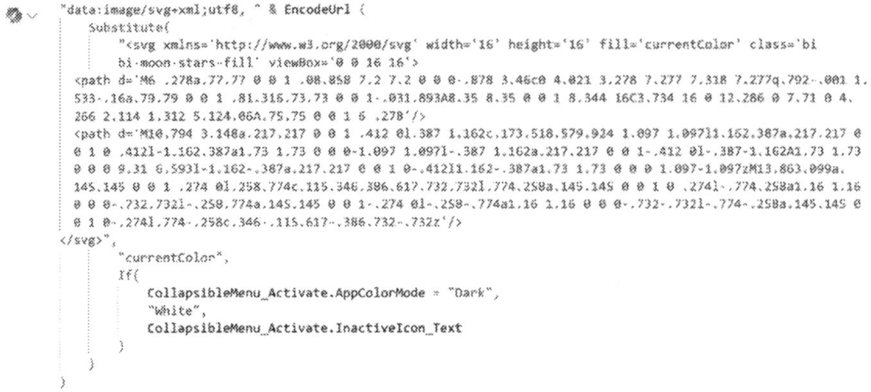

```
"data:image/svg+xml;utf8, " & EncodeUrl (
    Substitute(
        "<svg xmlns='http://www.w3.org/2000/svg' width='16' height='16' fill='currentColor' class='bi
        bi-moon-stars-fill' viewBox='0 0 16 16'>
    <path d='M6 .278a.77.77 0 0 1 .08.858 7.2 7.2 0 0 0-.878 3.46c0 4.021 3.278 7.277 7.318 7.277q.792-.001 1.
    533-.16a.79.79 0 0 1 .81.316.73.73 0 0 1-.031.893A8.35 8.35 0 0 1 8.344 16C3.734 16 0 12.286 0 7.71 0 4.
    266 2.114 1.312 5.124.06A.75.75 0 0 1 6 .278'/>
    <path d='M10.794 3.148a.217.217 0 0 1 .412 0l.387 1.162c.173.518.579.924 1.097 1.097l1.162.387a.217.217 0
    0 1 0 .412l-1.162.387a1.73 1.73 0 0 0-1.097 1.097l-.387 1.162a.217.217 0 0 1-.412 0l-.387-1.162A1.73 1.73
    0 0 0 9.31 6.593l-1.162-.387a.217.217 0 0 1 0-.412l1.162-.387a1.73 1.73 0 0 0 1.097-1.097zM13.863.099a.
    145.145 0 0 1 .274 0l.258.774c.115.346.386.617.732.732l.774.258a.145.145 0 0 1 0 .274l-.774.258a1.16 1.16
    0 0 0-.732.732l-.258.774a.145.145 0 0 1-.274 0l-.258-.774a1.16 1.16 0 0 0-.732-.732l-.774-.258a.145.145 0
    0 1 0-.274l.774-.258c.346-.115.617-.386.732-.732z'/>
    </svg>",
        "currentColor",
        If(
            CollapsibleMenu_Activate.AppColorMode = "Dark",
            "White",
            CollapsibleMenu_Activate.InactiveIcon_Text
        )
    )
)
```

Figure 11-101. *Formula code to add the moon SVG icon*

You can copy the code from here as well:

```
"data:image/svg+xml;utf8, " & EncodeUrl (
    Substitute(
        "<svg xmlns='http://www.w3.org/2000/svg'
        width='16' height='16' fill='currentColor'
        class='bi bi-moon-stars-fill' viewBox='0
        0 16 16'>
    <path d='M6 .278a.77.77 0 0 1 .08.858 7.2 7.2 0 0
    0-.878 3.46c0 4.021 3.278 7.277 7.318 7.277q.792-
    .001 1.533-.16a.79.79 0 0 1 .81.316.73.73 0 0
    1-.031.893A8.35 8.35 0 0 1 8.344 16C3.734 16 0 12.286
    0 7.71 0 4.266 2.114 1.312 5.124.06A.75.75 0 0 1
    6 .278'/>
    <path d='M10.794 3.148a.217.217 0 0 1 .412 0l.387
    1.162c.173.518.579.924 1.097 1.097l1.162.387a.217.217
    0 0 1 0 .412l-1.162.387a1.73 1.73 0 0 0-1.097
    1.097l-.387 1.162a.217.217 0 0 1-.412
    0l-.3811-1.162A1.73 1.73 0 0 0 9.31 6.593l-1.162-
```

```
.387a.217.217 0 0 1 0-.412l1.162-.387a1.73 1.73
0 0 0 1.0911-1.097zM13.863.099a.145.145 0 0 1
.274 0l.258.774c.115.346.386.617.732.732l.774
.258a.145.145 0 0 1 0 .274l-.774.258a1.16 1.16 0 0
0-.732.732l-.258.774a.145.145 0 0 1-.274 0l-.258-
.774a1.16 1.16 0 0 0-.732-.732l-.774-.258a.145.145 0
0 1 0-.274l.774-.258c.346-.115.6111-.386.732-.732z'/>
</svg>",
         "currentColor",
         If(
             CollapsibleMenu_Activate.AppColorMode
             = "Dark",
             "White",
             CollapsibleMenu_Activate.InactiveIcon_Text
         )
     )
 )
```

This code changes AppColorMode to "Dark" because
it is now implementing the dark theme.

13. Select the SwitchContainer_Dark container and
    in the Fill property, add the following code. Make
    sure the AppColorMode is set to "Dark", as shown in
    Figure 11-102.

```
If(
    CollapsibleMenu_Activate.AppColorMode = "Dark",
    CollapsibleMenu_Activate.InactiveIcon,
    RGBA(0,0,0,0)
)
```

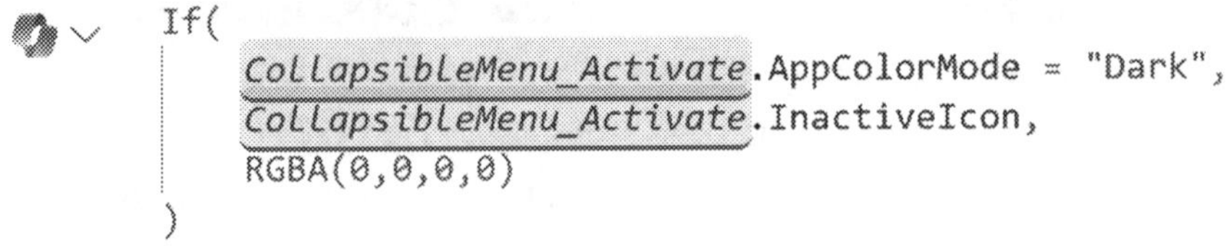

```
If(
    CollapsibleMenu_Activate.AppColorMode = "Dark",
    CollapsibleMenu_Activate.InactiveIcon,
    RGBA(0,0,0,0)
)
```

Figure 11-102. *Formula code to activate the dark color theme*

14. Now you need to create a toggle that will auto-
    align when the menu is expanded. To do that,
    select the AppThemeSwitcher container (which is
    also called the responsive container), choose the
    LayoutDirection property from the Formula bar,
    and add the following code:

    If(
        CollapsibleMenu_Activate.MenuExpanded,
        LayoutDirection.Horizontal,
        LayoutDirection.Vertical
)

    This code will sets the layout to horizontal if the
    menu is expanded or make it vertical if it is not
    expanded.

    Figure 11-103 shows the code of the
    LayoutDirection property of the AppThemeSwitcher
    container.

Figure 11-103. *Formula code of the LayoutDirection property of the AppThemeSwitcher container*

15. Now, fixing the `height` and `width` of the
     `AppThemeSwitcher` container. To do this, set the
     `width` using this code in the Formula bar:

```
If(
    Self.LayoutDirection = LayoutDirection.Horizontal,
    60,
    30
)
```

This code evaluates the orientation of a container
and adjusts its dimensions accordingly. If the
container's direction is horizontal, the width is set
to 60, while the height is set to 30. Conversely, if the
container is not horizontal, the width is set to 30
and the height to 60. This ensures that the container
maintains appropriate proportions regardless of
its orientation. Set the height with the following
formula from the Formula bar.

```
If(
    Self.LayoutDirection = LayoutDirection.Horizontal,
    30,
    60
)
```

16. Once this is done, set the toggle container, which
is named AppThemeSwitcherContainer to take
its width and height from the inner responsive
container. Select the AppThemeSwitcherContainer
container, choose the width from the Formula bar
and add the following code:

AppThemeSwitcher.Width

Here, AppThemeSwitcher is the inner responsive
container under AppThemeSwitcherContainer.

Also, set the height using the following
formula code:

AppThemeSwitcher.Height

17. Let's add a border now. Select the
AppThemeSwitcherContainer container and set the
following parameters to design the border.

Border Thickness = 2
Border Color = *CollapsibleMenu_Activate*.InactiveIcon
Border Radius = 20

Figure 11-104 shows the preview after changing the
parameters.

Figure 11-104. *AppThemeSwitcherContainer preview after changing
the parameters*

18. Now set the Border Radius property for SwitchContainer and SwitchContainer_ Dark to 20, matching the changes in the AppThemeSwitcherContainer. Figure 11-105 shows the preview of the toggle icon.

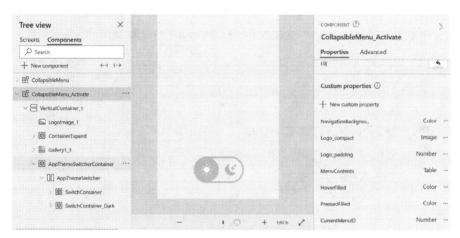

Figure 11-105. *Preview after changing the border radius in SwitchContainer and SwitchContainer_Dark*

19. Now add a button inside AppThemeSwitcherContainer to ensure that the entire container is clickable. I renamed it AppThemeSwitcherButton. Change the following parameters of the button:

Text = ""

X = 0

Y = 0

Width = Parent.Width

Height = Parent.Height

Fill = Color.Transparent

Border Style = None

Pressed Fill = *CollapsibleMenu_Activate*.PressedFilled

Hover Fill = *CollapsibleMenu_Activate*.HoverFilled

Note   CollapsibleMenu_Activate is the name of the
component. Check your component name and replace it if required.

---

20. The last step is to configure the button to
    change the color or theme. To do this, select the
    AppThemeSwitcherButton, choose the OnSelect
    property from the Formula bar, and add the
    following code:

```
If(
    varAppColorMode = "Light",
    Set(
        varAppColorMode,
        "Dark"
    ),
    Set (
        varAppColorMode,
        "Light"
    )
);
```

This formula checks the value of the global variable
varAppColorMode. If the value is Light, it sets
the variable to Dark. If the value is Dark, it sets
the variable to Light. The result is the last value
assigned to the variable.

21. Turn on the Access App Scope feature from the
CollapsibleMenu_Active properties, as shown in
Figure 11-106.

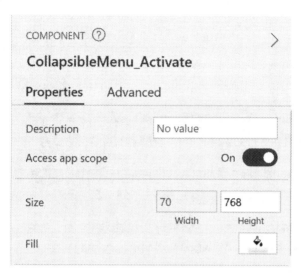

Figure 11-106. *Turning on the Access App Feature of the
CollapsibleMenu_Activate component*

With this setting turned on, your component can
now access:

- Global variables

- Collections

- Controls and components on screens, such as a
TextInput control

- Tabular data sources, such as Dataverse tables

When this setting is turned Off, none of these are
available to the component. The Set and Collect
functions are still available, but the resulting
variables and collections are scoped to the
component instance and not shared with the app.

22. Go to the screen, select App, and choose the
    formulas. Add the following code to the formulas:

```
PrimaryColor = If(varAppThemeMode = "Dark",
RGBA(9,15,37,1), RGBA(255,255, 255,1));

PrimaryColor_Text = If(varAppThemeMode = "Dark",
"RGBA(9,15,37,1)", "RGBA(255,255, 255,1)");

AccentColor =  If(varAppThemeMode = "Dark", RGBA(254,
189, 47,1), RGBA(254, 189, 47, 1));

AccentColor_Text =  If(varAppThemeMode = "Dark",
"RGBA(254, 189, 47,1)", "RGBA(254, 189, 47, 1)");

TertiarColor = If(varAppThemeMode="Dark",RGBA(16,25,50,
1),RGBA(244,244,244,1));

TertiarColor_Text =If(varAppThemeMode="Dark","RGBA(16
,25,50,1)","RGBA(244,244,244,1)");

PrimaryTextColor = If(varAppThemeMode="Dark",RGBA(247,
247, 247, 1),RGBA(37, 52, 100, 1));

PrimaryTextColor_Text = If(varAppThemeMode="Dark","RG
BA(247, 247, 247, 1)","RGBA(37, 52, 100, 1)");

SecondaryTextColor = If(varAppThemeMode="Dark",RG
BA(115, 131, 176, 1),RGBA(115, 131, 176, 1));
```

SecondaryTextColor_Text = If(varAppThemeMode="Dark",
"RGBA(115, 131, 176, 1)" , "RGBA(115, 131, 176, 1)");

AccentTextColor = If(varAppThemeMode = "Dark", RGBA(22,
25, 39, 1), RGBA(22, 25, 39, 1));

AccentTextColor_Text = If(varAppThemeMode = "Dark",
"RGBA(22, 25, 39, 1)", "RGBA(22, 25, 39, 1)");

HighlightColor = If(varAppThemeMode = "Dark", RGBA(23,
33, 69, 1), RGBA(215, 219, 230, 1));

HighlightColor_Text = If(varAppThemeMode = "Dark",
"RGBA(23, 33, 69, 1)", "RGBA(215, 219, 230, 1)");

varHoverFilled=If(varAppThemeMode="Dark",RGBA(255,255,
255,0.1),RGBA(0,0,0,0.1));

varPressedFilled=If(varAppThemeMode="Dark",RGBA(255,
255,255,0.2),RGBA(0,0,0,0.2));

This color scheme is designed to automatically
adjust the theme color when switching to light or
dark mode.

Figure 11-107 shows the code in the App formulas.

Figure 11-107. *Theme color code in the App formulas*

657

23. Now update the values of the custom properties
using the values specified in the theme color file that
you previously created.

Select the specified custom properties and update
their default values as follows:

NavigationBackground = TertiaryColor

HoverFilled = varHoverFilled

PressedFilled = varPressedFilled

TextColor = PrimaryTextColor

AppColorMode = varAppThemeMode

For example, choose the NavigationBackground
custom property and add the value TertiaryColor,
as shown in Figure 11-108.

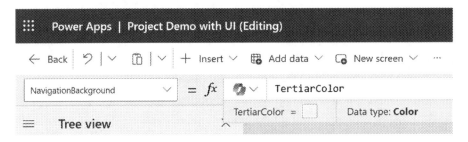

Figure 11-108. *Changing the NavigationBackground default value
with a color variable*

24. Select the SelectedIconBG custom property and
    apply the following formula code to adjust its color
    based on changes to the theme:

```
If(
    varAppThemeMode = "Dark",
    HighlightColor,
    PrimaryColor
)
```

25. Go to the Media section and upload a white version
    of your logo. This is necessary because in dark
    mode, a colored logo might become invisible.

26. Select the Logo_Expanded custom property and add
    the following formula code:

```
If(
    varAppThemeMode = "Dark",
    'Full logo white',
    'Full logo'
)
```

This code will determine if the theme is set to dark,
in which case it will display the white logo. If the
theme is not dark, the colored logo will be shown
instead.

27. You are done! Figure 11-109 shows the difference
    between the light and dark themes in compact and
    expanded menus.

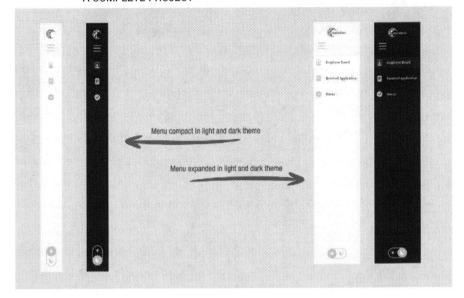

Figure 11-109. *Menu preview in light and dark mode, also in compact and expanded mode*

To activate the menu, just add this menu to the screen container. Figure 11-60 shows how to add custom components in Power Apps.

Creating Complex UI Using Microsoft Copilot

You have reached the final part of this demo. This section demonstrates how to create a unique design interface using Copilot for Power Apps. To complete this demo, I use three websites for different purposes:

- **Color Hunt** (https://colorhunt.co/): To select an appropriate color scheme.

- **Microsoft Copilot Web** (https://bing.com/chat): To generate unique images for the application.

- **ILoveImg** (https://www.iloveimg.com/): To upscale the images created with Microsoft Copilot.

There are many other free tools available online, so feel free to choose your own alternatives. Follow these steps to get started:

1. Go back to your project. Open Color Hunt (https://colorhunt.co/) and choose a color scheme. For this demo, I chose the color schema shown in Figure 11-110.

Figure 11-110. Choosing a color scheme for the Power Apps UI

2. As shown in Figure 11-110, both the color code and the color name are crucial for providing commands in Copilot and for manual UI design in Power Apps. Use this Copilot prompt to design a clean, modern, and professional image to use in Power Apps:

   Generate a professional, modern and clean image for an office management webapp mainly for desktop browser. The app color scheme should include white (rgb(246, 241, 238)) main color, Orange (rgb(237, 125, 49)) as

the primary color, brown (rgb(108, 95, 91)) as the
supplementary color. The page should feature a welcome
message and include 3 menu items. The menus should
be clearly labeled and visually distinct. The design
should be clean, user-friendly and professional. Do not
generate any additional components. Do not add any text
to the image.

3. Add this prompt to Microsoft Copilot Web
    (https://bing.com/chat) and attempt to generate
    a suitable image. Note that the image you receive
    will not be the same as in the demo, as Copilot
    creates unique images each time. You may also need
    to modify the prompt according to your specific
    requirements. I chose the image from Copilot shown
    in Figure 11-111.

Figure 11-111. AI generated image by Microsoft Copilot

4. Super! Download the image and take a screenshot of the banner part only, as shown in Figure 11-112.

Figure 11-112. *Separate the banner image from the AI generated image*

5. After taking the screenshot, the quality of the image has diminished. Therefore, you need to upscale the image to enhance its quality, ensuring it is suitable for high-quality use. Open ILoveImg (`https://www.iloveimg.com/`), select the Upscale option, and upload the image, as shown in Figure 11-113.

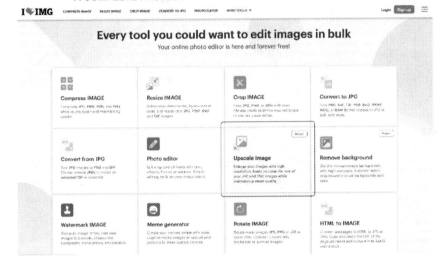

Figure 11-113. *Upscale Image option in the ILoveImg tool*

6. After uploading the image, you will notice that the
   tool displays the upscale resolution, as shown in
   Figure 11-114.

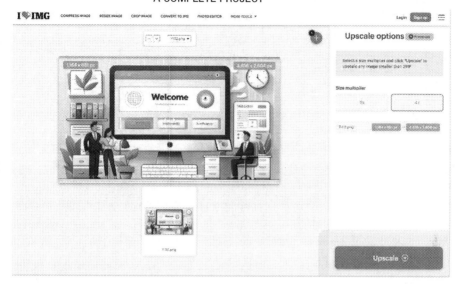

Figure 11-114. *Upscaling image quality using the ILoveImg tool*

7. Upscale the image and download it.

8. Go back to the project and add three more screens—
called EmployeeBoard, ReceivedApplication, and
Status—as shown in Figure 11-115.

665

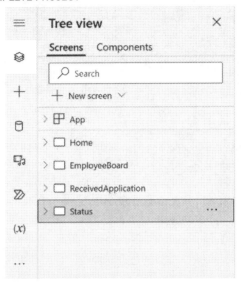

Figure 11-115. *Creating three new screens in the Power Apps project*

9. Compose the following prompt in Copilot to add
    three more horizontal containers inside the vertical
    container named Container10 (see Figure 11-116):

    Add 3 containers in "Container10"

Figure 11-116. *Copilot prompt to create new containers inside a vertical container*

10. Let's configure the container first. Select the top container, rename it HeaderContainer, and set the following parameters:

    Flexible Height = Off
    Height = 100

11. Rename the middle container BodyContainer and the bottom container FooterContainer. Select the three containers from the Tree View and change the Drop Shadow property to None, as shown in Figure 11-117.

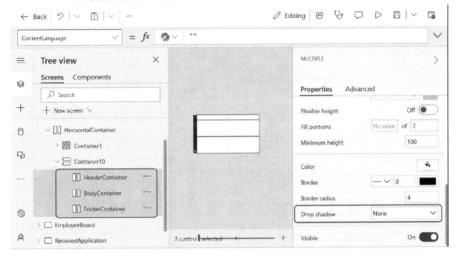

Figure 11-117. *Renaming the container names and selecting None for the Drop Shadow option*

12. Upload the downloaded upscaled image in the Power Apps project.

13. Change the background color from RGBA(246,255,255,1) to RGBA(246,241,238,1). This is the color that you got from Color Hunt. Refer to Figure 11-110.

   To change the color, select Apps from Tree View, and choose Formulas from the Formula bar. After that, change the values of PrimaryColor and PrimaryColor_Text. Only change the value of light theme. Figure 11-118 shows the actual changes.

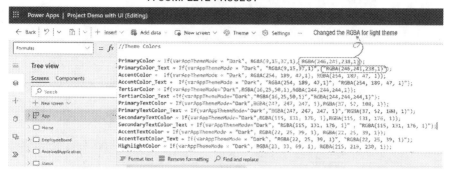

Figure 11-118. *RGBA code to change the background color to the new color code*

After changing the background color to RGBA (246, 241, 238, 1), you can see that the background changes from White to Whitesmoke color.

14. Choose the HeaderContainer and add a new non-responsive container. Inside the new container, add a new text label and set the following parameters from the Formula bar:

Text = "Welcome to Backend Office Management Application"

Font = Font.'Lato Black'

FontWeight = FontWeight.Bold

Size = 18

Height = Parent.Height

Width = Parent.Width

PaddingTop = 10

PaddingBottom = 10

PaddingLeft = 25

PaddingRight = 10

BorderStyle= BorderStyle.None

PaddingRight = 10

Also, in the Color property, add the following formula code, as shown in Figure 11-119.

```
If(
    varAppThemeMode = "Dark",
    AccentColor,
    RGBA(237,125,49,1)
)
```

Figure 11-119. *Adding formula code to the Color property of the text label*

This code means that if dark mode is enabled, the text color will be AccentColor. Conversely, in light mode, the text color will be RGBA (237,125,49,1), which is the primary color from Color Hunt, as shown in Figure 11-120.

Figure 11-120. *Color codes from Color Hunt*

Press F5 or run the app to see the preview. You will
see something like Figure 11-121.

Figure 11-121. *Preview of the text label and background after
changing the color*

15. Select BodyContainer and add two more
    containers called RightBodyContainer and
    LeftBodyContainer, as shown in Figure 11-122.

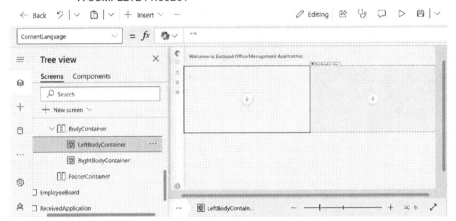

Figure 11-122. *Adding two new non-responsive containers inside BodyContainer*

Set the following parameters for both containers:

Border Radius = 0
Drop Shadow = None

16. In LeftBodyContainer, add a text label and a
button, as shown in Figure 11-123.

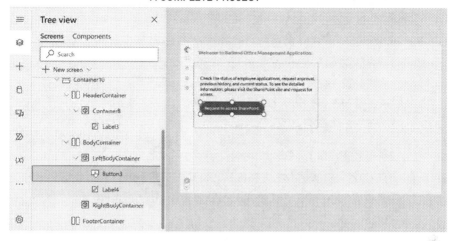

Figure 11-123. *Adding a text label and button to LeftBodyContainer*

Select the Text label, choose the color properties
from the Formula bar, and add this code:

```
If(
    varAppThemeMode = "Dark",

    RGBA(255,255,255,1),
    RGBA(79,74,69,1)
)
```

This means that when the theme switches to dark
mode, the content or text will be white. Otherwise, it
will be dark brown.

17. In RightBodyContainer, add a new image and set
the following properties from the Formula bar:

```
Image = 'UpscaleImage'
Height = Parent.Height
Width = Parent.Width
```

X = 0

Y = 0

PaddingLeft = 25

PaddingRight = 10

BorderStyle= BorderStyle.None

PaddingRight = 10

Note that, in the Image property, I used
UpscaleImage. This is the image that you upscale
for your project. You can also use any other image if
you want.

18. After changing these parameters, you will see
something like Figure 11-124.

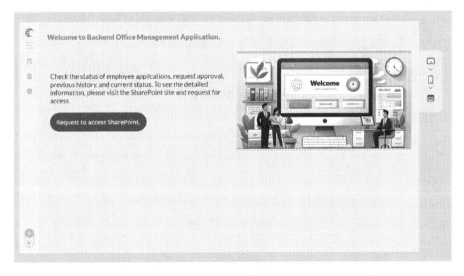

Figure 11-124. *Adding an AI image that was generated by
Microsoft Copilot*

19. In FooterContainer, add a new container. Inside the
     container, add a Copilot component and connect
     your data source, as shown in Figure 11-125. As
     demonstrated in previous chapters, I have a ready
     data source. You can either use your existing data
     source or create a new one.

Figure 11-125. *Adding a Copilot component and choosing a
data source*

20. Set the following parameters of the Copilot
     component:

Height = Parent.Height
Width = Parent.Width
X = 0
Y = 0

21. After you set these parameters, you will see the page
shown in Figure 11-126.

Figure 11-126. *Preview after adding the Copilot component and
setting its parameters*

22. As you are now focusing on the UI, you can adjust
some parameters of `FooterContainer`. Set the top,
bottom, left, and right padding to 20, as shown in
Figure 11-127.

Figure 11-127. *Adjusting the padding of FooterContainer*

23.   Press F5 or run the app to see the preview. You will see something similar to Figure 11-128.

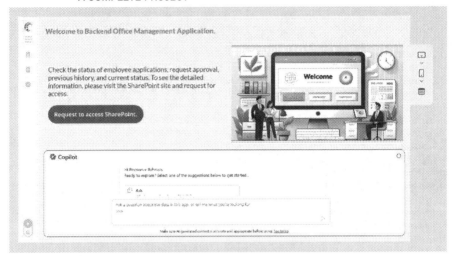

Figure 11-128. *Preview of the homepage of the app after adding the Copilot component*

If you switch to dark mode, you will see the dark mode shown in Figure 11-129.

Figure 11-129. *Preview of the dark mode*

24. To the other pages (Employee Board, Received Application, and Status), add your data source and set the color conditions explained in this demo.

Summary

This chapter demonstrated how to use Microsoft Copilot in Power Apps to create a dynamic, modern UI with features like collapsible menus and theme switching. It walked through the process step-by-step, using Power Fx and Copilot to design an intuitive and visually appealing application, enhancing both functionality and user experience.

Chapter 12 explores the future of Copilot and Power Apps, focusing on the latest trends in app development. You'll look at how AI, automation, and new integration capabilities are set to revolutionize the way we build and interact with applications. That chapter provides insights into the innovations that will shape the future of app development.

Visions of the Future: Copilot's Evolving Landscape

The previous chapter explored the capabilities of Microsoft Copilot, and you learned how to transform a standard Power Apps interface into a modern, user-friendly design with advanced features like collapsible menus and theme switching. This hands-on experience showcased how to elevate an app's usability and aesthetics using the latest tools.

This chapter shifts focus to the future of app development. It explores the emerging trends that are set to redefine how applications are built and used, with a particular emphasis on the evolving landscape of AI integration, low-code platforms, and cross-platform development. This chapter provides a forward-looking perspective on the innovations and strategies that will drive the next wave of app development, preparing you to stay ahead in this rapidly changing field.

© Rezwanur Rahman 2024
R. Rahman, *Microsoft Copilot for Power Apps*, Inside Copilot,
https://doi.org/10.1007/979-8-8688-0512-7_12

Trailblazing Trends: The Next Wave in App Development

In the rapidly evolving landscape of app development, staying ahead of the curve is essential. Emerging trends are continuously reshaping how developers approach creating applications, offering new tools and technologies that promise to revolutionize the industry. From integrating cutting-edge artificial intelligence to embracing the power of blockchain, these innovations are setting the stage for the next wave of app development. This section explores the most promising trends that are poised to transform the way we build and interact with applications.

AI Integration

Artificial intelligence (AI) is increasingly becoming a cornerstone of modern app development. AI integration enables the creation of smarter, more intuitive applications that can understand and predict user needs. AI-driven features like natural language processing (NLP), machine learning (ML) algorithms, and personalized recommendations are transforming user experiences. For example, chatbots and virtual assistants, powered by AI, provide real-time customer support and automate repetitive tasks, improving efficiency and user satisfaction. Additionally, AI is enhancing app security through advanced threat detection and fraud prevention mechanisms.

Low-Code/No-Code Platforms

The rise of low-code and no-code platforms is democratizing app development, allowing users with minimal coding experience to build robust applications. These platforms offer drag-and-drop interfaces, pre-built templates, and easy-to-configure components, significantly reducing development time and cost. Tools like Microsoft Power Apps enable businesses to quickly create custom solutions without relying heavily on traditional development resources. This trend is empowering more people to participate in app development, fostering innovation, and addressing specific business needs more efficiently.

Cross-Platform Development

Cross-platform development tools and frameworks are revolutionizing how developers build applications, ensuring that they work seamlessly across multiple devices and operating systems. Technologies like React Native, Flutter, and Xamarin allow developers to write code once and deploy it across platforms such as iOS, Android, and the web. This approach not only saves time and resources but also ensures a consistent user experience across different devices. As a result, businesses can reach a broader audience with their applications while maintaining high-quality performance and functionality.

Augmented Reality (AR) and Virtual Reality (VR)

Augmented Reality (AR) and Virtual Reality (VR) are no longer confined to gaming and entertainment; they are now integral parts of various app development projects. AR and VR technologies are enhancing user experiences by providing immersive and interactive environments. For instance, AR can be used in retail apps to allow customers to visualize products in their real-world environment before making a purchase. VR is being utilized in education and training apps to create realistic simulations that enhance learning and skill development. As these technologies continue to evolve, their application in app development will expand, offering new possibilities for engagement and interaction.

Blockchain Technology

Blockchain technology is making a significant impact on app development, particularly in areas concerning security, data integrity, and decentralization. Blockchain's decentralized nature ensures that data is stored securely across multiple nodes, reducing the risk of data breaches and fraud. This technology is being leveraged to create decentralized applications (dApps) that operate on peer-to-peer networks, thereby enhancing transparency and trust. In industries such as finance, supply chain, and healthcare, blockchain is revolutionizing how data is managed and shared, providing greater security and efficiency. By incorporating blockchain, developers can build apps that offer enhanced security features, fostering user confidence in data handling and transactions.

Upcoming Innovations in Copilot Technology

Digital productivity is set to experience a significant transformation with the upcoming innovations in Copilot technology. As artificial intelligence advances, Microsoft is introducing more sophisticated, intuitive, and efficient AI-driven features across its product suite. These enhancements aim to revolutionize user interactions with software, making tools smarter, more responsive, and seamlessly integrated into daily workflows. From intelligent assistance in note-taking and compliance management to personalized themes and advanced meeting preparation, the next wave of Copilot innovations promises to empower users with unprecedented levels of productivity and insight. The following sections discuss the detailed features, benefits, and release schedules of these exciting new developments.

Microsoft Copilot (Microsoft 365)

Microsoft Copilot is evolving to integrate advanced AI-driven features across its suite of tools, significantly enhancing productivity and user experience. From expanding Copilot's capabilities with plugins to providing graph-grounded insights in Excel, Copilot is set to revolutionize how users interact with their data and workflows.

Plugins in Copilot

Users can now use plugins via `copilot.microsoft.com` to expand Copilot skills. This feature integrates various plugins to extend Copilot's capabilities, increasing productivity and customization. It is currently in development and is expected to be released in December CY2024. This feature will be available on the web platform and is intended for worldwide (standard multi-tenant) cloud instances.

Copilot in Excel: Graph Grounded Chat

You will be able to ask Copilot for answers grounded in your work content from the Microsoft Graph—your chats, documents, meetings, and emails—beyond your active Excel workbook. If you're analyzing a workbook and want to enhance your understanding using information from another source in your tenant, just ask Copilot in Excel. This feature provides contextual insights from across the Microsoft Graph, enhancing data analysis and decision-making. It is currently in development and is slated for release in August CY2024. This feature will be available on web, desktop, and Mac platforms, and is intended for worldwide (standard multi-tenant) cloud instances.

Usage Reports: Microsoft Copilot with Graph-Grounded Chat

Microsoft Copilot with graph-grounded chat usage metrics will be included in the Copilot for Microsoft 365 Usage report. This new feature provides additional usage insights and informs adoption strategy decisions for Microsoft Copilot in your organization. It offers detailed usage metrics to help organizations track Copilot adoption and optimize its use. Currently in development, it is expected to be released in September CY2024 with a preview in March CY2024. This feature will be available on the web platform and is intended for worldwide (standard multi-tenant) cloud instances.

Microsoft Viva

Microsoft Viva integrates Copilot's AI capabilities to enhance employee experience and organizational productivity. With features designed to improve workplace satisfaction, track goals, and boost engagement, Viva is poised to transform how teams collaborate and grow.

Copilot in Viva Glint

This feature highlights top issues and potential solutions harnessing Copilot AI capabilities in Viva Glint. It helps managers and HR teams quickly identify and address employee concerns and improve workplace satisfaction. Currently in development, it is expected to be released in November CY2024 with a preview in June CY2024. This feature will be available on the web platform and is intended for worldwide (standard multi-tenant) cloud instances.

Viva Goals: M365 Chat Plugin

This feature empowers users to track goals and progress via a chat plugin in Microsoft 365. It simplifies goal tracking and increases team collaboration and accountability. Currently in development, it is expected to be released in November CY2024 with a preview in August CY2024. This feature will be available on the web platform and is intended for worldwide (standard multi-tenant) cloud instances.

Copilot in Viva Engage

Experience the power of Copilot in Viva Engage, providing intelligent insights and assistance. This feature enhances engagement and collaboration with AI-driven insights. Currently in development, it is expected to be released in October CY2024. This feature will be available on the web platform and is intended for worldwide (standard multi-tenant) cloud instances.

OneNote

OneNote integrates Copilot's advanced AI to enhance creating and managing notes, making it a more powerful tool for users on the go. With intelligent suggestions and automated organization, OneNote on iPad is set to elevate productivity.

Copilot Chat on OneNote for iPad

OneNote Copilot on iPad is your intelligent assistant for capturing and structuring information. This feature enhances productivity by providing intelligent suggestions and automated organization of notes. Currently in development, it is expected to be released in December CY2024. This feature will be available on the iOS platform and is intended for worldwide (standard multi-tenant) cloud instances.

Outlook

Outlook is getting a productivity boost with Copilot's AI-driven features, making it easier to prepare for meetings and personalize the email experience. These enhancements aim to streamline user workflows and improve efficiency.

Prepare for Meetings with Copilot in the New Outlook for Windows and Web

With so many people in back-to-back meetings, it can be a real struggle to stay on top of pre-reads, action items, and even what each meeting is about. Copilot can identify and summarize the key points so you can show up prepared in just a few minutes. When you have an upcoming meeting, Copilot proactively shows you a Prepare button in your inbox, which helps you quickly get context for the meeting by providing a summary of the meeting and showing and summarizing relevant files leveraging the power of the Microsoft Graph. This feature helps users prepare for meetings quickly by summarizing key points and relevant files, enhancing meeting productivity. Currently in development, it is expected to be released in July CY2024. This feature will be available on desktop and web platforms and is intended for worldwide (standard multi-tenant) cloud instances.

Outlook Themes Generated by Microsoft Copilot

Make Outlook yours with themes generated by Copilot. You will be able to find these themes in Settings. This feature personalizes the Outlook experience with AI-generated themes. Currently in development, it is expected to be released in July CY2024. This feature will be available on iOS and Android platforms and is intended for worldwide (standard multi-tenant) cloud instances.

Microsoft Purview

Microsoft Purview is enhancing its compliance capabilities with the integration of AI, centralizing tools, and insights for a streamlined approach to managing risks and regulatory requirements. This evolution promises to improve efficiency and effectiveness in compliance management.

AI Hub in Compliance Portal

The AI Hub in Microsoft Purview is a centralized location for all AI-driven compliance tools and insights. This feature streamlines compliance processes by leveraging AI to identify risks and ensure regulatory adherence. Currently in development, it is expected to be released in November CY2024 with a preview in May CY2024. This feature will be available on the web platform and is intended for worldwide (standard multi-tenant) cloud instances.

You can view the full Microsoft 365 Copilot roadmap and upcoming innovations in Copilot technology using the following URL or the QR code shown in Figure 12-1.

```
https://www.microsoft.com/en-us/microsoft-365/roadmap?filters=
Microsoft%20Copilot%20(Microsoft%20365)%2CIn%20development#
owRoadmapMainContent
```

Figure 12-1. *Microsoft 365 Copilot roadmap QR code*

Predicting Future Trends in Power Apps Development

As we look to the future, Power Apps is poised to undergo significant advancements that will shape its development and usage in the years to come. Driven by the evolving needs of businesses and the rapid pace of technological innovation, Power Apps will continue to enhance its capabilities, offering more robust and versatile solutions for users. The following sections explore the key trends expected to influence the development of Power Apps, providing insights into how Microsoft plans to make the platform more powerful, user-friendly, and integrated with other services. By understanding these trends, organizations can better prepare to leverage Power Apps to its fullest potential.

Greater Customization

One of the most anticipated trends in the development of Power Apps is the push toward greater customization. As organizations seek to create apps that are more closely aligned with their unique workflows and requirements, Microsoft is likely to enhance the customization capabilities within Power Apps. This will include more advanced and user-friendly tools for designing app interfaces, defining custom business logic, and integrating with proprietary systems. Additionally, the introduction of more flexible and granular control over app components will enable users to tailor their applications to specific business needs, resulting in more effective and efficient solutions.

Integration with Other Microsoft Services

Power Apps is expected to further integrate with other Microsoft services, such as Office 365, Dynamics 365, Azure, and Microsoft Teams. This deeper integration will facilitate a more seamless experience for users who rely on multiple Microsoft products for their day-to-day operations. For example, enhanced connectivity with Office 365 will allow for more efficient data sharing and collaboration, while integration with Dynamics 365 will enable businesses to create custom applications that leverage CRM and ERP data. As Power Apps continues to evolve, you can anticipate more robust and intuitive integrations that streamline workflows and improve productivity.

AI and Automation Features

The incorporation of AI and automation features into Power Apps is set to revolutionize the way users create and manage applications. Microsoft is likely to introduce more AI-driven tools that simplify the app development process, such as intelligent app suggestions, automated workflows, and predictive analytics. These features will not only make it easier for users to build and maintain their apps but will also provide valuable insights that can help optimize business processes. Furthermore, the use of AI for tasks such as natural language processing, image recognition, and data analysis will open new possibilities for creating innovative and intelligent applications.

Expanded Template Libraries

As Power Apps gains popularity, the demand for pre-built templates that cater to various industries and use cases will continue to grow. Microsoft is expected to expand its library of templates, offering a wider variety of ready-to-use solutions that can be easily customized to meet specific business needs. These templates will cover a broad range of functions, from simple task management to complex enterprise solutions, and will help users get started quickly without the need for extensive development knowledge. The availability of more sophisticated and versatile templates will empower users to create high-quality applications with minimal effort.

Community Contributions

The Power Apps community of developers and users is rapidly growing, and their contributions are becoming increasingly significant. This vibrant community is expected to play a crucial role in shaping the future of Power Apps by sharing knowledge, best practices, and custom solutions. Community-driven content, such as custom connectors, components, and templates, will enrich the Power Apps ecosystem and provide users with a wealth of resources to draw from. Additionally, the collaborative nature of the community will foster innovation and encourage the development of new features and capabilities that address the evolving needs of users.

The Future of AI Builder and Power Apps: What's Next?

This section discusses the future updates of AI Builder and Power Apps, exploring the exciting innovations and enhancements on the horizon. As these tools continue to evolve, new features promise to revolutionize the way users build and deploy applications, making them more intelligent, intuitive, and efficient. From advanced AI capabilities to seamless integrations, these upcoming developments will empower users to create smarter, more responsive solutions. The following sections explore the specifics of what lies ahead for AI Builder and Power Apps.

AI Builder

AI Builder is a pivotal tool and is set to receive several exciting updates. This section explores the future enhancements planned for AI Builder, highlighting the features that will elevate its capabilities to new heights.

1. **Admins can enable or disable extension credits for AI Builder.**

   Admins now have enhanced control over credit extension requests in the Power Platform Admin Center, thanks to new tenant settings that allow them to specify who can request these extensions. They can choose separately whether admins or makers are permitted to request credit extensions, providing better oversight on how AI Builder credits are utilized. With this update, admins can configure the availability of the Request an Extension button for both makers and admins when an environment exceeds its allocated credits. Previously, this button was always available to both groups in their respective interfaces, regardless of the environment's status. This feature is available from September 2024 as part of the AI Builder 2024 release wave 1, enables administrators, makers, marketers, and analysts to manage credit consumption more effectively. It will be enabled automatically, ensuring seamless integration into existing workflows.

2. **Admins can govern access to AI Builder models
    through the Admin Center.**

    Admins now can control who has access to AI
    capabilities across their tenant, helping them
    comply with internal responsible AI requirements
    and potentially increasing AI Builder adoption. The
    AI Builder connector can be configured through
    the Power Platform Admin Center, allowing admins
    to manage access and usage of AI Builder models
    within their organization. This feature enables
    admins to turn access to specific AI models on or off
    across various environments, providing full control
    over the governance of AI capabilities powered by
    AI Builder. Available to both admins and makers,
    this update was revised on April 4, 2024, and is
    now generally available. Part of the AI Builder 2024
    release wave 1, this feature is automatically enabled
    for administrators, makers, marketers, and business
    analysts, ensuring seamless implementation and
    enhanced governance over AI model usage.

3. **Companies can monitor usage of AI Builder
    models, including GPT outputs.**

    Companies can now monitor the usage
    and performance of AI Builder models with
    preconfigured monitoring reports, facilitating the
    adoption of AI Builder in production scenarios.
    These reports allow users to track which AI Builder
    models are used, how frequently they are used,
    and their associated credit consumption. This
    enhanced tracking capability ensures more efficient
    deployment of AI Builder models in production

settings. By effectively managing the historical data generated by Power Automate flows, Power Apps, or other Microsoft Power Platform products, companies can maintain efficient and cost-effective Dataverse environments.

The AI Builder activity page provides a comprehensive view of AI model activity, including usage in Power Apps and detailed tracking of inputs and outputs for GPT text generation models. Users can customize the data by applying filters for specific timeframes or models. This data is valuable for makers who want to monitor their AI models' usage and for environment admins who need to oversee all activity and credit consumption within an environment. Available to both admins and makers, this feature was last updated on April 17, 2024, and became generally available in September 2024 as part of the AI Builder 2024 release wave 1. It is automatically enabled for administrators, makers, marketers, and business analysts, ensuring seamless integration and enhanced monitoring capabilities.

4. **Companies can try AI Builder capabilities in developer environments before committing to AI.**

If you created a developer environment using the Power Apps developer plan, you can utilize AI Builder, customize AI Builder models, and integrate them into your flows and apps. You receive 20,000 credits every month for use within your developer environment, offering a valuable opportunity to explore AI Builder's possibilities without immediate commitment.

Available to both admins and makers, this feature was last updated on May 9, 2024.

It entered public preview in September 2024. Part of the AI Builder 2024 release wave 1, this feature is automatically enabled for administrators, makers, marketers, and business analysts. This automatic enablement ensures users can seamlessly experiment with AI Builder's capabilities in a development setting, fostering innovation and experimentation.

5. **Admins can use the new AI capacity management experience.**

   Admins can now monitor the usage of AI Builder with preconfigured monitoring reports in the Power Platform Admin Center. This facilitates the setup of an AI center of excellence using AI Builder, providing greater tracking capabilities that allow organizations to deploy AI Builder models more easily in a production setting and more accurately forecast credit usage.

   Utilizing the "Get insights into currency and storage consumption" release, preconfigured monitoring reports are available for admins to track where AI Builder models are used, how often they are used, and how many credits they consume. These reports provide admins with a comprehensive view of AI model usage across an organization.

   Available to both admins and makers, this feature was last updated on April 4, 2024. It will enter public preview in March 2025. Part of the AI Builder 2024 release wave 2, this feature is automatically enabled for administrators, makers, marketers, and business analysts, ensuring seamless integration and enhanced monitoring capabilities.

6. **Admins can define GPT output formats in JSON with Prompt Builder.**

   Admins can now utilize the GPT Prompt Builder to structure information in specific formats, going beyond basic text processing. This feature allows makers to generate and test specific output formats directly within the Prompt Builder experience, enabling usage across multiple scenarios, including automation, and extending app behaviors where reliable data formatting is crucial. During the public preview, JSON formatting is the first supported output format. AI Builder prompts that generate JSON formatting are accessible from Power Automate and Power Apps, including PCF controls and custom Copilots.

   Available to users, this feature was last updated on April 17, 2024, entered public preview in May 2024 and became generally available in September 2024 as part of the AI Builder 2024 release wave 1. This feature must be enabled or configured by administrators, makers, or business analysts to be available for their users, ensuring seamless integration and enhanced data formatting capabilities.

7. **Users experience advanced settings and model selection in Prompt Builder.**

You gain several advantages by using GPT-4, including a larger context window, more current knowledge, and more capable reasoning. When you open Prompt Builder, you can adjust these settings, allowing you to achieve results that meet your expectations with fewer attempts using various prompts.

In Prompt Builder, you can choose your preferred LLM to associate with individual prompts. In this release, you can select either GPT-4 or GPT-3.5. Additionally, you can control the model temperature to customize the creativity of the output response. GPT-4 is more capable and has knowledge of world events up to April 2023. It offers a larger context window, fitting the equivalent of more than 300 pages of text in a single prompt. GPT-4 also performs better than previous models on tasks requiring careful instruction-following, such as generating specific formats like JSON.

Available to both admins and makers, this feature was last updated on April 17, 2024, entered public preview in May 2024 and became generally available in September 2024 as part of the AI Builder 2024 release wave 1. This feature is automatically enabled for administrators, makers, marketers, and business analysts, ensuring seamless integration and enhanced prompt customization capabilities.

Power Apps

This section explores the future enhancements planned for Power Apps, highlighting the features that will elevate its capabilities to new heights. These advancements aim to make app development more accessible and powerful, enabling users to create applications with greater ease and sophistication. From improved user interfaces to expanded data integration options, the forthcoming updates promise to significantly enhance the functionality and versatility of Power Apps.

1. **Use Copilot easily in Canvas apps.**

   Copilot functionality is turned on by default in Canvas apps that connect to Microsoft Dataverse data, requiring no special configuration. This means that Copilot is available immediately to users, helping them better understand their data by answering questions. For instance, users can ask which employee has the highest sales or which warehouse is out of stock for a certain SKU. Copilot queries Dataverse tables to provide the answers.

   Microsoft is expanding Copilot to more apps and users. Available to both admins and makers, this feature was last updated on March 27, 2024, and entered public preview in July 2024 as part of the Power Apps 2024 release wave 1. This feature is automatically enabled for administrators, makers, marketers, and business analysts, ensuring seamless integration and enhanced data querying capabilities.

2. **Use the Power Platform Environment Settings app.**

The Power Platform Environment Settings app provides a modern, performant, accessible, secure, and extensible settings-management experience, offering a unified experience for application developers to create settings for their applications.

The Power Platform Environment Settings app replaces the legacy web client experience, delivering the same security, access control, and extensibility features. This release involves incremental rollouts, starting with the replacement of the settings application itself and followed by updates. Existing extensions created by customers to extend the settings sitemap will be preserved, and any solution imports that include extensions to settings will be routed to the new Power Platform Environment Settings app.

As part of the initial release, existing links for advanced settings in various Power Platform locations will be redirected from the legacy Settings web client to the new Power Platform Environment Settings app. Until this feature reaches general availability, tenant or environment administrators can turn off the advanced settings redirection to the new app by setting the Advanced Settings Redirection option to Off in the Power Platform Admin Center.

Available to both admins and makers, this feature was last updated on March 6, 2024, and entered public preview in September 2024, and is scheduled for general availability in January 2025. Part of the Power Apps 2024 release wave 1, this feature is automatically enabled for administrators, makers, marketers, and business analysts, ensuring a seamless transition to a unified settings management experience.

Some of the functionality described in this release plan has not been released. Delivery timelines may change, and projected functionality may not be released.

3. **Select columns downloaded to mobile devices.**

You can now select the columns of tables that are downloaded on mobile devices for offline use. The fewer columns you select, the faster the app downloads the data on the device for usage without connectivity.

In the settings of your offline-enabled app in the maker portal, you can customize the offline profile for an optimized data-loading experience for your users. For each table, you can select the columns that are required in the app by either using the suggested columns computed by the system or by manually selecting the columns. On the main page for the offline profile, you can see how many columns are selected for download for each table.

Available to both admins and makers, this feature was last updated on January 25, 2024. It will enter public preview in January 2025, and is scheduled for general availability in April 2025. Part of the Power Apps 2024 release wave 1, this feature is automatically enabled for administrators, makers, marketers, and business analysts, ensuring a seamless and efficient offline data-loading experience.

4. **Modernize maker experience security settings.** Makers can now use a modern and accessible security role editor while creating apps.

Makers can configure security role settings in Power Apps using a new Security Role editor. This feature includes a new panel called New Role, allowing makers to configure column security profiles.

Available to both admins and makers, this feature was last updated on March 25, 2024, entered public preview in May 28 2024, and became generally available from July 14, 2024. Part of the Power Apps 2024 release wave 1, this feature is automatically enabled for administrators, makers, marketers, and business analysts, ensuring a seamless and efficient security configuration experience.

Summary

This chapter explored the future of app development, focusing on how AI integration, low-code platforms, and cross-platform development are set to change how users build and use applications. I also highlighted the upcoming innovations in Microsoft Copilot and how these advancements can enhance productivity and user experiences.

The next chapter moves from discussing future trends to showcasing real-world applications. It includes success stories of companies that have effectively integrated Microsoft Copilot into their operations, demonstrating how these AI-powered tools have improved efficiency, streamlined workflows, and empowered teams to achieve greater success.

Copilot Success Stories: Lessons from the Field

The previous chapter explored how emerging technologies like AI, low-code platforms, and cross-platform development are set to reshape the future of app creation. This chapter turns the spotlight on real-world examples that demonstrate the impact of these innovations.

This chapter shares inspiring stories of organizations that have successfully implemented Microsoft Copilot to enhance their operations. Through these examples, you'll see how AI-driven tools are not just concepts of the future but are already driving significant improvements in productivity, efficiency, and team empowerment.

Inspirational Stories of Success

This section explore the transformative experiences of several companies that have significantly boosted their productivity, streamlined operations, and strengthened their workforce capabilities by incorporating Microsoft Copilot into their daily workflows. By integrating this powerful AI tool into Microsoft products such as Power Platform and Microsoft Teams,

© Rezwanur Rahman 2024
R. Rahman, *Microsoft Copilot for Power Apps*, Inside Copilot,
https://doi.org/10.1007/979-8-8688-0512-7_13

these organizations have not only saved considerable time but also enhanced their operational efficiency. These detailed accounts explain how Microsoft Copilot has become an integral part of their success, enabling smarter decision-making and fostering a more empowered team environment.

KPMG: Harnessing the Power of AI-Driven Productivity with Microsoft 365 Copilot

The success narrative of KPMG's integration of Microsoft 365 Copilot in the professional services industry exemplifies a journey marked by strategic innovation and thoughtful execution. KPMG, a leading global provider in professional services, embarked on an initiative to harness the capabilities of Microsoft 365 Copilot, aiming to enhance productivity, stimulate creativity, and adeptly manage the evolving workplace dynamics. This initiative extended beyond the simple adoption of new technology; it encompassed a comprehensive change-management strategy, ensuring the effective adoption and integration of Copilot into their existing modern workplace framework.

KPMG's approach to implementing Microsoft 365 Copilot was meticulous and multifaceted. They focused on building a compelling business case by evaluating Return on Investment (ROI) and establishing key performance indicators (KPIs) to measure success. Through defining personas, assessing strategic value, and aligning deployment with business priorities, KPMG laid a solid foundation for the adoption of Copilot. The readiness and rollout phase involved assessing licensing needs, data governance, privacy, security, and configuring Copilot for seamless integration. Data governance emerged as a critical factor for the successful utilization of generative AI in the workplace. KPMG emphasized sound content management, permissions adherence, and data security to ensure integrity and regulatory compliance. By optimizing search functionalities and updating governance processes, KPMG established a robust data governance framework to support the effective use of Microsoft 365 Copilot.

Additionally, KPMG expanded the functionality of Copilot by accessing datasets, defining integration methods, and enhancing user experience. This phase aimed to create a more customized Copilot integration that addressed specific organizational needs and challenges, thereby unlocking the full potential of Copilot. Change management played a pivotal role in KPMG's success story, with a focus on empowering users through training, awareness of responsible AI use, and establishing a Copilot Center of Excellence. By fostering an informed and engaged workforce, KPMG ensured that employees could maximize the benefits of Microsoft 365 Copilot and drive innovation within the organization.

Ultimately, KPMG's journey with Microsoft 365 Copilot exemplifies a strategic and comprehensive approach to leveraging AI in professional services. By combining technological innovation with robust change-management practices, KPMG successfully navigated obstacles, empowered its workforce, and embraced the future of work through the transformative capabilities of Microsoft 365 Copilot.

To read the full story, visit `https://customers.microsoft.com/en-us/story/1749522406496386350-kpmg-microsoft-365-copilot-professional-services-en-united-states` or scan the QR code in Figure 13-1.

Figure 13-1. *Success story of KPMG after adopting Microsoft 365 Copilot*

Nsure: Streamlining Insurance Operations and Enhancing Customer Experiences with the Power Platform

Nsure.com, a licensed digital insurance agency based in Florida, United States, enables people to buy home and auto insurance online across all 50 states. The company, founded in 2018, has been using Microsoft Power Platform to automate complex business processes since its early adoption of the platform. Between 2020 and 2023, Nsure's revenue grew at a Compound Annual Growth Rate (CAGR) of over 100 percent.

Nsure.com matches customers with insurance carriers by comparing their requirements with a database of information from over 20 data sources and over 50 top-tier insurers across the nation. The company faced challenges as it quickly grew to nearly 1 million unique users of the platform. With the overwhelming human involvement required in customer contacts, Nsure.com had to deal with over 1 billion data points for its customers, including information about their homes and vehicles. Each month, around 100 customer representatives processed over 100,000 interactions with customers through calls, emails, and texts.

To address these challenges, Nsure.com leveraged Microsoft Power Platform and generative AI to automate various business processes. Power Automate was used to gather responses from multiple systems, which were then consolidated and transformed using generative AI models into specific formats that could be presented to customers and transferred to other systems.

Generative AI was also used to analyze unstructured text from insurance documents, extract key information, and determine the best policy coverages for customers based on real-world data. Next-best actions and email reply suggestions were automatically generated and combined with other transactional data, activity data, and the communication history of the customer.

As a result of these automations, Nsure's customer service representatives reduced their time on manual tasks by more than 60 percent, allowing them to focus on more valuable and meaningful tasks, such as engaging with high-priority, complex escalations; building customer relationships; and increasing satisfaction. Instead of processing every contact, the team could oversee the communications started by AI and make the final decisions.

By adopting Microsoft Power Platform and generative AI, Nsure. com reduced manual processing time by over 60 percent and costs by 50 percent. The company plans to further optimize its operations by eliminating mundane and repetitive tasks with generative AI and Copilot capabilities, as well as having virtual assistants handle more than 90 percent of incoming requests for insurance quotes and policies.

To read the full story, visit `https://powerautomate.microsoft.com/en-us/blog/insurance-agency-nsure-com-leverages-microsoft-power-platform-and-generative-ai-to-reduce-manual-processes-by-60/` or scan the QR code in Figure 13-2.

Figure 13-2.   Success story of Nsure.com

Hargreaves Lansdown: Revolutionizing Efficiency with Microsoft Copilot

Hargreaves Lansdown, a prominent financial services organization in the United Kingdom, has achieved remarkable success by integrating Microsoft Copilot for Microsoft 365 and Teams Premium into its operations. This strategic move aimed to enhance productivity and client service by empowering employees to excel in their strengths and rapidly acquire new skills. The outcome has been nothing short of impressive, with advisors expecting to complete client paperwork four times faster, employees saving two-three hours weekly, and an overwhelming 96 percent of employees finding Microsoft 365 Copilot helpful for daily tasks.

The seamless integration of Copilot has revolutionized the workflow at Hargreaves Lansdown. The company has experienced a significant reduction in the time spent searching through documents and emails. Copilot's advanced AI capabilities swiftly grasp context and generate relevant input in minutes, streamlining information retrieval and simplifying daily tasks. This has enabled employees to focus on high-level, high-value work, allowing leaders to reimagine their business models and pursue once-impossible, bold opportunities.

The implementation of Copilot has also had a profound impact on the company's neurodivergent workers. The ability to record meetings and listen to them later, or receive summaries of what they have missed, has significantly reduced stress and made work more enjoyable for these employees. This unexpected yet welcome benefit of technology has been a testament to the inclusive nature of Microsoft Copilot.

Furthermore, the integration of Copilot has enabled Hargreaves Lansdown to better support its employees in their roles. By providing them with the tools to work more efficiently, the company has reduced the administrative burden and allowed employees to focus on high-value tasks. This has led to increased job satisfaction and a more positive work environment.

In addition to the benefits for employees, Hargreaves Lansdown has also seen improvements in client service. The time saved using Copilot has allowed advisors to focus more on understanding client needs and providing personalized solutions. This has resulted in higher client satisfaction and stronger relationships with customers.

The adoption of Microsoft Copilot has also had a positive impact on the company's bottom line. By streamlining processes and increasing efficiency, Hargreaves Lansdown has reduced costs and improved profitability. This has enabled the company to invest in further innovation and growth, positioning it for long-term success in the competitive financial services industry.

In conclusion, the adoption of Microsoft Copilot has been a significant success for Hargreaves Lansdown, enabling the company to work more efficiently and effectively while improving the work experience for its employees and enhancing client service. The integration of Copilot has opened new possibilities for the company, allowing it to reimagine its business models and pursue bold opportunities.

To read the full story, visit `https://customers.microsoft.com/en-us/story/17009442995316119513-hargreaves-lansdown-microsoft-365-copilot-united-kingdom` or scan the QR code in Figure 13-3.

Figure 13-3. *Success story of Hargreaves Lansdown*

PG&E: Transforming Operations with Microsoft Copilot and Teams

Pacific Gas & Electric (PG&E), a leading energy company in the United States, has achieved remarkable success by leveraging the power of Microsoft Copilot and Microsoft Teams. The company streamlined its operations, enhanced productivity, and drove significant cost savings through the adoption of these innovative technologies.

PG&E initially faced significant challenges in managing its help desk demands, which were consuming a substantial number of resources. The company was receiving a high volume of help desk requests, ranging from password resets to software troubleshooting, and its support team was struggling to keep up with the workload. This resulted in longer response times, frustrated employees, and increased costs for the company.

To address these challenges, PG&E decided to explore the potential of Microsoft Copilot. The company integrated Copilot with Microsoft Teams, its primary communication and collaboration platform, to create a seamless and efficient help desk solution.

By leveraging the natural language processing capabilities of Microsoft Copilot, PG&E automated up to 40 percent of its help desk demands. Employees could simply chat with Copilot in Microsoft Teams to request assistance, and the virtual assistant would automatically triage the request, provide relevant information, or escalate the issue to the appropriate support team. This automation not only reduced the workload of the support team but also provided employees with faster and more efficient assistance.

The integration of Microsoft Copilot and Microsoft Teams has resulted in significant cost savings for PG&E. The company estimates that it has saved over $1 million annually by automating help desk demands and reducing the need for manual intervention. These savings have allowed PG&E to reallocate resources to more strategic initiatives and invest in other areas of its business.

Moreover, the adoption of Microsoft Copilot and Microsoft Teams has had a positive impact on employee experiences at PG&E. By providing employees with efficient and user-friendly tools for their daily tasks, the company has increased employee engagement and loyalty. The seamless integration of Copilot and Teams has also improved collaboration among teams, as employees can easily share information, work on projects together, and stay connected regardless of their location.

PG&E's success with Microsoft Copilot and Microsoft Teams demonstrates the potential of these technologies to transform business operations and drive significant cost savings. By automating repetitive tasks, enhancing productivity, and improving employee experiences, companies like PG&E can gain a competitive edge in their respective industries. As more organizations recognize the benefits of AI-powered solutions and collaborative platforms, the adoption of technologies like Microsoft Copilot and Microsoft Teams is expected to continue growing in the years to come.

To read the full story, visit https://customers.microsoft.com/en-us/ story/17095390496068998613-pacific-gas-and-electric-microsoft- power-apps-energy-usa or scan the QR code in Figure 13-4.

Figure 13-4. *Success story of PG&E*

Air India: Elevating Airline Operations with Microsoft Copilot and Teams

Air India, a prominent airline in India, embarked on a journey to enhance its operational efficiency by leveraging the power of AI and Microsoft tools. The airline aimed to streamline its processes, improve communication, and reduce costs. To achieve this, Air India adopted Microsoft Copilot for Microsoft 365, integrating it with Microsoft Teams.

The airline began by implementing Microsoft Copilot, freeing up staff to focus on more strategic and creative work. This integration enabled Air India to optimize its travel and transportation operations, ensuring seamless coordination and communication among various teams. Microsoft Copilot's AI capabilities helped the airline analyze and predict passenger demand, optimize flight schedules, and manage resources more effectively.

To facilitate this transformation, Air India adopted Microsoft Teams, which allowed the airline to create dedicated channels for different teams, ensuring that critical information and updates were accessible to the right people at the right time. This enhanced collaboration and reduced the time spent on manual tasks, allowing staff to focus on higher-value activities.

The integration of Microsoft Copilot and Microsoft Teams enabled Air India to achieve significant operational improvements. The airline reduced manual errors, improved response times, and enhanced overall customer satisfaction. By leveraging AI and Microsoft tools, Air India created a more efficient and agile organization, better equipped to meet the evolving needs of its passengers.

Overall, Air India's adoption of Microsoft Copilot and Microsoft Teams marked a significant milestone in its journey toward operational excellence. By harnessing the power of AI and collaborative technology, the airline streamlined its operations, improved communication, and enhanced the overall passenger experience.

To read the full story, visit https://customers.microsoft.com/en-us/story/17500595187858575413-airindia-microsoft-teams-travel-and-transportation-en-india or scan the QR code in Figure 13-5.

Figure 13-5. *Success story of Air India*

Summary

This chapter explored real-world success stories where organizations have effectively implemented Microsoft Copilot to boost productivity, streamline operations, and empower their teams. These examples highlighted the transformative power of AI-driven tools across various industries, demonstrating their practical benefits in everyday business activities.

The next chapter shifts focus to provide you with essential resources that will support your ongoing journey with Microsoft Copilot and related technologies. You'll find a detailed glossary, comprehensive learning materials, and access to vibrant online communities, all designed to deepen your knowledge and help you further explore and innovate with Microsoft Copilot, Power Apps, and AI-driven solutions.

Comprehensive Resources

In the previous chapter, you learned about organizations that successfully leveraged Microsoft Copilot to transform their operations, demonstrating the real-world impact of AI-driven tools. These stories provided practical insights into how technology can enhance productivity, streamline processes, and empower teams.

As you enter the final chapter of this book, the focus shifts from examples of success to providing you with the resources needed to continue your journey with Microsoft Copilot and related technologies. This chapter offers a comprehensive glossary, curated learning materials, and connections to active online communities. These resources are designed to deepen your understanding and equip you with the tools necessary to innovate and succeed in your own digital transformation efforts.

The Copilot Lexicon: Glossary and Key Definitions

This section presents a comprehensive glossary of key terms and definitions crucial to understanding Microsoft Copilot, Power Apps, Copilot Studio, and app development. This lexicon serves as a valuable

© Rezwanur Rahman 2024
R. Rahman, *Microsoft Copilot for Power Apps*, Inside Copilot,
https://doi.org/10.1007/979-8-8688-0512-7_14

reference for developers, business users, and anyone involved in creating and managing applications with these powerful tools. The following list of keywords provides detailed explanations to help you navigate the concepts, technologies, and functionalities that underpin these innovative platforms.

1. **Adaptive Cards**

   - **Definition**: User interface components designed to deliver content and inputs in a flexible, adaptable way.

   - **Explanation**: Adaptive Cards enable developers to create responsive and dynamic layouts that automatically adjust to the content and container. They are used in applications like Microsoft Teams, Outlook, and Windows Timeline to create rich, interactive experiences.

2. **AI Builder**

   - **Definition**: A feature in Microsoft Power Apps that brings artificial intelligence capabilities to the platform.

   - **Explanation**: AI Builder allows users to integrate AI models into their apps without needing deep technical knowledge. It supports functionalities like form processing, object detection, and predictive analysis to enhance app capabilities.

3. **AI-Driven Insights**

   - **Definition**: Insights generated by artificial intelligence through data analysis and pattern recognition.

- **Explanation**: AI-driven insights help organizations make informed decisions by analyzing large datasets to identify trends, anomalies, and patterns. This capability is crucial in fields like business intelligence and customer relationship management.

4. **AI-Powered Code Generation**

   - **Definition**: The automatic creation of code by artificial intelligence based on user input or predefined rules.

   - **Explanation**: AI-powered code generation simplifies the development process by allowing users to describe the functionality they need in natural language. The AI then translates these descriptions into working code, reducing development time and errors.

5. **App Customization**

   - **Definition**: The process of modifying an application to meet specific user needs or preferences.

   - **Explanation**: App customization involves changing the user interface, adding new features, or integrating with other systems to tailor the app to specific business requirements. This ensures the application is more relevant and useful to its users.

6. **App Development**

   - **Definition**: The process of creating software applications for various platforms.

- **Explanation**: App development encompasses the entire lifecycle of creating an application, from initial design and coding to testing, deployment, and maintenance. It involves a range of skills including programming, UI/UX design, and project management.

7. **Application Lifecycle Management (ALM)**

   - **Definition**: The process of managing an application's lifecycle, from development to retirement.

   - **Explanation**: ALM involves tracking and managing the entire lifecycle of an application, including planning, development, testing, deployment, maintenance, and decommissioning. Effective ALM practices ensure software quality, reliability, and maintainability.

8. **Azure**

   - **Definition**: Microsoft's cloud computing platform and service.

   - **Explanation**: Azure provides a range of cloud services, including computing, analytics, storage, and networking. It supports various programming languages, tools, and frameworks, making it a versatile platform for developing and deploying applications.

9. **Azure Cognitive Services**

   - **Definition**: A suite of AI services and APIs to build intelligent applications.

- **Explanation**: Azure Cognitive Services offer capabilities such as natural language processing, computer vision, speech recognition, and decision-making algorithms. These services enable developers to add AI features to their applications without extensive AI expertise.

10. **Business Intelligence (BI)**

    - **Definition**: Technologies and strategies used by enterprises for data analysis and business information.

    - **Explanation**: BI involves collecting, processing, and analyzing data to help organizations make better business decisions. BI tools provide insights through data visualization, reporting, and analytics, enhancing strategic planning and operational efficiency.

11. **Business Process Automation**

    - **Definition**: The use of technology to perform repetitive tasks or processes in a business.

    - **Explanation**: Business process automation aims to increase efficiency, reduce costs, and minimize errors by automating routine tasks. Tools like Power Automate can automate workflows, integrate applications, and handle data processing.

12. **Chat Experiences**

    - **Definition**: Interactive conversational interfaces in applications.

- **Explanation**: Chat experiences involve integrating chatbots or live chat features into applications to facilitate user interaction. These interfaces can provide customer support, gather feedback, or assist with navigation and decision-making.

13. **Chatbots**

   - **Definition**: AI-powered software designed to simulate human conversation.

   - **Explanation**: Chatbots can handle customer inquiries, provide information, and automate tasks through text or voice interactions. They are used in customer service, marketing, and personal assistance applications to enhance user engagement and efficiency.

14. **Citizen Developers**

   - **Definition**: Non-professional developers who create applications using low-code/no-code platforms.

   - **Explanation**: Citizen developers use tools like Power Apps to build applications without deep programming knowledge. This democratizes app development, allowing business users to create solutions that address their specific needs and improve productivity.

15. **Code Suggestions**

   - **Definition**: Recommendations provided by AI to improve or complete code.

- **Explanation**: Code suggestions help developers by offering snippets, optimizations, and best practices. These suggestions can speed up coding, reduce errors, and ensure adherence to coding standards.

16. **Collaboration Tools**

- **Definition**: Software applications that enable team collaboration and communication.

- **Explanation**: Collaboration tools like Microsoft Teams, Slack, and SharePoint facilitate teamwork by providing features for chat, video conferencing, file sharing, and project management. They help teams work together efficiently, regardless of location.

17. **Connectors**

- **Definition**: Integrations that allow applications to communicate with external data sources or services.

- **Explanation**: Connectors enable apps to access and interact with data from various systems like databases, web services, and other applications. Power Apps and Power Automate use connectors to integrate seamlessly with services like SharePoint, SQL Server, and Dynamics 365.

18. **Continuous Deployment (CD)**

- **Definition**: The practice of automatically deploying code changes to production environments.

- **Explanation**: CD ensures that new features, bug fixes, and updates are released quickly and reliably. It involves automated testing and deployment pipelines to streamline the delivery process and maintain application stability.

19. **Continuous Integration (CI)**

   - **Definition**: The practice of frequently integrating code changes into a shared repository.

   - **Explanation**: CI involves automated testing and builds to detect and fix issues early in the development cycle. This practice helps maintain code quality, reduces integration problems, and accelerates development.

20. **Context IQ**

   - **Definition**: An AI feature that provides relevant suggestions based on user context and data.

   - **Explanation**: Context IQ enhances productivity by understanding user actions and offering proactive suggestions, such as relevant files, contacts, or information. This feature leverages AI to streamline workflows and improve decision-making.

21. **Copilot**

   - **Definition**: An AI-powered assistant integrated into Microsoft products to aid users.

   - **Explanation**: Copilot provides intelligent assistance by understanding user commands, offering suggestions, and automating tasks. It enhances productivity in applications like Word, Excel, and Power Apps by leveraging AI capabilities.

22. **Copilot AI Technology**

- **Definition**: The underlying AI technology powering the Copilot assistant.

- **Explanation**: This technology includes natural language processing, machine learning, and predictive analytics. It enables Copilot to understand user input, generate responses, and provide intelligent assistance across various applications.

23. **Copilot Capabilities**

- **Definition**: The range of features and functions provided by Copilot.

- **Explanation**: Copilot's capabilities include code generation, data analysis, task automation, and personalized recommendations. These features help users perform complex tasks more efficiently and effectively.

24. **Copilot Customization**

- **Definition**: The ability to tailor Copilot's functionality to specific user needs.

- **Explanation**: Users can customize Copilot by adding plugins, configuring settings, and integrating it with external data sources. This ensures that Copilot meets the unique requirements of different users and applications.

25. **Copilot Extensibility**

- **Definition**: The ability to extend Copilot's functionality through plugins and integrations.

- **Explanation**: Extensibility allows developers to add new features and capabilities to Copilot. This can include integrating third-party services, creating custom connectors, and enhancing Copilot's AI models.

26. **Copilot Features**

- **Definition**: The specific tools and functionalities offered by Copilot.

- **Explanation**: Copilot features include natural language processing, predictive analytics, intelligent design suggestions, and real-time collaboration. These tools enhance user productivity and streamline workflows.

27. **Copilot Framework**

- **Definition**: The underlying structure that supports Copilot's functionality.

- **Explanation**: The Copilot framework includes APIs, AI models, and integration points with Microsoft products. This framework enables seamless interaction between Copilot and various applications, ensuring consistent performance and reliability.

28. **Copilot Integration**

- **Definition**: The process of embedding Copilot into Microsoft products and services.

- **Explanation**: Integration involves connecting Copilot with applications like Power Apps, Word, and Excel to provide AI-driven assistance. This enhances the functionality and user experience of these applications by leveraging Copilot's capabilities.

29. **Copilot Licensing**

- **Definition**: The terms and conditions for using Copilot within Microsoft products.

- **Explanation**: Licensing details the usage rights, subscription plans, and limitations associated with Copilot. Understanding these terms ensures compliance and optimal use of Copilot's features.

30. **Copilot Plugins**

- **Definition**: Add-ons that extend Copilot's functionality.

- **Explanation**: Plugins enable users to enhance Copilot by adding new features, integrating with external services, and customizing its behavior. This extensibility makes Copilot more versatile and adaptable to different use cases.

31. **Copilot Revolution**

- **Definition**: The transformative impact of Copilot on software development and productivity.

- **Explanation**: The Copilot revolution refers to the significant changes brought about by integrating AI into development and productivity tools. It democratizes software development, enabling more people to create applications and solutions with minimal coding knowledge.

32. **Copilot Service**

- **Definition**: The AI-powered service provided by Microsoft as part of its product suite.

- **Explanation**: The Copilot service includes AI capabilities like natural language processing, predictive analytics, and intelligent assistance. It is designed to enhance productivity and streamline workflows across Microsoft applications.

33. **Copilot Studio**

- **Definition**: A platform for developing and managing Copilot extensions and customizations.

- **Explanation**: Copilot Studio provides tools and resources for developers to create plugins, integrate with external data sources, and customize Copilot's functionality. It supports the development and deployment of tailored AI solutions.

34. **Copilot Suggestions**

- **Definition**: Recommendations provided by Copilot to assist users.

- **Explanation**: Copilot offers suggestions based on user input, context, and data analysis. These suggestions can include code snippets, design improvements, and workflow optimizations to enhance productivity and decision-making.

35. **Custom Connectors**

- **Definition**: User-defined integrations that enable applications to communicate with external data sources.

- **Explanation**: Custom connectors allow developers to integrate their applications with specific services or data sources not supported by default connectors. This expands the functionality and interoperability of applications like Power Apps and Power Automate.

36. **Data Governance**

    - **Definition**: The management of data availability, usability, integrity, and security in an enterprise.

    - **Explanation**: Data governance involves policies, procedures, and standards to ensure data is managed effectively throughout its lifecycle. It aims to maintain data quality, compliance, and security across the organization.

37. **Data Integration**

    - **Definition**: The process of combining data from different sources into a unified view.

    - **Explanation**: Data integration involves consolidating data from various databases, systems, and applications to provide a comprehensive and accurate view. This is essential for analytics, reporting, and decision-making.

38. **Data Management**

    - **Definition**: The practice of organizing and maintaining data processes to meet an organization's information needs.

- **Explanation**: Data management includes data storage, retrieval, security, and governance. Effective data management ensures that data is accurate, accessible, and secure, supporting business operations and analytics.

39. **Data Security**

- **Definition**: The protection of data from unauthorized access, corruption, or theft.

- **Explanation**: Data security involves implementing measures like encryption, access controls, and audits to protect sensitive information. It ensures data confidentiality, integrity, and availability.

40. **Data Visualization**

- **Definition**: The graphical representation of data to facilitate understanding and insights.

- **Explanation**: Data visualization involves using charts, graphs, and other visual tools to present data in a way that is easy to understand and interpret. It helps users identify trends, patterns, and outliers in their data.

41. **Dataverse**

- **Definition**: A scalable data platform used in Microsoft Power Platform to store and manage data.

- **Explanation**: Dataverse provides a secure and compliant data storage solution with built-in support for business logic, data relationships, and workflows. It integrates seamlessly with Power Apps, Power Automate, and other Microsoft services.

42. **Debugging**

- **Definition**: The process of identifying and fixing errors or bugs in software code.

- **Explanation**: Debugging involves using tools and techniques to detect, diagnose, and correct issues in an application. This process is critical for ensuring software quality and functionality.

43. **Development Environment**

- **Definition**: The set of tools and resources used for software development.

- **Explanation**: A development environment includes code editors, compilers, debuggers, and other tools that support the development, testing, and deployment of applications. It provides a controlled setting for writing and managing code.

44. **Digital Transformation**

- **Definition**: The integration of digital technology into all areas of a business to improve operations and value delivery.

- **Explanation**: Digital transformation involves leveraging technologies like AI, cloud computing, and IoT to enhance business processes, customer experiences, and business models. It aims to increase efficiency, agility, and innovation.

45. **Dynamics 365**

- **Definition**: A suite of intelligent business applications offered by Microsoft.

- **Explanation**: Dynamics 365 includes applications for customer relationship management (CRM) and enterprise resource planning (ERP). It helps organizations manage their business operations, customer interactions, and data insights.

46. **Enhancing App Quality**

- **Definition**: Improving the performance, reliability, and user experience of an application.

- **Explanation**: Enhancing app quality involves implementing best practices, optimizing code, and conducting thorough testing. It ensures that the application meets user needs and performs well under various conditions.

47. **Enterprise Solutions**

- **Definition**: Comprehensive software applications designed to support business operations and processes.

- **Explanation**: Enterprise solutions include ERP, CRM, and other systems that integrate various business functions. They help organizations streamline operations, improve efficiency, and make data-driven decisions.

48. **Extensibility Options**

- **Definition**: Features that allow users to add new functionality to existing applications.

- **Explanation**: Extensibility options enable developers to customize and enhance applications by adding plugins, integrations, and custom code. This ensures that applications can evolve to meet changing business needs.

49. **Graph API**

    - **Definition**: An API that provides access to Microsoft cloud services and data.

    - **Explanation**: The Microsoft Graph API enables developers to interact with a wide range of Microsoft services, including Azure Active Directory, Office 365, and OneDrive. It allows for seamless integration and data access across the Microsoft ecosystem.

50. **Graph Connectors**

    - **Definition**: Tools that connect external data sources to Microsoft Graph.

    - **Explanation**: Graph connectors enable users to integrate data from third-party services and applications into the Microsoft ecosystem. This expands the capabilities of Microsoft 365 applications by providing access to additional data and insights.

51. **Human Expertise**

    - **Definition**: The knowledge and skills possessed by individuals.

    - **Explanation**: Human expertise complements AI by providing the critical thinking, creativity, and experience necessary for complex decision-making and problem-solving. In software development, human expertise ensures that AI tools like Copilot are used effectively.

52. **Interactive Dashboards**

- **Definition**: Data visualization tools that allow users to interact with and explore data.

- **Explanation**: Interactive dashboards provide dynamic and responsive views of data, enabling users to filter, drill down, and analyze information in real-time. They are essential for business intelligence and data-driven decision-making.

53. **Intelligent Assistance**

- **Definition**: AI-driven support that helps users perform tasks more efficiently.

- **Explanation**: Intelligent assistance involves using AI to provide recommendations, automate tasks, and enhance user productivity. Examples include Copilot's suggestions in applications like Word and Excel.

54. **Licensing Needs**

- **Definition**: The requirements for legally using software and services.

- **Explanation**: Licensing needs detail the terms, conditions, and costs associated with using software. Understanding these needs ensures compliance and optimal utilization of the software's features.

55. **Low-Code Development**

- **Definition**: A development approach that uses visual tools and minimal coding to create applications.

- **Explanation**: Low-code development platforms like Power Apps enable users to build applications quickly and with less effort. This approach democratizes app development, allowing more people to create solutions without extensive programming knowledge.

56. **Low-Code/No-Code Solutions**

- **Definition**: Platforms that allow users to create applications with minimal or no coding.

- **Explanation**: These solutions provide drag-and-drop interfaces, pre-built templates, and integration tools to simplify app development. They enable business users to create and deploy applications quickly, addressing specific needs without relying on professional developers.

57. **Machine Learning Algorithms**

- **Definition**: Computational methods that enable machines to learn from data.

- **Explanation**: Machine learning algorithms analyze and model data to make predictions, identify patterns, and improve over time. They are fundamental to AI applications, including those used in Copilot for providing intelligent assistance.

58. **Microsoft 365**

- **Definition**: A suite of productivity and collaboration tools offered by Microsoft.

- **Explanation**: Microsoft 365 includes applications like Word, Excel, PowerPoint, Outlook, and Teams. It integrates with cloud services to provide a comprehensive solution for productivity, collaboration, and communication.

59. **Microsoft Entra ID**

- **Definition**: Microsoft's identity and access management service (previously known as Azure Active Directory).

- **Explanation**: Entra ID provides secure authentication, single sign-on, and access management for users and applications. It helps organizations manage identities, control access, and protect data across their IT environment.

60. **Microsoft Flow**

- **Definition**: A cloud-based service that allows users to create automated workflows (now known as Power Automate).

- **Explanation**: Microsoft Flow enables users to automate tasks and processes across various applications and services. It supports integration with Microsoft 365, Dynamics 365, and third-party applications, enhancing productivity and efficiency.

61. **Microsoft Graph**

- **Definition**: A unified API endpoint that provides access to Microsoft services and data.

- **Explanation**: Microsoft Graph enables developers to interact with a wide range of Microsoft services, including user profiles, emails, files, and activities. It supports the integration of data and functionality across the Microsoft ecosystem.

62. **Mobile App Development**

- **Definition**: The process of creating software applications for mobile devices.

- **Explanation**: Mobile app development involves designing, coding, testing, and deploying applications for smartphones and tablets. It requires consideration of different operating systems, screen sizes, and user interactions.

63. **Natural Language Processing (NLP)**

- **Definition**: A branch of AI that focuses on the interaction between computers and human language.

- **Explanation**: NLP involves the analysis and generation of human language by machines. It enables applications to understand, interpret, and respond to text and speech, making interactions more intuitive and natural.

64. **Natural Language Understanding (NLU)**

- **Definition**: A subset of NLP focused on understanding the meaning and context of human language.

- **Explanation**: NLU enables machines to comprehend the intent and context behind user input. It is crucial for applications like chatbots and virtual assistants, where accurate interpretation of user queries is essential.

65. **Office Productivity Software**

- **Definition**: Software applications designed to facilitate office tasks and workflows.

- **Explanation**: Office productivity software includes tools like word processors, spreadsheets, presentation software, and email clients. These applications help users create, edit, manage, and share documents and communications efficiently.

66. **Optimization**

- **Definition**: The process of making something as effective or functional as possible.

- **Explanation**: Optimization involves improving performance, efficiency, and quality. In software development, this can include code optimization, resource management, and process improvements to enhance the overall functionality of an application.

67. **Organizational Efficiency**

- **Definition**: The ability of an organization to achieve its goals with minimal waste of resources.

- **Explanation**: Organizational efficiency involves streamlining processes, reducing costs, and maximizing productivity. It is achieved through effective management, technology integration, and continuous improvement.

68. **Personalized Recommendations**

- **Definition**: Suggestions tailored to individual users based on their preferences and behavior.

- **Explanation**: Personalized recommendations leverage data analysis and machine learning to provide relevant and customized suggestions. This enhances user experience by delivering content, products, or actions that align with user interests.

69. **Plugins**

- **Definition**: Add-on software components that extend the functionality of an application.

- **Explanation**: Plugins enable users to customize and enhance applications by adding new features, integrating with other services, or modifying existing behavior. They provide flexibility and adaptability to meet specific user needs.

70. **Power Apps**

- **Definition**: A suite of apps, services, and connectors provided by Microsoft for app development.

- **Explanation**: Power Apps allows users to create custom business applications with minimal coding. It integrates with various data sources and services, enabling the development of scalable and functional applications for diverse business needs.

71. **Power Automate**

- **Definition**: A cloud-based service that automates workflows across applications and services.

- **Explanation**: Power Automate, formerly known as Microsoft Flow, allows users to create automated workflows to handle repetitive tasks, integrate systems, and streamline business processes. It enhances productivity by reducing manual effort and increasing efficiency.

72. **Power BI Integration**

- **Definition**: The integration of Power BI with other applications and data sources.

- **Explanation**: Power BI integration enables users to incorporate advanced data visualization and analytics into their applications. This allows for the creation of interactive reports and dashboards, providing valuable insights and supporting data-driven decision-making.

73. **Power Platform**

- **Definition**: A suite of Microsoft products that includes Power BI, Power Apps, Power Automate, and Power Virtual Agents.

- **Explanation**: The Power Platform provides tools for data analysis, app development, workflow automation, and intelligent virtual agents. It enables organizations to build comprehensive and integrated solutions to enhance business processes and decision-making.

74. **Predictive Analytics**

    - **Definition**: The use of statistical techniques and algorithms to predict future outcomes based on historical data.

    - **Explanation**: Predictive analytics involves analyzing past data to identify trends and make forecasts. It is used in various applications, such as risk management, marketing, and operational optimization, to support proactive decision-making.

75. **Productivity Enhancement**

    - **Definition**: The improvement of efficiency and effectiveness in performing tasks.

    - **Explanation**: Productivity enhancement involves using tools, techniques, and strategies to increase the output and quality of work. This can include automation, process optimization, and the use of intelligent assistants like Copilot to support users.

76. **Proactive Suggestions**

    - **Definition**: Recommendations provided in advance to assist users in performing tasks.

- **Explanation**: Proactive suggestions leverage AI to anticipate user needs and offer relevant advice or actions. This helps user's complete tasks more efficiently and prevents potential issues before they arise.

77. **Real-Time Updates**

- **Definition**: Changes or information delivered immediately as it occurs.

- **Explanation**: Real-time updates ensure that users have access to the most current data and information. This is essential for applications that require up-to-date content, such as collaborative tools, financial systems, and monitoring applications.

78. **Role-Based Access Control**

- **Definition**: A security model that restricts system access based on user roles.

- **Explanation**: Role-based access control (RBAC) assigns permissions to users based on their roles within an organization. This ensures that users have the appropriate level of access to perform their tasks while protecting sensitive information.

79. **Scalability**

- **Definition**: The capability of a system to handle increased load without compromising performance.

- **Explanation**: Scalability ensures that applications can grow and accommodate more users, data, and transactions. It involves designing systems that can expand efficiently, whether through hardware upgrades, software optimizations, or cloud resources.

80. **SDKs (Software Development Kits)**

- **Definition**: A set of tools and libraries for developing software applications.

- **Explanation**: SDKs provide developers with the resources needed to create applications for specific platforms or services. They include APIs, documentation, code samples, and development environments to streamline the development process.

81. **Security and Compliance**

- **Definition**: Measures and practices to protect data and ensure adherence to regulatory standards.

- **Explanation**: Security and compliance involve implementing policies, controls, and technologies to safeguard information and meet legal and industry requirements. This includes data encryption, access controls, audits, and adherence to standards like GDPR and HIPAA.

82. **Semantic Analysis**

- **Definition**: The process of understanding the meaning and context of words in a language.

- **Explanation**: Semantic analysis involves interpreting and analyzing the relationships between words to understand their meaning. It is used in natural language processing to improve the accuracy and relevance of AI-generated responses.

83. **Software Development**

- **Definition**: The process of designing, coding, testing, and maintaining software applications.

- **Explanation**: Software development encompasses the entire lifecycle of creating software, from initial requirements gathering to deployment and maintenance. It involves various disciplines, including programming, project management, and quality assurance.

84. **Task Automation**

- **Definition**: The use of technology to perform tasks without human intervention.

- **Explanation**: Task automation involves using tools and scripts to handle repetitive or time-consuming tasks. This increases efficiency, reduces errors, and frees up human resources for more complex and strategic activities.

85. **Teams Message Extensions**

- **Definition**: Add-ons that extend the functionality of Microsoft Teams messages.

- **Explanation**: Teams message extensions enable users to integrate additional features and services into their Microsoft Teams chats. This includes actions like creating tasks, pulling data, and interacting with external applications directly within Teams.

86. **Third-Party Integrations**

- **Definition**: The process of connecting external applications and services to enhance functionality.

- **Explanation**: Third-party integrations allow applications to leverage the capabilities of other systems and services. This expands the functionality of the primary application and provides a more comprehensive solution to users.

87. **User Authentication**

- **Definition**: The process of verifying the identity of a user.

- **Explanation**: User authentication involves validating credentials, such as passwords or biometric data, to grant access to a system. It ensures that only authorized users can access sensitive information and perform certain actions.

88. **User Data Ecosystem**

- **Definition**: The collection of data generated and used by users within an application.

- **Explanation**: The user data ecosystem includes all the information related to user activities, preferences, and interactions. This data is used to provide personalized experiences, improve application functionality, and inform decision-making.

89. **User Experience (UX)**

- **Definition**: The overall experience of a person using a product, especially in terms of how easy and pleasant it is to use.

- **Explanation**: UX design focuses on enhancing user satisfaction by improving the usability, accessibility, and efficiency of an application. It involves research, design, and testing to create intuitive and engaging user interfaces.

90. **Version Control Systems**

- **Definition**: Tools that manage changes to source code over time.

- **Explanation**: Version control systems, like Git, track modifications to code, enabling developers to collaborate, revert to previous versions, and maintain a history of changes. They are essential for managing software development projects and ensuring code integrity.

91. **Virtual Agents**

- **Definition**: AI-powered bots that interact with users to provide assistance and perform tasks.

- **Explanation**: Virtual agents use natural language processing and machine learning to understand user queries and provide relevant responses. They are used in customer service, technical support, and personal assistance applications to enhance user engagement and efficiency.

92. **Visual Development Tools**

- **Definition**: Software that allows users to create applications using graphical interfaces instead of traditional coding.

- **Explanation**: Visual development tools provide drag-and-drop components, visual workflows, and pre-built templates to simplify app creation. They enable users with limited coding skills to build functional applications quickly and easily.

93. **Workflow Automation**

- **Definition**: The process of automating the flow of tasks and activities in a business process.

- **Explanation**: Workflow automation uses tools like Power Automate to streamline processes, reduce manual effort, and increase efficiency. It involves defining rules and triggers that automate the movement of data and tasks between different systems and applications.

Beyond the Book: Extended Resources

To further enrich your journey, I have compiled a selection of online resources, links, and additional information for those eager to explore beyond the content of this book. These resources are designed to offer deeper insights, practical tutorials, and the latest updates on Microsoft Copilot, Copilot Studio, Power Apps, and AI Builder. Whether you are just starting out or already have experience, these resources will provide valuable knowledge and keep you informed about the newest developments in these powerful tools.

Resources for Microsoft Copilot

To help you maximize the potential of Microsoft Copilot, I have gathered a selection of valuable resources. These links and guides provide you with detailed tutorials, best practices, and the latest updates to enhance your understanding and usage of Copilot. Dive into these resources to fully utilize the capabilities of this innovative tool.

1. **Copilot Learning Hub (Microsoft Learn)**

    The Copilot Learning Hub is the official source for learning about Microsoft Copilot. Visit the Microsoft Learn website at `https://learn.microsoft.com/en-us/copilot/` to access a comprehensive collection of resources and learning materials for Microsoft Copilot. Or you can scan the QR code shown in Figure 14-1.

Figure 14-1. *QR code of the Microsoft Copilot Learning Hub (Microsoft Learn)*

    You can also learn how to use Microsoft Copilot based on your specific role. Table 14-1 provides the URLs for role-based learning resources.

Table 14-1. *URLs for Role-Based Learning Resources*

Role	URL
Administrator	https://aka.ms/clh-administrator
App maker	https://aka.ms/clh-app-maker
Data analyst	https://aka.ms/clh-data-analyst
Developer/solution architect	https://aka.ms/clh-developer
Functional consultant	https://aka.ms/clh-functional-consultant
Independent software vendor	https://aka.ms/clh-isv
Partner	https://aka.ms/clh-partner
Security engineer	https://aka.ms/clh-security-engineer
Service adoption specialist	https://aka.ms/clh-service-adoption-specialist
Startup founder	https://aka.ms/clh-startup-founder
Student	https://aka.ms/clh-student
Technology manager	https://aka.ms/clh-technology-manager

2. **AI Learning Hub (Microsoft Learn)**

    Like the Copilot Learning Hub, the AI Learning
    Hub is another official source for learning artificial
    intelligence. You can learn how to build your own
    Copilot with Azure AI Copilot Studio. Visit https://
    learn.microsoft.com/en-us/ai/ or scan the QR
    code shown in Figure 14-2.

Figure 14-2. *QR code of the Microsoft Copilot Learning Hub (Microsoft Learn)*

Resources for Microsoft Copilot Studio

Explore a set of invaluable resources to master Microsoft Copilot Studio. These materials include detailed tutorials, practical tips, and the latest updates, all aimed at helping you effectively utilize Copilot Studio's features.

1. **Microsoft Copilot Studio in Microsoft Learn**

   Microsoft Learn serves as the authoritative hub for all educational content related to Microsoft Copilot Studio. This resource offers an extensive collection of materials, including official tutorials that guide you through various functionalities, practical tips for efficient usage, and thorough documentation to deepen your understanding. Additionally, it features instructional videos that demonstrate key concepts and workflows. The platform also keeps you informed about any limitations, known issues, and the latest updates, ensuring that you have the most current information at your fingertips. To access these resources, simply visit the designated URL or scan the QR code displayed in Figure 14-3.

Figure 14-3. *QR code of the Microsoft Copilot Studio (Microsoft Learn)*

Resources for Microsoft Power Apps

Discover a comprehensive collection of resources designed to help you master Microsoft Power Apps. These materials include in-depth tutorials, practical tips, and the latest updates, all aimed at enabling you to effectively leverage Power Apps features. Whether you're new to Power Apps or looking to enhance your skills, these resources will guide you in creating powerful and efficient applications.

1. **Microsoft Power Apps in Microsoft Learn**

   Microsoft Learn is the definitive platform for mastering Microsoft Power Apps. It offers an array of resources tailored for both beginners and seasoned developers interested in deepening their expertise with Canvas apps and model-driven apps. This educational hub guides you through the process of creating successful applications using the Canvas framework and introduces innovative approaches to building apps interactively with AI Copilot. The platform also provides detailed tutorials on how to start conversations within your apps, enhancing user interaction and functionality. For those looking to extend their applications' capabilities, there are instructions on integrating with external data sources, allowing for richer, more dynamic app content. Furthermore, Microsoft Learn covers how to harness real-time insights using Azure Synapse, providing powerful analytics that drive decision-making.

Additionally, Microsoft Learn is a treasure trove of best practices, offering numerous ideas and strategies to optimize app design, functionality, and user experience. Whether you're a beginner aiming to create your first app or a professional looking to refine your skills, Microsoft Learn provides the tools and knowledge you need to succeed. For comprehensive learning materials, visit `https://learn.microsoft.com/en-us/power-apps/` or scan the QR code shown in Figure 14-4.

Figure 14-4. *QR code of the Microsoft Power Apps (Microsoft Learn)*

2. **Official Power Apps Blog**

   Microsoft Power Apps blog is a comprehensive
   resource for developers and users of Power Apps,
   providing updates, technical how-to guides,
   and product announcements. The blog features
   contributions from Microsoft program managers
   and other experts in the field, including frequent
   posters like Denise Moran, Greg Lindhorst, and
   Adrian Orth. It covers a broad range of Power
   Apps topics, making it an essential read for
   anyone looking to stay informed about the latest
   developments and best practices in Power Apps.
   The blog is particularly useful for developers, as
   it offers detailed technical guidance and insights
   into the capabilities and features of Power Apps.
   Additionally, it provides inspiration and real-world
   examples of how Power Apps are being used to
   digitally transform businesses, making it a valuable
   resource for anyone interested in leveraging low-
   code development for their own projects.

Visit the official Power Apps blog at https://
powerapps.microsoft.com/en-us/blog/ or scan
the QR code shown in Figure 14-5.

Figure 14-5. *QR code of the official Power Apps blog*

Resources for AI Builder

Unlock the full potential of AI Builder with this curated set of resources.
Here, you will find detailed tutorials, best practices, and up-to-date
information to help you make the most of AI Builder's capabilities.
These materials are tailored to provide you with the knowledge and tools
necessary to integrate AI into your projects seamlessly and efficiently.

1. **AI Builder in Microsoft Learn**

   AI Builder is a powerful Microsoft Power Platform
   capability that enables organizations to leverage
   the power of AI without requiring coding or data
   science expertise. The AI Builder documentation
   on Microsoft Learn provides a comprehensive
   overview of this tool, including information on
   pre-built and custom AI models, how to add
   intelligence to business processes, and resources for

learning to use AI Builder effectively. By reading this documentation, users can gain insights into how AI Builder can optimize their business processes, automate tasks, and generate valuable insights from their data. The documentation also covers important topics such as AI Builder's release status, licensing, and administration, making it an essential resource for anyone looking to harness the potential of AI within their organization. You can access the AI Builder in Microsoft Learn by visiting `https://learn.microsoft.com/en-us/ai-builder/` or scanning the QR code in Figure 14-6.

Figure 14-6. *QR code of the official AI Builder documentation*

Resources for Microsoft Power Automate

Enhance your proficiency with Microsoft Power Automate using this curated set of resources. They include comprehensive tutorials, practical tips, and the latest updates to maximize the features of Power Automate. These resources provide the insights and skills you need to fully utilize Power Automate.

1. **Microsoft Power Automate in Microsoft Learn**

   Power Automate, formerly known as Microsoft
   Flow, is a cloud-based workflow automation tool
   that allows users to create automated workflows
   between various applications and services. The
   Microsoft Learn platform offers comprehensive
   documentation on Power Automate, including
   sections on creating and designing workflows,
   integrating with other products, administering
   and extending Power Automate, and using flows.
   This resource includes training courses, videos,
   and tutorials to help users automate workflows,
   synchronize files, get notifications, and collect data.
   It provides a one-stop learning resource, covering
   product capabilities, administration, and usage
   to help users streamline business processes and
   enhance productivity. Learn more at `https://`
   `learn.microsoft.com/en-us/power-automate/` or
   scan the QR code in Figure 14-7.

Figure 14-7. *QR code of the official Power Automate documentation*

Online Communities and Forums

In today's internet era, we are fortunate to have access to online communities, virtual friends, and forums for help and learning. This section includes some of the best online communities and forums where you can get assistance, learn daily, and share your insights. Some of these communities are managed by Microsoft, others by Microsoft Most Valuable Professionals (MVPs), and some by both.

1. **Microsoft 365 Copilot Community**

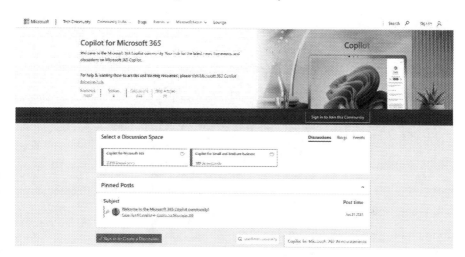

Figure 14-8. *The Official Microsoft 365 Copilot community*

The Microsoft 365 Copilot community (as shown in Figure 14-8) is a collaborative space where you can connect, share ideas, and explore the possibilities of Microsoft 365 Copilot. Serving as a hub for the latest news, live events, and discussions on Copilot, this community offers a variety of resources, including how-to articles, training materials, and expert advice. By joining the Microsoft 365 Copilot

Community, you can enhance your productivity, learn more about Microsoft AI, and stay updated with the latest releases. You can also engage with Microsoft experts, participate in digital events like Ask Microsoft Anything (AMA), and connect with fellow Microsoft 365 enthusiasts. This community aims to help you elevate your skills, empower your organization, and embark on an exciting journey of digital transformation with Microsoft 365 Copilot.

Visit `https://bit.ly/CopilotCommunity` or scan the QR code shown in Figure 14-9.

Figure 14-9. *QR code for the official community of Copilot for Microsoft 365*

2.   **Microsoft 365 Copilot Community**

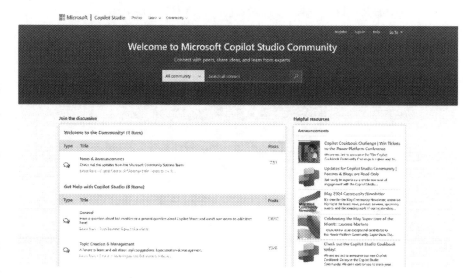

Figure 14-10. *Official Microsoft Copilot Studio community*

The Copilot Studio community (as shown in Figure 14-10) is a vibrant and engaging platform for you to connect, learn, and share your experiences with Microsoft's powerful AI assistant. By joining this community, you can stay informed about the latest trends, tips, and tricks from Copilot experts and fellow members. The community offers a variety of resources, including videos that provide insights into using Copilot Studio effectively, webinars for engaging with the product team, and challenges that showcase user creativity while offering exciting prizes. Additionally, the community forums serve as a valuable resource for asking questions, getting help, and sharing ideas. By actively participating in the Copilot Studio community, you can expand your network, build lasting relationships, and contribute your own stories, solutions, and successes to inspire and educate others.

Visit https://go.microsoft.com/
fwlink/?linkid=2058639 or scan the QR code to
join the community, as shown in Figure 14-11.

Figure 14-11. *QR code for the official community of Copilot Studio community*

3. **Microsoft Power Platform Community**

The Microsoft Power Platform community is a
vibrant and growing online hub for users of the
Power Platform to connect, learn, and collaborate.
This community includes over 880,000 members
across 480 user groups and highlights 94,000
solutions and 150,000 discussions. It provides a
central place for Power Platform enthusiasts to
explore the various products like Power Apps, Power
Automate, Power BI, and Power Virtual Agents, ask
questions, share knowledge, and find support from
experts and peers. Figure 14-12 shows the first look
of the community page.

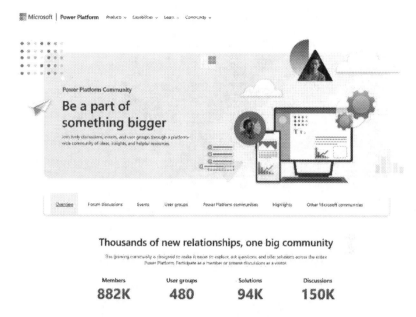

Figure 14-12. *Official Power Platform community of Microsoft*

Whether you're a novice or an experienced Power
Platform user, joining this community will help
you stay up to date with the latest developments,
learn new skills through tutorials and videos, and
tap into the collective wisdom of the community
to solve business challenges more effectively. The
community's forums, LinkedIn page, and social
media groups enable users to personalize their
experience and engage in meaningful conversations
around the Power Platform.

Visit https://powerusers.microsoft.com/ or
scan the QR code shown in Figure 14-13 to join the
community.

Figure 14-13. *QR code for the official Power Platform community*

4. **Microsoft 365 Technical Community: DACH**

    The Microsoft 365 Technical Community: DACH
    is a global network that transcends geographical
    boundaries, uniting individuals worldwide
    who share a common interest in Microsoft 365
    technologies. While the name may suggest a focus
    on the DACH region (Germany, Austria, and
    Switzerland), this community is inclusive and
    welcomes members from all corners of the globe.
    Figure 14-14 shows the welcome page for Microsoft
    365 Technical Community: DACH.

Figure 14-14. *The welcome page for the Microsoft 365 Technical Community: DACH*

Led by Microsoft MVPs, MCTs, regional directors, and other esteemed community leaders, this platform is dedicated to fostering collaboration, continuous learning, and knowledge sharing. As an active member and Microsoft MVP, I contribute to the community by regularly sharing free blogs, webinars, and training sessions every month, providing valuable insights and hands-on learning opportunities for members. Through these initiatives, members have the opportunity to stay informed about the latest trends, connect with industry peers and experts, access valuable resources, and engage in global discussions and events. By being a part of this dynamic community, individuals can expand their skills, stay abreast of Microsoft 365 advancements, and forge meaningful connections with professionals worldwide.

You can join the webinars, community calls, or training sessions by visiting the official website of Microsoft 365 Technical Community: DACH (https://www.m365community.eu/) or scanning the QR code shown in Figure 14-15.

Figure 14-15. QR code of the Microsoft 365 Technical Community: DACH

Summary

This final chapter provided essential resources to support your journey with Microsoft Copilot for Power Apps. Following the inspiring real-world applications, this chapter serves as a vital resource hub, offering detailed explanations, extended learning materials, and information on thriving online communities.

Starting with "The Copilot Lexicon" section, the chapter includes key terms and definitions crucial for understanding Microsoft Copilot, Power Apps, Copilot Studio, and app development. This glossary helps developers, business users, and anyone involved in creating and managing applications.

To enhance your learning, the chapter also included online resources, including the Copilot Learning Hub and AI Learning Hub on Microsoft Learn. These hubs feature role-based learning resources, tutorials, practical tips, and the latest updates. For those looking to master Microsoft Power Apps, AI Builder, and Microsoft Power Automate, comprehensive guides and best practices are available.

Recognizing the importance of community support, the chapter highlighted online communities such as the Microsoft 365 Copilot Community, Copilot Studio Community, Microsoft Power Platform Community, and Microsoft 365 Technical Community: DACH. These platforms offer spaces to share ideas, access resources, and engage in discussions about Microsoft's AI technologies.

As you conclude this book, my goal has been to introduce you to the transformative power of Microsoft Copilot for Power Apps and to provide you with the tools, knowledge, and community support necessary to continue your journey. Embracing these technologies can significantly enhance productivity, streamline operations, and empower your workforce. With the resources and communities highlighted in this chapter, you are well-equipped to explore, innovate, and harness AI for a brighter, more efficient future.

Thank you for joining me on this journey. May the insights, tools, and communities discussed inspire you to accomplish your digital transformation and achieve new heights with AI.

Index

A

Aesthetic design, UX/UI
  color, 273
  color palette, 273, 274
  color schemes, 275–277
  fonts/sizes, 278, 279
AI Builder
  AKS, 114
  Azure services
    AKS, 109
    CI/CD, 110
    cognitive services, 108
    insights/analytics, 110
    ML, 107
    security/compliance, 111
  business intelligence, 87, 88
  code/development,
      revolutionizing, 82–84
  compliance/security, 114
  connections/functions, 81
  core capabilities, 84, 85
  custom AI models, 113
  features, 86
  licensing, 89, 90
  ML, 114
  Power Apps, 87
  pre-built AI scenarios, 113

prompts, 90
technologies
  machine learning
    techniques, 106
  NLP, 104
  Power Fx/Power Fx Apps
    Studio, 105
  system architecture/data
    privacy, 106
AI prompts
  custom prompt option
    adoption website, 537
    confirmation, 545
    creation, 535
    dynamic value, 540–542,
      544
    GPT model, 543
    initial screen, 536
    input option, 539, 540
    modal box, 538
    name changing, 539
    prompt engineering
      guide, 546
    prompt page, 535
    response, 545
    smart features, 534
    testing process, 544

© Rezwanur Rahman 2024
R. Rahman, *Microsoft Copilot for Power Apps*, Inside Copilot,
https://doi.org/10.1007/979-8-8688-0512-7

P, Q

V, W, X, Y

Z